T0288244

A BICENTENNIAL COMMEMORATIVE
OF THE PRAIRIE STATE

A BICENTENNIAL COMMEMORATIVE OF THE PRAIRIE STATE

Readings from the Journal of the Illinois State Historical Society

Edited by David W. Scott

Foreword by Leah Joy Axelrod

Published for the Illinois State Historical Society

Southern Illinois University Press
Carbondale

Southern Illinois University Press
www.siupress.com

21 20 19 18   4 3 2 1

Publication of this book was supported financially by the Illinois State
    Historical Society.

Jacket illustrations (*clockwise from upper left*): presidential candidate
    Abraham Lincoln, photographed by Alexander Hesler, Springfield,
    Ill., June 3, 1860 (*Library of Congress*); Old State Capitol, Springfield,
    Ill. (*photograph by William Furry*); Chicago Fire, lithograph by F. Sala
    and Company, 1871 (*Chicago History Museum, ICHI-63773*); painting
    of Joseph Smith, ca. 1842 (*courtesy of Community of Christ archives,
    Independence, Mo.*).

LIBRARY OF CONGRESS CATALOGING-IN-PUBLICATION DATA
Names: Scott, David W., [date] editor.
Title: A Bicentennial Commemorative of the Prairie State : Readings
    from the "Journal of the Illinois State Historical Society" / edited
    by David W. Scott ; foreword by Leah Joy Axelrod.
Other titles: Journal of the Illinois State Historical Society.
Description: Carbondale : Southern Illinois University Press, 2018. |
    Includes bibliographical references and index.
Identifiers: LCCN 2017055148 | ISBN 9780809336883 (hardback)
Subjects: LCSH: Illinois—History. | BISAC: HISTORY / United States
    / State & Local / Midwest (IA, IL, IN, KS, MI, MN, MO, ND, NE,
    OH, SD, WI). | HISTORY / Essays. | HISTORY / United States / General.
Classification: LCC F541.5 .B53 2018 | DDC 977.3—dc23 LC record
    available at https://lccn.loc.gov/2017055148

Printed on recycled paper. ♻

This paper meets the requirements of ANSI/NISO Z39.48-1992
    (Permanence of Paper) ∞

CONTENTS

Contents

Contents

ILLUSTRATIONS

The work of the Illinois State Historical Society is neatly summed up in a single sentence:

"The mission of the society is to foster awareness, understanding, research, preservation, and recognition of history in Illinois."

A more lengthy statement from 1930—yet still timely—is that the society aims to "arouse and stimulate a general interest in the history of Illinois, to disseminate the story of the state as widely as possible, to encourage historical research, and secure its promulgation."

The bicentennial of Illinois statehood is a perfect opportunity to fulfill the society's mission of fostering awareness and telling the story of the state. Illinois has gone from a frontier territory of forty thousand pioneers in 1818 to a major player in the nation two centuries later with a population of almost thirteen million. A lot has happened in those two hundred years, and this book tells that story.

A rich source of material that illuminates Illinois history is found in the *Journal of the Illinois State Historical Society*, published continuously for 110 years. From the hundreds of articles appearing in its quarterly issues, thirty-three have been chosen for this bicentennial book. In these pages, you will meet soldiers, politicians, farm women, musicians, civil rights leaders, coal miners, entrepreneurs, and more. Some were heroes; a few were villains. No doubt many would be surprised to have their diverse stories told today, but they are all part of the fabric of Illinois history.

Additionally, this book offers a unique history of the Illinois State Historical Society, established in 1899 as an adjunct to the State Historical Library and reorganized as a freestanding organization in 1998. The journal of the society has been one of its most important contributions—a respected publication that continues to present the Illinois story, both in grand scale and personal detail, over the years.

In this bicentennial year, the Illinois State Historical Society is doing more to celebrate our past and prepare for the future. The society has secured saplings from an original Johnny Appleseed tree that are being planted in each county. It is making available a framed portrait of Abraham Lincoln to be hung in every county courthouse. It has members serving on the state bicentennial commission. It is collaborating with local historical societies to help share their stories.

We can all be part of the bicentennial celebration. Let us carry on the mission of the society to "foster awareness and understanding" as we tell the colorful story of our state.

Leah Joy Axelrod
President, Illinois State Historical Society

PREFACE

The year 2018 marks the two-hundredth year of statehood for Illinois. This bicentennial recognition provides an incentive for communities, historical societies, museums, and other groups to pay particular attention to their past as well as their future, whatever the date of their founding.

Although not nearly as old as the state itself, the Illinois State Historical Society has been around for a long time, having been founded in 1899. A major activity since 1908 has been providing those interested in Illinois history with a regular source of information in the form of articles published in a journal of history. One major way that the society has chosen to celebrate its past is by publishing this book containing thirty-three selected articles that appeared in the *Journal of the Illinois State Historical Society* over its 110-year history (known as the *Illinois Historical Journal* from 1984 to 1998). Each of the six parts covers a specific period of time; the first part is "Early Illinois" and the sixth is titled "Mid-Twentieth Century." Many articles were published in recent decades, but some date from early in the *Journal's* history. Most of the authors are academics, but some come from outside the academy. Accompanying these articles is an overview of the history of the society. It places some emphasis on the *Journal* but covers other programs and activities of the society as well. There were many sources of information for this overview, but by far the principal ones were the *Dispatch*, initiated in 1958 as the newsletter for the Illinois State Historical Society and some of the earlier annual reports.

This book has its precedents—two books prepared in celebration of the Illinois sesquicentennial by historians with long and distinguished association with the Illinois State Historical Society in editorial and executive positions. One is titled *Prairie State: Impressions of Illinois, 1673–1967, by Travelers and Other Observers*, compiled and edited by Paul M. Angle. The other is *An Illinois Reader*, edited by Clyde Walton. It has five chapters and twenty-five articles, most of which were taken from the *Journal*. Of the two books, Walton's *Reader* more directly relates to this book.

As this book, like Walton's, was prepared for the general reader, the editor did not include the notes that appeared in the articles as published in the *Journal*. Some articles were edited for length, yet retain text central to main themes of the article. The reader can use JSTOR to find the articles as originally published, complete with footnotes or endnotes, and can view them on the computer screen and print them out. Information on JSTOR is found in a separate section of this book. The reader may also find the articles in bound volumes of the *Journal* in local libraries.

Each article is introduced with a brief summary statement; for some, one or two additional articles are cited as "related reading" due to their closely linked content. A separate section contains brief information on each author.

Executive Director William Furry initiated the idea of a book of selected *Journal* articles as an Illinois bicentennial project of the society. He asked me as the chairman of the publications committee of the board of the society to prepare a proposal for publishing this book of readings and coordinating the selection process. The members of the committee were Mike Kienzler, a society advisory board member and retired newspaper editor; Herbert Russell, a director of the society who holds a PhD in English from Southern Illinois University; and me. I hold an MA in American history from the University of Wisconsin and a PhD in political science from Northwestern University. I am a former president of the society and have published in the *Journal* and elsewhere. Among the functions of the publications committee has been to determine the Harry E. Pratt Award winner for the best article in the *Journal* published in the four issues of the previous year. Some of these winning articles have been included in this book. Glenna Schroeder-Lien served as a consultant, evaluating articles identified in the first round of selection by the committee and providing helpful ideas on criteria for choice. She is an author and editor and recently retired from the Abraham Lincoln Presidential Library where she was a full-time researcher. Committee members and the consultant chose for inclusion articles of varying topics and eras that the average reader would find informative and interesting and that cover many important groups, persons, events, activities, and places in state history. However, given the multiplicity of topics in state history, it is inevitable—yet regrettable—that many topics could not be included in this survey.

William Furry, current executive director, and Jon Austin, former executive director, have been most helpful in the preparation of the section on recent society history. I am grateful for the advice provided by the editorial staff at SIU Press. Much appreciated is the editorial and proofreading work so ably provided by my wife, Virginia.

David W. Scott
January 2018

A BICENTENNIAL COMMEMORATIVE
OF THE PRAIRIE STATE

THE ILLINOIS STATE HISTORICAL
SOCIETY AND ITS *JOURNAL*

David W. Scott

The Early Years to the 1940s

The first historical societies in Illinois were formed in the early days of statehood and were short lived. Organized in 1827, the Antiquarian and Historical Society of Illinois lasted only a few years. Societies formed in 1831 and 1843 also ended after brief periods. Each had similar purposes. The 1843 society was created for "collecting, preserving and disseminating information relative to the history of Illinois." The first permanent historical society in Illinois was formed in Chicago in 1856. It soon took on a scope broader than the city and began collecting materials of general statewide interest.

Responding to concerns of inadequate collecting and preserving of historical materials, the state legislature in 1889 established the Illinois State Historical Library, overseen by a three-member board of trustees appointed by the governor. Ten years later in 1899 the Illinois State Historical Society was chartered by the state as a not-for-profit organization. In 1903 legislation provided a home for the society under the auspices of the Illinois State Historical Library, which was authorized to pay some of the expenses of the society to supplement membership fees and donations. The first president of the Society was Hiram W. Beckwith, an attorney from Danville. He was one of the first gubernatorial appointments to the library board and was elected the first president of that board. He served from 1899 to 1903. The second society board president was John F. Snyder of Virginia, a physician and amateur historian who served from 1903 to 1905.

The location of the society was resolved in the 1903 decision, when Springfield was chosen over the University of Illinois. Other issues focused on how much influence academics would have on the society relative to those not associated with a college or university, how the society would be financed, and the nature of the society's relationship with the library, notably the extent of its autonomy.

The history from 1827 to 1905 is covered by Roger Bridges in his 1975 article, "The Origins and Early History of the Illinois State Historical Society," *Journal of the Illinois State Historical Society (Journal of the ISHS)* vol. 68, no. 2 (April 1975). According to Bridges,

> Despite the early conflicts between university-affiliated historians and citizens interested in history, the Historical Society, by 1905, was firmly established as a statewide institution with a permanent headquarters in the Historical Library at Springfield. The dedicated service rendered by Jessie Palmer Weber, who became de facto administrative officer when she was elected the Society's first secretary-treasurer in 1903, gave the organization the stability, continuity, and direction it needed.

Jessie Palmer Weber not only served as society administrator but also publications editor. These positions were added to her existing role as librarian.

Over the years, mission statements adopted by the society varied somewhat in wording. Typical is one from 1930: the society was "to arouse and stimulate a general interest in the history of Illinois; to disseminate the story of the state as widely as possible; to encourage historical research and secure its promulgation; and to collect and preserve all data relating to the history of Illinois and its peoples" (*Journal of the ISHS*, vol. 34, no. 3 [September, 1941]). Reflecting the society's involvement with the Historical Library was the goal "to collect and preserve all data relating to the history of Illinois and its peoples."

The society's initial effort at institution-building was to organize an annual meeting where people interested in Illinois history could gather to network, socialize, read and hear papers, and select officers and directors. The founders wanted to develop relationships with local societies, encouraging their formation, growth, and involvement with the society and each other. Holding each annual meeting in a different part of the state was an attempt to realize that early goal. Another approach was to appoint a number of vice presidents from different local historical societies or regions of the state.

Publication was a principal activity of the society from the start. First issued at the very beginning of the society's existence in 1900 was *Transactions of the Illinois State Historical Society*. Included in this publication were papers read at the annual meeting of the society as well as "the proceedings" of the last annual meeting, such as the secretary's annual report, the election of officers and board members, and other business of the society. It appeared annually as *Transactions* until 1937, when it was renamed *Papers in Illinois History*.

The society hoped that a regular publication would emerge that would provide reports of meetings and items of interest to local historical societies, that would contain reviews of historical publications, and that would "contain [in each number] at least one paper or address of real historic value and interest." Such content appeared in volume 1, issue 1 of the *Journal of the Illinois State Historical Society*, first printed in 1908. The *Journal* had considerably expanded upon this content by issue 4, which included a report on the Woodford County Historical Society, two letters written by Governor John Reynolds, a listing of the death of a State Historical Society member, and a short essay on Lincoln as the typical American. Also included was a more academic article on Indian mounds.

By the early 1930s the number of articles "of real historic value and interest" appearing in each issue of the *Journal* had increased substantially; for example, issues 3 and 4 of volume 26, which came out in 1934, together contained seven such articles. Still, the *Journal* included a number of items focused on the meetings and events of local groups, obituaries of members, letters to the editor, and several short pieces. The editor of the *Journal* at this time was Paul Angle, whose distinguished career included authorship of many books on Lincoln and Illinois history and a stint as director and secretary of the Chicago Historical Society.

At Angle's initiative, the society's Markers Program was established in 1934 and continues to flourish today. Through this program, the society works with local groups to erect outdoor signs that display information about persons, places, and events of historic interest locally and beyond.

Angle served from 1932 to 1945 as the third editor of the *Journal*, and he is credited with enhancing its academic quality. As editor, he followed Jessie Palmer Weber (1908–26) and Georgia L. Osborne (1926–32). In addition to *Journal* editors, these three were also chief administrators of the society, a position first called "secretary" and later "executive director." These early leaders were chosen specifically because they had been appointed by the State Library Board as director of the library. This merging of positions, although not required by statute, continued until the 1990s. It was designed to facilitate the coordination of State Library activities with those of the

Historical Society and to symbolize their equal status. The title of the head of the Historical Library was changed in the 1940s from librarian to state historian. Over the years, the executive director of the society became more the executive editor of the *Journal*, as the responsibility of day-to-day editing increasingly fell to a staff of library employees. While not required by statute, the board of directors of the society continued to choose as its executive director the library board's appointed state historian.

Angle, in the 1934 *Transactions* issue, explained the intended difference between the quarterly *Journal* and the annual *Transactions*, stating that "shorter papers and those of general interest will be printed in the quarterly *Journal*." *Transactions* was to contain longer contributions and was to continue its tradition extending back to the founding of the society of containing the official proceedings of the previous annual meeting and the papers read there.

However, by the 1940s fewer papers were read at the annual meeting; thus, there was less reason to continue such a publication. Justifying the decision to drop the *Papers* (to which *Transactions* had been renamed), Angle wrote that "the Society's official proceedings can easily be published in the *Journal* and most of the articles which have appeared in the annual volume can also be accommodated in our quarterly publication" (*Journal of the ISHS* vol. 37, no. 4 (December 1944). While issues of *Papers/Transactions* contain rich sources of articles, they are not, unlike the *Journal*, available for reading at home through JSTOR. JSTOR is the comprehensive online service that archives academic journals including the *Journal of the Illinois State Historical Society*. Indexes are available to identify the content of *Papers/Transactions*. See "Using JSTOR" in this book.

A New Publication, New Programs, and a New Home: 1950s–60s

In 1958 another publication joined the *Journal* when the society established a quarterly newsletter, the *Dispatch*. One of its purposes was to disseminate news about historical events around the state, such as the celebrations of Lincoln-Douglas debates being held that year at some of the sites. Also included in the *Dispatch* were brief articles on historical topics. Over the years such articles became longer and more frequent, in some cases exceeding two pages. Representative of the *Dispatch*'s content is a sampling of articles over its first six issues through 1959: staff changes and additions at the library, the receipt of a $5,000 gift to the society, the Lincoln essay contest for high school students, the list of members of the society's board and committees, notice of tours, a report on society annual meetings, notice of the death of a former board member, and news of local society activities. There was an essay on what readers want and expect in their publications and an article asking who is teaching Illinois history to teachers. (The answer: "Almost nobody.") Not surprisingly, the topic of membership and membership growth was found in initial issues of the *Dispatch*. At the time there were about three thousand society members, each paying three dollars in annual dues.

Despite the arrival of the *Dispatch*, the *Journal* continued providing information on the activities of local societies and overlapped in other content areas as well. Of course, the *Journal* continued its unique contribution of publishing book reviews and longer articles on a range of historical topics with varying degrees of original research and scholarly approaches.

The *Dispatch* was just one of several major ways in which society programs broadened under Clyde Walton. Serving from 1956 to 1967, he held the usual plurality of titles, including executive director of the society, editor of the *Journal,* and state historian, the title given to the director of the State Historical Library. As already noted, this arrangement reflects expectations of equal status of the society with the library and the need to coordinate activities, including the library staff handling administrative matters of the various society or joint programs. Walton was preceded as indicated by Weber, Osborne, and Angle, and also by Jay Monaghan (1946–50) and Harry Pratt (1950–56). Following Walton were William Alderfer (1967–81), Olive Foster 1981–85), Michael Devine (1986–91), and E. Duane Elbert (1991–93). Walton was trained as a librarian; following his years with the State Library and Society, he became a university library director. He was an editor of several books and authored many articles on Illinois and Civil War history.

Clyde Walton in his reports in the mid-1960s surveyed the accomplishments of the society's publications for adult readers but also of society/ library publications for younger ones. New was a four-page leaflet entitled *My State Reader* for pupils in the second and third grades, distributed to schools throughout the state. Walton reported on the continuing popularity of *Illinois History: A Magazine for Young People*, introduced in 1946, one of several school service programs carried out over the years. Awards were offered for students who wrote articles for the magazine. Teachers were recognized for their contributions to *Illinois History*. These and other awards were part of the annual Student Historian Awards Day. For an example of such an event, see *Journal of the ISHS* vol. 54, no. 3 (Autumn 1961). The governor was often on hand at this recognition ceremony to present awards. Other society/library school service programs included regional and state history fairs and workshops for teachers. The 1968 Sesquicentennial Year of Illinois Statehood was the occasion for the society to issue special publications oriented to students. Although limited in later years, the society remains involved with teachers and students. Continuing education credits are available to teachers who attend the society's symposia. Also offered are the Olive Foster Award for outstanding teaching of Illinois history and the Verna Ross Orndorff Scholarship for an outstanding Lincoln or Civil War essay by a high school student. (There is no known relationship between Orndorff and Alfred Orendorff, a founding president of the society.) Prior to becoming state historian and society executive director, Olive Foster directed the school service programs for many years.

A long-standing goal of the society, going back to its origins, was to encourage the formation and development of local societies and assist them in their work. In 1967 Executive Director Clyde Walton and the board of the society formalized this goal by creating the Congress of Illinois Historical Societies and Museums. The State Historical Society was to provide administrative assistance and serve as a clearinghouse of information. The Congress was to have an annual meeting and conduct workshops. It grew rapidly, employed an executive secretary, and soon began giving "awards of merit" at its annual meeting. More than thirty local groups were qualified to attend the society-sponsored second annual meeting of the Congress in 1968.

Toward the end of the Walton years, the society was on the verge of occupying new quarters. The Centennial Building, just southeast of the Illinois State House, had been the home of the library and society since they moved out of the State House in the 1920s. By the early 1960s their space was becoming overcrowded, and society leaders looked forward to the possibility of finding a new space as part of the proposed renovation of the Sangamon County Building, which had been the Illinois capitol from 1837 to 1878. In 1968 the State Historical Library and Society moved to the underground level of the recently reconstructed Old State Capitol.

Expansion of Academic and Journal Activity: 1960s–80s

In 1966 the society set up a fellowship fund for graduate study in Illinois history. Up to $2,000 was available to a graduate student whose study was directly related to Illinois history. An award committee comprising representatives of several Illinois colleges and universities was formed to review applications.

In 1969 the society created an award for the best *Journal* article published in the previous year. The award was named after Harry E. Pratt (1901–56), a noted Lincoln scholar with numerous books and articles to his credit. Pratt served as executive secretary of the Abraham Lincoln Association for seven years (1936–43). His years of involvement with the society as editor and administrator ran from 1950 to 1956.

The winner of the first Pratt Award (two hundred dollars and a plaque) was John H. Keiser, a faculty member at Eastern Illinois University, for his article "The Union Miners Cemetery at Mt. Olive, Illinois: A Spirit Thread of Labor History." A more extensive statement explaining the award was used in later announcements of the winner: "The award is presented to one author each year in recognition of the exceptional value of his or her article as a contribution to Illinois history and as an acknowledgment of the general excellence, style and accuracy of the original manuscript—a testimonial to Dr. Pratt's extraordinary accomplishments in the field of Illinois history" (*Dispatch,* Winter 1998).

By the 1970s the *Journal* was a well-established publication with visibility in the higher-education community. According to the 1974 annual report, fifty-three manuscripts had been received and twenty-three accepted. In that year, the *Journal* published fifty-two book reviews. Five years later, the 1979 annual report showed that fifty-seven contributors wrote articles or book reviews for the four issues of the *Journal*. Thirty-three were faculty or graduate students at colleges and universities, and eight were employees of historical agencies. Other professionals included freelance journalists and genealogists (Annual Report, *Journal of the ISHS* vol. 73, no. 4). The support provided by the library staff in producing the *Journal* was housed in the library's Publications Division, which included in the mid-1970s senior editor Mary Ellen McElligott and associate editor Janice Petterchak. The Publications Division supervisor was Ellen M. Whitney (Annual Report, *Journal of the ISHS* vol. 68, no. 2; vol. 72, no. 4).

Enhancing the scholarly character of the *Journal* was the 1984 appointment of an editorial advisory board to assist library staff in soliciting and choosing articles for the *Journal*. This board was made up of history scholars throughout the state. Also advancing the scholarly character of the society was the first Illinois History Symposium on December 5–6, 1981. It was designed to provide an annual opportunity for both established and beginning scholars to read and get reactions to their research papers. The first symposium offered eleven sessions, including "Illinois Pioneers," "Frontier Illinois," and "Coal Mining in Illinois." A committee of academics was formed to receive and evaluate proposed papers for presentation at the subsequent symposium. Symposia have been held on university or college campuses and have had specific themes, such as "Religion and Society" in 2005 and "Illinois and the War of 1812," held on the two hundredth anniversary of the war. The theme for the 2017 Illinois History Symposium was "1917, Year of Turmoil: War and Suffrage," held on the campus of Lincoln Land Community College.

Special issues of the *Journal* have been published from time to time that focused on a particular topic. Among such topics have been the Civil War, Lincoln, African Americans, Native Americans, Mexicans, women, Mormons, the Emancipation Proclamation, the 1970 Illinois Constitutional Convention, and Illinois State University.

The Society's Links to the Public: 1970s–80s

Dedications of historical markers placed by the society were often well-attended events, sometimes combined with other society activities. For example, attendees at the annual meeting in Vandalia in 1975 took part in the tradition of touring the host community. The tour included a stop to dedicate a marker containing information on the history of Vandalia—part of the Markers Program established by the society in 1934. The society has long operated this program in cooperation with local groups, and there are more than four hundred markers in the state. Today through the society's web page (www.historyillinois.org) one can locate historic markers in all parts of Illinois, such as those commemorating the Underground Railroad and the first of the Walgreen drugstores.

Another link to the public is the Centennial Business Program, set up in 1984 to recognize Illinois businesses that have been in existence for at least one hundred years. According to State Historian/society director Olive Foster, "It is essential that we stimulate an interest in preserving Illinois' most important commercial and industrial heritage for future generations. The people of Illinois can benefit through the donations of corporate histories to the Illinois State Historical Library" (*Dispatch,* March/April 1984). For many years the recognition ceremony was held at the elegant Empire Room of the Palmer House in downtown Chicago. Serving as master of ceremonies in the early years was sports broadcaster Jack Brickhouse; later, his widow performed the honor. However, the event has moved to other locations, and its focus changes from time to time, such as specifically honoring sesquicentennial churches.

Much of the work of the society has been performed by volunteers. The 1984 joint Annual Report of the library and society gave particular attention to their central role; it listed four officers (president, vice president, secretary, and treasurer) and fifteen directors, an arrangement that continues to this day. In addition, in 1984 there were twenty-one vice presidents, each specifically appointed to represent a local society or region of the state. Today an advisory board of some two dozen members has replaced this array of vice presidents. An important role of all these volunteers has been to serve on society committees. In 1984 there were five ad hoc committees and twelve standing committees. Among the committees then and which still exist today are Centennial Business, Publications, Scholarly Symposium, Markers, and Awards. Recommendations from committees have helped shape society programs, policies, and procedures.

Of all the volunteers, the president, of course, has been the most visible face of the society to the membership and the general history-oriented public, second only to the visibility of the executive director. As there have been seventy presidents, it is beyond the scope of this article to focus on the priorities and accomplishments of any one or more of them. Presidents were elected for a one-year term and could succeed themselves, but a tradition of single terms allowed the honor to be spread around. In 1993 the presidential term was expanded to two years, allowing more time for a president to work on priority concerns.

The following list presents presidents in two categories. The first category shows the founding presidents—those who held that office upon the founding of the society in 1899 and later upon the establishment of the *Journal* in 1908. The second group lists those who have served from 1993 to the present under the two-year-term policy. By including the hometown of the president holding office, the list illustrates the fact that society volunteers have come from all over Illinois. Some presidents have been professional historians, but many over the years have not.

David W. Scott

Founding Presidents
Hiram W. Beckwith, Danville, 1899–1903
John F. Snyder, Virginia, 1903–5
Alfred Orendorff, Springfield, 1905–9

Recent Presidents with Two-Year Terms
Robert J. Klaus, Chicago, 1993–95
Michael J. McNerney, Carbondale, 1995–97
Robert McColley, Urbana, 1997–99
Barbara M. Posadas, DeKalb, 1999–2001
Rand Burnette, Jacksonville, 2001–3
David W. Scott, Springfield, 2003–5
Marvin W. Ehlers, Deerfield, 2005–7
John Weck, Elgin, 2007–9
Mark Sorensen, Decatur, 2009–11
Russell Lewis, Chicago, 2011–15
Randall Saxon, Peoria, 2015–17
Leah Joy Axelrod, Highland Park, 2017–19

1985–98: Reorganization, Fund-Raising, New Publication

The governmental structure under which the society operated changed significantly with the creation of the Illinois Historic Preservation Agency (IHPA) in 1985. The three trustees of the library were expanded in number to six and given responsibility for additional programs—namely, historic sites and other programs transferred to the agency from the Illinois Department of Conservation.

There continued to be a sense that the library and society were equal in organizational standing, but the introduction of historic sites and preservation services to the mix created a more complex organizational structure. The formal interrelationships are indicated by several job titles being assigned to one person. Michael Devine was not only state historian but also executive director of the Illinois State Historical Society and overall editor of the *Journal*. He served in these positions from 1986 to 1991. Yet on a 1990 organization chart, the society was listed as just one of six units in the agency. Others were the library, historic sites, preservation services, the Lincoln Legal Papers, and public affairs (the location of the Publications Section where the *Journal* was prepared).

The support for the various society programs—Awards, Markers, Centennial Businesses, the symposium, and the publications—remained strong to assure their continuation for some time to come. Regarding publications, for example, a 1988 membership survey found that 37 percent read each issue of the *Journal* "from cover to cover," while 63 percent "read selected articles." The format and content of the *Dispatch* were approved by 87 percent. The survey also found, not surprisingly, an older, well-educated membership (*Dispatch,* March–April 1988).

These years were ones of much improved financial conditions. The three-year Second Century Campaign, spearheaded by the society in the years 1987–90, raised more than $1.5 million from corporations, foundations, and individuals. These funds supported library acquisitions and new equipment, increased considerably the society's endowment, and funded other programs and projects.

Very beneficial to the society were major bequests from the estate of King V. Hostick, who died in 1993. Hostick was a well-known collector of Lincolniana who had been active with the society for many years. The society acquired $1.43 million for its endowment from the Hostick estate, with an equal amount directed to the library division of the preservation agency. Society leaders worked to gain the entire bequest that they thought the will granted to the society. However, the IHPA challenged that interpretation, and a court decided to divide the total in half.

Through another provision in the Hostick will, the Illinois State Historical Society received original glass-plate positives of images of Abraham Lincoln made by photographer Alexander Hesler during the 1860 presidential campaign. The society continues today to receive income through the sale of framed prints. Part of the Hostick bequest reinstated an annual award previously given to doctoral students preparing a dissertation on Illinois history. The society and the agency jointly have paid for and administered the program.

With the higher income generated by this increase in endowment and a membership level of about twenty-six hundred, the society's programs were able to function more independently of the IHPA's administration, and the society itself could pay for an executive director, several staff positions, and its own office space. By 1993 the society was required to do this, as the agency trustees voted that year to cease covering the cost of society administration. The last person to hold the joint position of society director and librarian/state historian was E. Duane Elbert (1991–93).

The following list from 1993 to the present includes those who have served as ISHS executive director during that time:

Carolyn Johnson (acting), 1993–95
Jon Austin, 1995–2000
Harry Klinkhamer, 2000–2001 (interim)
Thomas Teague, 2001–4
William Furry, 2004–present

The *Illinois Heritage*, a major new publication and popular history magazine, launched in 1997. It was to be printed on glossy paper and feature four-color photos. It was considered a membership builder, in that it would attract those interested in history but who might not join the society solely to receive the scholarly *Journal*. Publications with such popular focus had been considered from time to time in society history. In his report to the membership in 1937, Society director/editor Paul Angle expressed his conviction that "almost nothing the Society could do would serve a better purpose or attract more favorable attention" than having a popular publication. Angle noted that the appearance should be attractive and the subject matter should have a broad appeal, be interesting, and have illustrations (*Papers,* Official Proceedings, 1937).

In 1997 Executive Director Jon Austin, who served as the first editor of the *Heritage,* stated that "we seek nonfiction articles that are carefully written, and solidly researched and amenable to illustration" (*Dispatch,* Summer 1997). William Furry assumed the editorship of the *Heritage* in 2001 and retains that position to the present, along with the society executive directorship, which he assumed in 2004. Previous to his society involvement, he was an editor/writer with a Springfield-based weekly newspaper, the *Illinois Times.* Today the *Illinois Heritage* is a highly regarded addition to the services provided by the society to its members and the public. It publishes six issues a year containing interesting, well-illustrated articles on a great variety of historic events, persons, and locations.

The Visions of Illinois History calendar was introduced in 1997, issued in addition to the society's other publications as a benefit to members. Among the sources for its monthly photographs were the Illinois State Historical Library and local historical societies throughout the state. The daily calendar spaces contained references to significant events in Illinois history, thereby reinforcing the calendar's educational purpose. However, when resources became tight, the Visions Calendar was retired. In 2001 the renamed *Dispatch/News* also was retired. It publicized society events as well as events of local groups who were members of the Association of Illinois Museums and Historical Societies (AIMHS), formerly called the Congress of Museums and

Historical Societies. Even with the eventual phasing out of the association due to the agency having developed a competitive program, local societies and museums remain an important category of the society's membership base. The society profiles such groups in the *Heritage*, publishes schedules of coming events on its website (www.historyillinois.org), and provides visibility for them through the Awards and Markers Programs.

The society does continue as an active bookseller. Over the years dozens of books on Illinois history from university presses and other publishers have been offered to members at discounted rates. Occasionally the society has served as publisher or copublisher. Books include Robert Howard's *Mostly Good and Competent Men*, a 1988 biographical book of Illinois' first thirty-seven governors, and Carl D. Oblinger's *Divided Kingdom: Work, Community, and the Mining Wars in the Central Illinois Coal Fields during the Great Depression,* 1991.

Characterizing the mid-1990s were efforts to understand and clarify the activities of programs involving both the society and the agency. It took a full-page statement in the *Dispatch* to identify which of these two entities had primary responsibility for what, and which one was responsible for financing what activities or some phase thereof (*Dispatch/News,* 1996). It is not difficult to see how one of the partners could be viewed as encroaching on what the other understood as its role.

After several years of strategic planning, the society in 1987 set forth as one of its missions to cooperate with the Illinois Historic Preservation Agency. Other mission statements made clear that the society had a basic role in publications, markers, conferences, education programs, consulting services, and awards (*Dispatch,* Summer 1997). The awards committee was evolving into one that judged as "meritorious, excellent, or superior" publications, nonbook material, preservation activities, and special projects of local museums and societies, recognizing these achievements at the annual awards banquet.

Independence from the Agency: 1998–2018

As the 1990s wore on, many of those active within the society became increasingly dissatisfied with the control its officers and board members perceived the agency exerted over the *Journal* and other programs that were originally established by the society and that continued to be identified with the society. In 1998, a milestone event occurred: the board of the society declared its independence from the agency. It was publicly justified in the following 1999 statement:

David W. Scott

Over the past few years, the Illinois State Historical Society and the Illinois Historic Preservation Agency have steadily drifted apart after a decade of amiable cooperation since the Agency's inception in 1985 during James Thompson's administration. Recent actions by the Agency led the Society's president and Board of Directors to assert its independence rather than allow the Agency to further absorb established programs and services, essentially making them a department of the Agency. (*Dispatch*, Summer 1999)

The leaders at the time of the break were President Robert McColley (1997–99) and President-Elect Barbara Posadas (1999–2001), both professors, longtime active members of the ISHS, and members of the *Journal*'s editorial advisory board. In the President's Message of summer 1998, justifying the board decision, the two jointly stated that "gradually the State employees have assumed control of the editorial practice and policy of the *Journal* and distribute to where they please" (*Dispatch*, Summer 1998).

The dispute between the society and the agency provides a case study of the conflicts that can arise in public-private partnerships. The agency threatened legal action to gain control of the *Journal*'s trademark and copyright and made public statements that the *Journal* belonged to the agency. Despite these threats, the 1998 declaration of independence by the society's officers and board of directors did succeed. When they left, they took with them the society's publications and other programs. The society's board had moved a step ahead of the agency. The executive director, Jon Austin, was given credit for working assiduously on copyright and trademark issues to preserve the society's title to its almost ninety-year-old *Journal* (*Dispatch*, President's Message, Fall 2000).

Prior to the break, the agency had created its own association of museums, and at the time of the break it began to operate its own journal and symposium. The position of the society was that doing so is an unnecessary and costly duplication of services. The society is performing them and relying heavily on volunteers, so there was no need for the IHPA to also perform them, and at taxpayer expense. Society income derives solely from nongovernment sources: membership dues, donations, and income from invested funds, the largest of which has been the Hostick endowment.

With the break from the IHPA in 1998, the editorship of the *Journal* transferred from Evelyn Taylor, director of the Publications Division of the

14

Public Affairs Division of IHPA, to Robert McColley, professor of history at the University of Illinois, Urbana-Champaign. One of the first acts was to return to the original name of this publication—*Journal of the Illinois State Historical Society*. For reasons not provided in the 1984 annual report (prepared by state historian and society executive director Olive Foster), the name of the society was removed from the title of the *Journal* and was changed to *Illinois Historical Journal* that year. Perhaps the motivation was an attempt to expand the readership base beyond the typical society member to those interested in and involved with museums or libraries.

McColley explained that because the *Journal* was no longer produced at taxpayer expense, some economies would have to be made, but it would not be inferior in appearance and quality to other history journals. "We will aim to improve the quality and quantity of historical writing in each issue," McColley stated. On the other hand, recognizing that most of the society members are not professors, "we will not be publishing articles which employ rarified jargon of advanced disciplines" (*Dispatch*, Fall 1998).

Some modifications were made that changed the formatting of the *Journal*. Footnotes became endnotes. The biographies of the authors were removed from the title page of their article to a special section that contained the biographies of all the authors in an issue. An "editor's page" was introduced to summarize and comment on all the articles in the issue. There was a tendency for articles to become longer and clearly more scholarly with an expanded number of notes. African American and Civil War history have been frequent topics.

The following list of editors of the *Journal* covers the time between the break with the agency and the present and includes their university affiliation and years of service along with the volumes they edited:

> Robert M. McColley, University of Illinois U-C, 1998–2002, vols. 91–95 (no. 2)
> Kay Carr, Southern Illinois University, Carbondale, 2002–7, vols. 95 (No. 3) through 100
> Eileen M. McMahon, Lewis University, 2008–13, vols. 101–6
> Mark Hubbard, Eastern Illinois University, 2014–present, vols. 107–

During this twenty-year period, the *Journal* has kept to a schedule of four issues per year, remained a peer-reviewed academic journal, expanded the membership of its editorial review board, periodically used guest editors for issues on special topics, and continues providing a number of book reviews in each issue.

Starting in 2012, the University of Illinois Press became the society's membership/subscription service. Resulting from this affiliation was the extension to society members of the benefits of JSTOR. Members now have free access online to each article in the *Journal* since its founding in 1908.

The state-level environment within which the society has operated has shifted several times since it became independent of the Illinois Historic Preservation Agency (IHPA) in 1998. In 2004 the Abraham Lincoln Presidential Museum opened, and it was linked with the Illinois State Historical Library as a distinct entity within the agency and renamed the Abraham Lincoln Presidential Library and Museum (ALPLM). A new library building adjoins the presidential museum. The ALPLM continues to duplicate several society functions. In 2017 a Governor's Executive Order made the ALPLM a separate state agency and, in the process, dissolved the IHPA. Its historic sites and other preservation functions were assigned to the Department of Natural Resources.

The year 2018 marks 119 years since the founding of the Illinois State Historical Society, 110 years since the first publication of the *Journal,* and 20 years since the society became independent of the Illinois Historic Preservation Agency. In those 20 years the society has continued operating the programs it initiated, albeit with modifications. In addition to the *Journal* (1908), the society sponsors the annual meeting (1900), tours (1900), the historical Markers Program (1934), some student and teacher recognition and services (1947), scholarly history symposiums (1981), the Centennial Awards Program (1984), graduate fellowships (1996), *Illinois Heritage* (1997), and the annual awards banquet recognizing achievement in publications, non-book material, preservation, and other fields. On the other hand, several programs have been phased out: *Dispatch/News* initiated in 1958, the Vision Calendar initiated in 1997, and the Association of Illinois Museums and History Societies (AIMHS) organized in 1967.

In 2014 the society moved its office from downtown Springfield to the historic Strawbridge-Shepherd House adjoining the campus of the University of Illinois at Springfield. This move has deepened the relationship that the society has been cultivating with the university in recent years. Twice since its break with the agency, the society has engaged in strategic planning, a reassessment of its mission and goals. Among the priorities identified in the most recent planning exercise was expansion of outreach to teachers at all levels and changes in the committee structure to focus more effectively on fundraising and membership growth. A related outcome was the creation of a new staff position, director of development.

With the arrival of the bicentennial year, the society—drawing on its strength in publications—sponsored special issues of the *Journal*. Scholars were recruited to prepare articles in their fields of expertise in Illinois history.

In 2018, the year of the Illinois bicentennial, the society's mission to "foster awareness, understanding, research, preservation and recognition of history in Illinois" continues strong and promises to remain so in the years ahead.

PART I

EARLY ILLINOIS

1.

THE FRONTIER
IN ILLINOIS HISTORY

Ray A. Billington

Journal of the Illinois State Historical Society
vol. 43, no. 1 (Spring 1950)

Early Illinois settlers came from the southern states, but they were joined in the 1830s by New Englanders and other Northerners and, later, European immigrants. Some turned to land speculation. Democratic values were strong in frontier Illinois, which were reflected in the Constitution of 1818. Illinoisans had a flexible approach to economic systems, believing in laissez-faire at times and leaning toward collectivism at others, "ready to demand national or state aid, even governmental ownership," notably in the case of the Internal Improvement Act of 1837. On the frontier, mechanical ingenuity was highly developed, a response to challenging natural conditions. The variations of soil quality influenced eventual institution-building.

First, the frontier was an area where man's inherited institutions were significantly altered by natural conditions. Illinois offers a unique example of this transformation, for within its borders are two differing soil areas, each of which influenced not only the settlement process but subsequent economic developments. These resulted from two of the glaciers that ground their way southward during the Pleistocene Age. One, the Illinoian Drift, covered the state as far south as the Ohio River, leaving behind as it receded a rugged hill country littered with glacial debris and a compact clay soil marked by the absence of such essential elements as sulphur, potassium, carbon, and nitrogen. At a later day in geological history a second ice sheet pushed slowly down from the north—the Wisconsin Drift. Grinding down hills into smooth prairies, this glacier left behind a level countryside and a light loam soil rich in both the humus and chemicals needed for fertility. The Wisconsin Drift, however, did not benefit all parts of the state equally. The extreme southern limit of its advance was marked by the clearly defined Shelbyville Moraine, the most important natural boundary in Illinois. Pioneers were quick to notice the difference between lands lying north and south of this dividing line. Above the moraine the countryside was level, the soil deep, and the swamps numerous—swamps that could readily be drained to form humus-rich fields of immense productivity. Below, the rugged hills and glacier-strewn waste discouraged frontiersmen.

For a century both land prices and agricultural yields confirmed the judgment of the first settlers. In 1904, for example, lands just north of the moraine sold from $75 to $125 an acre; those to the south for $30 an acre. In the same year fields in Coles County, lying in the glaciated area, yielded thirty-six bushels of oats or forty of corn to the acre; in Cumberland County, just to the southward, only twenty-eight bushels of oats or thirty of corn were produced. Higher yields, in turn, allowed a greater degree of population concentration; a typical county north of the moraine contained 42 percent more people than another to the south. This reflected a more advanced stage of urbanization, on which depended cultural progress. The counties north of the Shelbyville Moraine, with more taxable wealth, could support better schools, colleges, libraries, and similar intellectual agencies. Although twentieth-century industrialization has lessened the effect of this natural boundary, Illinois' early history provides an outstanding example of that impact of nature on man, which typified the Americanization process.

Secondly, the frontier was an area where men of all sections and all nations met to form a new society, enriched by borrowings from many lands. In few other areas of the West did the accident of migration result in such a thorough blending of many racial strains as in Illinois. From the Southeast, from the Middle States, from New England, from older states of the Northwest, and from Europe came the state's pioneers, each contributing new flavor and new strength to the social order that evolved.

The first settlers were from the South. Some came from the seaboard regions, but more left homes in the uplands of the Carolinas, Virginia, Tennessee, or Kentucky, where a mingling process had already produced a mixed population from Scotch-Irish, German, and English strains. Skilled in the techniques of conquering the wilderness, these sturdy woodsmen were crowded from their old homes by the advance of the plantation frontier during the first quarter of the nineteenth century. Moving northward over Kentucky's Wilderness Road or drifting down the Ohio River on flatboats, they reached such embarkation points as Shawneetown by the thousands, then fanned out over the trails that led to the interior: some along the Great Western Road through Kaskaskia and Cahokia to St. Louis, others along the Goshen Road toward Alton, still others northward through Carmi to Albion after that town was founded in 1818. Filling in the rich bottom lands of the Ohio and Mississippi first, they soon spread over the forested portions of southern Illinois, seeking always the dense timber that testified to good soil. There they girdled the trees, planted their corn, raised their log cabins, split rails for their worm fences, shook through regular attacks of malaria, and steadily extended their civilization over a widening area.

The predominantly southern character of Illinois' early migration cannot be overemphasized. In 1818, when the first rough survey was taken, 38 percent of the settlers were from the South-Atlantic Seaboard, almost 37 percent from Kentucky and Tennessee, 13 percent from the Middle States, 3 percent from New England, and 9 percent from abroad. Thus 75 percent of the people were from the South, as opposed to 25 percent from all the rest of the United States and Europe. Nor did this ratio change during the next decade; as late as 1830 observers believed that Illinois was on its way to becoming a transplanted southern commonwealth, with all the institutions—including slavery—of its sister states south of Mason and Dixon's Line.

Then the tide turned. The Erie Canal was responsible. The opening in 1825 of that all-water route between the Hudson River and Lake Erie shifted the center of migration northward as New Englanders and men from the Middle Atlantic States found the gateway to the West open before them. Now the Great Lakes, not the Ohio River formed the pathway toward the setting sun. From Buffalo, New York, steamboats carried pioneers to new towns that sprang up as embarkation points: Cleveland, Toledo, Detroit, and Chicago. In 1834, eighty thousand people followed this route westward; eleven years later the number reached ninety-eight thousand. Michigan and Ohio attracted some, but Illinois, which was scarcely settled north of Alton, was the mecca of more. As they landed on the Chicago wharfs, that frontier hamlet blossomed overnight into a booming city. Such was the demand for buildings to house the newcomers that lots which sold in the spring of 1835 for $9,000 fetched $25,000 four months later. Most stayed in the cramped city only long enough to lay in supplies for the overland trip to the farm at the end of their rainbow. As they flooded over the countryside, the statistics of the government land offices told a dramatic story: a quarter of a million acres were sold in 1834, two million in 1835, almost four million in 1836.

The newcomers were as predominantly northern as the earlier immigrants were southern; fully 75 percent from north of the Mason and Dixon Line. Some came in groups from their native New England, fully equipped with pastor, schoolmaster, and eastern ways of life. Rockwell, Tremont, and Lyons were planted in this way between 1833 and 1836; a year later Wethersfield was laid out by Yankees whose childhoods had been spent in the shaded streets of that old Connecticut village. More came as individuals or in families, bringing with them the habits of their native New England and an insatiable thirst for land that did not, as one advertiser put it, stand on edge. As they came they transformed northern Illinois into a replica of the Northeast, just as southern Illinois was a duplicate of the Southeast. "Each of these two fountains of our civilization," wrote the editor of the *Democratic Monthly Magazine* in 1844, "is pouring forth its columns of immigrants to the Great Valley, forming there a new and third type that will reform and remold the American civilization.

Yet no frontier state could be typically American without the invigorating impact of European migration. Illinois benefited from the transfusion of this fresh blood during the 1840s. First to come were Irish peasants who drifted westward as laborers on canals and railroads; many eventually settled along the path of the Illinois and Michigan Canal. They were soon joined by German pioneers who had been driven from their homes by a devastating potato famine. Taking advantage of the cheap transportation offered by returning cotton ships, they reached New Orleans then traveled up the river to the cheap lands of Missouri, Illinois, and Wisconsin. With them came a sprinkling of intellectuals fleeing the political tempests of 1848. Few in numbers but large in influence, these leaders injected German customs and thought into the Illinois social order to a degree rarely equaled in other states.

If an Illinoisan had paused to take stock of his state at the close of the settlement period, he would have been proud of what he saw. In few commonwealths was acculturation so complete. Here in 1850 lived 334,000 native sons, 138,000 born in the South, 112,000 from the Middle Atlantic States, 37,000 from New England, 110,000 from the other states of the Old

Northwest, and 110,000 foreign born. Each group contributed something to the composite whole; each made Illinois more completely American. "The society thus newly organized constituted," wrote a Westerner, "is more liberal, enlarged, unprejudiced, and, of course, more affectionate and pleasant, than a society of people of *unique* birth and character, who bring all their early prejudices, as a common stock, to be transmitted as an inheritance in perpetuity."

Thirdly, the frontier was a region where mechanical ingenuity was highly developed in the never-ending battle between man and nature. In Illinois, settlers were forced to display a higher degree of adaptability than on most frontiers, for they faced a natural barrier that would have proved insurmountable to men of lesser stature: the vast central grassland. This was a forbidding obstacle to pioneers trained by two centuries of experience in the technique of clearing wooded areas. They had learned to judge the fertility of land by the density of its forests, to build their homes and fences from the plentiful wood supply, to secure their fuel from the wilderness, to obtain water from springs or streams, and to depend for shelter on the bands of timber left standing when fields were cleared. The habits of woodland pioneering were so deeply engrained in the average pioneer that any deviation was difficult if not impossible.

Yet that adjustment had to be made before Illinois could be settled. In the northern portions of the state, vast fields blanketed by six-foot-tall grass were interlaced with forest lots or crisscrossed by the bands of timber that followed every stream, but in central Illinois the prairies stretched away to the horizon on every side. Every instinct told the pioneer to avoid these grasslands. How could soil that would not support trees grow crops? Where could he get wood for his cabin, his fences, and his fuel? How could he obtain drinking water in a region where sluggish streams were thick with silt? How could he farm fields that were turned into swamps by every rainfall? And, most important of all, how could he bring the prairies under cultivation when tough sod shattered the fragile cast-iron plows which had proved adequate in timbered areas? Those were the problems that had to be solved before central and northern Illinois could be settled.

Little wonder, in view of these obstacles, that the shift from forest to prairie was made slowly. Farmers in the wooded areas along the Fox and Rock Rivers first began pasturing their cattle on nearby grasslands, then experimentally turned under some of the sod. When the land proved productive, others imitated their example, until a ring of farms surrounded the open grassland. Each year the cultivated fields were expanded until eventually they met. By 1850 all the grasslands of Illinois were under the plow save the central portions of the Grand Prairie. Not until the Illinois Central Railroad penetrated that region five years later was the last unsettled area occupied.

No simple account of the settlement of the state reveals the inventiveness, ingenuity, and boldness displayed by the Illinois pioneers. They overcame one of their most deep-seated prejudices when they learned that a soil's richness could not be determined by the density of its timber. They discovered that "stone coal" could be brought in more easily than wood for heating. They learned how to sink wells, and developed both well-drilling machinery and windmills to ease the back-breaking task of providing water. They discovered that cooperative efforts were necessary for drainage. And they invented special plows, pulled by four to six oxen, to break the tough sod. The expense involved in the use of these cumbersome contraptions, which could be hired from a local operator at a rate of two to five dollars an acre, created a demand for more efficient equipment which sent inventors to their drafting boards; one landmark was passed in 1837 when John Deere gave the world the steel plow. They learned to plant a "sod crop" by cutting upturned furrows at intervals with an ax, then dropping in a few kernels of corn. Although these fields could not be cultivated, the good Illinois soil produced yields up to fifty bushels to the acre, while the roots helped break up the rotting sod.

Learning new techniques and inventing new implements, the Illinois farmer not only solved one of the most troublesome problems faced in the conquest of the continent but by his very ingenuity stamped himself as a typical product of the American frontier.

Fourthly, the West was a region where democratic theory was enshrined and democratic practices perpetuated. Living in a land where all men were reduced to equality by the greater force of nature, conscious of the economic opportunity that promised to make the poor rich, and impatient of restraints from uninformed Easterners who knew nothing of western problems, the frontiersman insisted that each man's right to rule himself was as fundamental as his right to good land. The Westerner made few contributions to the mechanics of democracy, for in the realm of theory he was imitative rather than inventive, but he did show a marked tendency to adopt the most liberal practices of the East he had left behind. Illinois, as a typical frontier state, exhibited this tendency admirably.

Its people's democratic faith was first reflected in the Constitution of 1818. At this time Southerners predominated; in the constitutional convention, twenty-one were from the South, two had been born in Illinois of Southern parents, five came from the Middle Atlantic States, and only one from New England. Despite this influence toward conservatism, despite even the perpetuation of slavery—in the form of indentured servitude—the Illinois constitution was a model of democratic practice. Based on the frames of government already adopted in Ohio, Tennessee, and Kentucky, but going beyond them in the direction of popular rule, it vested virtually sovereign power in the legislature while reducing the governor to a mere figurehead. True, the chief executive, together with the justices of the state Supreme Court, constituted a council of revision empowered to veto acts of the assembly, but as laws could be passed over the veto by a mere majority vote, this meant nothing. Property qualifications for voting and office holding were swept away, and all adult males who lived in the state for six months were allowed to vote. Mounting western nationalism was reflected in a provision that the governor must have been a citizen of the United States for at least thirty years.

The Constitution of 1818, democratic as it was, only paved the way for still more liberal changes during the next years; eventually even the state judges were popularly elected. Illinois, a frontier state, believed, even before Lincoln's classic statement, in rule of the people, by the people, and for the people.

Fifthly, the frontier was a region of optimism, of boundless belief in the future. The Illinois frontiersman shared with his fellow Westerners an exuberant faith in progress; like them, too, he had a rambunctious confidence in his ability to make his dreams come true. One manifestation of this spirit was his willingness to support colleges. Although primary education was not fully established until the passage of the school law of 1855, institutions of higher learning began to multiply a quarter century earlier, many of them church-supported schools dedicated to the task of producing intelligent congregations and learned ministers. By 1840 the thinly settled, poverty-ridden Prairie State boasted no less than twelve colleges. Pioneers unable to read and write were anxious to contribute time and money to assure their children a better opportunity, their community a richer culture. In few other states were frontiersmen willing to invest so heavily in the future.

On a less elevated plane, frontier optimism in Illinois found expression in speculative land buying. In no other wilderness commonwealth were so many acres engrossed by jobbers, so many "paper towns" laid out, so much absentee capital invested in the years before 1850.

They were legion, the starry-eyed speculators who gobbled up the forests and prairies of the state. Many were farmers who bought more land than they could use, hoping to sell off the remainder to later comers; in 1850, seven million acres of Illinois land that had been sold but not unimproved was largely held by such purchasers. Others were local businessmen or politicians who accumulated strategically located lands against the price rise they believed inevitable. Still others were wealthy Easterners or Southerners whose careers were devoted to speculation. Men of this ilk engrossed six million acres in Illinois between 1847 and 1855 by buying up soldiers' warrants from fifty cents to a dollar an acre; others of the same fraternity bought seven million acres of rich countryside near Springfield between 1833 and 1837. A favorite occupation of all these speculators was the accumulation of prospective town sites. Scarcely a bend or fork of a stream deep enough to wade in, scarcely a bay on Lake Michigan that would shelter a rowboat, scarcely a spot on any imagined canal or railroad that might conceivably be built in the future, that was not grabbed up by some land jobber. Most of these never got beyond the "paper" stage—where maps were drawn to induce gullible Easterners to buy town lots—yet in one northern Illinois "town" that had only one house, lots sold for $2,500 each, while a Chicago observer, witnessing the mad scramble for town sites, seriously proposed reserving one or two sections in each township for farming!

Finally, the frontier was an area where opportunism, rather than an enduring belief in any one theory or system, shaped the character of economic life and thought. Students of the westward movement, failing to recognize this, have frequently insisted that the West was a region of economic radicalism, of laissez-faire, of rugged individualism. True, the frontiersman was an economic radical on occasion, but he was just as likely to be found among extreme conservatives; he was an individualist if such a course seemed feasible, but he did not hesitate to embrace the cause of collectivism if that path promised greater profits. He did believe in laissez-faire—some of the time—but he was ready to demand national or state aid, and even governmental ownership of essential services, if such a course seemed wiser. The frontiersman, in other words, was a practical realist who believed in following the path that promised greatest immediate returns, regardless of past precedents. An opportunist rather than a theorist, he showed no embarrassment when forced to shift his thought with the changing times. The Illinois pioneer reflected this point of view. His vacillating opinion on the question of state-operated transportation facilities and on matters of finance illustrated how well he fitted into the frontier mold.

He first became aware of the transportation problem in the 1820s and 1830s, when accumulating agricultural surpluses in interior Illinois brought home the need for highways to the main trade arteries of the West: the Mississippi River system and the Great Lakes. Statisticians were everywhere present to demonstrate the profits that would go to the pioneer if these could be built. A bushel of corn, they pointed out, sold in the interior for twelve to twenty cents; at Chicago or on the Ohio River that same bushel fetched fifty cents. As the average farmer produced sixty bushels to the acre, lead-pencil engineers needed only enough ciphering paper to prove the stratospheric profits that would be the farmer's with better outlets. For every hundred-acre farm, the increased return would be $1,800 a year; for the ten million acres soon to be in production the saving would be $180 million! Roads and canals would transmute Illinois' poverty into luxurious affluence. So all agreed, and they were equally sure that these outlets could only be built by the state government, which alone boasted resources and credit adequate for the giant task. By the beginning of the 1830s all Illinois was advocating an important experiment in state socialism.

Thus was the stage set for the fabulous internal improvement program launched during the next decade. An approving populace watched delightedly as the legislature authorized construction of the Illinois and Michigan Canal, secured a land grant from Congress, and placed the credit of the state behind the canal bonds that were marketed in the East and England to finance the project. This simply whetted the popular appetite for more. The canal benefited only one corner of Illinois; why should the rest be neglected when state-constructed railroads and canals would not only pay for themselves and enrich shippers but assure such profits that taxes could be abolished? Swept along on this wave of enthusiasm, Illinois adopted its famous Internal Improvements Act of 1837. This fantastic measure pledged the four hundred thousand poverty-ridden inhabitants of the frontier state to spend more than $10 million on a network of railroads and canals which would crisscross in every direction. If the program had been less grandiose, and the times more auspicious, Illinois' dreams of a state-operated transportation system might have been realized. Instead the mere magnitude of the plan, the lack of managerial skill among those entrusted with its administration, and the Panic of 1837 brought a speedy end to the whole project. By 1841 work was at a standstill.

The effect of this debacle on public opinion was great. As Illinois farmers viewed the visible remains of their wrecked hopes—half-completed roadbeds, untidy slashes that marked the beginning of canals, a $15 million state debt, a 50 percent increase in land taxes, debt repudiation—a feeling of revulsion against state ownership swept across the state. During the next few years the one completed railroad, the Northern Cross, which had cost $250,000, was sold for $21,000 without a voice being raised to protest. The people wanted no more public control; private enterprise could run the risks in the future. For the next generation the citizens of Illinois advocated laissez-faire as strenuously as they had governmental ownership a few years before.

Their frontier-like tendency toward opportunism was even better illustrated when two panics during the pioneer period brought them face to face with an age-old question: what banking and currency system would assure security and prosperity for their state? Twice they tried to solve the problem, and each time their answers differed.

The issue first arose in the era of hard times following the Panic of 1819. What was needed to stem the downward trend, all agreed, was more money. This could best be provided by local banks, backed by the faith and credit of the state which could issue paper currency. On the crest of this pro-bank sentiment, the legislature in 1821 chartered the Bank of Illinois, capitalized at $300,000 to be subscribed by the state and authorized to issue bank notes in small denominations to the full extent of its capitalization. The notes were made legal tender for all public and private debts; any creditor who refused to accept them was prohibited from seizing property pledged as security for at least three years. This, in other words, was an inflationary measure, designed principally to increase the amount of circulating currency. Popular meetings in Illinois and elsewhere went even farther along the path toward inflation by demanding a complete paper currency bearing no relationship to specie.

The inflationary trend was accentuated during the prosperous 1830s when money was in great demand for land speculation, business expansion, and the internal improvement program. By this time the State Bank of Illinois, with headquarters at Springfield, had joined the Bank of Illinois in catering to the state's financial needs. Both of these institutions were called upon to aid the public works program that was launched in 1837. This was done by increasing their capitalization, turning over to them state bonds in return for shares of bank stock, and then borrowing back the bank notes issued on the basis of the state's own securities. Officials honestly believed that this flimsy process would not only supply money for internal improvements but eventually pay for all construction, as the bank stock was expected to pay annual dividends of 8 to 10 percent. These returns, plus tolls from canals and railroads, would soon retire the entire investment and provide so much income that taxes could be abolished! This was the talk, not of wild dreamers, but of sober businessmen and state leaders.

Illinois learned its lesson when the Panic of 1837 tumbled down its speculative house of cards. With hard times, antibank feeling swept across the state. Farmers who owed money to the banks grumbled that they could not continue their payments. Others who were paid for their produce in the depreciated notes of the two institutions complained that they were being swindled. Still others lost heavily when the banks finally collapsed. More were convinced that there was a direct connection between the banks and the panic. The depression, they told themselves, was a product of the wild currency fluctuations that followed the overissue of state bank notes. These might benefit eastern capitalists, but every fluctuation drove the poor man, who could never understand such financial mysteries, deeper into debt. His only protection was to abolish banks and paper money, returning to the security of a solid gold and silver currency. "A bank of earth is the best bank," wrote one, "and a plow share the best share," while another declared: "Banks to help the farmer appear to me like feudal lords to defend the people." The Illinois farmer of the post-panic era was the most conservative of all Americans on financial questions.

The reaction of the state's pioneers to the panics of 1819 and 1837 demonstrated the opportunistic nature of frontier economic thought. In one case they moved leftward along the road to inflation; in the other they swung so far to the economic right that the nation's business leaders and bankers seemed financial radicals by comparison.

Reactions such as these stamped the Illinois frontiersman as typically American. He was typical, too, in his optimism, his democracy, his ingenuity, and his faith in progress. Molded by the frontier environment and strengthened by contacts with fellow pioneers from all the Western world, he served as a perfect answer to Hector St. John de Crèvecoeur's famous query: "What then is the American, this new man?"

Ray A. Billington

RELATED READING

Robert M. Sutton, "Illinois' Year of Decision, 1837," *Journal of the Illinois State Historical Society* vol. 58, no. 1 (Spring 1960).

The General Assembly enacted an expensive and impractical scheme of internal improvements. In the end, thanks to bad planning and worse timing, Illinois was left with a debt of $15 million and a grand total of twenty-four miles of complete railroad track of the thirteen hundred planned throughout the state.

2.

TAVERN THEATRE
IN EARLY CHICAGO

Arthur W. Bloom

Journal of the Illinois State Historical Society
vol. 74, no. 3 (Autumn 1981)

Chicago's first recorded theatrical performance was by one Mr. Bowers, an itinerant "Professeur de tours Amusant." It was an unpromising start, presented on the second floor of a tavern, but typical of the first wave of American theater. In 1837, a traveling company of actors set up shop in a derelict hotel rather than a tavern. Its three-month season was so successful that the company decided to build its own theater for the next year. This led into a new phase involving larger companies and expectations of returning to perform in spaces specifically constructed as theaters. The focus here is the first phase.

The beginning and growth of the theatre in Chicago followed a national pattern. The pattern's discoverer, Professor Douglas McDermott of California State College, Stanislaus, found that "once towns were established, theatre grew according to a three-phase process of transformation, which, because of its persistence, constitutes a working definition of frontier theatre in America."

McDermott described the first phase as "the theatre of the strolling player," which was composed of "magicians, variety performers, partners like Mark Twain's King and Duke, and small repertory companies made up of one or two families." Those companies performed in Lexington,

First McVicker's Theatre, in an 1865 engraving (altered here to eliminate newspaper text from upper left). Theatrical performances have always been a part of Chicago's cultural and entertainment atmosphere. McVicker's was destroyed by the Chicago Fire in 1871. *Image courtesy Chicago History Museum.*

Frankfort, Louisville, Cincinnati, and Pittsburgh as early as 1810. But by the 1830s such cities as Cleveland and Detroit had become part of a more complex second-phase circuit in which companies with as many as twenty-four members performed in spaces specifically constructed of theatres.

Chicago's limited population and rugged climate, however, kept it in the first phase of American theatre until 1838. Charles Joseph Latrobe, who passed through the town in 1833, described it as "one chaos of mud, rubbish, and confusion." The lone itinerant performers of 1834 and the first band of strolling players in 1837 had to perform in what is euphemistically described in the modern period as "found space." One hundred and fifty years ago in Chicago it was virtually the only space available—the local tavern.

The first site of Chicago tavern theatre was "the house of Mr. D. Graves," where on Monday, February 24, 1834, a Mr. Bowers—billed as "Professeur de tours Amusant"—gave a two-part presentation. The announcement of the performance appeared in the classified advertisements of the *Chicago Democrat* under "Exhibitions," and the act was described as follows:

Part First

Mr. Bowers will fully personate Monsieur Chaubert, the celebrated Fire King, who so much astonished the people of Europe, and go thro' his wonderful Chemical Performance. He will draw a red hot iron across his tongue, hands, &c. and will partake of a comfortable warm supper, by eating fire balls, burning sealing wax, live coals on fire, melted lead. He will dip his fingers in melted lead, and make use of a red hot spoon to convey same to his mouth.

Part Second

Mr. Bowers will introduce many very amusing feats of ventriloquism and legerdemain, many of which are original, and too numerous to mention. Admittance is 50 cents, children half price.

Bowers is representative of the pioneers of the first wave of American theatre, about which McDermott writes: "Its members were amateurs with no particular theatrical background. . . . They played in found spaces, in barns, warehouses, courthouses, stores, and unfinished dwellings. Above all, they were itinerant, seldom remaining for more than one season in a region, and hardly ever visiting the same town twice."

Nothing is known about Bowers except that he performed a similar act in Cleveland a month before arriving in Chicago. His program was not reviewed by the Chicago press, nor was he mentioned in the memoirs of other frontier performers. The circumstances of his performance, however, can be surmised from information about frontier Chicago.

At the time of Bowers's appearance, Chicago was a community of approximately 3,200 inhabitants. It was said to be the "largest commercial town in Illinois," with fifty-one stores, thirty groceries, one bank, one newspaper, and ten taverns. The terrain, nevertheless, in the words of resident John Dean Caton, was "low wet prairie." So "impassable" were the roads, according to Caton, that guests at a ball held one month before Bowers's performance could travel only "on lumber-wagons or ox-carts, or other similar heavy conveyance."

The tavern of Dexter Graves, later called the Mansion House, was newly enlarged in 1834. According to Chicago historian A. T. Andreas, in 1831 Graves had built an "unpretentious log tavern" east of the corner of Dearborn Street on the north side of Lake Street. By July 1833, Graves was ordering nails from merchant Philo Carpenter for a two-story addition. When Harriet

N. Warren Dodson passed through the town in November 1833, she observed that the tavern was "nearly enclosed." And by December members of the Board of Trustees of Chicago were meeting there.

The second story of Graves's house—referred to as the "Assembly Room" —remained unfurnished, although it was equipped with fireplaces at either end. Charles Fenno Hoffman, an eastern visitor, described the area in January 1834, as "a tolerably-sized dancing-room." He also observed that an "orchestra [stand] of unplaned boards was raised against the wall in the centre of the room." Such a platform would have sufficed as a stage for Bowers. The fact that managers of a ball there in February 1834 printed a total of two hundred tickets supports Hoffman's claim that the room had a good capacity.

Tickets to Bowers's performances were "to be had at the bar," which typically functioned as the registration desk and lobby in an early nineteenth-century tavern. Adults were admitted to the candlelit performances for fifty cents, children for twenty-five cents. Seats were "preserved for Ladies" in an attempt to provide for the comfort and convenience of the spectators. Thus, although Virginia Baxley, the wife of Fort Dearborn's commanding officer, was willing to attend balls at Graves's "Assembly-Room," newspaper advertisements in the 1830s treated the presence of women in the theatre as if it were a somewhat unexpected and felicitous occurrence.

Although Bowers's performance was the first recorded theatrical event in Chicago, other entertainment was available in the town's early period. Charles Butler, a real estate speculator, wrote in his diary entry of August 5, 1833, of attending the "monthly concert." The musicians were probably members of the Chicago Academy of Sacred Music, which practiced every Friday night in the municipal courtroom, under the leadership of George Davis. The account books of John Calhoun, Chicago's earliest printer, indicate that at least three balls were held each year during the 1832–55 period. Also, an advertisement in the *Chicago Democrat* of June 11, 1834, informed patrons that tickets for an exhibition of ventriloquism at another tavern were available "at the usual places." "At the usual places" implies that by 1834 the selling of tickets had become quite common enough to have developed a traditional set of purchase sites, one of which was probably the bar of the Travellers' Home.

The Travellers' Home was originally and better known as the Wolf Point Tavern. Rechristened by its owner, Chester Ingersoll, in October 1833, it was a double log house built by James Kinzie in 1828 or 1829 on the west side of the Chicago River, just north of the main branch. Henry R. Hurlbut, a Chicago historian writing in 1881, described its site as "a triangular point of ground embraced with the three streets, W. Lake, Canal, and W. Water Streets." The appearance of the building has been much debated—particularly because of a frequently reproduced engraving that first appeared in the *Chicago Magazine* of June 1857 and that Hurlbut described as a "hideous deformity." Eyewitness accounts seem to agree, however, that by the summer of 1833 a second floor had been added. Guests slept in what one of its later owners, Mary Taylor, described as "the big unfinished room over the store." Mrs. Taylor's recollection that balls were held in that room creates the possibility that the ventriloquism performance of June 1834 was also held there, although the "spacious dining room" or "long room on the first floor" mentioned by early Chicago resident Leonora Hoyne would have been adequate.

The Travellers' Home ventriloquist, a Mr. Kenworthy, like Bowers before him, was a lone itinerant who performed "whims, Stories, Adventures &c. of a Ventriloquist, as embodied in his entertaining monologue of the Bromback family." Kenworthy was apparently traveling east, because he had performed in Columbia, Missouri, in February and was to surface in Cleveland in August. Unlike ventriloquists of later days, he worked without a dummy and instead threw his voice to various parts of the room.

The first major advance in Chicago theatre beyond the tavern level occurred in 1837, when an eastern scene painter and minor actor named Harry Isherwood converted the dining room of the Old Sauganash Hotel into a performance site for Chicago's first theatrical company.

Like Dexter Grave's house and the Travellers' Home, the Sauganash Hotel, located on the southeast corner of Lake and Market Streets, was the extension of a one-room log cabin. The cabin was eventually turned into a barroom. In 1831, a two-story frame addition—housing a dining room, sleeping rooms, and a second-floor parlor—was attached to the cabin's south side. Some twenty years later, Juliette Kinzie recalled the structure as a "pretentious white, two-story building." In 1870, John Dean Caton remembered it as "a fashionable boardinghouse." But writing in 1853, Patrick Shirreff pictured the inn as "extremely crowded" and "dirty in the extreme." Charles Joseph Latrobe described it as a "vile, two-storied barrack, which, dignified as usual by the title of Hotel, afforded us quarters." In it, he said, was "appalling confusion, filth, and racket."

By 1836, the Sauganash had changed hands and had been renamed the United States Hotel by its new proprietors, Harriet and John Murphy. Yet when Harry Isherwood began a search for a home for his theatre company in 1837, the building was deserted and available. In light of Harriet Murphy's comment that "we had no ballroom in our house but danced in the dining room," Andreas's contention that performances took place in the dining room is probably accurate.

Many of the descriptions of Chicago's first theatrical company and season must be corrected because of newspaper accounts from the Illinois State Historical Library, the American Antiquarian Society, and the University of Chicago. The seating capacity of the Sauganash, for example, has been inflated. In 1884, James McVicker contended that it seated two hundred; Andreas placed the capacity at about three hundred. Subsequent historians—including Bessie Louise Pierce, Milburn John Bergfald, and Ernestine and Harold Briggs—have accepted McVicker's figures. Yet contemporary newspapers state that when "upwards of 100 tickets were sold, the house was a complete jam."

The length of Chicago's first theatrical season, conversely, has been underestimated. Robert L. Sherman's *Chicago Stage* places the first performance of Isherwood's company on Monday, October 23, 1837; the Briggses and Gordon Van Kirk put the event "late in October." According to the *Chicago American* of October 21, 1837, however, the company had been performing for "nearly a fortnight," which would indicate an opening date shortly after October 7. There are similar problems with the closing date. Andreas claims that "it is known that the theater was not kept open longer than six weeks"; but contemporary newspapers show that Isherwood's company stayed in Chicago through the week of January 3, 1838—nearly three months after the opening.

Finally, the extent of the company's repertoire and the level of its professionalism must be re-evaluated. Douglas McDermott contends that the first-phase company "presented a repertory of no more than a dozen of the established classics of the time." But contemporary sources indicate that at least thirty-four plays were presented by Isherwood during the 1837 season in Chicago.

McDermott has mistakenly placed the troupe into a phase of frontier theatre characterized by Mark Twain's King and Duke. But the members of the troupe organized by Harry Isherwood and his partner Alexander MacKenzie were not "amateurs with no particular theatrical background," as McDermott implies. They were seasoned performers. Their company was a professional offshoot of the Jefferson family troupe, which had begun operations in 1830 and disbanded in 1835. MacKenzie had been the partner of Joseph Jefferson II from 1832 to 1835 in Washington, Baltimore, and the Pennsylvania cities of York, Lancaster, Reading, and Pottsville.

The company that performed at Chicago's Sauganash Hotel in October 1837 had been formed in Buffalo, New York, in the spring of that year, when managerial problems, an actors' strike, and a lack of audience forced Edwin Dean and D. D. McKinney, operators of Buffalo's Eagle Street Theatre, to move their theatrical forces westward to the City Theatre of Detroit. There, on May 31, 1837, the company opened for a summer season that lasted until September.

In early September 1837, Isherwood had set out for Cleveland, leaving the company to play a three-night engagement at the Detroit Museum. In Cleveland, he fitted up the Italian Hall as a theatre and announced a twelve-night season. The company opened on Tuesday, September 12, just three days after their last performance in Detroit. They had picked up several new actors, including a juvenile hornpipe dancer named Master Lavett (sometimes spelled Lavette). They remained in Cleveland until Tuesday, September 26.

Meanwhile, Isherwood proceeded westward, arriving in Chicago in late September or early October 1837. In the pelting rain, he wandered through town and finally found the Sauganash Hotel. Fifty years later, he wrote McVicker: "It was a queer-looking place. It had been a rough tavern, with an extension of about fifty feet in length added to it. It stood at some distance out on the prairie, solitary and alone. I arranged with the owner and painted several pretty scenes."

The company that performed at the Sauganash was managed by Isherwood and his partner, Alexander MacKenzie, a bookseller turned box-office manager. At its nucleus were Isherwood and MacKenzie and the daughters of actor Joseph Jefferson I (1774–1832)—Hester Jefferson MacKenzie, wife of the partner, and Mary Anne Jefferson Ingersoll, a dancer/actress. Other members were William Childs, a comedian; Thomas Sankey, who specialized in playing elderly men; Madame Arreline, a "French" dancer who played the ingénue parts; and Henry Leicester, the leading man.

The company had ridden the steam packet *Pennsylvania* from Cleveland around the Great Lakes, docking at Green Bay, Wisconsin, two days before they arrived in Chicago. A French traveler, Count Francesco Arese, was among the passengers, and he described the troupe with patronizing humor:

There was also on board a theatrical company on its way to Chicago, whose two conspicuous members were the leading lady and the head dancer. Mrs. or Miss Ingerson (*sic*) for I am not certain which, was neither young nor good looking, but indeed quite the contrary; but to make up for that she paced the deck with an air of as much importance as either Semiramis or Cleopatra could have worn. The dancer, who called herself French, or more truly advertised herself as French, had apparently had terrible misfortunes with her shoes, whether low or high, for she wore a pair of her husband's boots, and such was the slimness of her legs, which would have done credit to a fighting-cock, and the fullness of her dresses, that you might have called her a butterfly-in-boots.

The company landed in Chicago and began performing in the newly "fitted up" Sauganash shortly after October 7, 1837. It was not until October 17, however, that they applied to the Common Council for a six-month license, indicating their intention to stay during the winter. They requested that a low fee be set because they anticipated no profits due to a lengthy run. But licensing fees were common and difficult to avoid in the period, and the Common Council established the amount of $150 for six months. Isherwood and MacKenzie protested the fee on the basis that their Buffalo license had cost only fifty dollars for the year and that expenses would be higher and receipts lower in Chicago. The validity of their contention is shaky, because license fees varied considerably in the period. In Detroit, the troupe of Dean and McKinney had paid twenty-five dollars per week in May 1834; twelve dollars per week in May 1835; and only fifty dollars for the entire year in 1836. In 1839, Dean was to pay one hundred dollars for a six-month license in Buffalo. John Miller was granted a license at five dollars per week for a circus exhibit in Chicago. And fees in the Kentucky town of Lexington and Frankfort were already ranging from thirty to forty dollars per week. The Common Council of Chicago had not been unreasonable. Nevertheless, MacKenzie's and Isherwood's protests were shrewd business. City councils often reversed their initial decisions, and upon the motion of Alderman John Dean Caton, the term was changed to three months for seventy-five dollars. Isherwood and McKenzie paid on October 27, 1837.

The shortening of the theatrical term is significant. When the company left Chicago in January 1838, they state that they wished to avoid "the severity of the weather," yet the decision may well have been influenced by the fact that their license had expired. They apparently had decided that renewal was unprofitable.

The fee was probably not a particular hardship, for it appears that the company's first season was reasonably successful. While there is no evidence for ticket prices charged in Chicago in 1837, Cleveland newspapers indicate that the MacKenzie-Isherwood troupe played there for fifty cents a ticket only a month before. Robert Sherman contends that the top ticket price in Chicago was seventy-five cents. Although there is no way of checking Sherman's unfootnoted information, his use of specific play titles and cast lists indicates that he may have been working from scrapbook clippings destroyed after his death. Moreover, much of what he says dovetails with extant editorial comments. Consequently, it is safe to assume a ticket range of fifty to seventy-five cents for the 1837 Chicago season.

Given that range of prices, an audience capacity of approximately one hundred, and a run of seventy-nine performances (excluding Sundays) from October 7, 1837, to January 6, 1838, the MacKenzie-Isherwood company could have played to approximately 7,900 people and taken in between $3,950 and $5,925. Editorial comments in newspapers during the season indicate that houses were excellent despite inclement weather. Moreover, the company returned for two more seasons and built their own theatre. Their objections to paying a six-month license demonstrates that they had little expectation of filling the house in a town that first impressed Isherwood as "no place for a show."

Many of the pieces that the MacKenzie-Isherwood company performed in Chicago were at least ten years old, while about one-third of them were the "most recent hits" of the last decade. Nearly all of the plays were English, and 68 percent of the titles that can be identified had been part of the Jefferson family's repertoire for fifteen years or more.

While the thirty-four plays known to have been performed in Chicago during MacKenzie-Isherwood's first season fall within the three-dozen maximum set by McDermott for a second-phase operation, they represent only 35 percent of the possible performance days. Consequently, the total repertoire is likely to have been far in excess of McDermott's limit. The reason for that lies in the nature of a nineteenth-century theatrical company.

Nineteenth-century companies would organize, perform, break up, re-form, and move on with a somewhat different constituency over and over again. A troupe such as the MacKenzie-Isherwood company was an assortment of actors, musicians, singers, and technicians whose professional and personal lives continually intersected. That explains why a small group of actors such as the MacKenzie-Isherwood company could produce what seems to the modern theatre practitioner an extraordinarily large number of plays in a short period of time. Their entire Chicago season was performed chiefly by six men and three women, although their forces were occasionally augmented by such townspeople as Mr. and Mrs. George Davis, who were well known locally for their abilities in music and dance.

Although playing under less than ideal conditions, the MacKenzie-Isherwood company was essentially the vanguard of a more professional operation. They were not just passing through Chicago, as were Mr. Bowers or Mr. Kenworthy. They played three seasons in the city (October 1837–January 1838; May 1838–October 1838; August 1839–November 1839), between which they made tours of Illinois, Iowa, and Minnesota. They were consciously attempting to establish a permanent theatrical base.

Moreover, they succeeded during their first season in nurturing a frontier audience. On Saturday, October 21, 1837, the *Chicago American* reported that "the acting is well spoken of and the crowded houses are constant." On Wednesday, November 8, the *Chicago Democrat* noted that "the audience is nightly increasing" and that the actors were frequently interrupted with "loud and protracted applause." On the twenty-second, the theatre was viewed as "flourishing in defiance of the embarrassment of the times" caused by the Panic of 1837. Women began to attend regularly in significant numbers. And despite torrential rains that began on November 21 and apparently continued through most of December, houses, according to the *Democrat*, were at least "respectable" if not full. When a benefit was held on December 17 for Henry Leicester, the company's leading man, the house was "a complete jam." By late December, Isherwood and MacKenzie had decided to build a theatre in the upper floor of a new building for the next season.

Isherwood's prediction that Chicago was "no place for a show" had been wrong. In January 1838, when the performers moved southward on tour, they promised to return in the spring. Chicago's tavern theatre phase was over, and the city was about to advance to the next step of its theatrical history.

3.

THE PIONEER SQUATTER

Robert W. McCluggage

Illinois Historical Journal vol. 82, no. 1 (Spring 1989)
Historians have identified three groups of migrants into a frontier area by the order of their arrival—first the pioneer squatters, then the settlers, followed by entrepreneurs. The author focuses on the first of these. One observer stated that "these men cannot live in regular society. They are too idle; too talkative; too passionate; too prodigal; and too shiftless to acquire either property or character. They are impatient of the restraints of law, religion and morality. They were hunters and moved often." In sum, the pioneer squatters represented a different culture.

The bicentennial of the Northwest Ordinance of 1787 invited attention to the people whose actions and needs led to adoption of the Ordinance and its sequels—that is, the migrants of European origin who populated the region in the name of the United States. Historians have tended to classify these groups into a sequence of two, or occasionally three, broad categories, one following the other. The first comers were the pioneer squatters; next, the settlers; and finally, the entrepreneurs who oversaw the transition to industrialization and urbanization. Least known and least studied of these groups is the first. John Mason Peck, an itinerant frontier preacher and booster of Illinois country, established the frontiersman's traits:

First comes the pioneer, who depends for the subsistence of his family chiefly upon the natural growth of vegetation, called the "range," and the proceeds of hunting. . . . He is the occupant for the time being,

pays no rent, and feels as independent as the "lord of the manor." . . .
[He] occupies till the range is somewhat subdued, and hunting a little
precarious, or, which is more frequently the case, till neighbors crowd
around . . . and he lacks elbow room.

Peck's judgment on the backwoodsmen is neutral. There is, however,
a great deal of testimony suggesting that those founding fathers did not
enjoy their contemporaries. J. Hector St. John de Crevecoeur summarized
his view of those hardy but unadmirable pioneers: "Thus are our first steps
trod, thus are our first trees felled, in general, by the most vicious of our
people." Timothy Dwight agreed: "A considerable part of all those who *begin*
the cultivation of the wilderness, may be denominated *foresters*, or *Pioneers*.
. . . These men cannot live in regular society. They are too idle; too talkative;
too passionate; too prodigal; and too shiftless; to acquire either property or
character. They are impatient of the restraints of law, religion, and morality."

Most observers deplored pioneer morality. One reporter, an Anglican
clergyman and admittedly prejudiced, "accused the back country fold of
'swopping wives as cattle' and estimated that 95 percent of the young women
he married were already pregnant . . . [and] that nine-tenths of the settlers
had venereal disease."

Even worse, they were indolent. "Too many," Henry C. Knight thought,
"instead of resting on one day in seven, work only on one day in six." Sir
William Johnson declared: "Many of these emigrants are idle fellows that
are too lazy to cultivate lands & invited by the plenty of game they found,
have employed themselves in hunting."

Undoubtedly part of that perception of the pioneers rested on the revulsion at the squalor of their persons and habitations. Their "miserable
Cabins" sheltered dirty women fostering filthy urchins all "pigged together"
in a single room, along with whatever passersby happened along. They were
reportedly no more fastidious in their persons than they were in their dwellings. William Cullen Bryant, traveling the Illinois frontier in 1832, described
some of the pioneers he met: "In looking for a place to feed our horses I asked
for corn at the cabin of an old settler named Wilson. Here I saw a fat dusky
woman barefoot with six children as dirty as pigs and shaggy as bears. She
was lousing one of them and cracking the unfortunate insects between her
thumbnails. I was very glad when she told me that she had no corn nor oats."

For some, however, the revulsion might be mitigated if the proprietor
turned out to be a man of substance. During a steamboat wooding stop,

Edmund Flagg went ashore for a stroll and, as he says, "entered easily into confabulation with a pretty, slatternly-looking female, with a brood of mushroom, flaxen-haired urchins at her apron-strings, and an infant at the breast very quietly receiving his supper." Flagg continued in that vein but then added that the husband was "proprietor of some thousand acres of *bottom*" in the vicinity. "Subsequently I was informed that the worthy woodcutter could be valued at not less than one hundred thousand! Yet, *en virite*, reader mine, I do asseverate that my latent sympathies were not slightly roused at the first introduction, because of the seeming poverty of the dirty cabin and its dirtier mistress."

Now hear Bryant again:

At the next house we found corn and seeing a little boy of two years running about with a clean face I told John that we should get a clean breakfast. I was right. The man whose name was Short had a tall young wife in a clean cotton gown and shoes and stockings. She baked us some cakes, fried some bacon and made a cup of coffee which being put on a clean table and recommended by a good appetite was swallowed with some eagerness.

Clearly this was no pioneer setting.

Other characteristics likewise contributed to the poor reputation of the pioneers. Hunting, for example, appears in virtually every inventory of the backwoodsman's traits. James Flint, who traveled through our region in the years after the War of 1812, reports that a "class of hunters, commonly called backwoodsmen" constituted the first occupants of the western forests. Fordham noted that for these men "their rifle is their principle means of support." Johann David Schoepf observed in 1874: "Their object is merely wild, altogether natural freedom, and hunting is what pleases them. . . . They get game from the woods: skins bring them in whiskey." He concluded: "They are often lucky on the hunt and bring back great freight of furs, the proceeds of which are very handsome."

George Flower, one of the founders of the early Illinois settlement on English Prairie, spoke of the backwoodsmen gratefully: "Dexterous with the ax, they built all our first log-cabins, and supplied us with venison. In a year or two, they moved into less-peopled regions." "The formation of a settlement in his neighborhood is hurtful to the success of his favorite pursuit," James Flint wrote, "and is the signal for his removing into more remote parts of the wilderness." At about the same time, Fordham commented, "This class cannot be called first settlers, for they move every year or two."

The restless mobility of the pioneer submits to various explanations. Increasing density of the settlement might indeed reduce the prospects of hunting, although that consideration was perhaps offset by the availability of a market for game. Peck was not alone in noting that the pioneer became nervous when neighbors crowded around. Schoepf reported, "By this wandering uncertain way of life, of which they are vastly fond, they become indifferent to all social ties, and do not like many neighbors about them."

Often, however, mobility reflected an indifference to title to land—or lack of funds. The registrar of the District Land Office at Kaskaskia, Michael Jones, reported to Secretary of the Treasury Albert Gallatin in 1808 that almost two hundred families in the Illinois country had not bothered to take advantage of preemption legislation to secure their right to remain on their claims. John Pulliam, who appears in John Mack Faragher's *Sugar Creek*, may have been one of that type. He moved several times among the bluffs and bottomlands above Kaskaskia before settling down to operate a ferry at what is now Fayetteville. That marked the end of a wandering that had begun in Henry County, Virginia, with a stop along the way in Kentucky. Pulliam's son, Robert, left home at twenty-six and likewise moved about—to Wood River by the Mississippi and eventually to Sangamon County, where he founded a settlement. While John Pulliam may never have held title to any of his claims (Illinois land from the public domain was not offered for sale until after his death), son Robert eventually did. So, no doubt, did many of his fellows. Nonetheless, in the eyes of contemporaries and of subsequent commentators as well, the title of pioneer was a synonym for squatter.

Charges against the backwoodsmen resemble in almost every particular the contemporary ideas about Indians. That fact, of course, did not escape the notice of reporters and historians of the frontier. Johann Schoepf, shortly after Independence, noted: "These hunters or 'backwoodsmen' live very like the Indians and acquire similar ways of thinking. They shun everything which appears to demand of them law and order, dread anything which breathes constraint."

Fordham observed that "daring and hardy race of men" resembled Indians in "dress and manners." His further observations bear out the notion: "Their women never sit at table with them: at least, I have never seen them. I cannot speak in high terms of the manners or of the virtue of their squaws and daughters. Their houses contain but one room, and that used as a sleeping room as well by strangers as by the men of the family, they lose all feminine delicacy, and hold their virtue cheap."

It well may be that the dislike, often antagonism, expressed toward those pioneers derived from the same sources as the Indian-hating described by Roy Harvey Pearce. In the foreword to *Savages of America: A Study of the Indian and the Idea of Civilization,* Pearce wrote:

> I have tried to recount how it was and what it meant for civilized men to believe that in the savage and his destiny there was manifest all that they had long grown away from and yet still had to overcome. Civilized men, of course, believed in themselves: they could survive, so they know, only if they believed in themselves. In America before the 1850s that belief was most often defined negatively—in terms of the savage Indians who, as stubborn obstacles to progress, forced Americans to consider and reconsider what it was to be civilized and what it took to build a civilization.

In many ways the pioneer squatter posed as much of a threat to the stability and respectability of American society and culture as the Indian, perhaps even more of a threat, since a bath and a shave could eradicate the most obvious stigmata of the backwoodsman. Those white Indians constantly reminded the established order how precarious "civilization" really was—and how attractive the alternative might be.

I think those observations point us toward an understanding of these vanguards of American expansion. They represented a different culture, a different society, with obviously different values. Clarence Walworth Alvord generalized his findings about the pioneer in his *Mississippi Valley in British Politics*: "The vanguard in the winning of the West has been composed of men of hardy nature with few social graces; and observers coming from better surroundings have frequently identified the external ugliness with the inward reality." Alvord thus tried to retain the pioneers within the bounds of American culture in much the way Cooper did with Natty Bumppo. Estyn Evans, discussing English attitudes toward the Irish, explains much of writers' treatment of pioneers as well as Indians: "The Indians, while accepting, for good or ill, the material goods of white civilization, found it so unattractive that they consciously refused to be absorbed." What follows is the telling point: "Consequently their degraded remnants appeared to nineteenth-century historians to confirm the views of their first conquerors." Similarly, historians with nineteenth- and twentieth-century middle-class standards have been predisposed to read literally the derogatory judgments of earlier cultured eastern observers. But less abstract arguments can be used to make the same point—that pioneer squatters simply represented a different culture. As we have seen, hunting was a major trait distinguishing the backwoodsman from the settler. Now western culture has always viewed hunting ambivalently. In medieval times, the nobility alone had the privilege of hunting; game animals belonged to the king. That prerogative often aroused jealousy in days when animal protein was scarce: the sentiment only intensified with the Enlightenment, the rise of the bourgeoisie, and the awakening of ideas of equality. At the other extreme of the social spectrum lurked the poacher, lawlessly taking what the peasant was forbidden. Both his envied and arrogant betters and the outcast poachers enjoyed the hunt; the peasant resented and distrusted the hunters.

Robert Forster and Orest Ranum, introducing their collection *Rural Society in France*, essays from the *Annales*, write about the "woodspeople" who appeared "suspect to the villagers, who saw them as 'shack people,' who hunted and poached, ate differently (their staples were game and herring), and had no milk of their own. Above all, the woodspeople did not lead regulated lives, either in work or with regard to their property or in human relationships."

Addiction to hunting, addiction to moving from place to place (Frederick Merk calls the pioneers "semi-vagrant"), and addiction to indolence certainly constituted for the industrializing western culture of the late eighteenth and early nineteenth centuries a damning indictment. From another point of view, Marshall Sahlins has argued,

> By common understanding an affluent society is one in which all the people's wants are easily satisfied: and though we are pleased to consider this happy condition the unique achievement of industrial civilization, a better case can be made for hunters and gatherers. . . . For "wants are easily satisfied" either by producing much or desiring little, and there are accordingly, two possible roads to affluence.

As work discipline assumed ever-increasing importance and the workshop and the city imposed more and more constraints, the life of the pioneer squatter—who was, after all, a hunter-gatherer—could look dangerously attractive.

"If the people did not live up to other people's ideas, they lived as well as they wanted to," wrote one of the apologists for pioneer squatters. "They didn't want to make slaves of themselves; they were contented with living as their fathers lived before them." One need not accept the identification of those frontiersmen with the Scotch-Irish, as Forrest McDonald and Grady McWhiney have proposed, to perceive that here was a different culture—and one bound to suffer the adverse opinion we tend to give those who are different.

And what happened to the backwoodsman in the course of the years? After all, there was a limit to the "tall timber" in which he could retreat. Buley, following Fordham, subdivided them into two categories—hunters and the "first settlers, half hunter, half farmer." In that view, there was the hunter-gatherer squatter and the upwardly mobile squatter. The latter is a transitional figure who aspires to the next phase in the evolution of society, a settler-farmer.

As to the hunter-gatherer squatter, the type may even yet be found on the fringes of the dominant society. Just recently a so-called mountain man and his son were tried for murder in the attempted abduction of a young woman. How many like them escape our notice? We may even see them in the cities—the shopping-cart people and similar types who decline to submit to the norms of American culture. In the nineteenth century no doubt many of the hunter-gatherers clung to their ways by supplying the rising towns and cities with game.

The case of the upwardly mobile squatter differs. I think they merged into the next phase of frontier development. Probably the principal obstacle to land ownership, then and now, was cost. The land system created the upwardly mobile squatter; the land system's evolution led to his passing. The Land Ordinance of 1785 provided for the sale of minimum tracts of whole townships alternately with townships sold by sections. The Ordinance fixed the price at one dollar per acre. The Act of 1796, however, raised the price to two dollars, although it allowed a year's credit with a down payment of half the purchase price. "We humbly conceive the smallest tracts too large for us to purchase and Risk the loss of half the purchase money," some petitioners from the Scioto complained in 1798.

Successive revisions of the land system brought reductions in the minimum tract to a half-section in 1800 and a quarter section in 1804. An eighty-acre minimum in acts of 1817 and 1820 coincided with a price reduction to $1.25 per acre as the great boom of development in the Old Northwest began. The one-hundred-dollar farm of 1820 became the fifty-dollar farm of 1832 when the minimum of forty acres was reached. The hundred-dollar

farm—or certainly the fifty-dollar farm—effectively eliminated the upwardly mobile squatter who had found cost an obstacle to land ownership.

In the boom years following the War of 1812, the period of the pioneers
in the Old Northwest ended. The problem of the squatter assumed different
dimensions, having more to do with securing desirable tracts than cost
considerations. After the War of 1812, new frontier types meeting different
conditions and different problems superseded the pioneer squatters.

4.

JOURNALISM IN ILLINOIS BEFORE THE THIRTIES

Carl R. Miller

Journal of the Illinois State Historical Society
vol. 11, no. 2 (July 1918)

This article provides an overview of conditions in Illinois at the time it became a state. Poor postal service was just one of the impediments a newspaper publisher faced in pioneer Illinois. Freight delay and, notably, the difficulty of collecting payments from advertisers and subscribers were among the others.

Illinois's early newspapers were also unabashedly partisan organs, "designed not to furnish news, but ideas," Miller writes. As such, they were an indispensable public forum.

L ate in the summer of 1818 a flatboat left Pittsburg headed down the Ohio carrying two newspapermen, who were to cast their future with the people of Illinois country. Packed on this flatboat were a clumsy hand press, several fonts of type, and probably enough paper for several issues of the newspaper they hoped to establish in some promising pioneer town. Henry Eddy, a young lawyer, and Peter Kimmel, a printer, together with the latter's sons, made up the part who aspired to try their hand at western journalism. When the men left Pittsburg, they intended to go to St. Louis, where the *Missouri Gazette* had been established for nearly ten years. However, fate seemed destined to play a part in establishing an Illinois newspaper, for when the boat arrived in Shawneetown, it struck a sandbar, where the people "induced him (Eddy) to start a newspaper" in their village. Thus was the *Illinois Emigrant* started, the second newspaper in Illinois.

The foregoing serves to illustrate the manner in which the territorial press gained its foothold in the early days. In 1814 Matthew Duncan published the first newspaper in Illinois at Kaskaskia, which he called the *Illinois Herald*. The editor of the first newspaper labored under not a few disadvantages. The population was small and widely scattered. Communication, transportation, education, and politics were in a pioneer state of development. In 1815 the total population seems to have been about fifteen thousand. The village of Kaskaskia and vicinity boasted of the largest population in 1815, which was estimated at seven hundred to one thousand people. On the eastern side of the territory, Gallatin County, with Shawneetown on the Ohio River, was the most populous county. In 1818 it contained only thirty-two hundred persons, a growth of twelve hundred in eighteen years.

Political reasons doubtless influenced greatly the establishment of newspapers in Illinois. Under a law passed by Congress in 1814, "the Secretary of State was authorized to cause the laws of the United States passed, or to be passed, during present or any future session of Congress, to be published in two of the public newspapers within each and every territory of the United States, *provided* in his opinion it shall become necessary and expedient." This meant that there were territorial laws to be printed. It was a source of revenue not to be overlooked by those who previous to this time were reluctant to start a paper because of lack of immediate financial support. Matthew Duncan, first Illinois printer, secured the printing of the first edition of the Illinois Territorial Laws through his friend, Ninian Edwards, first territorial governor. In the *Illinois Herald* he announced himself as "printer to the Territory and publisher of the laws of the Union to 1815." Before coming to Shawneetown, Henry Eddy, through Nathaniel Pope, territorial delegate in Congress, had been authorized to publish United States laws.

Another fact that drew newspapermen to Illinois was the rapid growth of the population and the movement started by prominent citizens for statehood. After the War of 1812 and the passage of the preemption act of 1813, a new era in the western movement began. A land office was opened at Kaskaskia in 1814. In the three years from 1815 to 1818 the estimated growth of population was twenty thousand, it being thirty-five thousand in the midsummer of 1818. Believing that the time was ripe for launching a movement for the admittance of Illinois into the Union, Daniel P. Cook, Auditor of Public Accounts for Illinois Territory, started a movement in the

Western Intelligencer, which he owned and edited. This was in 1817, when Cook was only twenty years of age. He, with Robert Blackwell, a printer, had purchased the *Illinois Herald* from Matthew Duncan, and the name of the paper was changed to *Western Intelligencer*.

The advent of the *Edwardsville Spectator* in 1819 indicated a shifting of the population westward. Edwardsville, the county seat of Madison County, had about sixty or seventy houses, a courthouse, a jail, and a land office. The *Spectator*, the third paper published in the State, was edited by Hooper Warren and was continued for eight years under the editorship of one man, an unusual incident for those times when newspapers were bought and sold with the coming and going of elections.

The difficulties under which the first newspapers in Illinois were estab-lished taxed the genius as well as the temper of the pioneer editors. First, means of communication—which were the connecting links between the pioneer village and the outside world—were meager and primitive. Mail routes were made in 1810 to St. Louis by way of Kaskaskia, Prairie du Rocher, and Cahokia; from Kaskaskia to Cape Girardeau, but by way of St. Gene-vieve; and from Louisville to Shawneetown. Shortly before this, Vincennes, Cahokia, and Shawneetown were connected by mail routes. When weather was not too bad or when the clay of southern Illinois roads was not too sticky, mail was carried over these routes once or twice a week. In the *Illi-nois Intelligencer* is found a notice by the Postmaster General of proposals wanted for carrying the mails. "For every thirty minutes delay," the notice reads, "(unavoidable accidents excepted) in arriving at times prescribed in every contract, the contractor shall forfeit one dollar."

The dollar fine for every half hour's delay, however, does not seem to have brought about the efficiency desired of the pony express mail service. The editor of the *Edwardsville Spectator* has cause for being angry with the services when he says, "No mail has arrived at this place during the past week, with the exception of the southern, which brought nothing but the Kaskaskia paper. The postmaster at Kaskaskia prefers sending the packets addressed to this place by a circuitous route of St. Louis, instead of the di-rect one by way of Belleville, and the postmaster at St. Louis has deemed it expedient to suspend all intercourse with us by mail."

The poor postal service from the East was the cause of much editorial wrath being exhausted on the subject by the proprietors of the *Western Intelligencer*. "A letter from a delegate in Congress, dated the tenth of De-cember," says an editorial, "reached her on the fifteenth instant, one month and five days on its passage from the city of Washington to this place. The case pointed out here is not the only instance. They occur every week." One can appreciate the dilemma of the editors when it is considered that the columns of the Illinois papers were made up largely of clippings and excerpts from eastern and foreign publications.

Delay in freight transportation often made the editors suspend publication of their journals temporarily. Paper, as well as type, ink, and other materials, had to be shipped tediously by steam or flatboat from eastern cities. Because paper shipped down the Ohio on June 13 was delayed by low water and did not arrive until more than two months later, the *Illinois Emigrant* issued no edition between June 23 and August 24, 1819. "After a lapse of several weeks (three months, to be exact) we are now enabled to resume the publication of our sheet," says James Hall in the *Illinois Gazette*, 1821. "Paper (the want of which has been the cause of the late interruption) was shipped for us early last fall, on board of a boat bound for St. Louis; to which place, owing probably to the forgetfulness of the master, it was carried, and has but just now come to hand. Our situation is such, and our means so inadequate to guard against these occasional interruptions by laying in large supplies of paper, ink, etc., that we are more or less affected by every change in the elements of defalcation in individual promises. High and low water, it seems are equally our enemies—that one is sure to delay the arrival of some article necessary to the prosecution of our labors, while the other hurries something of which we stand in the most pressing need, down the current beyond our reach. And high winds, and warm and cold weather, equally delight to make us their sport. But we assure our subscribers that, however much they may regret missing a paper for a week, they can not regret it more than we; for after all, we are the losers."

It is evident that the general character of the newspapers in Illinois before the thirties was political. They were often established by aspirants to public office—lawyers for the most part—or else they espoused some State issue, such as the movement for statehood or the struggle against slavery. Daniel P. Cook, Elias Kent Kane, Henry Eddy, Thomas Reynolds, Edward Coles, and David Blackwell were men prominently in the public eye at this time, and all of them, at one time or other, were proprietors of newspapers or active in newspaper work. Each of them felt the power of the press in moulding public opinion. "It is obvious that the editor held the whip in hand," writes Thompson of the political influence of the press in the State, "for, unless he supported a candidate or at least remained neutral, he seriously handicapped any and all candidates by refusing them publicity; and without publicity, such as the press afforded, any aspirant for office had slim chances for success." Therefore, every prominent politician was compelled to have the support of one or more papers. In case the office seeker was unable to secure the assistance of the press already established, new sheets were established in the more populous localities. This explains the reason why so many of the early newspapers were so short lived. Many were run at a loss to the proprietor and were discontinued after the campaign was over.

"The attitude of the typical editor toward his political opponents was one of severity. He espoused or opposed issues with unreasonable vehemence, and abused and slandered when required. Such an attitude may have been due to deliberate choice, but is more likely that it was forced on him by the political ideals of the time. Consequently a neutral newspaper would have been out of place in such environment; and had such an editor attempted to stand on middle ground, or even temporized with opposition, his political influence would have been at an end."

Unlike many modern newspapers, the early journal was designed not to furnish news, but ideas. Modeling his paper largely after the English journal, the editor resorted freely to pastepot and scissors and clipped excerpts from Pittsburg, New York, Boston, Louisville, and sometimes from London exchanges. For example, an early issue of the *Illinois Gazette* contained paragraphs on Louis XV, Charles II, Cromwell, Sir Robert Walpole, Richelieu, Doctor Johnson, and Queen Elizabeth. Many of the articles were copied directly from recently published books or from periodicals of that time devoted to literature. "Want of room alone," explained one of the editors, "has prevented us from fulfilling an intention which we earlier formed, of devoting a portion of our columns to literature. Our own resources at this isolated spot, where we can calculate on but little assistance and where we seldom receive new books, must of course be small; but the columns of many of the eastern papers are tastefully variegated with those lighter productions which delight the fancy, and on them we may sometimes draw for the amusement of our readers." Local news found little space in these early publications. The editors had the opinion that local events were dwarfed by accounts of happenings in other places—and doubtless they were right. In such small communities isolated from the outside world, so to speak, the newspaper must needs contain the combined qualities of a local recorder of current events and a literary journal. It also had to serve as a sort of public forum, where formulating policies of the State and National Government were threshed out.

Usually these early newspapers were a little larger than the popular magazine of today—about nine by fourteen inches. The publication of State and national laws or proposed laws occupied a large portion of the news columns. Three dollars per year in advance of four dollars paid at the end of the year was the prevalent subscription price. Pleasing, indeed, was the rugged pioneer who came into the printshop and "planked down" the welcome three dollars. He made the editor rejoice, for there were many names on the subscriptions list who were never credited with the desired merchandise, farm produce, or cash. Subscriptions were usually paid with pork, cabbage, potatoes, beeswax, cordwood, or coon skins—mediums of exchange much more familiar to the pioneer community than money. Methods of extracting the subscription prices often vexed the editor. Delinquents were urged to pay up by wordy exhortations scattered throughout the news columns. Henry Eddy went so far as to publish a "black list" in the *Illinois Gazette*, in which he gave the names of those for whom he "had labored and paid out money without receiving any further remuneration than the honor of their patronage."

Advertising rates usually asked by the early newspapers were a dollar for first insertion for space "not exceeding a square"—that is, one column wide—and fifty cents was charged for each succeeding insertion. A discount of 25 percent was made for advertising by yearly contract. The early printer, lacking display faces, was compelled to set his advertisements from body type. Roman caps and italics were about the only fonts in his cases that could lay any claim to being display type.

Runaway negroes, strayed horses, town sites, hotels, lotteries, as well as liquor advertisements, are to be found very frequently. The following notice of a pioneer merchant, appearing in the *Edwardsville Spectator*, is typical of the times:

R. POGUE, MERCHANDISE.
Prime green coffee, Cognac Brandy, New
England Rum, Saddle Bags, Superfine
Black Cloth, Straw Bonnets, MEDICINES,
Etc., etc., &c, &c.

———

P. S.—Persons having accts. of long
standing and actually due, will please
to call & settle the same.

In a word, the pioneer newspaper was not essentially different from the modern journal in an attempt to play the role of moulder of public opinion. The early editor's influence over the people of his community can scarcely be estimated. His verbose editorial, laboriously composed as he was setting a stick of type, reached as many ears as the thundering voice of pioneer circuit rider. To the sturdy pioneer newspapermen of Illinois we owe an everlasting debt of gratitude. Undaunted by the hardships and vicissitudes of a new land, they fought for the political and social ideals of an embryonic commonwealth. They battled and planted the fruits of civilization which we now enjoy.

PART II

BEYOND THE FRONTIER

5

THE UNDERGROUND
RAILROAD IN ILLINOIS

Larry Gara

Journal of the Illinois State Historical Society
vol. 56, no. 13 (Autumn 1963)

This article is a comprehensive review of the reputation and reality of the Underground Railroad. It points out the tendency of people to recall as participation what might well have been a mere public statement of approval. The article identifies leading abolitionists, the role of free Negroes, the informality of an essentially disjointed operation, relations between Missouri slaveholders and Illinois abolitionists, and the impact of the Fugitive Slave Law of 1850.

In 1874 Illinois' governor John Lourie Beveridge, himself a former abolitionist, addressed a welcome to a convention of veteran abolitionists meeting in Chicago. He began with a description of Owen Lovejoy, who had laid out a railroad. "That road," said the governor "was one line of the underground railroad—chartered not by law, but in moral convictions; engineered not by science, but through charity; constructed not with money, but out of love; freighted not with commerce, but with down-trodden humanity; operated not for the benefit of stockholders, but for the escape of the fugitive fleeing from the hand of his oppressor." The road began in the land of slavery and ended in Canada. It operated in spite of all obstacles, and its passengers were a "constant reminder of the inhumanity and barbarity of African slavery." The fugitives "excited sympathy, awakened moral sentiment, aroused the public conscience, and brought agitation."

Governor Beveridge's remarks summarized the traditional concept of Illinois' underground railroad: it was a humanitarian institution created to undermine slavery, an enormous immorality; and it dealt a deadly blow to the evil system. Although he viewed the underground railroad as an abolitionist participant, he correctly emphasized its dual function in the antislavery movement: at the same time that abolitionists gave assistance to the fleeing bondsmen, they used the fugitive slave issue itself as a most important weapon in their propaganda war against slavery. In reality, the drama of the underground involved ordinary humans in a complicated series of circumstances which do not easily lend themselves to the oversimplified, moralistic point of view of either set of participants.

Traditional accounts of the underground railroad in Illinois are numerous and persistent. Stories of a series of stations stretching from various southern points of entry across the state to Chicago and Canada frequently rest on vague testimony handed down orally from generation to generation. Similar evidence has provided the raw materials for constructing a romantic interpretation of the underground epoch in which benevolent abolitionists and despicable slavecatchers operated in a setting of hairbreadth escapes, clever disguises and hiding places, and glorious freedom in Canada for the "passengers." All was done with the utmost of secrecy. With only minor variations, the story has been repeated in popular newspaper accounts and various local and county histories, and has even found its way into a number of more scholarly historical writings.

Illinois tradition includes a number of people and places renowned for their underground railroad contributions. Writing in 1882, a well-known abolitionist described the Theopolis branch of the Quincy Mission Institute as "station number one" and added that it "soon became the special object of hatred by the slaveholders in Missouri." A history of Knox County alleged that from its founding, Galesburg "was noted as the principal depot of the Underground Railroad in Western Illinois, if not in the whole state." When historian Wilbur H. Siebert asked aged survivors of the abolition movement and their descendants about the Illinois lines of the road, he got a variety of replies. One correspondent said the "Under-ground rail-road was established in forty-six or seven at Bureau County, Ill, the home of Owen Lovejoy"; another recalled that in the early days of the movement, Sparta, in Randolph County, was the "most prominent, and what may be called headquarters in all efforts in behalf of the fugitive"; and still another maintained that Brighton, in Macoupin County, was generally recognized as the road's "Headquarters."

Many other places shared a similar reputation, sometimes combining underground railroad tradition with other Civil War memories. In the latter part of the nineteenth century, a Cairo hotel, the Halliday, advertised the building as its headquarters, the cells for military prisoners off the basement, and the place under the pavement where "well founded rumor has always contended a busy station of the 'Underground Railway' was located."

Among Illinois' underground railroad heroes, Owen Lovejoy of Princeton was probably the best known. His reputation for underground service received added weight because of his political career, his prosecutions for harboring fugitives, and the fame of his martyred brother Elijah. Others from the state also gained fame in the cause. Peter Stewart of Wilmington gladly accepted the title "President" of the underground railroad, though he shared it with Indiana's Levi Coffin and several others as well. One of Professor Siebert's correspondents informed him that John Hossack was a prominent abolitionist and conductor on the "tunnel route," and another told him of an Illinois resident who "was an officer in the Underground Road." One elderly veteran of the antislavery cause recalled that John Cross was "a regular old war horse who . . . *laid out* the U.G.R.R. from Quincy to Chicago." Such reputations constituted a significant aspect of traditional history, a history which had foundation in the pre–Civil War scene as well as in the memories of aged participants.

One of the contemporary bases for the underground railroad tradition was the suspicion of abolitionist activity which slaveholders frequently expressed when slaves ran away. It was difficult for some of them to accept the idea that a slave would abscond without outside suggestion or that a Negro could succeed in escaping without assistance. Advertisements for runaway slaves and newspaper accounts of escapes often mentioned the probability of such aid, but those stories neither proved nor disproved the existence of abolitionist activity.

When a series of group escapes occurred in 1845 in St. Louis, a newspaper reported the belief that the slaves had been enticed away by abolitionists and that they had gone "by the 'great under-ground railway'" through Alton and Chicago to Canada. The following year a newspaper stated, "The frequent attempts made in this city during the last year to decoy away slaves, prove that there are Abolitionists in our midst who require close watching." In 1850, when five slaves from various part of St. Louis escaped within a period of a few days, the report stated, "Either our atmosphere must be impregnated with a morbid spirit of freedom or our city harboring some enthusiasts in the cause of abolitionism." Four years later a domestic servant from the same city escaped, taking money and clothing from her owner. "It is supposed," commented the *Daily Intelligencer,* "that she was decoyed off and conducted on the 'underground' by some white villain." Very few St. Louis news announcements concerning runaway slaves failed to include mention of such suspicions.

Political spokesmen for Missouri's slaveholding class also interpreted the problem of runaway slaves as a result of abolitionists at work in the state. In 1842 Governor Thomas Reynolds told the legislature that recent events showed that Missouri's slaveholders were "constantly exposed to the depredations of the organized bands of abolitionists, residing in sister States," who seduced slaves from their masters, aided them to escape into non-slaveholding states, and often into Canada. The remedy the governor proposed was more severe punishment, and he suggested life imprisonment as a possibility.

Abolitionist activity in assisting fugitive slaves also provided a basis for later underground railroad tradition in Illinois. Some of the abolitionists did little but talk, although others offered more concrete forms of aid to the fleeing bondsman. Practically all those who considered themselves abolitionists favored the idea of helping escaped slaves to elude pursuit and reach a haven in Canada. Countless resolutions passed at antislavery meetings endorsed this principle. In 1843 the Putnam County Anti-Slavery Society resolved that despite the penal laws of Illinois, the "colored brethren" who were escaping were "peculiarly entitled to the sympathy, advice, assistance and comfort of the abolitionists." In giving such assistance, resolved the reformers, they were "obeying the precepts of the Bible, the dictates of humanity and justice," and therefore they did not feel themselves "bound to act secretly, but openly in view of the world so far as not needlessly to jeopardize the hunted fugitive."

Other gatherings endorsed similar resolutions. In 1842 the Illinois Anti-Slavery Society urged fellow citizens in the state "to extend the hand of kindness and hospitality in *all things necessary for his escape,* to every panting fugitive from the Southern Prison House, who may come within reach of their benevolence." In 1844 the same society, meeting at Jacksonville, resolved that helping a fugitive escape was "only an act of common humanity, and that the contempt, bitterness, and angry feeling," which were so often shown toward those who performed such acts, were "sad evidence of the influence slavery has had in corrupting the heart of the northern people."

Passing resolutions while under the emotional stimulus of an antislavery gathering was one thing; actual participation in underground railroad work was something else. Not all abolitionists had an opportunity to participate directly in such activity, and some were involved in only one or two fugitive slave incidents. A few of the reformers who were engaged in this phase of abolitionism kept records which indicate that the work was carried on with a minimum of organization; as revealed in the very scanty evidence available, the Illinois underground was a makeshift, improvised method for helping fugitive slaves rather than a smoothly operating system.

Although most people who considered themselves abolitionists, as well as many who did not, would provide food, shelter, and possibly transportation to a fugitive slave, very few of them approved of running slaves out of the South. In 1858 an abolitionist who was actually engaged in helping fugitives in Illinois wrote Jonathan B. Turner that though he was willing to assist a Negro who was in want, he "would not go into a Slave State to entice a man to leave his master or in any way to induce him to leave a state of bondage." He would entice slaves from the South if he thought doing so was his duty, but he considered it "neither wise nor prudent thus to do." Owen Lovejoy expressed similar sentiments. He frequently boasted of his willingness to help a fugitive slave, which he likened to "snatching a lamb from the jaws of a wolf," but going into the South would be to court disaster. "It is simply a question whether it will pay to go down into the den where the wolf is," said Lovejoy.

A few incidents involving abolitionist activity in Missouri and other slave states received a great deal of attention and helped convince many southerners that a branch of the underground railroad extended into their section. One of the most widely publicized episodes involved two students and an older resident from the Mission Institute at Quincy. In this summer of 1841 Alanson Work, James E. Burr, and George Thompson went into Missouri and talked with some slaves who said they wanted to go north. The three arranged to meet a group of slaves at night, but the meeting proved to be a trap and the slaves betrayed them. A Missouri court sentenced the three to twelve years in prison

None of the abolitionists served more than five years of the sentence, and all were eventually pardoned by Missouri's governor. Abolitionist friends of the three published a sympathetic account of the incident, making clear, however, that though the motives of the group were beyond reproach, they erred seriously in judgment and chose the wrong way to attack slavery. The men themselves agreed not to engage in similar practices in the future. In explaining his change in thought, George Thompson refused to acknowledge that he had done anything morally wrong but agreed that his act was rash and imprudent and had been taken without full consideration of the danger involved. On purely expedient grounds he agreed not to repeat his attempt to aid slaves in escaping from the South.

The imprisonment of Work, Burr, and Thompson became the focal point for abolitionist propaganda. The Garrisonians, who looked upon constant agitation as their main weapon against slavery, were especially alert to the publicity value of such incidents. When the three were jailed, the *Boston Liberator* alleged that they were victims of slaveholders' cruelty and power and stated that they had not violated either the laws of God or of Missouri. The paper urged abolitionists to hold protest meetings in every city, town, and village, and to "let the ball be put in motion without delay." Illinois abolitionists saw a connection between an increase in slave escapes and publicity given the Work, Burr, and Thompson imprisonment.

Antislavery workers gave similar publicity to prosecutions under Illinois and federal statutes which grew out of assistance given to fugitive slaves in, or traveling through, the state. In 1843 the Chicago abolition newspaper the *Western Citizen* devoted considerable space to such court actions, including the fines imposed upon Dr. Richard Eells of Quincy and Julius Willard of Jacksonville, and the cases which were brought against Owen Lovejoy of Princeton, Samuel G. Wright of Stark County, and John Cross of Knox County. Abolitionists appealed to the concern for civil liberties which their neighbors shared with them, and did not hesitate to boast openly of their underground railroad activity.

The abolitionist press frequently carried stories about fugitive slaves and underground railroad operations. Some gave the details of a particular escape, while others were couched in general terms. In 1844 the *Western Citizen* reported the arrival of five fugitives "at the termination of Cross' underground Rail Road, . . . all *emancipated by their own executive power, and in accordance with wills* of their own." The editor added that the five, who would soon be in Canada, wished to send compliments to their masters.

Reporting such material gave the abolitionists an opportunity to refute pro-slavery allegations that slaves were contented with their lot. The plight of the fugitive slave naturally evoked sympathetic response from those who had no direct interest in the South's peculiar institution. By the 1850s such sympathy was widespread in Illinois. In 1854 the *Chicago Tribune* used an article entitled "Passengers on the Underground Railroad" to discredit Stephen A. Douglas and his controversial Nebraska Bill. The report told readers that though "its trains run through our streets regularly," and with greatly increased business, there was no word of "speculation in its stock" or failure of its machines. "A large corps of trusty conductors" had been secured, the stations were "well fitted up, and the officers and passengers on the road furnished with 'irons' to be used against all who may have the audacity to interfere with trains or passengers" who had been "greatly increased by the notorious Nebraska Bill, the offspring of Judge Douglas."

On occasion, rendering assistance to fugitive slaves also provided an important morale-building contribution to the abolitionists themselves. Participating in such work or in mass meetings connected with the work gave the zealous reformers a sense of accomplishment and often enabled them to reach others who were not usually sympathetic to their cause.

While some abolitionists seemed to find work in the underground railroad merely an exciting diversion, Negroes in Illinois took a more sober view of the events relating to its operations. Free Negroes were often involved in fugitive rescues, and frequently such rescues were reported in the press as the activity of a "Negro mob." Both the free Negroes and fugitive slaves had a more vital and personal interest in the fugitive question than the abolitionists, who viewed it partly as an indirect method of attacking the institution of slavery. The abolitionist point of view was ideological. On at least one occasion, the *Western Citizen* went so far as to suggest that some fugitives might best contribute to the cause by accepting martyrdom, and consenting "to return awhile to slavery as propagandists of liberty, and as a standing appeal to the humanity of the North." To the abolitionists, the propaganda war against slavery sometimes took precedence over rendering assistance to its refugees.

In retrospect, the role of the Negro is frequently neglected in discussions of the underground railroad. Those who lived in the pre–Civil War period, however, did not overlook the Negro's contribution. The presence of free Negroes in slave states was sometimes considered to be an open invitation to slaves to escape. From time to time St. Louis newspapers called attention to this danger. In 1841 an item in the *Daily Evening Gazette* pointed out that free Negroes and hired slaves working on riverboats had an opportunity to talk with slaves of other southern states and also with the free Negroes and abolitionists of Illinois and other free states. "This communication," argued the writer, "renders the slaves restless and induces them to run away, and furnishes them with means to escape." Several years later another St. Louis paper attributed the active operations of the underground railroad to the presence of the hundreds of free Negroes then in the city.

While free Negroes and abolitionists could usually be depended upon to assist the fugitive slave, the assistance rendered was not always essential to the success of the escape. The fugitives often planned and carried out their escapes wholly on their own initiative. They sometimes traveled at night and hid by day, trusting no one whom they might encounter along their way. When John Anderson left slavery in Missouri, it took him several weeks to reach Illinois. There he received a night's lodging and food at the home of an English settler and occasional aid from other farmers. Finally, at Rock Island, he came into contact with abolitionists who paid his railroad fare to Chicago. A fugitive from the Deep South followed the Mississippi River to St. Louis, where he crossed into Illinois. There he obtained shelter, food, and information about the roads from a free Negro. In Indiana he found abolitionists who helped him get to Michigan. William Hall of Tennessee made three unsuccessful escape attempts before he was able to leave the South. In Illinois several colored residents assisted Hall, and at Ottawa he came into contact with an abolitionist who helped him get to Chicago. Still another former slave later recalled that when he escaped, he had some trouble getting through Illinois since there were many "slaveholders in heart here." But he managed to reach Canada safely.

Not all the fugitive slaves going through Illinois avoided capture. Whatever degree of organization the abolitionists may have put into their underground railroad, it was not efficient enough to contact all who needed its services or to protect them from their would-be captors. Several fugitives were betrayed by Negroes to whom they had appealed for help, and others were turned in by white settlers. The informers were usually motivated by a desire for rewards rather than any concern for the slaveholders' economic interests. The capture of fugitive slaves in Illinois sometimes elicited comment from the abolitionist press. When three Negroes were arrested in Springfield on suspicion that they were escaped slaves, the *National Anti-Slavery Standard* remarked, "Illinois is usually reckoned a *Free* State, but occurrences like this would seem to indicate that she is on the other side of the line."

The testimony of those fugitive slaves who recorded their experiences or dictated them for others to publish indicates that it was their own will and determination as much as assistance from others that made it possible to escape from slavery. Yet the various propaganda uses which abolitionists made of the fugitive issue tended to call attention to their own part in the escape drama. Defenders of slavery attempted to deal with what they believed was an actual threat to their property interests and with the propaganda attack of abolitionists. From time to time Missourians organized anti-abolition societies to take measures to protect slave property from abolitionist interference. Meetings of such societies sometimes encouraged vigilante action against individuals suspected of aiding slaves to escape. One, in Lewis County in 1843, demanded that several alleged abolitionists leave the county within four days or face punishment of fifty lashes or hanging. The same meeting recommended that one Illinois abolitionist be brought to Missouri for each slave he helped to escape. In 1846 a St. Louis meeting organized a committee to ferret out "the secret agents of the abolitionists" and passed resolutions demanding severe restrictions on the movement and activity of free Negroes in the state. An 1853 meeting in Howard County demanded that the practice of slave hiring cease and that all free Negroes be required to leave the county.

Neither the formation of southern anti-abolition committees nor newspaper attacks on the reformers indicates the extent of underground railroad activity in Illinois or neighboring states. Some Missourians denied that there was any great loss to slaveholders as a result of abolitionist interference. In 1859 a St. Louis newspaper commented, "Occasionally, the Old John Brownites get on the underground road and run off a few slaves to Canada, and the Black Republicans assist them in doing it, but the number is not so great as to materially help that party in their labor of love, in ridding Missouri of slavery." Shortly afterward the same newspaper published assessors' returns for 1858 and 1859 to show how groundless the charges were that northern counties of the state were rapidly losing their slave population. The returns indicated that the border areas had not "lost any considerable number" of slaves and that the total slave population of those counties had actually increased.

Illinois abolitionists usually answered statements made about them in the Missouri press and commented on pro-slavery activity as well. While they delighted, at times, in boasting of their participation in successful slave escapes, they also denied that they had any organized system for transporting fugitives from the South. In 1843 the editor of the *Western Citizen* noted that pro-slavery spokesmen accused abolitionists of having a complete organization which induced slaves to run away and then helped them on their way to Canada. "Now we would assure all who entertain such opinions," commented the editor, "that they labor under a great mistake. There is no organization whose object is to induce the slaves to escape."

A partial answer to abolitionist activity was the Fugitive Slave Law of 1850, but it was also much more than that. The law, an amendment to an earlier one of 1793, was a vital part of the sectional Compromise of 1850. Southern spokesmen insisted upon it more for the constitutional guarantee which it appeared to give them than for the relatively few fugitive slaves who might be returned under its provisions. It was the single major concession to the South included in the Compromise, and its enforcement in good faith was viewed as a test of northern sincerity in preserving the Union.

Southerners viewed every abolitionist attack upon the Fugitive Slave Law with grave concern. Shortly after Congress passed the law, a St. Louis newspaper commented that the "test of the Union's permanency is fairly presented to the North in the fugitive slave law." If the free states lacked the moral power to maintain the law and the general government had not the moral and physical power to enforce it, the southern states would be compelled to defend their rights, take leave of their northern brethren, and "dissolve all connection to the Union." The next year Missouri's governor Austin A. King echoed similar sentiments in remarks before the state legislature. "In insisting upon the rigid execution of that law," he said, ". . . the people of the slaveholding States assert only a plain constitutional right, guaranteed to them when they entered the Union, and of which they cannot be deprived as long as the constitution and Union stand."

In Illinois the majority of residents accepted the Compromise, in principle at least, even though many of them resented the Fugitive Slave Law itself. Stephen A. Douglas and other political leaders spoke frequently and convincingly throughout the state, pointing out the grave crisis through which the Union had passed and the importance of the Compromise in preventing disruption and possible civil war. However, after 1854, with the furor over the proposed Kansas-Nebraska Bill and the question of extending slavery into the new territories, the already unpopular law became a symbol of southern aggression and virtually unenforceable in the northern states. By 1859 the fugitive issue was a heated one in politics, and that year the attempted return of a fugitive slave in Ottawa and the ensuing rescue provided an effective issue for the Republicans, enabling them to win a victory in a district which was generally safe for the Democrats.

To the abolitionists, the Fugitive Slave Law was without parallel an issue for reaching others outside their ranks. They held countless meetings, passed numerous resolutions, and printed and distributed pamphlets and sermons denouncing the law. A meeting in Somonauk, Illinois, resolved to "agitate! agitate!! Back petition by petition, till this infamous law is repealed." A group in Eden announced that its members would refuse to vote for anyone who had voted for the law or who had refused to take a stand against it. Several incidents involving rescues of alleged fugitives and prosecutions for violating the law provided ample material for the abolitionist propagandists. As the sectional rift deepened, the abolition attack on the harsh and unpopular statute helped to convince many in Illinois and other states that the South was making unreasonable and immoral demands on their people, demands that included returning the slaves whom their masters could not keep in bondage except by brute force.

Much of Illinois' underground railroad tradition rests on exciting events connected with the Fugitive Slave Law. It was in the years after the Civil War, however, that the tradition became firmly entrenched in the minds of Americans. It was in those years that the former abolitionists, whose once unpopular cause had been fully vindicated, recalled the stirring events of the underground epoch for newspapers, writers of local history, and admiring relatives. The underground railroad material which found its way into local history and legend repeated the abolitionists' version of institution. It was a thrilling story replete with narrow escapes, secret operations, numerous clever hiding places, and a flood of helpless refuges from southern bondage. The abolitionist conductors were the heroes; those unsympathetic to their cause, the villains; and the fugitives, only grateful passengers.

The story of the underground railroad as recounted in the years after the events transpired is often told in generalities, with a minimum of concrete information. One or two incidents sometimes provide the basis for a widespread and often-repeated legend, and it is rare that such accounts are adequately documented. Some of the stories came from garrulous old men who delighted in repeating the tales of their contribution to the antislavery cause. One investigator who made a determined effort to track down some concrete underground railroad material relating to the area around Jerseyville, Illinois, reported that when he first talked with the elderly abolitionists, he was led to believe he would get a great deal of information. "I find," he lamented, "that while they will talk very volubly and at great length what they say, when boiled down so as to get what they *know* shows but little on paper."

Professor Wilbur H. Siebert's correspondence in the 1890s with numerous Illinois abolitionists revealed a great variety of impressions which those people had of the underground railroad. When asked as precise a question as the dates of its greatest activity, Siebert's correspondents gave many different answers. One thought it was the years 1854 to 1858; another 1840 to 1848; and a third, "from 1850 perhaps until before until the emancipation." The inability of the abolitionists to agree on so specific and unemotional an aspect of the road's history underscores the need for great caution in using such reminiscent material as a historical source.

The local reputation that certain well-known persons acquired for underground railroad service could also be deceptive. One of Jacksonville's most famous inhabitants, Jonathan B. Turner, provides a case in point. In 1896 several people from Illinois called Professor Siebert's attention to Turner's work on the underground railroad, and one referred to him as "a station agent." Turner's daughter later described her father as a "member of the Underground Railroad," though "not very zealous in its work," and the historian of Illinois College wrote that Turner had taken "a very prominent part in the activity of the Underground Railway in Jacksonville."

As a matter of fact, however, Turner's reputation resulted entirely from a single incident. In 1846 he had helped protect three women fugitives from their pursuers. He escorted the slaves to a home of a pro-slavery Presbyterian elder who temporarily abandoned his abstract principles and hid them safely for two weeks. Then another abolitionist transported them to Farmington. In recalling the incident, Turner commented, "and this is all I ever knew about the Underground Railway, or its stations."

The contrast between Jonathan B. Turner's fame as an underground railroad conductor and his own statements concerning that activity further emphasizes the need for caution when dealing with the traditional material. Far too much of the published history of the Illinois underground railroad has no other basis than oral traditions or local legend; it disregards the subtleties of a complex situation. In the period since the war the subtleties have disappeared and history has been modified. The underground railroad has assumed a larger importance than it had during its period of operation, and much that was merely talk of action has been accepted as proof of activity. The significant deeds and courageous acts of the Negroes who made the break from slavery have largely been overlooked. The aid that abolitionists provided has assumed a more formal and highly organized appearance than it actually had. On this score, the term "underground railroad" is in itself somewhat misleading.

Nevertheless, the scholarly revision presents only a modification of the familiar. The tradition exaggerates and oversimplifies a history which had

a basis in fact. The historical picture, however, is still incomplete. Many local legends await a careful examination of the contemporary sources upon
which they rest. In 1896 an elderly resident of Maple Grove answered Professor Siebert's inquiry in a way which neatly but ungrammatically summed
up the vagaries of Illinois underground railroad tradition: "We have herd
the Underground Railrode Spoken of in my younger days but thought it
was only Campaign buncom but do not know that it raily ever existed herd
a goodeal said about it before the war when there was lots of hard things
said about those who were engaged in helping Negroes to escape from their
masters. While thare were slaves smuggles through this county, we do not
[know] of any underground Rail Rode as a matter of fact."

RELATED READING

Carol Pirtle, "Andrew Borders v. William Hayes: Indentured Servitude and
the Underground Railroad in Illinois," *Illinois Historical Journal* vol. 89,
no. 3 (Autumn 1996).
Merton L. Dillon, "Abolition Comes to Illinois," *Journal of the Illinois State
Historical Society* vol. 53, no. 4 (Winter 1960).

6.

JOHN JONES
A Study of a Black Chicagoan

Charles A. Gliozzo

Illinois Historical Journal vol. 80, no. 3 (Autumn 1987)

The Fugitive Slave Law and the opposition to it is a central focus of this article on John Jones, the first black Chicagoan to be elected to political office—Cook County commissioner. A free African American, he and his wife took up residence in Chicago in 1845, where he enjoyed considerable business and political success. He was a leading opponent of the state's Black Laws, which were not repealed until 1865. Jones played an active role in national and state black conventions.

On a spring day in 1875, surrounded by fellow Cook County commissioners and members of Chicago's elite, John Jones recalled the triumphs of his memorable life as the city's most distinguished black citizen. The occasion for the celebration was the thirtieth anniversary of Jones's arrival in Chicago. Although he had come with only $3.50 in his pocket, he had amassed a considerable fortune. Hard work and canny business sense had resulted in successful careers in real estate, business, and politics. Yet, Jones concluded that none of the labors of his busy life had given him more satisfaction than his "warfare upon the black laws of the state" waged until their repeal in 1865. Up to the time of the repeal, he told a reporter, "the black man in Illinois had no standing. He could not accumulate property; and he had no inducement to be either industrious or saving."

John Jones, the first African American in Chicago to be
elected to a political office—Cook County commissioner.
Image courtesy Chicago History Museum.

Jones was born not in Chicago but on a plantation in Greene County,
North Carolina, in 1816, to a free mulatto mother and a father of German
ancestry. Although Jones was considered free, his mother feared that his
father might attempt to reduce him to slavery, and therefore she apprenticed him at an early age to a man by the name of Sheppard, who agreed to
teach him a trade. Subsequently, when Sheppard moved to Tennessee, Jones
was apprenticed to Richard Clere, a tailor who lived at Somerville, Fayette
County, about fifty miles from Memphis. Clere, in turn, hired Jones out to
various tailors throughout the state. While working for a tailor in Memphis,
Jones became acquainted and fell in love with Mary Jane Richardson, the
daughter of Elijah Richardson, a free Negro blacksmith. The couple were
separated when the Richardsons moved to Alton, Illinois. Jones meanwhile

completed his Memphis apprenticeship and, after working for three years and accumulating a savings of approximately one hundred dollars, at the age of twenty-seven went north to Alton, where he and Mary Jane were married in 1844. Very little is known of their life in Alton. In March of 1845 the Joneses journeyed to Chicago. The trip took nearly a week—by stage to Ottawa and then from Ottawa by canal to Chicago. En route, they were detained on suspicion of being fugitive slaves. The stagecoach driver vouched for their freedom, however, and—notwithstanding the severity of their journey and racial harassments—they finally arrived in Chicago on March 11.

What prompted John Jones to make the trip from Alton to Chicago? The lure of broader opportunities and the more liberal climate of Chicago toward blacks were major factors. Chicago in the 1840s, although still in a frontier stage of development, was gradually being transformed into an urban center. The first waterworks had been constructed in 1841, and the first meatpacking plant followed three years later. A permanent public school building was built in 1845, and in 1846 Chicago was made a port of entry. The city was attracting adventurous, active, and ambitious people from throughout the nation as well as from foreign countries. Like those arrivals, Jones envisaged Chicago as a land of opportunity, capable of satisfying his economic expectations. He was aware from conversations in Tennessee and Alton that Chicagoans were regarded as progressive in their relationships with blacks. In Chicago there was a quickening of the public conscience concerning the institution of slavery. The *Cairo Weekly Times and Delta* said of Chicagoans, "They are undoubtedly the most riotous people in the state. Mention Negro and slave catcher in the same breath and they are up in arms."

According to the Illinois State Census of 1845, blacks numbered 140 out of a total Chicago population of 12,088. The black population was fairly well concentrated—81 of the 140 lived in the Second Ward, bounded by State Street, Clark Street, and the Chicago River. In that area the Jones family rented a one-room apartment on the corner of Madison Street and Fifth Avenue (now Wells Street). Jones also set up a small tailoring shop in the west side of Clark Street between Randolph and Lake, near what became the entrance to the Sherman House. His was one of the first black business establishments in Chicago. Within time, "J. Jones, Clothes Dresser & Repairer" enjoyed a thriving business at his home at 119 Dearborn. An 1851 advertisement in the city directory announced,

I take this method of informing you that I may be found at all business hours at my shop, ready and willing to do all work in my line you may think proper to favor me with, in the best possible manner. I have on hand all kinds of Trimmings for repairing Gentleman's Clothes. Bring in your Clothes, Gents, and have them Cleaned and Repaired. Remember that all Clothes left with me are safe, because I am responsible and permanently located at 119 Dearborn Street.

Jones was fortunate in obtaining the aid of two local abolitionists, the eminent physician Charles V. Dyer and the noted lawyer Lemanuel Covell Paine Freer, who were to remain steadfast friends throughout his life. During the earliest days of Jones's residency in Chicago, Freer wrote all of his correspondence, and eventually he taught Jones the fundamentals of reading and writing. Denied formal education because of his race, Jones realized that a knowledge of such basic skills was essential to the operation of his business.

Jones was the first black to become a notary public in Illinois, and in 1871 he was elected a Cook County commissioner, the first black man so honored. In 1872 he was reelected for a three-year term. The antecedents of his distinguished career are to be found in his role in the black convention movement and in his successful campaign for the repeal of the Illinois Black Laws.

Jones was convinced that the Black Laws—which date back to the earliest days of statehood—were the principal reason for the poverty of Negroes. Based on the assumptions that slaves were property, not persons, and that blacks, either slave or free, had to be kept in a subordinate position, the Illinois Black Laws restricted every aspect of Negro life. Following Illinois statehood, the first general assembly in 1819 had adopted laws stipulating that blacks had no legal rights: they could not sue or be sued; they could not testify against whites, although testimony could be given against a slave or a free Negro; their oath was not binding; and they could not make a contract. Ownership of property or merchandise was generally forbidden. Blacks could not visit the homes of whites or entertain them in their homes. They had no right to an education. Even the right of more than three blacks to assemble for dancing was forbidden unless white persons were present.

The earliest Black Laws stemmed from an obsessive fear of slave insurrections and, according to historian John Hope Franklin, were designed "to insure the maximum protection of the white population and to maintain discipline among the slaves." In Illinois, all free blacks or mulattos were required to file a certificate of freedom, with bond, with the clerk of the county court. Thus, in accordance with state law, both John and Mary Jane Jones obtained from the clerk at Madison County the essential certificates of freedom in 1844. Jones's first attempt at repeal of the Black Laws began in the heated debate surrounding the Constitutional Convention of 1847. A common fear prevailed among delegates that an increase in free blacks would have a severe impact on white labor. In an 1847 series of articles in Chicago's *Western Citizen*, Jones defended the rights of blacks. Jones pointed out that the Founding Fathers had refused to insert the word "white" into their definition of free citizens. The enlightenment of the nineteenth century, he said, the standards of republican government, and the Revolutionary War record of blacks were sufficient reasons for recognizing black citizenship. He insisted that blacks were entitled to the right of equal representation and equality before the law.

Jones's arguments were not sufficient to prevent passage of the anti-immigration provision, however. Article XIV of the 1848 Illinois Constitution, which was submitted to a popular vote as a separate article, instructed legislators to "pass such laws as will effectually prohibit free persons of color from immigrating to and settling in this state, and to effectually prevent the owners of slaves from bringing them into the state for the purpose of setting them free." Voters approved the anti-immigration article by a wide majority, and Jones responded, "I view it with regret and alarm, because it attempts to prohibit natural-born citizens of the United States from settling in this state on account of the color of their skin." Yet, despite his failure to suppress the anti-immigration provision, Jones was achieving a reputation as a spokesman for black rights. On August 7, 1848, black Chicagoans meeting at the Baptist Church selected Jones and Reverend Abraham T. Hall as delegates to the Colored National Convention of black freemen called for the following month in Cleveland. They instructed Jones and Hall to report to the convention on the moral and intellectual development of blacks in Illinois, their financial status, and their interest in freedom.

Between fifty and seventy delegates assembled at Cleveland on September 6. Most were self-made men from west of the Appalachians and north of the Ohio, including several representatives from Canada. They represented a cross section of free blacks in the North—printers, carpenters, blacksmiths, clergymen, barbers, grocers, tailors, editors, dentists, engineers, painters, and farmers. Frederick Douglass, already nationally known, was chosen president, and Jones was named vice president.

Of primary interest to the Cleveland delegates was the improvement of the status of blacks in the United States. They encouraged education, temperance, and community cooperation. They were especially sensitive to occupations not considered "honorable." Jones believed that equality of persons could be achieved only by quality of attainments. Mechanical trades, business, farming, and the learned professions were honorable occupations, he believed, that should be pursued by blacks. He demeaned menial labor, calling upon delegates to "deem it our bounded duty to discountenance such pursuits, except when necessity compels the person to resort thereto as a means of livelihood."

The Cleveland convention debated at length the possibility of endorsing a presidential candidate. First, members adopted Jones's resolution that "the two great political parties of the Union [i.e., Democrats and Whigs] have by their acts and nominations betrayed the sacred cause of human freedom." Would delegates ally themselves with the Free-Soil party, whose candidate was Martin Van Buren? Resolutions in support of the Free-Soil movement as the "dawn of a bright and more auspicious day" were subsequently rejected, but delegates did "recommend" the Free-Soil movement to black voters. Also, they accepted a preamble offered by Jones that the slogan "Free Soil, Free Speech, Free Labor, and Free Men" was in the interest of the downtrodden. Cautiously, the convention had moved closer to political action.

Upon Jones's return to Chicago, he concentrated on the repeal of the Black Laws. On September 11, working with other prominent Chicago blacks—notably William Styles, Henry O. Wagoner, William Johnson, and Rev. Abraham T. Hall—he established a correspondence committee that passed a series of resolutions condemning as unconstitutional any statutes that deprived free men of constitutional rights. The committee was charged with two functions: to ascertain the feasibility of circulating a petition for the repeal of the Black Laws and to canvass the Fourth Congressional District (which included Chicago) for the names of all blacks. Their efforts proved to be a model for repeal associations and petition drives throughout the state. At the 1849 session of the Illinois General Assembly, the Senate passed an anti-immigration bill, but committee delays prevented passage in the House.

When Congress passed the Fugitive Slave Act in September of 1850, another obstacle had been placed in the way of black emancipation. Vesting the federal government with almost unlimited powers for the apprehension and return of fugitive slaves, the act denied the alleged fugitive a trial by jury and the right to summon witnesses or testify in court. Ownership was determined by a single affidavit of the person claiming the slave, and the affidavit was protected by the United States commissioner's certificate from "all molestation . . . by any process issued by any court, judge, magistrate, or other person whosoever." Heavy penalties were to be inflicted on officials who failed to observe the law, as well as on those who harbored or aided in the escape of the fugitive. The severity of the act and the dehumanizing view of "man-hunting" created considerable alarm among Chicago blacks. For Jones, the law also was not only unconstitutional but also inconsistent with the view that all men are created equal; it was a measure dictated by the vested interests of the South, ignoring the rights of every party save those of the master.

More than three hundred Chicago blacks rallied on September 30, 1850, at the African Methodist Church on Wells Street to decide upon a course of resistance to the Fugitive Slave Act. The meeting ended with the selection of a committee on resolutions, whose members included Jones. Two days later, before a capacity black audience at the church, Jones released the committee's findings. He reported the existence of strong, deep resolve to resist every attempt to bring back to bondage any black, and a determination to defend each other at the risk of imprisonment, fine, or life itself. "We are determined to defend ourselves at all hazards, even should it be to the shedding of human blood," he announced. "We who have tasted of *freedom* are ready to exclaim in the language of the brave Patrick Henry, 'Give us liberty or give us death.'" The committee believed that the tendency of the law was "to enslave every colored man in the United States, because no provisions are made in the bill to guard against false claims, inasmuch as the slaveholder's claim . . . is to be considered as prima facie evidence of its validity." The committee called the law a glaring instance of Northern subserviency to slaveholding dictation, being nothing less than the sanctioning of a hunting ground for slaveholders. As a means of "protecting each other from being borne back in bondage," a vigilance committee was created, consisting of a black police force of seven divisions, with six persons in each division to patrol the city each night and 'keep an eye out' for interlopers." The police patrol was to exist as long as it was deemed necessary to maintain the safety of black Chicagoans. In October, the Chicago Common Council supported the resolutions of Jones and his committee. Members called on "the citizens, officers and police of this city" to "abstain from any and all interference in the capture and deliverance of the fugitives." The Council contended that the Fugitive Slave Act was not only unconstitutional but also contrary to the practice and propagation of Christian principles. Other areas of the state were not in agreement with Chicago's antislavery view, however. The *Belleville Advocate* reported, "We of the south do not regard Chicago as belonging to Illinois. It is as perfect a SINK HOLE OF ABOLITION as Boston or Cincinnati."

In December, Jones circulated yet another petition to state legislators for the repeal of the Black Laws: "The undersigned, inhabitants of the State of Illinois, respectfully petition your honorable body, for the immediate and total repeal of all laws now existing upon the statute books of this State. Whereby discriminations are made among the people on account of their complexion."

In defiance of the Fugitive Slave Act, Jones doubled his efforts. His daughter, Lavinia Jones Lee, recalled that he was responsible for "sending hundreds of fugitives to Canada." The Jones home, she said "was a haven for escaped slaves" and became the "local headquarters of the underground railroad." The Jones house was a rendezvous site for white as well as black abolitionists, including John Brown and Frederick Douglass. Mary Jane related one conversation with Brown about proposed raids into Pennsylvania and Virginia. Jones perceptively remarked, "Why, Mr. Brown, that is all wind, and there is nothing to it; and besides, you would lose your life if you undertook to carry out your plans." Brown retorted with a snap of his fingers, "What do I care for my life, if I can do what I want to do—if I can free these negroes." Both Mary Jane and John Jones viewed Mr. Brown's schemes as impracticable, and they believed that his ideas would never be fulfilled.

Frederick Douglass was accompanied by Jones on an antislavery tour through the West, and related this story:

> [We] stopped at a Hotel in Janesville and were seated by ourselves to take our meals where all the barroom loafers of the town could stare at us. Thus seated I took occasion to say, loud enough for the crowd to hear me, that I had just been to the stable and had made a great discovery. Asked by Mr. Jones what my discovery was, I said that I saw there black horses and white horses eating together from the same trough in peace, from which I inferred that the horses of Janesville were more civilized than its people. The crowd saw the hit, and broke out in a good-natured laugh. We were afterwards entertained at the same table with the other guests.

The severity of the Fugitive Slave Act and the intensity of black discrimination promoted the revival of the black national convention movement. In
1853 Douglass called for a convention of "free colored people . . . to confer and
deliberate upon their present condition, and upon principles and measures
important to their welfare, progress and general improvement." In response,
some 140 delegates representing nine states assembled in Corinthian Hall
of Rochester, New York, on July 6. Delegates selected Reverend James W. L.
Pennington of New York as president. Several vice presidents were named,
including Jones and Douglass. The purposes of the convention as stated in
a resolution by Dr. James McCune Smith of New York were "improving the
character, developing the intelligence, maintaining the rights, and organizing a Union of the Colored People of the Free States." State councils were
appointed for each state, and Jones and James D. Bonner of Chicago were
appointed to lead the movement in Illinois. In addition, four standing committees were established: Manual Labor School, Protective Unions, Business
Relations, and Publications. The goals were establishment of an industrial
college for black youths; developing protective unions for the "purchase
and sale of articles of domestic consumption"; maintaining a registry of
black businesses that would serve as a clearinghouse of persons willing to
teach trades and professions; and creating a reading room for materials by
and about blacks. That last committee would also respond to publications
attacking the character or status of blacks. The Rochester convention did not
attempt to establish a separatist society for blacks but to demand justice in
American society. It was the answer of Jones, Douglass, and other traditional
leaders to the challenge of colonizationists who proposed that emigration
to Africa was the only solution to black discrimination.

In October, three months after the Rochester convention, the first Black
Illinois State Convention convened in Chicago. Delegates elected Jones president, and he subsequently became chairman of the colonization committee.
His report denouncing colonization schemes was enthusiastically adopted.
"Any form of colonization was calculated to increase pro slavery prejudice,"
he argued, "to depress our moral energies, and to unsettle all our plans for
improvement." He moved that the convention adopt the language of the
Rochester convention—"We will plant our trees in American soil, and repose
under the shade thereof." Delegates not only supported his resolution but
denounced the call by Martin R. Delany for a National Emigration Convention as "fatal to our hopes and aspirations." Jones's report was hailed in
a letter to the *Chicago Tribune* as "a manly well written document which

would do credit to any man in our midst." The convention gave Illinois blacks an opportunity to publicize their sentiments and aspirations. Jones, as president of the convention, was praised for presiding "both with dignity and with truly surprising parliamentary accuracy."

The Illinois convention, like the Rochester convention, however, was unsuccessful in the attainment of equal opportunities for blacks. Inadequate finances, factional disputes regarding emigration, and the exodus of some blacks to Canada after the passage of the Fugitive Slave Act led to the collapse of the program objectives. Yet the convention movement was one of great significance. The strong anti-emigration resolution doomed colonization efforts, and the convention movement did more than any other to refute the view of black inferiority. For, as Philip Foner indicated, the conventions "brought Northern Negroes together as no other body did and provided them with an opportunity to arrive at a common perspective of problems and resolutions." At the conventions, each delegate "spoke, wrote and petitioned not as an individual but as a member of the convention of American Negroes. The convention movement developed national and local leaders, such as Jones, who were to play formidable roles in erasing Black Laws and other abuses of human rights.

The Illinois legislature enacted the anti-emigration article into law on February 12, 1853, providing that any person who brought a black or mulatto (defined as one having one-fourth black blood), free or slave, into the state would be fined not less than one hundred dollars nor more than five hundred dollars, and imprisoned for not more than one year. Blacks entering the state under their own volition and remaining ten days would be subject to a fine of fifty dollars and—if the fine was not paid—sold to any person who would pay the fine.

Throughout the 1850s there were occasional attempts to repeal, but none were successful. Education of blacks in public schools, the right to vote, and equity in the courts continued to be the principle issues of black convention movements. As a delegate to the 1856 Black Illinois State Convention at Alton, Jones continued to demand those legal rights.

The Civil War increased the number of blacks in Illinois because under the Federal Confiscation Act the slaves of rebel planters were given the status of contrabands and were shipped north. Many were sent to Cairo, Illinois, and distributed over the state. The *Chicago Tribune* reported in 1864 that "to credit of the people, as well as to the lasting disgrace of their lawmakers, it must be said that the 1853 statute has been a dead letter in all but two or three counties of the state, namely Jonesboro, Union County, and Nashville, Washington County." Even Jones admitted that many sections of the Black Code were not enforced, but he argues that "some of the disabilities laid upon Negroes were a *living active reality.*"

On November 4, 1864, Jones published at his own expense a sixteen-page pamphlet titled *The Black Laws of Illinois and a Few Reasons Why They Should Be Repealed.* He addressed his remarks to the people of Illinois and to newly elected members of the legislature. "We ask you in the name of the Great God, who made us all; in the name of Christianity and Humanity, to erase from your statute book that code of laws commonly called the Black Laws," he began. Jones proceeded to quote and to denounce the thirty sections of the Revised Statutes of 1845, including sections of the Civil Code. He based his arguments on moral, economic, legal, and constitutional principles. He contended that Section One of the Black Laws, which demanded a bond of $1,000 and a certificate of freedom from any black or mulatto residing in Illinois, was in direct violation of both the Illinois Constitution and the United States Constitution. Jones wrote:

> The Constitution of our State . . . declares that *all* men are born free and independent, and have an indefeasible right to enjoy liberty and pursue their own happiness. But this section denies the colored man equal freedom, to settle in this State. It is also a gross violation of the Constitution of the United States, the second section of the fourth article of which declares, that the citizens of each State shall be entitled to all the privileges and immunities of the several States.

To those individuals who did not consider blacks as citizens, Jones argued, "[I]f being natives, and born on the soil, of parents belonging to no other nation or tribe, does not constitute a citizen in this country under the theory and genius of our government, I am at a loss to know in what manner citizenship is acquired by birth." He declared that blacks were citizens by the courage and fidelity displayed by them in defending liberties and in achieving the country's independence. Jones concluded by citing a speech by William Eustis, late governor of Massachusetts, who spoke of the gallant role of blacks who had a participated in the Revolutionary War. He also cited a speech by Dr. Robert Clarke to the New York Constitutional Convention in 1821 extolling the heroic deeds of blacks in the War of 1812.

Jones was particularly embittered about Section Five of the Black Laws, which decreed that blacks or mulattos who failed to secure a certificate of freedom would be deemed runaway slaves and committed to the custody of the sheriff and given six weeks to produce a certificate or give evidence of freedom. Thereafter, the fugitive could be sold to the highest bidder. That section, wrote Jones, was most cruel indeed, subjecting blacks to the auction block with cattle, sheep, and swine. "[W]ithout any complaint or warrant describing the person to be seized, . . . a person may be arrested, thrown into prison, and subjected to be sold into involuntary servitude, without having committed any crime or offense except being born black," he wrote.

Jones then directed his attention to the Civil Code. He denounced Section Sixteen, which stated that "no black or mulatto person, or Indian, shall be permitted to give evidence in favor of or against any white person whatsoever." He wrote:

> It is not the complexion or shades of men that we are discussing; it is the rights of all inhabitants of the State, that we are advocating, for we are equally concerned and interested—the white, the black, and the colored. The interest of one, is the interest of all. We are inseparably and rightfully connected, in our business relations, with each other, and for this reason, if no other, we ought to be allowed to testify for or against you in the courts of justice. . . . Have we not eyes to see, intellect to understand, and hearts to feel, what other men see, understand and feel? . . . Your love of Christianity, humanity and equal rights to all, demand the repeal of this section, with the whole code.

As a businessman, Jones appealed to the economic interests of the legislators, most of whom were men of property: "Are we not to be found in all the industrial pursuits of life that other men are? . . . You ought to, and must repeal those Black Laws for the sake of your own interest, to mention no higher motive. . . . And I thank God the day has come when you will give us employment, notwithstanding you are subjected to a fine of five hundred dollars for so doing."

Jones's final argument was that the Black Laws encouraged discrimination against blacks by foreigners. "The cruel treatment that we receive daily at the hands of a portion of your foreign population, is all based on those enactments. They, seeing that you by your laws, have ignored us, and left us out in the cold, think it is for some crime we have committed, and therefore take license to insult and maltreat us every day on the highways and byways as we pass by them. They think we have no rights which white men are bound to respect, and according to your laws they think right." His final appeal to the Illinois legislature was on humanitarian grounds. "Our destiny is in your hands. Will you lift us out of our present degradation, and place us under the protection of wholesome laws, and make us responsible for the abuse of them as other citizens are?"

An editorial in the *Chicago Tribune* urged that the public read Jones's pamphlet. The *Chicago Evening Journal* also decried the Black Laws:

> Mr. Jones has exposed their inhumanity and injustice in an able manner, and his appeal to the good sense and magnanimity of the legislators and people for their repeal, cannot be resisted by any liberal mind. He has taken hold of this matter with zeal and earnestness, and is determined that if petitions and other honorable efforts can accomplish it, these statues—outlawing himself and his race—shall no longer disgrace our State. He has the sympathy of all right thinking men.

As the editorial indicated, Jones did not rely solely on his pamphlet. Throughout the winter, he continued circulating petitions and organizing correspondence committees and repeal associations.

The January 1865 session of the Illinois General Assembly seemed ripe for repeal of the Black Laws. On January 2, outgoing governor Richard Yates (who was resigning in order to take a seat in the United States Senate) urged lawmakers to "sweep the black laws from the statute books with a swift, relentless hand." It is difficult to say to what extent Yates was influenced by Jones. From boyhood, Yates had considered slavery a grievous wrong, and throughout his political career he had opposed slavery. In an 1864 speech at Bryan Hall in Chicago he had declared,

> Now, I am for the abolition of slavery, not because I am for the white man or the red man, or the black man, but because I am for man, for God's humanity. . . . I am for conferring upon every human being the right to the proceeds of his own labor, and to all the advantages which he has a right to under the constitution of the United States and our glorious declaration of the American Independence. I am not here to utter these sentiments to-day for the first time; these have been my opinions, well known and understood for a long time past. I am not afraid to utter them now. I have not been afraid to utter them for the past thirty years.

Yates, like Jones, based his appeal on legal grounds—that the Black Laws were contrary to the state and federal constitutions.

On January 4, the first working day of the session, bills repealing the Black Laws were introduced in both chambers of the general assembly. For the next two weeks, petitions flooded lawmakers. One such petition from Quincy, bearing the names of thousands of white citizens, was introduced by Senator Francis A. Eastman of Cook County, a member of the Judiciary Committee. According to the *Chicago Tribune,* petitions poured into the legislature "from all parts of the State for the repeal of the infamous Black Laws and all the other laws upon statute books placing disabilities upon the black race in this State." Jones lobbied vigorously, occasionally with mixed results. Senator William H. Green of Cairo, for example, was willing to support a special act enfranchising Jones, for whom he had sympathetic feelings, but would not support one for the entire race.

Meanwhile, the Thirteenth Amendment to the United States Constitution was being debated in Congress. Congress acted on February 1, and that very day Illinois became the first state to ratify the measure. Governor Richard J. Oglesby signed the repeal of Illinois Black Laws on February 7. The Illinois Senate had voted thirteen to ten on January 24, 1865, and the House followed with a vote of forty-nine to thirty on February 4. In commemoration of the momentous occasion, Springfield blacks fired a salute of sixty-two guns—one for each member of the Senate and House who voted for the bill. Jones was individually honored by being chosen to ignite the cannon fuse, symbolically ending the Black Laws. Afterward, the group proceeded to the African Methodist Episcopal Church, where Jones gave a "most interesting and able speech." Chicago and other cities throughout the state had simultaneous celebrations.

The repeal of the Black Laws provided an open door for prospective black immigrants to Illinois. By 1870 the black population in Illinois had increased more than threefold over prewar statistics, reaching a total of more than twenty-eight thousand. The passage of the civil rights bill in 1866 assured equal protection under the law, but segregation still existed in public schools. In 1869 Governor John M. Palmer announced that blacks were eligible for any political office, and shortly after he appointed Jones as the state's first notary public. A corollary to office eligibility was suffrage. Ratification of the Fifteenth Amendment in March 1870 allowed blacks to participate for the first time in Illinois elections. Within a year, John Jones was elected a Cook County commissioner, becoming the first black man elected to public office in Chicago.

Charles Branham indicated that Jones's election in 1871 was not the beginning of the emergence of black politics in Chicago but rather the fulfillment of the abolitionist Republican tradition of the city. It was, after all, the Republican Party that offered blacks protection and some hope of political advancement. Jones's candidacy resulted from his success in establishing himself as a "distinguished member of the larger Chicago community with important and powerful Republican contacts." His political ideas were forged in the repeal campaign of the 1860s and represented the postwar, postabolitionist tradition of nonmilitant civic protest and civil rights.

Jones's life was a testimonial to what could be achieved in spite of prejudice and injustice. He had faith in the American system and was optimistic about the future of his race. In 1874, five years before his death, he said,

> Everywhere the black man has sprung of his own free will and determination, in spite of Church and State, from the position of slavery and its consequences, to the bar, the pulpit, the lecture-room, the professorship, the degrees of M.D., and D.D. . . . His eloquence electrifies thousands of listeners; his pen instructs the millions; his merchandise travels over sea and land; his property is reckoned by millions; his strong arm upholds the American Government.

Jones's role in the black convention movement and in the repeal campaign against the Black Laws produced a leader of the black liberation movement.

RELATED READINGS

David Joens, "Illinois Colored Conventions of the 1880s," *Journal of the Illinois State Historical Society* vol. 110, nos. 3-4 (Fall-Winter 2017).
Victoria Harrison, "We Are Here Assembled: Illinois Colored Conventions, 1853–1873" (Special African-American Issue), *Journal of the State Historical Society* vol. 108, nos. 3-4 (Fall-Winter 2015).

7.

EDUCATION IN ILLINOIS
BEFORE 1857

Robert Gehlmann Bone

Journal of the Illinois State Historical Society
vol. 50, no. 2 (Summer 1957)

This article describes the landmark laws affecting common school education going back to the Land Act of 1784 and extending to the establishment of Illinois State Normal University in 1857. The author identifies the key events, individuals, groups, and periodicals supportive of state-sponsored teacher education and state-supported free schools. Success was finally achieved with the enactment of the Free School Act of 1855. For the first time, the law provided extensive financial state assistance to school districts.

From the very founding of our Republic, our growth as a democratic nation has been dependent to a degree upon an intelligent, educated electorate. A number of the Founding Fathers, such as Jefferson, Franklin, Washington, and Benjamin Rush, felt strongly that a people faced with the task of self-government must be an educated people. Washington referred to this need in his first message to Congress, and in a speech given in 1789 he said, "As in civilized Societies the welfare of the State and happiness of the People are advanced or retarded in proportion as the morals and good education of the youth are attended to." With our ever-increasing power among the nations of the world, with our progress in science and in many other areas, it is more vital than ever that we properly educate our leaders and citizens. Today Americans, as a whole, take for granted that our children will be given a free education through high school and will have an opportunity to enter college. Yet, if we study the history of education in our country, we discover that there has been a long, slow development for schools and that there were many problems and struggles in this development.

At the opening of the nineteenth century, however, the vast majority of Americans felt that education was for the few who could afford it. While it is true that the New England states had laws establishing free schools—Massachusetts had adopted such a law in 1674—not all communities availed themselves of the opportunity. Nonetheless, a good many people moving west in the early decades of the nineteenth century dreamed and hoped for the future and wanted their children to have equal rights. In many frontier settlements in Illinois, parents got together and hired a teacher or sent their children, at least the sons, to subscription schools. These schools increased in number, and just prior to the Free School Bill of 1855, there were 4,215 schools officially reported in Illinois. Most of these were private, parochial, or subscription schools. Very few were public schools; a few towns such as Joliet, Jacksonville, Alton, Griggsville, Galena, Galatia, and Springfield supported some education by public revenues. Some of these 4,215 schools did not have their own buildings but were held in homes, meetinghouses, churches, or even abandoned buildings. Nearly half of the school buildings were of log cabin construction. The report showed no graded schools or high schools. More than two-thirds of the teachers were men who received an average monthly salary of twenty-five dollars; women teachers received an average salary twelve dollars.

Largely because of the Free School Bill of 1855, schools increased by nearly eighty percent in the following three years. The official *Report on the Schools* for 1857 showed 7,694 free public schools. Of these, 181 were graded and these included a few high schools, some of which were in Jacksonville; Peoria, which opened a free public school in July 1856; Chicago, in October 1856; Springfield, in September 1857; and Bloomington, in October 1857. In the latter year Illinois boasted fourteen colleges and a state-supported normal university, which opened its classes in Bloomington on October 5, 1857.

From one point of view it might be said that the educational system and philosophy in the Midwest began in 1785, when the Continental Congress first enacted legislation concerning the land north of the Ohio. Lot No. 16 of every township was reserved for the maintenance of public schools within the township. Article III of the Northwest Ordinance of 1787 began, "Religion, morality, and knowledge being necessary to good government and the happiness of mankind, schools and the means of education shall forever be encouraged."

The next legislative reference to education in Illinois came in 1818 when, on April 18, Nathaniel Pope (1774–1850), territorial delegate in Congress, witnessed the passage of the enabling act which he had introduced for the creation of the State of Illinois. The people of Illinois should be most grateful to Pope. He wrote into the bill paragraphs which not only gave the state the northern boundary of forty-two degrees and thirty minutes rather than forty-one degrees and thirty-nine minutes, which had been first recommended, but also stipulated that three percent of government sales of land should be used for education, as well as two percent for roads. The bill further stipulated that monies from Section 16 in each township should be used for schools, and that funds from a whole township should be set aside for an educational seminary. The Constitution of the State of Illinois, which was written soon after Pope had engineered the enabling act through Congress, made no mention of education.

Except for granting some charters to a few towns for academies, there was practically no legislation concerning education until the meeting of the fourth General Assembly in 1824–25. Joseph Duncan (1794–1844) of Morgan County, later the fifth governor of Illinois, introduced "An Act Providing for the Establishment of Free Schools." This document placed Illinois as a leader in the field of education. None of all the New England states had such excellent school laws. The Act provided, among other things, that any township with fifteen families must supply a free school for at least three months of the year, and it provided further for officials and for taxation to carry on the school.

Both houses passed and approved the act on January 15, 1825. Schools were just being established, however, when the sixth General Assembly, 1828–29, retarded the progress of education in Illinois many decades by repealing Sections 15, 16, and 17 of the 1825 Act. These sections had provided the districts with taxing powers, and it was many decades before like taxing powers were again enacted. There was still strong feeling that no one should have to pay taxes for the children of other men. Furthermore, there were still many pioneers who were from the southeast and who felt that subscription schools were better.

However, in spite of lack of good free school laws, schools all over the state increased, and children were exposed to the three R's. In the 1830s there was a growing demand for trained teachers. A few public-spirited persons in the New England states encouraged young people to go west to teach. William Slade, ex-Governor of Vermont, sent numerous young women and some young men to Illinois. Catherine Beecher of the famous Beecher family encouraged many young ladies to go west and teach. As early as 1829 a rather famous group of young men from Yale had migrated to Illinois to preach and teach.

The majority of the teachers, however, were very poorly educated. Theodore C. Pease in his *Story of Illinois* wrote, "The earliest schools were most casual affairs. They were kept by drunkards, by men with the barest smattering of knowledge, unfitted for other purposes by physical or moral defects." Many examples referring to the character and training of teachers of the early decades can be found in reading early county histories and other documents. There were, of course, a number of teachers with the training of Jacob Poe and John Purviance, of Daniel Wilkins and John Brooks. However, many of those who actually migrated for the purpose of teaching created certain difficulties. The women teachers often married and with the prospect of the first child, they left the classroom. Largely because of low salaries and the fact that classes were held for only three or four months a year, most of the men held other jobs, and many of them, like the Vermonter Stephen A. Douglas, left teaching entirely. At the same time it must be remembered that the pioneer became proud of his area and his state and was easily led to find fault with the easterner who "was brought" specifically to teach. The pride of the pioneer was hurt. Public speakers and newspapers protested against the "importing of teachers." The *Belleville Advocate* quoted Judge William H. Underwood as late as 1857 as saying, "We want teachers raised up from among our own people, teachers acquainted with our habits, customs, and modes of life. . . . Imported teachers will not answer this purpose." Even Douglas spoke ardently against the imported teachers who were trying to "Yankeefy" and "abolitionize" the people of Illinois.

Long before Douglas and Underwood complained of importation of teachers, education leaders were trying to establish a teacher training institution. These leaders agreed that prepared teachers were necessary to the future of the state, and in 1833 an educational convention met in Vandalia just prior to the convening of the legislature. This group, known as the Illinois Institute of Education, met again in 1834 and in succeeding years under the leadership of the Rev. John Mason Peck (1789–1858), one of the great men in early Illinois history. He not only founded Shurtleff College (begun as Rock Spring Academy in 1827) but was an active and ardent missionary, one of the most active and ardent supporters of education, a capable lobbyist, and an able publisher and editor. Largely as a result of the early meetings of the Institute in the state capitol just prior to the legislative session of 1834, the State Senator from Gallatin County, William J. Gatewood (d. 1842), a close friend of Jacob Poe and a strong supporter of education, introduced a bill in 1835 to provide for a uniform system of free schools and for a system of seminaries to train teachers. The bill did not pass; and although it was introduced again in the following session, it lost again.

Massachusetts was more successful at this time in its attempt to create a school to train teachers, for it authorized the first Normal School in the country, which opened in Lexington in 1839 (later located in Framingham). The establishment of this school and others in the East during the succeeding decade spurred leaders in Illinois to agitate again for a normal school.

In the forties and the fifties, the attitudes in general toward education in Illinois changed, and the long, slow struggle for free education and for the proper preparation of teachers was won. A few men had begun hoping and agitating in the twenties and thirties. Referring to the Midwest in these two decades, one historian wrote that "in the hard toil of community building, not a little sentiment had sprung up against education in the frontier settlements." There were a good many who felt that "book larning" might go to one's head and fail to prepare a person for reality. Many factors, however, contributed to a gradual change in the attitudes toward education. Jacksonian Democracy, with the coming of manhood suffrage and the rise of the laboring groups, gave men a new feeling about the value of education. Many leaders renewed the philosophy of such men as Jefferson, believing that a real democracy would succeed only if there were an educated electorate. The common man, and there were few who were not "common men" in the pioneer states, wanted his children to read, write, and figure simple numbers. He wanted his children to have a free, public education.

Once started, the rise of the free schools in the new west was more rapid than elsewhere in the country. In Illinois, for instance, there were fewer shibboleths of the wealthy aristocracy; there were fewer private, subscription, or parochial schools to play their vested interests against free public schools. Some of those existing did strive to keep free school legislation from passing. On the other hand, there were many unselfish, public-spirited men, like Daniel Wilkins and John F. Brooks, who strongly urged the passage of such legislation, knowing that it might well close their own private schools.

The new states in the west had fewer sectarian controls and fewer wealthy persons or interests opposing the public funds for universal free education. By 1850 education was not only recommended as beneficial to a growing democracy but it "was also offered as a panacea for every other ill." It was beneficial in that it educated a rising electorate; the rising labor group did not believe that only the aristocracy should receive education. The campaign slogan of 1840, "From log cabin to White House," only accentuated the fact that a frontier boy of a poor family could rise to the top in the new Republic and that "he should be ready." Some of those who previously had opposed free education were won over by speakers and by writers of editorials and articles. Some felt that the foreign-born should be given an American education; that "would-be radicals" might be educated to think "properly"; that young prospective "hoodlums" might be disciplined; and that the parochial schools might become too numerous and too influential. For many reasons, men's attitudes on education were changing.

There were still those who thought "too much education" was dangerous for young people. Quite a number of property owners and businessmen were incensed that any man's property should be taxed to educate another man's children and all too often it seemed that the poorest people, the near pauper class, the "lazy, good-for-nothing class," had the most children. Yet in spite of these objections, more and more men were won over to the philosophy that democracy for all necessitated education for all. The changing attitudes were the result to a large extent of organized and influential newspapers and periodicals. The Illinois Teachers Association had been organized in Jacksonville in 1836, led by the able Jonathan B. Turner. The ITA published the *Common School Advocate* from 1837 to 1839. Later *The Illinois Common School Advocate* was published for a short period in the early forties. Two other periodicals which continued much longer and strongly supported education were *The Pioneer and Western Baptist*, edited by that early missionary and educator, the Rev. John Mason Peck; and *The Prairie Farmer*, edited by John S. Wright (1815–74). According to one historian of education, *The Prairie Farmer*, while edited by Wright, was the largest single force in bringing about legislation for the free school and for a teacher training institution in Illinois. A tireless worker in the field of education, John Wright became secretary of the Union Agricultural Society in 1839 and editor of the very influential periodical *The Union Agriculturist* (renamed *The Prairie Farmer* in 1843). He had been a wealthy Chicago merchant and had given the money for the construction of the first school building in that city. He had lost everything in the Panic of 1837 and had taken the secretarial position with the new organization. For many years, he published numerous strong articles in favor of education and of a normal school. Wright pleaded for the latter because "at least four-fifths of the teachers in the common schools of Illinois would not pass an examination in the rudiments of our English education, and most of them have taken to teaching because they hadn't anything in particular to do."

Because of growing interest in public schools, the General Assembly passed a school bill in 1841. This bill consisted of 109 sections. While it was an improvement over all previous bills, it did not bring about free public schools, because there was no provision for local taxation. A school law in 1845 added little to the bill of 1841 except that it provided for a state official to study and report on education. The Secretary of State was named the ex officio State Superintendent of Common Schools.

Interested and agitated groups wrote to and talked to Horace C. Cooley (1806–50), Secretary of State and ex officio Superintendent of Common Schools, urging him to call a convention of people interested in education; as a result, a four-day meeting was held in Springfield in January 1849. The main discussion centered about free schools and a teacher training institute. Among the more prominent speakers strongly urging state support were two future governors, William H. Bissell (1811–60) of Monroe County and Richard Yates (1815–73) of Morgan County.

New impetus was given to developing public education at Griggsville, Illinois, on May 13, 1850, when Professor Jonathan B. Turner presented "A Plan for a State University for the Industrial Classes." Professor Turner, a graduate of Yale, came to Illinois to teach in Illinois College at Jacksonville in 1833. As a teacher and a farmer, he was vitally interested in education throughout his life, and he spoke and wrote in its behalf with a missionary zeal.

Newspapers and periodicals gave a great deal of publicity to Turner's plan, and he was called to speak on numerous occasions during the following months. On November 18, 1851, he was a leading participant at a gathering of farmers and laborers in Granville, Illinois. This group not only strongly endorsed Turner's plan for a university for the common man with departments for teacher training, agricultural techniques, and mechanical skills, but they also created the Industrial League. Many of their principles and beliefs became the basis for the famous Morrill Act of 1862.

One of the most important meetings on the subject of education took place in December 1853. The prime mover on this particular occasion was the president of the Central Female Academy of Bloomington, Daniel Wilkins. He, with Harry Lee, a school principal in Chicago, and James Hawley, a book agent from Dixon, got Alexander Starne, Secretary of State and ex officio Superintendent of Common Schools, to join them in calling a statewide meeting on free public schools and other educational matters. This meeting was held in the Methodist Church of Bloomington on December 26–28.

The members of this group decided to form an organization so that they might act, not merely discuss and pass resolutions. These men were unanimous in their desire to have the state legislature create free public schools, and they felt that the creation of a separate office for education in the state was essential. They passed three resolutions and set up committees to implement each of them:

1. They organized the Illinois State Teachers Association, which became the Illinois Education Association in 1936. (Officers were elected, the Rev. William Goodfellow of Illinois Wesleyan University was named president, active committees were set up, and arrangements were made for a second meeting in Peoria in the following December.)

2. They resolved to legislate for an office of Superintendent of Education. (At a special session called by Governor Joel Matteson in February, 1854, the legislature approved the office of Superintendent of Public Instruction and Ninian W. Edwards was named to hold the office until the next general election.)

3. They authorized the publication of a periodical devoted to education. (The *Illinois Teacher* began publication in February 1854 under the joint editorship of Daniel Wilkins and W. F. M. Arny. In 1855 Charles E. Hovey [1827–97], principal of the Boys Stock School of Peoria, became editor, and he greatly expanded the subscription list and the influence of the periodical.)

The Bloomington meeting stressed free public schools and before adjourning passed another resolution recommending that the legislature create a normal school. The organization appointed an agent, Newton Bateman (1822–97), to tour the state on behalf of its interests and to talk to legislators. In 1857 he was succeeded by the equally able and dynamic Simeon Wright (d. 1876).

As noted above, Ninian W. Edwards (1809–86), son of ex-Governor Ninian Edwards, was named the first Superintendent of Public Instruction. He took his job very seriously and after only a few weeks in office invited some men to help him prepare a free public education bill for the legislature. An excellent bill was drawn up and presented to the proper legislative committees. The bill included many of the best features of the famous Education Act of 1825, plus some excellent sections on taxing rights and powers. The bill passed the Senate but ran into difficulties in the House. After some modifications and the deletion of a few sections, the Education Act of 1855 was passed and signed by Governor Matteson (1808–73). Fortunately, four sections, 67, 69, 70, and 71, granting taxing powers, were left in. Illinois, at long last, was able to provide free education for those who wanted it.

The State Teachers Association, with the aid of many interested groups and individuals, played a large part in the creation of the Office of State Superintendent and in the passage of the free education act. Schools increased in number and enrollment, and high schools were established. There was now greater need than ever for the creation of a normal school. While it is true that there were a number of colleges in Illinois, their graduates were not trained specifically for teaching in elementary or high schools. The State Teachers Association had gone on record in support of a normal school, but it had been far from a unanimous decision. While the members were agreed on many things, there were three groups in evidence when a normal school was discussed. The Rev. William Goodfellow of Illinois Wesleyan and many of his colleagues among other private colleges, academies, and seminaries hoped that the State's Seminary and College Funds might be distributed among them if the state did not create a state-supported college. Jonathan Turner, Bronson Murray, and others were insistent that the state create an industrial university, which would not only train teachers but would also train farmers and mechanics. A third group pressed for a state-supported teachers college.

In the meeting of the Association in Springfield in December 1855, all the officers elected were from the latter group, and Hovey was not only elected president but was also named editor of *The Illinois Teacher*. The officers made very careful plans for the 1856 meeting in Chicago and listed as the two main speakers Dr. Henry Barnard, a leader in the normal school movement in Connecticut and Rhode Island, and William H. Wells. Charles E. Hovey presided. On the morning following Barnard's talk, the Association passed a resolution which strongly urged the legislature to immediate steps to create a normal school. Immediately following the passage of the resolution, Newton Bateman obtained the floor and read a letter written by Jonathan Turner. The latter stated that he and the Industrial League had hoped for an industrial university which would include among other curricula one for the training of teachers. However, because it seemed doubtful as to whether an institution such as the League desired would be given legislative approval at the time, he and the League would cooperate in a program requesting a normal school. Turner's generous and famous letter ended with, "It is high time, my friends, that you had your Normal School, whether we ever get an Agricultural Department to it or not. Let us all take hold together and try to obtain it in such form as you may, on the whole, think best." It is no wonder that Hovey said years later that this event was the turning point in the creation of a state-supported normal school.

With a sweeping majority the Association voted that a committee be appointed to wait on the legislature. Charles Hovey, Daniel Wilkins, and President-elect Simeon Wright were named to meet with their colleague, William H. Powell, the Superintendent of Public Instruction-elect, and draft a bill for the legislature. These men prepared a bill in January 1857, and Representative Samuel W. Moulton (1822–1905), who had helped with education bills previously, sponsored the bill in the House. Captain J. S. Post (1816–86) of Decatur agreed to sponsor it in the Senate.

The bill passed the Senate sixteen to four and the House thirty-nine to twenty-five, and on February 18, 1857, Governor William C. Bissell signed the act creating a normal university—the first state-supported institution of higher education in the state and the first normal school in the Mississippi Valley. The bill also named a state Board of Education composed of fifteen members, including the Superintendent of Public Instruction.

[A number of towns competed] for the site of the normal university. Under the management of Jesse Fell of North Bloomington, the site (created the town of Normal by act of May 4, 1867) was selected on May 7, 1857. A few weeks later, on June 23, Charles Hovey was chosen president over William F. Phelps, principal of the New Jersey State Normal School. Horace Mann, strongly considered for a while, withdrew his name shortly before the board meeting.

Hovey and a number of the board members spent a great deal of time during the summer developing a curriculum, studying and agreeing upon architectural plans for a permanent building, obtaining temporary classrooms, and selecting a suitable staff. On September 29 ceremonies were held for the laying of the cornerstone of the Old Main. On the following Monday, October 3, classes opened in the upper stories of Major's Hall, a building on the southwest corner of East and Front Streets, in Bloomington. On the first day nineteen students enrolled. This number increased to twenty-nine by the end of the second day and to one hundred and twenty-seven (seventy-four women and fifty-three men) by the end of the first year.

By 1857, one phase of educational development in Illinois had been completed. The hopes and dreams, the thoughts and efforts of our pioneer leaders in education had met a good deal of success by that date. Free public schools had been established, a number of high schools had been organized, the office of Superintendent of Public Instruction had been created, and a normal university had opened classes. However, much still needed to be done in 1858; buildings were inadequate, teachers were underpaid and often inadequately prepared, and school attendance was not compulsory. Each decade since 1857 has found in Illinois improvement in the education of its citizens. In 1957, when one looks back on the history of the educational system in Illinois, he marvels at the progress that has been made, and he realizes the debt he owes certain leaders and groups who gave of their time and physical and mental energy to create a worthwhile program. As he looks ahead, he needs to dedicate himself to participate in the continuing growth and development of education, so well begun and developed by our forefathers decades ago.

RELATED READING

Kay J. Carr, "Community Dynamics and Educational Decisions: Establishing Public Schools in Belleville and Galesburg," *Illinois Historical Journal* vol. 84, no. 1 (Spring 1991).

This well-researched Pratt Award–winning article describes the different ways schooling developed in the mid-nineteenth century in two communities and the varying ways the 1855 law was addressed in them. The variations were based on differences in their economic and social characteristics. Particularly important was the influence of the large number of Germans, many foreign born, in Belleville, in contrast to the influence of the mostly native-born "Yankees/Yorkers" in Galesburg.

8.

A VANISHING FRONTIER
The Development of a Market Economy in DuPage County

Stephen J. Buck

Journal of the Illinois State Historical Society
vol. 93, no. 4 (Winter 2000/2001)

Formed in 1839 from the western part of Cook County, DuPage County rapidly transitioned to a market economy due to its proximity to Chicago. DuPage and Chicago became dependent on each other, as Chicago needed a place to sell its merchandise and DuPage needed a shipping point for its agricultural products. Improvements in transportation from dirt roads to plank roads to railroads promoted the rise of the market economy. Landowners and towns competed for railroads to route their tracks through their area. The nearby Illinois and Michigan Canal promised further economic development.

One of the great issues debated by historians is that of the transition in rural society from the sturdy, independent, self-sufficient yeoman farmer to that of the market-oriented capitalist farmer. While this process took centuries in British North America and the early United States, it proceeded at a vastly accelerated pace in the middle of the nineteenth century. This was especially true in the area surrounding the rapidly growing metropolis of Chicago, which included DuPage County. The economy rapidly changed from one focused primarily on local exchange to one focused on market relationships. That is to say it changed from a focus on trading goods, produce, and labor within the local community to a focus on connecting to regional, national, and international markets based on the market demand for various commodities. The majority of DuPage County settlers, just like settlers in the rest of Illinois and the nation, desperately wanted to create certainty and permanence in their lives. Even in the frontier stage of development as they pursued a variety of ways to supplement their incomes, most people worked very hard to become commercial farmers and businessmen. They welcomed the breakthroughs connecting them to distant markets. As they worked to better their condition, these people developed a particular view of what it meant to be a citizen of the United States. This, in turn, shaped the political lens through which county residents viewed events locally, in the state, and in the nation.

Located in the northeastern corner of Illinois, DuPage was set off from Cook County in 1839, nine years after the first white settlers arrived. Economic success, if and when it occurred, took place within an agricultural economy: 90 percent of the working population of the county labored in agriculture in 1840, and most of the rest held occupations dependent on farmers and their needs. By 1880, however, the total farm workforce in the county dropped to 60 percent of the working population. Continuing a trend which started in the 1850s, a growing percentage of the county's population no longer lived on farms but in the towns and villages. New arrivals to the county found opportunities other than farming available. Every non-farming occupation in the county experienced significant increases during the 1860s as immigrants and residents alike sought employment in the towns and villages.

In spite of these changes, the county economy remained overwhelmingly oriented toward agriculture, especially commercial agriculture. The transition to a market economy occurred rapidly in DuPage due to the proximity of Chicago. DuPage depended on Chicago as a shipping point for agricultural produce, but this dependency worked both ways. The *Chicago Democrat* remarked that "Chicago is completely dependent upon . . . the surrounding county." The editor admitted that the countryside of course needed the city as "its depot" and as "a place of deposit for merchandize [*sic*] and a point for trade," but emphasized the need of the city for the countryside for "every breath of its existence."

This interdependent development required the existence of a workable transportation system to and from the broader national markets, particularly

Stephen J. Buck

that of the eastern United States. The development of such a system occupied county boosters almost from the beginning of settlement. The first crucial element in this system was efficient lake transportation which brought the initial settlers as well as the vast majority of those who followed. These same ships provided the means to export the agricultural products of northern Illinois to eastern markets. At first, however, there was little to export as settlers were concerned with establishing their homesteads. From 1836, when the first shipments left Chicago, until 1839, the value of all exports leaving Chicago amounted to about $62,000. DuPage-area settlers complained that economic conditions were such that they were "very illy [sic] prepared to contribute beyond the current expenses of our families." Despite these concerns, DuPage farmers produced surplus products, but with new settlers arriving in or passing through the area every day, the emerging economy centered on them. Farmers traded grain for items brought by the new immigrants, but they also transported grain to Chicago and traded it for goods sold by merchants.

In 1840 exports skyrocketed to over $228,000 as farmers and merchants brought increasing amounts of surplus grain to market. Throughout the 1840s this trend continued; in 1847 Chicago exported goods worth almost $2.3 million which nearly equaled her imports. Grain, almost exclusively wheat, was the primary export. Before the late 1840s, every bushel shipped out arrived overland in wagons pulled over dirt roads. This made the arrival of grain in the city sporadic at best as transportation and trade fluctuated wildly from season to season. In spite of this, by 1840 farmers within a 250-mile radius of the city hauled grain to Chicago. By the middle of the decade, hundreds of farmers could be seen in Chicago every day. DuPage farmers and merchants actively participated in this massive flow of produce to market. One county resident marveled at the "string of wagons almost uninterrupted for two or three miles, farmers taking their wheat to Chicago." Another estimated that "more than 100 teams a day pass by here with wheat to Chicago." He was amazed that people came "from Fox River, Rock River and even from Iowa, some of them coming 200 miles to sell their wheat in Chicago."

Intensive efforts to improve transportation connections with Chicago and eastern markets began very early. After the formation of the county in 1839, most efforts focused on the creation of dirt roads connecting various communities to each other and with the main roads to Chicago.

Illinois and Michigan Canal

Other, simultaneous, efforts to improve access to markets were also underway from an early date. The planned route for the Illinois-Michigan Canal only touched the southeast tip of DuPage County, but market-oriented residents appreciated the canal's economic importance. They realized that the canal would increase the economic importance of Chicago, which in turn would increase the markets for agricultural products and the value of landed property. Although Congress had granted the land along the canal route to the state government in 1827, progress was agonizingly slow. The inept handling of state finances coupled with the depression of the late 1830s combined to cripple every effort to complete construction. In January of 1845 Whigs and Democrats from La Salle, Kendall, Kane, DuPage, and Cook Counties held a meeting in Naperville to draft resolutions expressing their concerns. Importantly, the resolution showed the unanimity of Illinois Whigs and Democrats concerning internal improvements and their willingness to incorporate both Whig and Democratic philosophies into the resolutions. The committee argued that the canal should be considered a national rather than a state work because the state government failed several times to complete the canal. Congress, therefore, "ought to make additional donations of land" to Illinois "to aid her in the completion of the aforesaid work." The resolution opposed direct federal construction of internal improvements, instead calling for federal aid channeled through state government in the form of more land, which the state could sell to finance the canal. Whigs were satisfied that, as a national endeavor, the federal government would finance the canal, and Democrats readily agreed, provided that aid was channeled through the state government.

The requested federal aid never appeared, and the state struggled with the canal's finances until its eventual completion in 1849. Farmers in the southeast portion of DuPage used the canal when it opened, but two other transportation networks proved much more important. The first of these, plank roads, did not radically change the nature of economic development but did intensify that development. Dirt roads turned into muddy quagmires during the spring and fall rains, often rendering them useless. Plank roads allowed the stream of traffic to and from the market to achieve a regularity not possible with dirt roads.

Illinois and Michigan Canal, which opened the interior of Illinois to commerce from the Great Lakes and hastened the growth of Chicago. *Library of Congress.*

From Plank Roads to Railroads

Citizens of the counties between Chicago and Rockford petitioned the State Legislature as early as 1844 to enact plank road legislation. Delegates from DuPage and six other counties met at Elgin in September and passed resolutions stressing the importance of plank roads to the economy and expressly calling for a plank road from Chicago to Rockford via Elgin and Belvidere. The delegates chose a committee to prepare a bill permitting the right to form a private corporation for that purpose. Unfortunately, the bill turned into a partisan measure and was defeated. Despite this setback, agitation for plank roads continued, and the necessary legislation eventually passed in 1848.

In the spring of 1848 the construction of privately financed plank roads from Chicago westward and within DuPage County began. Several wealthy county residents invested heavily in the two major routes extending out of Chicago throughout DuPage County and also combined to form plank road companies which built extensions off the main routes. The enthusiasm for plank roads even extended to county government, which appropriated $5,000 to buy plank road stock.

At the same time that the Illinois-Michigan Canal finally opened and the plank roads began to cross the county, the construction of a far more significant form of transportation was also underway: the Galena and Chicago Union Railroad. The directors of the railroad opened their stock subscription books in August of 1847 and worked feverishly to secure a right-of-way. The original plan included Naperville and Warrenville on the route, but it ran into opposition from Joseph Naper and Julius Warren, the founders of these communities. Both men were heavily invested in the various plank roads under construction and also owned inns and stores along those routes. At a public meeting organized by Naper and Warren in Naperville, the directors of the railroad found that the two men had created intense opposition. Citizens shouted that they "couldn't see the difference between a plank and a rail." Many swore that if the railroad came through, they would let their cattle run loose on the tracks. This would have forced the railroad to expend more funds to fence the right-of-way in the vicinity of Naperville, an expense the company could not afford. After this rebuff the surveyor for the railroad, Richard P. Morgan, changed his survey to eliminate both communities from the route and instead designated what eventually became Turner's Junction as the junction for the two planned branches of the railroad.

While the directors of the railroad wrestled with finding a right-of-way, people speculated as to the route. Realizing the economic gain which might result from selling land to the railroad or by having land close to the right-of-way, several landowners drove hard bargains with railroad agents. After securing the right-of-way as far as Babcock's Grove, company agents ran into opposition from farmers who refused to accept railroad stock as partial payment for their land or tried to achieve a windfall by greatly increasing the asking price for their land. The *Chicago Democrat* warned them to restrain their greed, reminding them that hard bargaining might cause the company to deal with more compliant landowners.

Others engaged in speculation as to the route of the railroad and lobbied company directors to send the railroad across their property. Elias Jewel built a railroad station on his property in anticipation of the projected route, and Erastus Gary hurriedly purchased land along what he thought would be the final route. Both men lost out to a pair of clever, and lucky, brothers. William Ogden and the other directors of the railroad made several trips through the county in an effort to secure the right-of-way. On one trip Warren and Jesse

Wheaton happened, by luck or by design, to meet Ogden and invite him to dinner. During dinner they offered Ogden the right-of-way across their land at no charge, a total of three and a half miles, if Ogden would slightly alter the projected course of the railroad to come through a town they planned to build. Ogden instantly accepted the offer, dashing the speculative hopes of Jewel and Gary and proving a boon to the Wheaton brothers.

The appearance of the railroad in the county created tremendous new business opportunities for landowners whose property abutted the right-of-way. Acutely aware of the financial gains to be made, a handful of men allowed the railroad to cross their property in exchange for station rights. They more than recouped the expense of building the station by selling or renting adjacent parcels of property to prospective entrepreneurs who hoped to profit from the trade generated by the railroad.

One key entrepreneur in the transition to a market economy was the grain warehouse operator. When farmers and merchants hauled grain to the station, the warehouse owner purchased the grain and made arrangements to sell it in Chicago. By the 1850s, Chicago had the most refined elevator system in the country, spearheading the transformation of grain marketing. Further accelerating this process was the creation of the Chicago Board of Trade in 1848. Over the next decade, the board regularized and systematized the marketing of grain. By 1856 farmers and shippers delivered grain to a warehouse and received a receipt redeemable by anyone. The owner of the receipt could sell the elevator receipt for a like quantity of grain to anyone. Sellers and buyers alike could then monitor the price of the various grades of grain in the newspapers which regularly printed market prices. Now, instead of setting aside three to five days to transport grain to Chicago, farmers and merchants arranged to ship grain to the city in a single day or less, depending upon their proximity to the seven stations built in the county during the 1850s.

Until the mid-1850s the plank roads shrugged off the competitive impact of the railroad. Yearly income continued to reach 40 percent or more of the original cost and the companies paid dividends of 14 percent. James Hunt, a Naperville businessman, noted that farmers came from miles around to use the plank road because it was the only good road to the city. He marveled that "the string of teams never ended. It was like a great pulley with sheaves at Chicago and Naperville." There were so many wagons around harvest time that "the wagons had to keep their places exactly as a rope. . . . If a kink got in the line anywhere, the whole machine stopped."

By 1857, however, competition from the Galena and Chicago Union Railroad drove the plank roads out of business. Hunt lamented that "the wheat was rolling into Chicago over the rails. . . . We tore up our plank road and distributed its planks to the stockholders." As the railroad extended across Illinois to the Mississippi River, freight volume increased, and freight rates progressively decreased. The plank roads also could not compete with the speed of rail transportation. The railroads utilized the power of steam to rapidly transport products to market and had the added advantage of saving the farmer the trip to Chicago. Plank roads still relied on slow, plodding animal power, and the farmer still had to make the trip to the city. The combination of better rates with shorter travel times for the individual farmer ensured the demise of the plank road companies.

Railroads and Town Development

The extension of the railroad during 1849–50 also led to the development of towns along its path, all of which catered to the business generated by the railroad. A few of these towns already existed, but for all intents and purposes they could not be called towns prior to 1849; most consisted of four or five buildings clustered around the intersection of two or more roads. Their real development began with the arrival of the railroad. For towns, the economic benefits of the railroad tended to be a zero-sum proposition: towns along the railroad prospered, but those which refused to allow the railroad to come through or were not located on its route experienced a negative impact on their economy. In the aftermath of its hostility to the railroad, Warrenville became a backwater village with little economic activity. Naperville remained economically vital, but not to the degree envisioned by its boosters.

Less than three years after Naperville tied its economic hopes to the plank roads, its business leaders began to complain that they were losing business. The editor of the *DuPage County Observer* warned his readers that "the Plank Road . . . is not quite the thing needed." He agreed that the road "is very convenient for people to ride into town upon, and for farmers living near it, who do all their marketing in Chicago," but that on the whole "it does not help [Naperville] much." He argued that Naperville needed a railroad if it was to grow. In a letter to the editor, "Stupeo" went even further, arguing that "Wherever railroads go, there business centers." He also stated that "a very large proportion of the business has been stopped and drawn from this place by the Railroad." This loss of business had resulted in the barring of "many doors and windows in our village," and he urged town residents to actively court the railroads. One anonymous county resident sought to refute Stupeo's arguments. The writer acknowledged that a railroad would certainly enhance the prosperity of Naperville's businessmen, but he challenged Stupeo to show "what business had been drawn away and stopped from this section of the county." He argued that "our merchants have never sold as many goods (during the same time) as the past year." In spite of this challenge, the perception remained that Naperville was losing business to towns along the railroad, and the fact remained that other towns now competed for business which once flowed exclusively into Naperville.

As business flowed away from Naperville, town business leaders, including the directors of the local plank road companies, pinned new hopes on the directors and stockholders of the Chicago, Burlington, and Quincy Railroad, which had completed its line to Aurora. The directors now had a decision to make: whether to continue the line to Chicago or make an arrangement with the Galena and Chicago to tap into their line at Turner's Junction.

Naperville's attempt to get a railroad through the town started early in 1852 when R. N. Murray discovered that the railroad was considering the Naperville route. Murray wrote to George Martin Jr. of "rumors in Chicago" that the railroad "had ordered a survey from Aurora to Chicago ... in the direction of our town." He remarked that the survey "was being made rather privately" and that Martin and some others ought to "go quietly over to the Big Woods and see what the prospects are." Martin found the prospects to be excellent, and in July the leading property holders around Naperville began to formulate a strategy to induce the C.B. & Q. to build a line to Chicago via Naperville. The people attending the meeting selected Joseph Naper, R. N. Murray, and Lewis Ellsworth, three major figures in both the town and the county Democratic Party, as a committee to address the situation. A second committee was to ascertain the amount of stock subscriptions which might be raised. Both committees made favorable reports: the first found the stockholders and directors of the railroad receptive to the plan, and the second returned with almost $22,000 in subscription pledges. The committee continued negotiations with the railroad directors, but financial considerations eventually prompted the directors to take the shorter route to the junction and to pay a yearly fee to the Galena and Chicago for the use of its track leading into Chicago.

Naperville and the southern townships next focused on events taking place in Whiteside County, along the Mississippi River. Three railroad companies competed for the financial backing of the citizens of Whiteside and other counties along the routes toward Chicago. The route proposed by the Chicago, Sterling, and Mississippi was to have gone through Naperville and received the enthusiastic backing of the same citizens who had courted the C.B. & Q. A rival railroad company, which planned to go through St. Charles in neighboring Kane County, broke ground first, which immediately produced a reaction from the Galena and Chicago. Determined to put a stop to this potential competition, the directors of the Galena and Chicago bought a majority of the company's stock and appointed Charles Dement, the major backer of the Chicago, Sterling, and Mississippi, as president of the Chicago and Galena's new branch railroad. The railroad went through St. Charles and then joined the Galena and Chicago's main line to Chicago at the junction.

The next opportunity for the southern townships to obtain a railroad occurred in 1858 when the C.B. & Q.'s lease with the Galena and Chicago expired. Once again, company directors explored the feasibility of building a line from Aurora to Chicago and appointed a committee to investigate the route. The southern townships immediately formed a committee to compile statistics showing the advantages of the Naperville route. The editor of the *Sentinel*, C. W. Richmond, printed the results in order to drum up support for the railroad. He lamented that previous efforts had not been unanimously supported by local inhabitants, claiming that "division of sentiment and effort" had doomed the attempts. He rejoiced that now, however, "a perfect unanimity of both effort and sentiment, prevails among our citizens."

This claim was premature, however, as some landowners along the proposed route resisted efforts to get them to grant right-of-way across their land. In another editorial, Richmond begged the recalcitrants to "estimate the damage to their lands arising from the construction of the road" and to "offset it against the advantage to be gained by the increase in the value of their farms." He also appealed to their presumed desire to be a part of the growing commercial attachment of the county to other markets in the nation. Richmond argued that farmers along the route could not only have a market for all their produce but also "the means of selecting the best market" for that produce.

Just when the pro-railroad group in the southern townships believed they had the directors convinced to build the line from Aurora to Chicago, the aftermath of the Panic of 1857 intervened. Despite the fact that the

C.B. & Q. paid over $100,000 per year in rental fees to the Galena and Chicago, in the face of the depression which followed the Panic the directors decided against paying the $700,000 they estimated it would cost to build the line. Instead, they signed another lease with the Galena and Chicago, once again dashing the hopes of the pro-railroad men in the southern townships. Not until 1864 did the C.B. & Q. build its own line across southern DuPage County into Chicago.

By 1857 the seven railroad depots located in the county handled over twenty-eight million pounds of freight. Centered on Chicago, the railroads fueled the rise of the city as the economic hub of the West. The city's continued growth created more demand for foodstuffs, which had to be supplied by the surrounding countryside. The *DuPage County Observer* acknowledged the importance of Chicago as a grain depot to the farmers in the county but focused on the city's potential as a market for foodstuffs in its own right. Noting that the rapidly escalating population of the city was predicted to reach one hundred thousand by the fall of 1855, the editor urged farmers to make "preparations to supply the butter, milk, eggs, poultry, and vegetables which this immense population will require." The editorial continued that the endeavor "will pay—pay infinitely better than raising wheat, if you engage in it systematically."

By 1860 agricultural production in DuPage County reflected the growing influence of the markets in Chicago, the eastern United States, and Europe. Market forces and the county's geographical location so near to Chicago dictated what items farmers produced, and these forces increased during the 1860s and the 1870s. A significant shift took place from a concentration on the production of grain for the market to a concentration on the production of wool, meat, and especially dairy products. Large scale meatpacking began in Chicago as early as 1835, but the creation of the Union Stock Yards in 1865 systematized and organized the entire process of getting animals to market. Just as with grain prices, newspapers regularly published animal prices, which gave buyers and sellers access to even more market information. While farmers did not grow any less grain, its primary purpose after 1865 was as fodder for animals rather than as a commodity for market. The *Illinoisan* commented that much of the grain remained because of the "dairy business" which "has stayed the current of grain exportation and it is all turned into milk and cheese." In 1870 DuPage farmers sold 968,665 gallons of milk, almost 10.5 percent of the statewide total. By 1890 DuPage, along with Kane and McHenry counties, led the state in the production of milk.

Population and Political Trends

Although most people did welcome the opportunities presented by the economic transitions of the mid-nineteenth century, the reality of competing in a market-oriented economy did not translate into instant success for all immigrants to DuPage County. The population itself changed constantly during these years, as fully 51 percent of the heads of household listed in the 1840 population census did not appear on the 1850 census. During the 1850s, despite the evolution of a supposedly more stable society caused by the passing of the frontier further to the west, the population of the county was actually more mobile than during the 1840s. As the county was drawn into the market economy, almost 58 percent of the people who resided in the county in 1850 were not listed on the 1860 census. Persistence rates stabilized during the 1860s at 50 percent and then increased to 55 percent during the 1870s. Some died in the intervening years, but others saw opportunity further west. Not all succeeded in DuPage; however, the very possibility of opportunity brought with it the possibility of failure. But, in an expanding nation, the opportunity for success elsewhere was always present.

The result was to create a community dominated by people with a similar economic worldview. In essence this view stimulated the development of free soil ideology among a population of farmers and shop owners. During the 1850s predominantly Democratic DuPage became overwhelmingly Republican. During the 1860 election, Lincoln carried 69 percent of the vote to Douglas's 31 percent. Although overwhelmingly Republican, DuPage County residents of both parties held similar views, which created a unity of purpose during the ensuing war years. The purpose of the Union, and the Constitution which defined it, was to guarantee the ability of white, commercially oriented freeholders to participate in a market economy. It was in this context that DuPage County residents approached the political events unfolding on the stages of Washington, D.C., and Springfield and, at the same time, sorted out politics at the community level.

9.

THE MORMONS
IN ILLINOIS, 1838–1846
A Special Introduction

Stanley B. Kimball

Journal of the Illinois State Historical Society
vol. 64, no. 1 (Spring 1971)

Part of a special issue on Mormons, this article provides a basic history of their time in Illinois—from the founding and rise of Nauvoo as a virtual city-state to its fall at the hands of its enemies. Contributing to the fall was the sect's involvement in state and national politics and the unusual nature of their doctrines, derived from Joseph Smith and outlined by the author in this article. The Mormons continue to be a topic of interest to scholars and the history-reading general public.

The Illinois phase of Mormon history is a pivotal one. Early Mormon history, from Joseph Smith's first vision in New York in 1820 and the founding of the faith in 1830, was climaxed in the "Kingdom on the Mississippi" with Smith's assassination in Carthage, Illinois, in 1844. Mormon history since that time stems from Nauvoo. In Illinois the Mormons (properly called the Church of Jesus Christ of Latter-Day Saints) partially realized their great desire to create a haven from past troubles and persecution by establishing a city-state (one that blurred the cherished American tradition of the separation of church and state). They hoped to make Nauvoo a great cultural and commercial center on the Mississippi River, and they began to realize their potential political strength as they expanded their relations

Nauvoo, the Mormon capital on the Mississippi, at its zenith in a photo taken probably in the mid-1840s. Within a decade the Latter-Day Saints would be relocated to Utah, and the temple would be rubble. *Photo courtesy Abraham Lincoln Presidential Library and Museum.*

with statesmen both in Illinois and Washington. In 1844 (one month before his death), Joseph Smith even became the candidate of the Nauvoo-based Reform Party for the office of the president of the United States.

During the Illinois period, missionary work was enormously expanded, and thousands of converts were made. Many of the Mormon Twelve Apostles went to England to enlarge that Old World beachhead that had been started in 1837, and nearly every state east of the Mississippi and Canada heard from Mormon missionaries. Also in Illinois the most esoteric doctrines, such as polygamy and temple ordinances, were first enunciated and practiced, attracting both attention and condemnation.

The beginning of Mormon history in Illinois may be traced to the notorious "Extermination Order" of Governor Lillburn W. Boggs of Missouri, dated October 27, 1838, which declared, "The Mormons must be treated as enemies, and must be exterminated or driven from the state if necessary for the public peace—their outrages are beyond description."

Fleeing the persecution this order generated, the Mormons left Missouri for Illinois and the Iowa Territory during the winter of 1838–39. Most of them crossed into Illinois on the ferry at Quincy, but some crossed at Louisiana, Missouri, and settled near Pittsfield. In western Illinois the refugees were generally made welcome by a people both sympathetic with the refugees and sorely in need of settlers and tax dollars.

At this critical time Joseph Smith was in prison in Liberty, Missouri, where he had been held since November 1838 on charges of treason. In April 1839, while being transferred from Liberty to the Boone County court for retrial, Smith was permitted to escape, and he quickly joined his followers in Quincy. (He and a few other Mormons had been in Illinois several times previously. In 1831, 1832, and 1834 they had passed through the state en route from Kirtland, Ohio, to the Mormon settlements in western Missouri.)

Faced with the necessity of resettling his scattered followers, Smith looked into the purchase of land and learned of a site for sale about fifty miles up the Mississippi. The area was a natural promontory jutting out into the river and one of the most beautiful natural locations on the entire river. At one time it was the site of a village headed by the Sauk chief Quashquame. Hancock County was organized in 1829, and a post-office town named Venus

The temporal and spiritual leader of the Church of Latter-Day Saints, Joseph Smith generated controversy with his church doctrines and political activities. *Image courtesy Abraham Lincoln Presidential Library and Museum.*

was founded at the old Indian village site. Later, representatives of land developers dropped the name of Venus and laid out the town of Commerce, and a few people settled in the community. In 1836 an adjoining town called Commerce City was platted. The general financial panic of 1837 nearly ruined both ventures, and the promoters were happy to sell the land to the Mormons on extremely easy terms. Joseph Smith made the first purchase on May 1, 1839, and quickly platted a city of more than six hundred acres.

The land was cleared and drained and a city soon appeared—not a temporary log cabin complex, but a sturdy New England village called Nauvoo. Smith gave the settlement its name, which was derived, he said, from a Hebrew root (*nawa*) meaning "a beautiful place." Nauvoo grew rapidly as members and new converts from the East and from Canada and the British Isles flooded the city. By the summer of 1841 Nauvoo had 8,000 to 9,000 inhabitants. The Illinois census of 1845 listed 11,052 residents, which made Nauvoo the largest city in Illinois.

Although the heart of the faith in Illinois was Nauvoo, there were other Mormon settlements throughout the state. Stakes (an ecclesiastical unit consisting of several congregations) were organized in Ramus, Lima, Geneva, Columbus, Payson, Springfield, Newark, and in Adams and Morgan Counties. Some of the Smith relatives lived in Plymouth, Colchester, Dixon, Amboy, and Macomb. Other Mormons resided at La Salle, Ottawa, Pleasant Grove, Walnut Grove, Oquawka, LaHarpe, Macedonia (now Webster), Indian Creek, Pittsfield, Big Vermilion (Vermilion County), and French Creek Cove (Bureau County).

Nauvoo provided the first opportunity for the Mormons to develop a community according to what they considered revelation. The streets, laid out grid fashion strictly according to the cardinal points of the compass, were usually three rods, or 49 1/2 feet, wide, and enclosed blocks of nearly four acres each. In this fashion, for the sake of the women, the amenities of city life were maintained in a largely agrarian setting.

Trouble in Ohio and Missouri led Smith to seek power to safeguard his people against repetition of persecution. In this effort he was successful, for politically Nauvoo had almost complete control of its own affairs under its charter, authorized by the Illinois legislature in December 1840. Abraham Lincoln and Stephen A. Douglas (then secretary of state) were among those who helped the Mormons get such a charter. The potential value of the Mormon vote was not lost on Illinois politicians. For a detailed study of this charter, see the article by James L. Kimball Jr., "The Nauvoo Charter:

A Reinterpretation," in this issue. The Nauvoo Legion grew to nearly two thousand men with its own armory and, much to the consternation of the surrounding countryside, was the largest standing body of armed men in the country next to the federal army. About the only limits placed upon the citizens of Nauvoo was that they do nothing contrary to the constitutions of Illinois and the United States.

The Mormons established many business and commercial enterprises, especially along the river and the wharf. They also made plans to utilize the power of the Des Moines Rapids immediately below Nauvoo and petitioned the federal government to construct a canal around the rapids so that the river could be navigated year round. Although Nauvoo never developed any heavy industry comparable to that in Chicago, Galena, or Alton, the grist- and sawmills, brick and lumberyards, limekilns, and home industries soon economically threatened nearby communities.

Nauvoo became a recreational center for the area, and excursion boats took many visitors there. Schools were opened, and the charter authorized a university. None was ever built, but instructors for the university were hired and classes for adults were held in various places. Several small hotels were built, and another large one planned and started. Nauvoo's Masonic Hall was probably the first to be built in Illinois by this fraternal organization and housed three lodges. By the mid-1840s the Nauvoo lodge was the largest in Illinois. For further information regarding the relatively unknown relations of Mormons and Masons, see Kenneth W. Godfrey's article, "Joseph Smith and the Masons," in this issue.

A combination printing plant, stereotype foundry, book-bindery, and stationery store published, among other things, three periodicals. The first and most important of these was the *Times and Seasons,* a monthly, later semi-monthly, publication that provided a variety of reading material for the stated purpose of communicating "to all men the principles of life and salvation and to declare glad tidings of great joy to the honest in heart." This paper lasted from November 1839 to the beginning of the exodus; the last issue came off the press on February 15, 1846. (Its successor in Utah was the *Deseret News*). Next came the short-lived *Wasp*, which appeared weekly from April 1843 to April 1844. It was succeeded by the *Nauvoo Neighbor,* a weekly, "devoted to a dissemination of useful knowledge of every description," through October 1845. Five other publications were printed elsewhere by the Mormons during the Nauvoo period—*The Gospel Reflector* (1841) in Philadelphia, *The Millennial Star* (1840–1870) in England, *The New York*

Messenger (1845) in New York, *The Prophetic Almanac* (1845–65) in New York, and *The Prophet* (1844–45) in New York and Boston.

No chapels were built at Nauvoo, and religious services were held in various places including a grove of trees. All energies and wealth in this direction were expended in erecting a large temple on which work was started in April 1841 and continued even after the exodus began in February 1846.

During the Nauvoo period the women of the church were organized into a Female Relief Society—the first of many "auxiliaries" to the priesthood for the teaching and effecting of the principles of the gospel to members at large. (The involvement of all members in the lay priesthood and auxiliaries is one of the secrets to the strength and cohesion of the Mormon church.) The purpose of the relief society, which is still in operation, was compassionate service: looking after the needs of the poor, searching for recipients of charity, and assisting in correcting the morals and strengthening the virtues of the community. Another auxiliary, the Young Gentlemen's and Ladies' Relief Society, a cultural venture, was also organized.

Joseph Smith was both the temporal and spiritual leader of the community. He was for several years mayor of the city as well as lieutenant general of the Nauvoo Legion and principal director of the church-operated business. As the recognized Prophet he based much of his action on revelation. Despite the common misconception, however, that Joseph Smith talked with God frequently whenever he felt the need to, he received by his own word only five revelations, or an average of one a year, during his life in Nauvoo, and the first of these came only after the Mormons had been in Nauvoo for nine months and twenty-two months after the last revelation in Missouri. (In addition, he set down in writing two letters and two statements of instructions which Mormons accept as based upon revelation.)

Collectively these nine revelations and letters dealt with missionary work, organizational and practical matters, and above all with principles of doctrine. Kings, presidents, governors, and the world in general were given notice in these revelations that the Mormons had been commissioned to "make a solemn proclamation of my [God's] gospel . . . in the spirit of meekness." They were told that the Lord would "soften their hearts." Missionaries were consequently soon widely dispatched. Brigham Young, for example, did so much traveling that one of the five revelations concerned the necessity of his staying home and taking care of his family.

Various important matters of organization and reorganization were attended to in accord with the revelations. The Mormons across the Mississippi in Iowa Territory were advised to remain there and "build up a city unto [God's] name." Later, when difficulties mounted, all of those Saints moved to Nauvoo. In accord with the revelations, a twelve-man High Council was organized, and men were appointed to the offices of presiding elder, patriarch, presiding bishop, counselors, president of the Council of the Twelve, and to the leadership of the High Priests, Seventies, and Elders.

The practical matter of housing those who would come to visit "Zion" was met by a revelation that called for building a hotel: "And let the name of that house be called Nauvoo House; and let it be a delightful habitation for man, and a resting place for the weary traveler, that he may contemplate the glory of Zion, the glory of this, the corner-stone thereof."

Many of the matters of doctrine pertained in one way or another to the temple and its ordinances and to the absolute necessity of building such a temple "for the Most High to dwell therein." As the temple rose, so did speculation about its use. The ordinances were sacred and therefore secret. This only increased speculation, curiosity, and rumor—usually suggesting sexual excesses to the non-Mormons.

As unusual and upsetting to traditional Christianity as these and other early Mormon doctrines and teaching may have been, they were nothing compared to the two revelations received in May and June of 1843 regarding "the new and everlasting covenant," which enunciated the doctrine of the eternity of the marriage covenant and the plurality of wives.

The troublesome doctrine of polygamy had appeared as early as 1831, but it was not practiced (save for one or two probable instances in Ohio) until 1841 when the Prophet and a few leading Mormons in Nauvoo secretly married additional wives. It was impossible to keep such a secret, and rumors began to spread. No point of doctrine before or since caused so much dissension either in the church or out of it. Finally, in July 1843, Joseph Smith set the revelation down in writing and read it to the Nauvoo High Council, but it was not openly taught until 1852, under Brigham Young in Utah, and not published officially until 1876.

Joseph Smith had brought the seeds of his martyrdom with him from Missouri, for in Illinois he was never entirely free of the enemies he had made previously. The Saints, having no choice, however, chose to forget their grievances against Missouri and soon ceased trying to get indemnification for their confiscated properties. The Missourians, on the other hand, perhaps in an effort to justify their treatment of the Mormons, continued to call Joseph Smith a criminal, and throughout the Nauvoo period Missouri authorities made several attempts to extradite him.

Trouble also seemed foreordained at Nauvoo because of the two disparate social orders, those of frontier Illinois and the Mormon community, which ultimately clashed. There are several reasons for the conflict. First there was resentment against Nauvoo because it was what Flanders calls a "communitarian" society (perhaps "self-contained" is a better term). During the nineteenth century many "communitarian" societies were founded in this country—those of the Harmonists, Shakers, and Jansonites, the latter at Bishop Hill. It was not even unusual for such bodies to move en masse to better carry out their beliefs and achieve their ends. But few of those groups met the kind of hostility the Mormons faced. The Mormons were feared particularly because of their potential political power and because Smith as prophet and leader was seen as a threat to the frontiersman whose values he seemed to overturn. Furthermore, the Mormons were more zealous and aggressive than members of other church-centered communities. And they were tireless and successful missionaries and too often imprudent—even arrogant—regarding their ascendancy in whatever areas they settled.

Mormons also practiced an irritating solidarity and exclusiveness. They generally acted economically, politically, and socially to the exclusion of others. This was even more true in Illinois than it had been in Ohio and Missouri. This solidarity was especially powerful at the polls, and non-Mormons feared the control thereby vested in Joseph Smith. At first, Whigs and Democrats wooed the Mormons for their vote; by 1843 both parties opposed the Saints.

In the days at Nauvoo, it often seemed to the Mormons that the greatest threats to their way of life were the apostates within the church who actively sought the Prophet's life. Joseph Smith himself said, "I am exposed to far greater danger from traitors among ourselves than from enemies without."

The final phase of the decline and fall of Nauvoo begins with the death of Joseph Smith on June 27, 1844, and ends with the "Mormon War" in September 1846. The specific action that culminated in the assassination of Joseph and Hyrum Smith was the city council's destruction in June 1844 of the anti-Mormon *Nauvoo Expositor* (of which only one issue ever appeared). Shortly afterward, Joseph Smith and other members of the council went to the county seat at Carthage to have a trial date set to answer for the destruction of the *Expositor*. Trial for the group was set at a subsequent term of the circuit court, and bonds were given for the appearance of defendants. Joseph returned to Carthage on June 24 and, while awaiting trial in the Carthage jail, was murdered by a mob on June 27. For a new contemporary account of this incident, see the article in this issue, "Mormons in Hancock County: A Reminiscence," by Eudocia Baldwin Marsh as edited by Douglas L. Wilson and Rodney O. Davis.

At first, the assassination did not appear to be the beginning of the end. In fact, there was relative peace between Mormons and non-Mormons after Joseph Smith's death. Nauvoo continued to grow and prosper, and work on the temple proceeded. Six months later, however, the Illinois General Assembly revoked the Nauvoo charter, and during the summer of 1845 old animosities against the Mormons were revived and civil war threatened. Governor Thomas Ford of Illinois was unable to stop the acts of violence against the Mormons, and to avoid further trouble, he appointed a commission headed by Stephen A. Douglas to work out a compromise with Brigham Young and other prominent Mormons. The result of these negotiations on September 30 and October 1, 1845, was that the Mormons agreed to leave the area the following spring. When it became evident in February, however, that they were still in danger, the Mormons were forced to commence their exodus. The negotiated peace lasted long enough to give the Mormons a breathing spell, and about 90 percent of them left the Nauvoo area before violence began again.

For a variety of reasons, including the fact that the few remaining Mormons gave no evidence of leaving and continued to work on the temple, the great symbol of Mormonism, violence began again in July and culminated in the Battle of Nauvoo in mid-September of 1846. After several days of fighting, Nauvoo surrendered September 13 to the seven-hundred-man Hancock County anti-Mormon posse commanded by Thomas S. Brockman. The treaty of surrender guaranteed the Saints protection until they could move across the river and provided for a committee of five to remain in the city for the purpose of disposing of property.

Even then not all the Mormons went west. Some individuals, including Joseph Smith's wife, children, and mother and some scattered groups remained behind in Illinois and elsewhere. In 1852 they reorganized and in 1860 persuaded Joseph Smith III to be their leader. These Mormons call themselves the Reorganized Church of Jesus Christ of Latter-Day Saints. Their headquarters were at Amboy and Plano, Illinois, until 1881, when they moved to Iowa.

10.

CRACKER BARREL DAYS
IN OLD ILLINOIS STORES

Gerald Carson

Journal of the Illinois State Historical Society
vol. 47, no. 1 (Spring 1954)

The owner of a country store in early Illinois was more than a vendor of necessities. He was a petty capitalist, a middleman for farm produce, an accountant, banker, and pharmacist, a jack-leg lawyer, sometimes a miller or tavern keeper, and often the proprietor of a community center and haven for town loafers. In short, country storekeepers were windows on the world for the isolated communities they served. Gerald Carson argues in this article that historians have given the pioneer merchant "markedly less than his due" as a civilizing influence in rural life.

Frequent acknowledgment has been made in our generation of the contribution to American life of the old-time country doctor, the lawyer, and the minister, whose special places in the community have been the subject of many appreciative and sympathetic studies. The proprietor of the general merchandise store, though he existed by the thousands, has received markedly less than his due as a leader and civilizing influence in rural life. Being a merchant was not a learned occupation, and there were all kinds of merchants, some quite temporary. It wasn't hard to get into storekeeping, as one Michigan wit used to remark; it was just hard to *stay* in.

Many men of low capacity or unstable temperaments tried storing, as they did farming, trapping, lumbering, or fighting. When a store failed to

First Berry-Lincoln Store in New Salem. The country store was more than a place to buy biscuits and brandy in early Illinois. And the proprietor was more than a rural merchant; he helped civilize rural America. *Photo courtesy Sangamon Valley Collection, Lincoln Public Library, Springfield.*

prosper and creditors became more numerous than debtors, the owners could always take shelter under lenient bankruptcy laws, or skedaddle to parts unknown, as did Denton Offutt, Lincoln's employer at New Salem, and many another.

Yet, if one were to set forth the character of the successful country trader, he would find himself considering a very durable man, tougher than green elm, with many impressive skills and accomplishments and a considerable knowledge of the world. The crossroads merchant managed a complex of buying and selling far more difficult than the merchandising of the twentieth century. He had an exhaustive knowledge of his community and served it in ways which were more continuous and more intimate than those of the doctor, lawyer, or minister. The country store was more than a communications center. It was the best hope that the four corners would one day become a town. As William Oliver, author of an immigrants' handbook on Illinois, said,

> A store, in this part of the country, and indeed in America generally, is a grand mélange of things of the most different qualities, and it proposes to supply the inhabitants with all the necessaries and luxuries they may require. They are sources of great profit; and a person with a little capital and some knowledge of the business, can scarcely fail, with ordinary prudence, to realize an independence.

The storekeepers, Rebecca Burlend told the people back in Yorkshire,

> supply the settlers with articles the most needed, such as food, clothing, implements of husbandry, medicine, and spirituous liquors: for which they receive in exchange the produce of their farms, consisting of wheat, Indian corn, sugar, beef, &c. As these store keepers exercise a sort of monopoly over a certain district, their profits are great, and they often become wealthy.

She also noted the rise of the store proprietor as petty capitalist and Illinois' first friend to industry: "[T]hey often have a saw-mill and a corn-mill, at which they grind the corn they obtain from the farmers, for the purpose of sending it to New Orleans."

It is not to be wondered at that a long-headed farm lad with a settled aversion to pulling stumps, shucking corn, packing salt pork, or cutting whip lashes out of a woodchuck skin would be attracted to "buying, tying and taking in the money." But there was much more to storekeeping in early Illinois than dusting the ribbon case, wearing a coat, and teaching a Sunday school class. The pioneer trader acted as middleman in a highly speculative two-way exchange, moving farm produce to New Orleans or some other primary market in exchange for store goods from the eastern seaboard cities. As issuer of long-term credit, he was, in effect, a banker, and underwrote the agriculture of the state. In a day before the traveling salesman had appeared, the local merchant journeyed to the wholesale markets and brought back not only goods but news, ideas, a touch of urbanity. He was a window on the world for a straitened people. As a person of wide experience, the country retailer was expected to demonstrate his versatility in astonishing ways. He could draw a farm lease, was able in a pinch to prepare a short-form will. If a doctor couldn't be found, the storekeeper prescribed for a "misery in the stummick [sic]." He supplied sulphur for the "Illinois mange," calomel for the "Illinois shakes." He was the natural choice to read the Declaration of Independence in a loud, clear voice down at the grove on the Fourth of July, when men still openly wiped tears from their eyes as they thought of their liberties. The storekeeper was also expected to be able to extract beans from small boys' noses.

Under the system of storekeeper-marketing, the trader gave the farmer low prices for his produce. The farmer could not hold his crops back. He had no capital, no other outlet, and was in debt to the store. For his part, the retailer took long risks, paid the high costs of transportation, and his speculative position in the commodity markets called for a strong stomach. The system worked. The crops did get to market. Those country store owners who were well fitted for the occupation almost invariably did make money over a lifetime. When business was slack, the resourceful merchant showed his mettle. He might dig a grave, peg shoes, run up a suit of clothes. Sometimes he kept a tavern as well as a store, probably under the same roof, taking out a license to sell by the drink as well as by the gallon. That's what Sam Hill, prosperous grocer, general merchant, and postmaster at New Salem did. Tradition has it that Hill lost the postmastership to Abraham Lincoln because of that tavern license. The women of New Salem objected to calling for their mail while rustic toughs made merry at the bar. Hill had underestimated the power of the women.

A grocery store, in the mid-nineteenth century, was not merely a food depot. The idea comes through clearly enough in a contemporary comment, "selling liquor *at the groceries* is the devil and all of a business." Although a grocery store "may be the receptacle of tea, coffee and sugar," says William Oliver, "it is not invariably so. It is, in fact . . . very often . . . entirely devoted to the selling of spirits."

Since the early accounts of Illinois life were invariably written from the point of view of the customer, there is much emphasis upon higher prices and rascally merchants. A yard of calico cost a bushel of wheat. It took five bushels to buy a pair of shoes. The buyer had to beware of short weight and adulterated goods.

To the extent that these practices were true of the store, they were also tolerated under the code of commercial morals followed by the barter customer when he had something to sell. We hear little of "stove-piping" the potatoes; but the practice was known when the farmer did the bagging.

A length of stovepipe was inserted into a gunny bag, the big potatoes poured around it, the runts and culls dumped into the inside, and the pipe gently removed; all in all, a neat western version of what was called in New England "deaconing the apples." Country butter from cool farm cellars was not always high-scoring. It could be "extended" with lard, although "the ordinary way of adulterating butter is by adding a large quantity of salt, so that it may absorb an excessive amount of water, and also increase the weight." "Candling and grading eggs was unknown," says Tom Haines of Missoula, Montana, remembering his youthful days at "clerking" in Rockport. "The farmer believed in letting the merchant get stuck. Many times when I was a boy I saw eggs hatch in the cases in the old Haines-Rupert store."

The equipment of one young clerk for general store merchandising was that in arithmetic he had gone through Erastus Root, Jonathan Grout, and Nathan Daboll. He had an easy acquaintance with decimal fractions, the rule of three, "single and double fellowship." He could spell accurately, read "tolerably," write a fair hand, and use "passable" grammar. He was also considered to be sharp at a bargain.

A "chore boy" of a general store of the 1880s was expected to perform a vast number of simple but exhausting duties. He swept out the store in the morning, took care of his employer's yard, straightened nails on the back step, rolled up oddments of string for the "string box." He waited on trade in small items, had his own cash box, and recorded his transactions in a giveaway memorandum issued by Dr. R. V. Pierce, known widely as the patent medicine millionaire of Buffalo, New York, but who preferred the modest accolade which he had bestowed upon himself, "the people's medical servant."

There were a number of ways in which a country merchant could keep his accounts in the days before the cash register or the early ticket register, such as the old McClaskey. He might calculate on a slate or a shingle, the wall or a notched stick, by some esoteric shorthand, hieroglyphic, or pictograph. But he had to keep accounts of some kind, and the only good ones were those which he himself could understand. If possible, he undertook to master single-entry bookkeeping and get a certificate from the "Professor," decorated with pen writing at its fanciest, dramatic thick-and-thin shadings, possibly a pair of doves on the wing. William M. Haines, who became a widely known merchant of Pike County, received such a certificate from Jonathan Jones in St. Louis, March 18, 1864. It recites that William M. Haines

has this day completed under my instruction a full course of Double Entry Bookkeeping embracing Mercantile, Manufacturing, and
Steamboat Bookkeeping, Individual Company and Compound Company, with Forms adapted to the Wholesale, Retail, Banking and Commission Business, . . . he is in every respect worthy of public confidence
as a Practical Accountant, and as such I do most cheerfully commend
him to the favorable consideration of those who may wish to employ
a Competent Bookkeeper.

When a general store folded up, or the owned died, the old leather-bound
folios often had a surprising subsequent history. Fitch Kelsey's ledger from
Liberty, Adams County, became a family scrapbook after he passed on.
Temperance tracts were pasted over the old records of debtor and creditor—newspaper verse, too, showing a nice taste for the sentimental poetry
of the period. A young miss, known to her mother as Eliza Lane, but in
her own secret dream world as Eliza Lanetta, started, but alas did not fin-
ish, an original composition entitled "Evening Hymn of a Child." It begins
promisingly enough:

> One evening I was wandering
> Beside a river fare . . . faire
> Wild roses and blue violets
> I'd pluck to deck my hair.

Here the poetess falters. Of the second stanza we have only this fragment:

> The birds were singing over me.

A new feminine hand shows up at this point, with a little jotting of tiny
family expenses, and of the earnings of a seamstress: "Cash for sewing in
Alton, $1.20."

Mrs. J. Q. Rapp, of Jeffersonville—a village whose population has shrunk,
and whose name has kept pace, being now shortened to Geff—used an old
ledger thriftily as a filing system. She made it over into an invoice book by
pasting over the closed accounts, for example, an invoice from Bishop Brothers, Cincinnati, for forty dollars' worth of crackers, cigars, nuts, candies,
and oranges, and one from Sprague, Warner & Company, Chicago, with a
scrawl across its face, "Too cold to ship cheese or ink."

Personal recollections and family traditions about the general store
come to mind most vividly either as a complex of extraordinary smells

and redolences or as memories of the stove-side sitters, those capped and bearded democrats who found in the store the American equivalent of the English pub as a center for congenial comradeship. The smells were a composite of machine oil, kerosene, coffee, onion sets, the sizing on the bolts of yard goods, tobacco smoke, local corn whiskey, harness, cowhide boots, raw humanity, and wet dogs.

The store loafers were a trial, occupying their places by a kind of right of eminent domain, dipping comfortably into the cracker barrel, munching the store cheese, hinting that a drink from the opened whiskey barrel would be acceptable, and buying little. Sometimes they were a source of entertainment, telling wonder tales and tall tales, getting off guys and jollies of store porch humor. Like a Greek chorus, they commented upon the people and the degenerate times. Sometimes they disputed over some troublesome theological doctrine, such as that of Immaculate Conception, and paused to notice local instances of the more ordinary kind. Again, they put their noses into the storekeeper's business, and rallied him upon his office of trustee of the district school, known ironically as "Cornstalk College." They ogled the more comely customers and were likely to raise a sudden cheer for Major McKinley or a tiger for Colonel Bryan.

It takes an effort of the historical imagination to reconstruct what was considered to be an exquisite prank in a nineteenth-century general store. Getting geese drunk on whiskey-soaked corn was a common practice. In the 1880s Jim Rupert of Rockford owned a dog called Jim Pug. Carson Rupert was always teasing the dog. One of his favorite tricks was to tie a string to a chunk of meat and give it to him. The dog would gulp it down, and then Carson would pull on the string. Jim would squat back, grunt, growl, scratch his feet, and create a general disturbance each time the string was pulled, much to the delight of the onlookers. Jim Pug was fond of eggs and would roll them out of the tubs and break them on the floor. He was choosy, too. If the egg was fairly fresh he would eat it. If not, he let it lie. The dog was quite an attraction and advertising medium for the store.

Another standard trick was for some of the boys to slip out and loosen the nuts on the buggy wheels of a store customer. After he got well on the way home, the buggy would shed its wheels, one by one. A jape of a more imaginative and monumental character occurred the time a small circus had its main and only tent pitched beside the railroad tracks at Fairbury, when the McDowell brothers, Elmer, Tom, and Johnny, had some kind of ruckus with the circus roustabouts. Feeling aggrieved, the McDowells tied a rope from the circus tent to the caboose of a freight train which was standing nearby. When the train pulled out, so did the tent.

The country store's great days came after the pioneering was over, when rail transportation, power farming, national markets, advertising, and quantities of store goods all seemed to arrive at once. A country trader typed the period when he remarked sadly, "Advertising seems to be kind of taking the place of dustin'." But advertising indubitably put some hurrah into storekeeping. "Highway Robbery, Murder, Treason, Codfish, Loco Foco Matches, and 4 cent Calico" was the attention-getter one general merchant used to align himself with the stirring new times. As advertising advanced, the tierces, barrels, piggins, firkins, and other forms of cooperage moved off the scene. H. J. Heinz, who gave away millions of little green plaster of paris pickle pins at the Columbian Exposition in 1893, took over the packaged, branded pickle business from the old bulk article. Barreled oatmeal became packaged Quaker Oats. Eatin' tobacco came to be called by such names as Star, Golden Rope, Something Good, Horseshoe. In the eighties the scene became crowded with new consumer-unit packages and trademarked names: Douglas Shoes, Lonsdale muslins, Ariosa Coffee, Yarmouth canned corn, McLean's patent medicines.

For almost a hundred years, the only competition the general store had was the pack or carting peddler. The itinerant merchant from the East was well, but not always favorably, known in Illinois. If a New Englander, it would be said of him, "Yankees are too quirky." For many young peddlers, the way up in the world was to pitch on a promising spot and set up as a country storekeeper with a permanent stand. Dexter Knowlton left the old family farm in the hills of Chautauqua County, New York, for a peddling trip to the western prairies. "I was gone from home over two months, having made my trip in over $300, over and above all expenses. . . . Being much pleased with northern Illinois, I decided to move there." At Freeport, Knowlton exchanged his pack for the counter and ruler of the sedentary merchant. Within a few years, "by close attention to my business," he owned a bank as well as a booming store, sat as director of the Galena and Chicago Union Railroad, had joined the railroad lobby in Springfield; and was nominated in 1852, though not elected, as governor of the state on the Free Soil ticket. In his last years, with a comfortable capital accumulated in Illinois, Knowlton reappeared in New York State as a substantial financier and promoter, purveyed Congress Water to the ailing at Saratoga, and died in the fullness of his years in a brownstone mansion on Brooklyn Heights. Carting gentleman, storekeeper, banker, politico, entrepreneur—peddler's progress, indeed!

The general store survived the competitive efforts of the peddler, the specialized "one line" store, the city department store, and also the vivacious and acrimonious era of the Chicago "wish books" ("Wish I had a Daisy Air Rifle"). The adversary which put the lights out along the old scarred counters was neither "Shears and Sawbuck" nor "Monkey-Ward." It was a short, simple name spelled a-u-t-o. When the red gas pump replaced the hitching rack, the drummers disappeared. The catalogue houses turned themselves into retail chain stores, and the customers trundled off to the nearest market town in the high, black, spidery, but reliable vehicle manufactured by Henry Ford and warranted to "Get You There and Get You Back."

The institution of the old, cluttered, leisurely general store is now largely a memory and a tradition, recalled with affection and humor and that wistfulness which often attaches to the remembrance of all things which have passed into oblivion. Starting as an American improvisation to meet new conditions in a vast and empty land, serving a scattered population which had no other facilities for buying its saleratus, powder, shot, and bed ticking, or of disposing of its little surpluses from home-use farming, the country store took on the local need, whatever it was, and tried to meet it.

Other methods of distributing goods came along better to serve the motor age. None ever equaled the original Pa and Ma store as a social as well as a commercial center. It's hard now to find even the semblance of a country store in Illinois, with old counters still in place, shelf goods along the wall, scythe snaths and hand tools in the rear, wash boilers, stalks of bananas and lanterns dangling from the rafters, all lines of general merchandise helter-skelter in a homey sort of confusion. There is Gully Haug's emporium at Golden Eagle. He still sells horse collars and cider barrels. Emil Schoen is at the old stand at Old Ripley. Carl Wittmond is an institution at Brussels. The traditional potbellied stove occupies the central point of interest at P. C. Schoenholz's bazaar at Scarboro, off U.S. Route 51, between Rochelle and Mendota. The ancient "Clat" Adams store facing the Mississippi River at Quincy and dating back to the 1830s has just closed its doors. Up to the time of its demise it continued to display the turnaround cabinet for "Merrick's Six Cord Spool Cotton," the settee by the stove, and the wooden drawers labeled in old-style lettering, sulphur, cassia, cinnamon, thyme, mace, sage, and alum.

As is the lot of all men, the proprietor of the crossroads store could not attend his own funeral, except in a highly unsatisfactory way. He could not hear the eulogy, or know the regard of the community for his life and work.

Perhaps he was no great "punkins" as men were measured in the greater world of state and nation. To those who traded at his store, providing that he was fair in matter of credit and gave "down weight" on the steelyard—to the neighbors who knew him in the good times and bad—he was the real grit.

We got some sense of what a country merchant meant to his township from the obituary columns of weekly newspapers. We read of Robert W. "Butch" Carr, who had conducted a general store and post office at Fayette. When Butch died, he was carried to the cemetery in charge of his lodge brothers, the Modern Woodmen of America. It was February. The store thermometer stood at zero. Long lines of heavy farm wagons fell into the ragged line, lighter spring wagons, buggies, and a few surreys teetered over the frozen ruts, all filled with Butch's neighbors and customers wrapped in buffalo robes, their feet feeling gingerly for the soapstone. No one said much, beyond the little phrases people use to conceal their thoughts. But the procession was one of the longest ever seen in Greene County.

11.

HIGHER EDUCATION
IN TRANSITION, 1850–1870

Ernest G. Hildner

Journal of the Illinois State Historical Society
vol. 56, no. 1 (Spring 1963)

The era 1850–70 was a time of change in higher education in Illinois. At the beginning of this period there were a number of private collegiate institutions, each generally affiliated with a church and providing a variety of levels of education. A major development was the entrance of the state into higher education with the advent of Illinois State Normal University (1857) and the University of Illinois (1867). By the end of the period, science and applied studies joined traditional curricula, fewer professors were members of the clergy, fraternities began to replace literary societies, and coeducation was established.

The Civil War affected these institutions in a variety of ways. After the war, work-study programs were reinstituted not only to provide financial aid to needy students but also to promote healthful forms of physical activity. Collegiate athletics were not yet on the scene, although baseball had become popular.

The financial panic of 1837 was a severe blow to the West, and it was not until the end of the following decade that full recovery was attained. The boom of the early fifties, along with the rapidly increasing population, especially in the northern half of the state, led to a multiplication of educational institutions on all levels. This is reflected in the private laws passed by the legislatures of the period, chartering colleges, seminaries, and academies. Although a general incorporation act had been adopted in 1848, the legislature continued to charter educational institutions until 1870. Because of the vague wording, it is impossible to tell exactly what level of education some of the charters contemplated. Not infrequently an academy was authorized to confer degrees. One rather common restriction appears in most of the charters of the decade of the fifties. It limited the amount of land these institutions could hold to not more than 160 acres; if they acquired more, it had to be disposed of in a period of three years. This may reflect a continuing distrust of higher education as expressed in the charters granted to the earlier colleges.

The legislature of 1855 chartered thirteen new distinctly collegiate institutions, the largest number by any General Assembly. These charters went to Chicago Theological Seminary; Peoria University, Peoria; Northwestern Masonic University, Keithsburg, Mercer County; North Illinois University, Henry, Marshall County; Marengo Collegiate Institute of the Presbytery of Chicago; Illinois Institute, Wheaton; Illinois Military Institute, Springfield; Garrett Biblical Institute, Cook County; Berean College, Jacksonville; Southern Illinois Female College, Salem; Hahnemann Medical College, Chicago; Abingdon College; and Eureka College. In contrast, the legislature of 1853 had incorporated only three educational institutions.

The granting of these charters cannot be regarded as representing the actual establishment of institutions. In some cases the colleges that were chartered were already operating as academies; in others the beginnings antedate the actual chartering. In still others the charters represented hopes rather than real beginnings. It is sometimes impossible to discover what happened after the issuance of the charter, for no other records of the institution or its founders seem to exist.

Nearly all of the charters of the 1850–70 period were sought and secured under the sponsorship of some religious body, but the period did see the beginning of state participation in higher education. This step had been advocated by Professor Jonathan B. Turner of Jacksonville, who in 1850 proposed an industrial and agricultural university. His plan was enunciated as the Granville Plan of 1851 and more fully developed in the months that followed. In February 1853 the Illinois legislature memorialized Congress, asking that such institutions be endowed by the public lands of the nation. It had been the intent of Turner and other like-minded men that the proposed institution in Illinois contain a teacher-training department, but the enactment of laws for free common schools in 1855 and the establishment of the office of the superintendent of public instruction in 1854 made action in this phase of the plan imperative immediately if teachers were to be obtained. Consequently, the state educational organizations pressed for the establishment of a normal school independent of the university. Turner hoped it would have industrial and agricultural departments but reluctantly agreed not to oppose, if he could not support, a normal school chartered independently. The result was the creation of Illinois State Normal University in 1857.

The act creating the university also named a state board of education, which was to locate the university. Competition for the school was intense but finally simmered down to a contest between Bloomington and Peoria. Through the influence and political maneuvering of Jesse Fell and others, it was finally secured for Bloomington. The state turned over to the school all the funds in the seminary and college accounts of the state treasury to be used as an endowment, with the proviso that none of the monies be used for the construction of buildings or the purchase of land. That part of the cost was to be borne by the area in which it was located. The financial panic made for difficulties and delay in the construction of a physical plant, but instruction began in the fall of 1857 in rented quarters. The curriculum was largely patterned after that of the arts colleges with the emphasis on composition, the classics, and mathematics. In strong contrast to later emphasis, it was then believed that students should have a sound academic training and that the method of imparting knowledge to pupils in the schools would naturally follow: in short, learning something to teach before learning how to teach.

Meanwhile, Turner and others interested in the establishment of an agricultural and industrial university continued to urge their claims. They achieved success when the Morrill Land-Grant Act was passed and signed into law by President Lincoln, July 2, 1862. Under the provisions of the act, each state was granted thirty thousand acres of the public domain for each representative and senator in the Congress to be used as an endowment for agricultural and industrial higher education, the states to determine just how the income should be spent. On account of the war, no immediate moves were taken to establish a university in Illinois, but by 1864 the matter had come to be quite controversial. The presidents of the old-line liberal arts colleges urged that the funds be divided among the already existing institutions; only President Julian M. Sturtevant of Illinois College refused to support this proposal and seconded the efforts of Turner and others to insure the establishment of a single institution supported from the land grants. Fortunately for Illinois, these men were successful, and the General Assembly of 1867 authorized the establishment of an industrial university.

Citizens of Champaign had been working to have the new school located in that city, but the legislature, under pressure from the state agricultural, horticultural, and educational societies, opened selection of a site to competitive bidding of towns, cities, and corporations. The most active bidders for the universities were Champaign, Logan, McLean, and Morgan Counties. A bitter contest ensued with the following offers: Champaign County, $285,000; McLean County, $470,000; Logan County, $385,000; Morgan County, $491,000. Although Champaign County made the lowest bid, it had the most effective political wire-pulling, and the legislature established the university there in an act of February 28, 1867. The opponents of the bill were not sure of the good faith of the Champaign County bid, however, and secured passage of an additional act, of March 8, providing that if the pledged funds were not paid in full to the trustees by June 1, 1867, the university was to be located in one of the other three counties. Champaign County fulfilled its obligations, and the university opened classes in March 1868 in the building provided by the county. Less than three years later, on September 13, 1871, when construction began on the new University Building, one of the most fitting ceremonies was the laying of the cornerstone by Professor Turner.

With the inauguration of the state university, one era in higher education in Illinois ended and another began. Nearly all of the private colleges and universities in Illinois at that time were on the model of the classical colleges founded before 1850. Greek, Latin, and mathematics were the core of the curriculum. Nonetheless, the effects of discoveries in the fields both of the natural and physical sciences were beginning to manifest themselves in the colleges, and more attention was paid to the sciences than formerly. Likewise, the private schools had begun to offer instruction in the modern languages, especially German and French. The student was given an opportunity to make some choice between courses, but his choice was extremely limited (not until the following decade was the revolutionary proposal of the free elective system to emerge). Faculties were also changing. At the beginning of the period not only were the colleges under the domination of churches but the faculties were largely composed of clergymen, many of whom regarded their college appointments as missionary activity. But by the end of the sixties, men without theological training composed a much greater proportion of the instructional staff.

Financially most of the colleges were in an extremely precarious state. The wave of optimism for the founding of new colleges engendered by the boom of the early fifties was turned into discouragement by the depression of the latter part of the decade. Peter Akers, president of McKendree College, was offered the presidency of Illinois Wesleyan in 1854 (it had been founded in 1850) but refused the post unless sufficient endowment could be secured. He stipulated the amount, and when it was not raised, did not accept. Other newly founded colleges had equal difficulty in raising funds. The older colleges, however, were able to recover the ground lost in the panic of 1837 and increase their assets slightly prior to the panic of 1857. But times were hard for these institutions. Perhaps the extreme case was that of the Illinois Conference Female College, which in 1861 was ordered sold to satisfy its debts (the school was purchased by three trustees and thus saved).

All colleges of the period felt the effects of the Civil War. During the decade of the fifties, college campuses, as well as the rest of the nation, had been agitated by the slavery question, which was debated vigorously in the college literary societies. At times the differences between students and faculty or between student and student erupted into fistfights. Bitter feelings over this issue also resulted in a decline in the enrollment of men from the slave states, especially in the latter part of the decade. With the beginning of hostilities many enlisted, while those remaining on the campus spent much of their time drilling, either under the direction of a faculty member or an undergraduate who had seen service.

Decreased enrollments, which meant less tuition income, multiplied the financial difficulties of the colleges; but even more serious was the inflation of the war period, when gold was at a high premium over paper, and coins practically disappeared from circulation. The financial straits of the colleges were particularly hard on faculties. Most instructors were on modest salaries, and families had difficulty in making ends meet. Faculty members were no doubt motivated as much by financial gain as by patriotic fervor in accepting commissions in the army. Hardly a college but furnished one or more of its faculty, usually as commander of an outfit having a large proportion of its members recruited from the student body. The Bloomington Regiment, the 33rd Illinois Infantry, was commanded by Charles E. Hovey, the president of Normal, while Company A was entirely composed of faculty and students. In 1864 Professor Rufus C. Crampton recruited all but one member of the senior class of Illinois College for service. Under such circumstances it was difficult for the institutions to continue to operate.

Contrary to our recent experience following World War II, there was no immediate increase in college enrollment after the war, and the rate of income from investments continued to decline. This financial difficulty was reflected in the fact that only two charters were issued from 1861 to 1867, both to state institutions, Illinois Agricultural College and Illinois Industrial University. In the latter year the state granted $25,000 for two years to the Illinois Soldiers' College, Fulton, Whiteside County, an institution about which no other information seems to exist.

The 1850–70 era marked the beginning of many curricular and social changes on the campuses of Illinois colleges. In 1865, for example, no physical education program was to be found anywhere in the state, and students were left to their own devices in working off surplus animal spirits. Informal games and horseplay, sometimes leading to disciplinary action, were the chief outlets. Following the war, baseball became a popular pastime, but not until after 1870 were collegiate or intercollegiate sports organized. This lack of regular exercise led to a curious revival. The earliest colleges of the state had been founded with manual labor programs designed to assist students in paying their way, but these failed everywhere. Following the war, however, there were proposals from many quarters that the plan be revived and that students, regardless of sex, devote three to five hours daily to manual labor, not so much for the money that might be earned but for the physical well-being of the student. These proposals were especially strong among the advocates of the agricultural and mechanical colleges, and in those schools, provisions were made for such labor. There seems to have been no attempt, however, to adopt such programs in most of the liberal arts colleges.

Another development of the 1850–70 period was coeducation. Of the older colleges, Illinois College was the only one which did not admit women by 1870 or soon thereafter. Nearly all of the newer institutions admitted them from the beginning. Only one degree-granting institution for women had been in operation during most of this period: the Northwestern Female College, which merged with the new Evanston College for Ladies in 1871 and a few years later was absorbed into Northwestern University. Other "female institutions" in the state, such as Monticello College, Rockford College, and the Illinois Conference Female College, did not yet offer degrees, although they may have had courses on a junior college level. No marked difference seems to have been made in college curricula as a result of coeducation. Such changes as were foreshadowed in this period were the result of other forces which were to become much more important in the following decade.

In the social life of the students, a new force, the social fraternity, was beginning to take the place of the literary society. The latter continued to function in the time-honored manner, conducting literary programs and furnishing library facilities to its members, but it was drawing toward the end of its usefulness. The appeal of the social fraternity was greater because of the secrecy of its meetings, its closer bond of fellowship, and more rigorous and selective choice of members. In addition, most of the fraternities offered as wide a literary program as the societies they were displacing. Although the fraternity system was nearly thirty years old when it reached Illinois, its expansion cannot be considered rapid. First in the field was Beta Theta Pi, with its first chapter at Knox in 1855, followed by others at Illinois College, 1856; Monmouth, 1865; and the University of Chicago, 1868. Phi Delta Theta soon followed, with chapters at Northwestern, 1859, and Chicago, 1865; Phi Kappa Psi located at Northwestern in 1864, and at the University of Chicago in 1865. Delta Tau Delta went to Monmouth in 1865 and to Lombard in 1869. Phi Gamma Delta located chapters at Monmouth and Illinois Wesleyan in 1866, at Knox and Northwestern in 1867. Psi Upsilon had one chapter at Chicago, started in 1869; and Sigma Chi entered Northwestern the same year. The only sorority chapter to appear before the end of the period was Pi Beta Phi, at Monmouth in 1867; this was the sorority's first chapter. By 1870, seven fraternities had established a total of sixteen chapters in seven Illinois colleges, though not all survived to the end of the period. The Beta chapter at Illinois College became inactive in 1866, and the Phi Gamma Delta group at Northwestern in 1870. In the years 1850–70 fraternities were most active at Monmouth, a situation which was to lead to the abolition of such organizations there in the next decade. As yet the social fraternities could not be justified on the grounds that they provided housing and meals on campuses where these were difficult to procure. On the contrary, their early history shows that meetings were most often held in the rooms of the members or in a meeting room secured from the college or in town. Rivalry was extreme, and college administrators and faculties looked upon the organizations with a great deal of suspicion and tended to oppose them.

The two decades following 1850 are of the greatest significance in the development of higher education in the state of Illinois. Liberal arts colleges, generally under the control of a religious body, continued to multiply. But, more important, the state entered the field, establishing a normal school and a state university. For the first time, practical and applied arts and sciences were offered on a collegiate level. Some revision of the standard classroom curriculum began toward the end of the period, foreshadowing the greater changes soon to come. College education for women on an equal basis with men was also a landmark of the period. By 1870, then, higher education had passed from the stage of pioneer rigidity to one marked by adaptability and continuous adjustment—characteristics that have continued to our own time.

PART III

THE CIVIL WAR ERA
AND LINCOLN

12.

MURDER AT A METHODIST CAMP MEETING
The Origins of Abraham Lincoln's Most Famous Trial

Daniel W. Stowell

Journal of the Illinois State Historical Society
vol. 101, no. 3–4 (Fall–Winter 2008)

As a prelude to the trial story, the author provides descriptions of camp meetings, their purpose of conversion and revival, and the role of Methodist preachers in running them; most prominently Peter Cartwright. Lincoln's life in New Salem is presented as relevant to the position Lincoln took at the trial. Defending a man accused of murder, Lincoln showed considerable skill in jury selection and instruction, examination of witnesses, introduction of scientific evidence, and dynamic oratory.

In May 1858, in a crowded courtroom in central Illinois, Abraham Lincoln defended a young man on trial for his life against a charge of murder. The one-day trial of *People v. Armstrong* was to become his most famous case. The events leading up to this famous legal drama are less well known. They occurred near a Methodist camp meeting in rural Mason County, Illinois, in the summer of 1857. Throughout the first half of the nineteenth century, camp meetings were an integral part of frontier religious life in the Old Northwest. Originating in the Great Revival in Kentucky in the turn of the nineteenth century, camp meetings flourished in the frontier regions of the

Daniel W. Stowell

South and the states emerging from the Northwest Territories. Methodists, Baptists, Presbyterians, and Disciples of Christ widely employed camp meetings to strengthen existing congregations and win new adherents. Early Methodist circuit riders had preached across the state as settlers arrived from eastern states. Systematic in everything, these pioneer preachers established churches, districts, and annual conferences. By the mid-1850s, the Methodist Episcopal Church was firmly established in Illinois, although not every community had a church building.

Although Christians across the nation continued to hold camp meetings throughout the nineteenth century, the assemblages took on a more orderly tone in the 1840s and 1850s. Initially characterized by intense enthusiasm and a democratization of participation, the camp meeting became more orderly and domesticated to denominational needs. In 1854, B. W. Gorham, a Methodist minister in Wyoming, published a *Camp Meeting Manual* to

Abraham Lincoln photographed in Beardstown, Illinois, during the famous Almanac Trial in 1858. *Photo courtesy Abraham Lincoln Presidential Library.*

142

defend the practice and to assist preachers and laity in organizing a successful camp meeting. In the middle states, he recommended holding a meeting between mid-June and mid-July or between mid-August and mid-September. The ideal spot would have "a bountiful supply of good water"; a canopy of shade trees; and available lumber for stand, seats, and tent poles. If possible, the meeting should be held in a neighborhood of Methodists "who will be likely to sympathize with, and sustain order in a meeting." Typically, a meeting of five to eight days was the proper length.

Gorham also recognized the need to preserve order: "Very much, both of the success and the reputation of a Camp Meeting, depends upon the due maintenance of proper police regulations on the ground." Unfortunately, "large numbers of people of reckless character attend Camp Meetings, although they seldom, if ever, visit any other place of worship." Furthermore, "nearly all persons, not decidedly religious, are disposed to take liberties in a forest, which they would not do in a church. . . ." The presiding elder of the district where the camp meeting was held was in charge of order on the campground, but Gorham also deemed it wise to have one or more civil officers on the ground to make arrests if necessary.

Rowdies at religious meetings had become so disruptive in antebellum America that the Illinois state legislature in 1833 made it a criminal offense to "disturb a worshiping congregation." The Act declared that anyone who "by menace, profane swearing, vulgar language, or any disorderly or immoral conduct" interrupted or disturbed "any congregation or collection of citizens assembled together for the purpose of worshipping Almighty God" or who sold, attempted to sell, or otherwise disposed of "ardent spirits or liquors, or any articles which will tend to disturb any worshiping congregation or collection of people, within one mile of such place" would be guilty of a high misdemeanor. If a jury found the accused person guilty, they could impose a fine not exceeding fifty dollars.

More than two decades later, individuals still skirted the violation of this law, as the events at a camp meeting near Walker's Grove in Mason County in the summer of 1857 demonstrated. The pastor of the local congregation was Reverend George D. Randle. Born in 1805 in Montgomery County, North Carolina, Randle had moved to Illinois as a child. His family settled near Edwardsville, and his father died when he was still young. Randle was converted at a camp as a youth, but he did not join the ministry until 1847, when he was licensed to preach. For several years, he served as a local preacher, filling in for the Methodist circuit riders when they were not available. Randle joined the

Illinois Annual Conference of the Methodist Episcopal Church at its meeting in Quincy in October 1856. There, Bishop Matthew Simpson appointed Randle to his first full-time appointment—the Walker's Grove mission circuit in eastern Mason and northwestern Logan counties in central Illinois.

The presiding elder of Randle's district was the veteran circuit rider Peter Cartwright. One of the earliest Methodist preachers to come to the Illinois frontier, Cartwright migrated to the state from Kentucky in 1824, six years before Abraham Lincoln's family moved to Illinois from southern Indiana. Converted in an outdoor meeting in Kentucky in 1801, Cartwright soon began preaching and was ordained as a preacher of the Methodist Episcopal Church in 1806.

After he moved to Illinois, Cartwright was the dominant figure in Illinois Methodism for the next four decades. In 1832 Cartwright won election over Abraham Lincoln for one of several seats in the Illinois state legislature representing Sangamon County. In 1846 the two men met again in electoral combat, when Democrat Peter Cartwright and Whig Abraham Lincoln vied to represent the Illinois Seventh District in Congress. That time, Lincoln triumphed and served as a one-term representative in Washington. By the 1850s both Cartwright and Lincoln were notable figures in Illinois society—Cartwright in religious circles, Lincoln in legal circles, both in matters of politics.

Reverend Randle moved to the Walker's Mission with his family in November 1856, "in a shower of rain, hail, and snow," and found "a Parsonage without any plastering." The mission had no church buildings in the still sparsely settled area. However, earlier preachers had established at least ten different preaching stations, usually a home or schoolhouse, which Randle visited periodically throughout the spring and summer of 1857. In the neighborhood of his first preaching appointment lived "Bro. James Walker and family, good, substantial Methodists," who "did a good part in the financial support of the church." The Walkers were just the kind of Methodists that Gorham had prescribed in his recipe for a successful camp meeting.

James Walker had moved to Mason County from Indiana in 1837. Walker settled near a fine grove of trees on four hundred acres, built the first frame house in the area, and raised a family of seven children. The grove contained oak, black walnut, sugar maple, hickory, butternut, and mulberry trees, as well as a variety of shrubs. Walker established a post office in his home in 1839 and served as the area's first postmaster. He held the position until the post office was moved across the Sangamon River into Menard County eighteen months later.

The Walker's Grove Mission held its fourth quarterly meeting on August 29, 1857, with Reverend Peter Cartwright presiding. Randle announced that thirty-three people had joined the church since the last quarterly meeting. In his report on the "state of religion" for the Walker's Grove Mission, Randle observed, "Most of the Classes appear to be prousperous [*sic*]. Some however are Rather Leuke [*sic*] Warm. . . . We Believe that the cause of God is Spreading." The ten small preaching locations had contributed $71.35 "for the support of the Gospel" during the quarter.

At this last quarterly meeting of the year, "which was held at Walnut Grove a few miles from the parsonage," Randle later remembered, "we had a glorious revival." Preachers at the camp meeting revival included Randle, Presiding Elder Cartwright, Reverend R. U. Davies, "Bro. Colwell of Quiver, and some local brethren were present also Bro. T. Bryant of Middletown circuit who helped much." The camp meeting began on Saturday August 29 and lasted for ten days.

Camp meetings had been a feature of frontier life for decades by 1857, though in some areas, they had begun to wane. When a Christian Church editor in Indiana criticized the meetings, the Methodist *Northwestern Christian Advocate* defended the meetings as both good and successful: "These convocations of the people in the wilderness this year have been greatly blessed. The spirit of opposition seems to have been held in check, and the Spirit of the Lord has been poured out." "From all quarters," the editor concluded, "we hear of glorious seasons—seasons of divine visitation in connection with these meetings."

In August 1856, Joseph B. Malony reported on a camp meeting just completed in neighboring Fulton County:

[T]his spirit continued without relax all afternoon dooring [sic] which time convictions and conversations followed in quick succession and the watchword of the afternoon was Mr or Miss such a one was down praying or had just got threw[.] as evening drew on the encampment becom [sic] to small and little groups scattered to the woods in all directions untill [sic] the entire grove appeared presented one of the grandest sein [sic] of confused sounds that mortal ear ever witnessed of grones cries screems [sic] shouts songs and prayers and as it begun to grow dark the sounds drew near the ground and we had to go out of carry som [sic] of the sisters in to camp who wer [sic] so filled with the Spirit as to be perfictually [sic] helpless . . .

As in other areas of Illinois, the camp meeting at Walnut Grove or Walker's Grove in Mason County was well attended by Methodists and by those seeking religious instruction. Other people also came to this large, multi-day religious and social gathering. Randle later recalled that "many of the huxter [sic] and whiskey family also came" to the meeting to sell their goods to those gathered at the meeting. The Methodist ministers and leaders "kept the whiskeyites a mile off and the huxters [sic] show that they did not sell anything that would intoxicate," in the hopes of avoiding trouble. Young men frequently came to camp meetings with everything but religion on their mind, and they gathered on the fringes of the meeting to race horses, drink, gamble, fight, and socialize.

A few days after the camp meeting concluded, Randle eagerly reported the success to the *Central Christian Advocate* in St. Louis, Missouri. In a letter to editor Joseph Brooks, Randle wrote,

> Our camp meeting for this charge, closed on the 7th inst. Our beloved elder was at his post, being on the ground at an early stage of the meeting. We had a pleasant quarterly conference. Our old hero, P. CARTWRIGHT, preached with great acceptability on Saturday and Sunday, but in order to meet his previous engagements, he left on Monday. The camp meeting continued for ten days; the people came and heard the word gladly; the Lord gave us a glorious revival; sinners were converted, some fell to the ground and cried for mercy, others ran away from the camp ground. We do not know the exact number of converts, but think we are safe in saying between thirty and forty were happily converted. Twenty-eight joined the M.E. Church. We look for better times. Several brethren from adjoining charges rendered us assistance; may the Lord reward them all, for their labor of love. Evening meetings are still kept up in the neighborhood with happy results. Praise the Lord!

In his glowing report to the newspaper, Randle did not mention what he later included in his reminiscence about his first year as a minister on the Walker's Grove Mission circuit—the death of a man on Tuesday, September 1, 1857, from a fight that had occurred near the whiskey wagons outside the camp meeting. According to Randle, the camp meeting continued for several days until unexpected news electrified the camp:

> This was a large camp meeting, and many of the huxter [sic] and whiskey family also came, but we kept the whiskeyites a mile off and

made the huxters [sic] show that they did not sell anything that would intoxicate and got along fine until Tuesday morning. The news came to camp meeting that a man was killed at the whiskey camp. This report proved true. This caused all the huxters [sic] and whiskeyites to leave forthwith. Our meeting being under good way became more interesting than ever. Continued with great interest until the next Tuesday morning. There were some young men converted that have been preachers for years, and good acceptable men.

The man killed at the "whiskey camp" was James Preston Metzker, and his death led to a trial that became legendary in the life of Abraham Lincoln.

James Preston Metzker was a young farmer in his mid-twenties who lived in nearby Menard County. On Saturday, August 29, 1857, he was among those young men on the outskirts of the camp meeting in Mason County. In addition, there were James H. Norris and William Duff Armstrong. Norris, a farmer in his late twenties, was married and had three or four children, but he was "intemperate." William Duff Armstrong was a twenty-four-year-old farmer from nearby Menard County. More importantly, Armstrong was the son of Jack and Hanna Armstrong.

The three young men—Metzker, Norris, and Armstrong—knew each other, and all had been drinking on that Saturday night near the whiskey wagons. During the evening, both Norris and Armstrong fought with Metzker, possibly together but probably separately. Metzker apparently left the camp meeting the next morning and died two days later. The Mason County sheriff promptly arrested both Norris and Armstrong for the murder of Metzker.

Although the average consumption of alcohol was on the decline by the 1850s from its peak in the 1830s and 1840s, communal binges still occurred, and camp meetings provided the social setting for such drinking sprees. Those who participated tended to be among the lower economic classes, such as farm laborers, were more likely in their twenties than older, and were more common in the West than in the East. When the Illinois Conference of the Methodist Episcopal Church met in Decatur on October 1, 1857, the Committee on Temperance reported, "The last year has been more replete with misery and death, occasioned by the sale and use of intoxicating drinks within the bounds of our work, than any year, perhaps, in the last ten."

The Mason County Circuit Court held its second semi-annual session for 1857 in late October and early November. The court impaneled a grand jury to consider indictments, and after hearing eleven witnesses against

Norris and Armstrong, the grand jury returned a true bill in the indictment for murder. The indictment declared that Norris and Armstrong, "not having the fear of God before their eyes, but being moved and seduced by the instigations of the Devil . . . unlawfully, feloniously, willfully and of their malice aforethought did make an assault" on James Metzker. This indictment claimed that Norris had used as a weapon a stick of wood about three feet long and that Armstrong had used a slingshot. The latter weapon was a small ball of metal, usually lead, encased in leather and attached to a strap.

Both Norris and Armstrong pleaded not guilty, and Armstrong requested a change of venue to a court in another county "on account of the minds of the inhabitants of Said Mason County being prejudiced against him." The judge granted the change of venue in Armstrong's case to neighboring Cass County, but Norris went to trial immediately. After the attorneys interviewed more than seventy-two potential jurors, the court impaneled a jury to hear the case. The jury found Norris guilty of the lesser charge of manslaughter and sentenced him to eight years in the state penitentiary—the maximum sentence for a manslaughter conviction.

Sometime before the Cass County Circuit Court met ten days later, William Duff Armstrong's mother asked Abraham Lincoln to defend her son against the charge of murder. Lincoln had known William Duff Armstrong's parents, Jack and Hanna Armstrong, since he was a young man in New Salem, Illinois. When he arrived in the town, his wrestling match against Jack Armstrong initiated him into the male culture of the town and won him the respect and loyalty of Armstrong's extended family and friends, the "Clary's Grove boys." When the governor of Illinois called for volunteers to drive the Sauk and Fox Indians from the northern portion of the state in the Black Hawk War, the men from New Salem elected Lincoln as captain of their company. Jack Armstrong served as one of his sergeants. Hanna Armstrong sewed leather onto Lincoln's pants to extend their usefulness, and Lincoln sometimes stayed at the Armstrongs' home a few miles from New Salem. Lincoln never forgot their kindnesses to him, and when the younger Armstrong faced a murder charge, Lincoln represented him and charged nothing for his services.

At the November term of the Cass County Circuit Court, the court continued the case to the next term to await the transfer of records in the case from the Mason County Circuit Court. Lincoln and Armstrong's other attorneys urged the court to allow Armstrong to post bail. Because Illinois law prohibited the court from releasing on bail a person accused of murder, the motion for bail was in effect a motion to reduce the charge to man-slaughter, which was a bailable offense. However, the court overruled the motion, and Armstrong remained incarcerated until the May 1858 term of the Cass County Circuit Court.

Armstrong's case came up for trial on Friday May 7, 1858, at the Cass County courthouse in Beardstown, Illinois. Judge James Harriott presided over the trial. State's Attorney Hugh Fullerton, assisted by J. Henry Shaw, represented the people of the State of Illinois for the prosecution. William Walker, Caleb J. Dilworth, and Abraham Lincoln represented the defendant Armstrong. For decades, participants and scholars have debated the progress and outcome of this trial. The first and second generations of historians in the mid- and late nineteenth century interviewed and corresponded with individuals who had been in the courtroom. Historical detectives inter-viewed attorneys, several jurors, the judge, witnesses, court officials, the mother of the defendant, and eventually the defendant himself to obtain their memories of the trial. Predictably, these memories, recorded from seven to thirty-nine years after the trial, diverge from and even contradict one another. However, they also provide details about the case and trial unavailable in the sparse official documentation.

What is clear is that Abraham Lincoln played a pivotal role in the case and that he had several strategies for victory. His first goal was to obtain the proper type of jury. "Lincoln was smart enough to get a jury of young men," recalled witness William O. Douglas. Young jurors would be more sympa-thetic to the passions aroused in other young men by too much whiskey. The oldest juror, foreman Milton Logan, was thirty-eight, and the average age of the jurors was twenty-eight.

During the trial itself, Lincoln carefully examined and cross-examined witnesses. Among the prosecution's principle witnesses was Charles Allen, a farm laborer from Menard County. Allen testified that he had seen both Norris and Armstrong strike Metzker in the head. Under cross-examination, Allen told Lincoln that he had seen the events from thirty yards away by the light of a nearly full moon high in the sky. Lincoln questioned Allen repeatedly about how he had seen so clearly the events to which he testified, so that Al-len's testimony regarding the moon was etched in the minds of the jury. Allen insisted that the moon was high in the sky and nearly full, lighting the scene of the assault. Lincoln then introduced an almanac for 1857 that showed that at the time of the fight, the moon was low in the sky and within one hour of setting. The moon set at just after midnight on August 29, 1857. According to one of the prosecuting attorneys, the almanac "*floored* the witness" and discredited his oft-repeated testimony in the eyes of the jury. One of the jurors later remembered, "The impression of the almanac evidence led the jury to the idea that if Allen could be so mistaken about the moon, he might have been mistaken about seeing Armstrong hit Metzker with a slung-shot [*sic*] . . ."

Lincoln also questioned witnesses for the defense, including Dr. Charles Parker, who testified that a blow to the back of the head, like the one Norris inflicted on Metzker, could cause injury to the front of the skull as well. Dr. Parker used a human skull to illustrate his testimony to the jury. Lincoln argued that the blow to the back of Metzker's skull by Norris had also cracked the skull in the front, near the right eye, where Armstrong was supposed to have struck Metzker. Judge Harriott later recalled, "The Almanace [*sic*] may have cut a figure, but it was Doct [*sic*] Parkers testimony confirming Lincolns theory" that led to Armstrong's acquittal.

In his closing argument before the jury, Lincoln summarized the testimony of the witnesses and the scientific evidence presented by Dr. Parker (regarding injuries to the skull) and by the almanac (regarding the location of the moon on the night of August 29). Finally, he recalled for the jury how the defendant's parents had been kind to him when he was a young man, friendless and alone. He insisted that he defended Armstrong without a fee because of his great love and respect for the young man's mother. William Walker, one of Lincoln's co-counsel, observed that "the last 15 minutes of his Speech [*sic*], was so eloquent, as I Ever heard, and Such the power, & Earnestness with which he Spoke that Jury & all, Sat as if Entranced, & when he was through found relief in a Gush of tears[.] I have never Seen Such mastery Exhibited over the feelings and Emotions of men, as on that occasion."

One of the prosecuting attorneys agreed, "Armstrong was not cleared by any want of testimony against him, but by the irresistable [*sic*] appeal of Mr. Lincoln in his favor. He told the jury of his once being a poor, friendless boy, that Armstrong's father took him into his house, fed & clothed him & gave him a home &c. the particulars of which were told so pathetically that the jury forgot the guilt of the boy in their admiration of the father. It was generally admitted that Lincoln's speech and personal appeal to the jury saved Armstrong." He later added, "[I]t was Lincoln's *speech* that saved that criminal from the Gallows, and neither money or fame inspired that speech, but it was incited by gratitude to the young man's father. . . ." Nearly forty years after the trial, the accused himself admitted that Lincoln's speech was critical: "[I]t seemed to me 'Uncle Abe' did his best talking when he told the jury what true friends my father and mother had been to him in the early days, when he was a poor young man at New Salem. He told how he used to go out to Jack Armstrong's and stay for days; how kind mother was to him, and how, many a time, he had rocked me to sleep in the old cradle. He said he was not there pleading for me because he was paid for it; but he was there to help a good woman who had helped him when he needed help. Lawyer Walker made a good speech for me, too, but 'Uncle Abe's' beat anything I ever heard."

At the end of the trial, both the prosecuting and the defense attorneys presented to the judge a series of instructions to be given to the jury. State's Attorney Fullerton proposed four jury instructions for the prosecution, and Abraham Lincoln proposed the following two jury instructions for the defense:

> That if they have any reasonable doubt as to whether Metzker came to his death by the blow on the eye, or by the blow on the back of the head, they are to find the defendant "Not guilty" unless they also believe from the evidence, beyond reasonable doubt, that *Armstrong and Norris acted by concert*, against Metzker, and that Norris struck the blow on the back of the head.
>
> That if they believe from the evidence that Norris killed Metzker, they are to acquit Armstrong, unless they also believe beyond a reasonable doubt that Armstrong acted in concert with Norris in the killing, or purpose to kill or hurt Metzker.

Judge Harriott gave all six proposed instructions to the jury. Caleb J. Dilworth, one of the other defense attorneys, later insisted, "What the case turned upon was the instructions given by the court. There was no question but what the fight with Armstrong and Metzker was an individual affair, and Norris was not present and had nothing to do with it. The assault of Norris was also a separate and distinct affair, and Armstrong was not present and had nothing to do with the matter. Norris had been convicted of the killing." After the court gave the jury the instructions proposed by Lincoln, "of course the jury found for the defendant, as the testimony was clear and conclusive that Armstrong had nothing to do with the assault which Norris made."

Whatever proved to be the decisive factor in the verdict, the case of *People v. Armstrong* reveals Lawyer Lincoln at his best. He used the structure of the court system to his advantage by selecting a jury of younger men and proposing brilliant jury instructions. He demonstrated his detective skills in the careful examination and cross-examination of witnesses. He employed scientific evidence to support or refute testimony. Finally, he marshaled his considerable oratorical skills to appeal to the jurors' emotions and sense of nostalgia by recalling the kindness of the defendants' parents to him when he was a directionless young man. Lincoln's adroit blend of tactics earned his client a rapid acquittal of a charge that could have cost him his life.

The most famous of Lincoln's cases began when a group of Methodists in central Illinois gathered for a season of spiritual renewal and revival. The Illinois legislature had made it a crime to disturb a worshiping congregation, and the organizers of the camp meeting had kept the "whiskeyites" away from the campground. Nevertheless, this camp meeting, like many others in antebellum America, drew both saints and rogues. Excluded from the immediate area of the worship services, scoffers gathered at whiskey wagons nearby to gamble, drink, and mock the devout. The combustible combination of youthful bravado and whiskey led to many fights, one of which turned deadly on the Illinois prairie in August of 1857. The aftermath of this tragedy led to one of Abraham Lincoln's greatest legal triumphs—the exoneration of the son of Jack and Hannah Armstrong, who had been so kind to him when he was a friendless young man.

RELATED READING

William D. Beard, "'I Have Labored Hard to Find the Law': Abraham Lincoln for the Alton and Sangamon Railroad," *Illinois Historical Journal* vol. 85, no. 4 (Winter 1992).

Lincoln contributed significantly to the development of law affecting corporations—specifically the rapidly growing railroads of the early 1850s. James Barret claimed that a change in route of the railroad nullified his contractual obligations to the company. Lincoln's skillful work convinced the Illinois Supreme Court to hold that a change in the route had many advantages to the public and the company, and Barret's claim was denied. Both the Stowell and Beard articles derive from the Lincoln Legal Papers, a documentary history of the law practices of Abraham Lincoln, 1836–61.

13.

RICHARD J. OGLESBY,
Lincoln's Rail-Splitter

Mark A. Plummer

Illinois Historical Journal vol. 80, no. 1 (Spring 1987)

Oglesby was involved with many aspects of Lincoln's life. Wanting to enhance Lincoln's appeal to the common man, Oglesby devised and successfully promoted the image of Lincoln the rail-splitter. Lincoln appointed Oglesby a brigadier general in the Civil War.

A central figure in Illinois government and Republican politics, Oglesby was elected United States senator once and governor three times—1864, 1872, and 1884. He made a fortune from California gold dust and Decatur real estate speculation. He died in 1899.

T he dozen or so men who were largely responsible for promoting Lincoln's nomination for the presidency in 1860 have been portrayed as the "Original Lincoln Men." Prominent among them was Richard J. Oglesby of Decatur, who enjoyed a distinguished career independent of Lincoln— including the honor of being the first thrice-elected governor in the history of the state.

Oglesby's achievements were long obscured by the lack of an adequate record, however, and it was not until 1960 that his personal papers were deposited in the Illinois State Historical Library. Over the past decade, I have examined the twenty-five thousand private letters in the collection, as well as Oglesby's gubernatorial papers at the Illinois State Archives. The Historical Library collection documents Oglesby's participation in the Mexican War, his extraordinary grand tour of Europe and the Holy Land, the gold rush to California, the Republican State Convention of 1860 in Decatur where Lincoln's rail-splitter image was born, the Civil War, his presence at the deathbed of Lincoln, his leadership in building Lincoln's Tomb, his service as governor and senator, and his involvement in the case of the Chicago Haymarket anarchists. In short, Oglesby was a participant in most of the important events in American history for a half century.

My purposes are to document the episode in which the rail-splitter image was born, to describe the broader relationship between Lincoln and Oglesby, and finally to highlight Oglesby's character and career.

Although the "Original Lincoln Men" of Illinois were committed to Lincoln's presidential candidacy in 1860, there was little reason for optimism. Even campaign manager Judge David Davis wrote on February 20, 1860, "Of course I should like it if Lincoln could be nominated . . . [but] it seems to me . . . now, as if it would be Mr. [Edward] Bates or Gov. [William] Seward" who will receive the nomination. Some Illinois newspapers thought Lincoln might receive the vice presidential nomination, and Lincoln himself thought the presidency out of reach. But Jesse W. Fell, founder of the *Bloomington Pantagraph*, was convinced that Lincoln fit the party's need. He told the reluctant candidate, "[W]hat the Republican party wants, to insure success in 1860, is a man of popular origin, or acknowledged ability, committed against slavery aggressions, who has no record to defend, and no radicalism of an offensive character."

Lincoln, Fell implied, did meet all of those qualifications, but he needed to establish himself more strongly as "a man of popular origin" with whom the working people of the country would identify. The necessary symbolism was inspired by Richard James Oglesby of Decatur. As the unofficial coordinator for local arrangements for the state nominating convention at Decatur, Oglesby solicited money from local Republicans for construction of a "wigwam"—the structure created by stretching canvas between a building and a wooden framework, over a street and two vacant lots. Wigwams symbolized popular involvement in politics, and the symbol was understood in the context of both the Decatur convention and the subsequent Republican National Convention in Chicago, but something more was needed to place Lincoln in the "man of popular origin" image. Oglesby remembered that the "common man" slogans had provided the only national victories for his and Lincoln's old Whig party. "Tippecanoe and Tyler Too" had won the "Log Cabin" campaign in 1840. Oglesby was in search of such a symbol for Lincoln.

A few days before the Decatur convention, Oglesby sought the help of old John Hanks, a relative of Lincoln's who had worked with him some thirty years before. What kind of work was Lincoln good at, Oglesby wanted to know. Hanks replied, "Well, not much of any kind but dreaming, but he did help me split a lot of rails when we made a clearing twelve miles west of here." Hanks was sure that he could identify the rails because he recalled that they had been made of black walnut and honey locust trees, and Oglesby therefore took him on a buggy ride to the area the next day. Hanks found stumps that appeared to be the right age, and he declared the rails found nearby to be the same ones that he and Lincoln had mauled thirty years earlier. Two fence rails were transported to Decatur and hidden in Oglesby's barn.

Although it was not the custom for candidates to appear at nominating conventions, Lincoln arrived in Decatur on May 8, the day before the balloting, saying, "I'm most too much of a candidate to be here and not enough of one to stay away." When the convention opened, three thousand persons crowded into the nine-hundred-seat wigwam. Lincoln seated himself inconspicuously in the crowd, but Oglesby arose to announce that Lincoln was in the audience and promptly invited him to take a seat on the platform. Lincoln's six-foot-four frame was passed horizontally over the crowd, and the disheveled candidate thanked the convention for their enthusiastic reception. But the best was yet to come. During a lull in balloting for governor, Oglesby again rose and announced that "an old Democrat of Macon county" desired to make a contribution to the convention. "Receive it," the crowd shouted on cue, and John Hanks and a friend marched in carrying two fence rails with a placard reading, "Abraham Lincoln, the Rail Candidate for President in 1860. Two rails from a lot of 3,000 made in 1830 by John Hanks and Abe Lincoln."

A fifteen-minute demonstration erupted, during which "the [canvas] roof was literally cheered off the building." A speech was demanded of Lincoln, and, after examining the rails, he allowed that although he had helped build a log cabin and split some rails near Decatur he could not swear that those were the identical rails. Moreover, he was sure that he had split some better than the rough-hewn ones presented. The correspondent for the *Springfield Illinois State Journal* editorialized that "many a delegate, in thoughtful mood, contrasted the present position of the noble, self-taught, self-made statesman and patriot, whose name is now mentioned in connection with the highest office . . . of the nation, with that of the humble pioneer and railmaker of thirty years ago."

The enthusiasm carried over into the second day of the convention, when ballots were cast for the presidential nomination. It was assumed that Lincoln would be supported on the first ballot as a courtesy, but delegates were expected to vote as well for their second choice. John M. Palmer rose to resolve that Lincoln be declared *the* choice of the Illinois Republican Party and that all delegates be instructed to support him at the national convention. The resolution carried unanimously.

Most Lincoln biographers have accepted Oglesby's rail-splitter slogan as having played an important role in the nomination and election. Allan Nevins concluded, "Oglesby's little drama which brought Lincoln before the country as the Rail Splitter, and thus identified him with all the pioneer virtues and the rousing cause of Free Labor had a great and fast-widening psychological impact." William Baringer notes that the Decatur convention transformed candidate Lincoln from a minor favorite son to a powerful dark-horse national candidate. He wrote, "The rail explosion, making him the beloved Rail Splitter, symbolizing the rights of free labor, had suddenly given the Lincoln boom an emotional strength which, in the West, no other candidate could approach."

One week later in Chicago, the enthusiasm generated at Decatur and the shrewd tactics of David Davis and his fellow Illinoisans parlayed the dark-horse candidate into the presidential nominee of the Republican Party. During the convention, reports from the *Chicago Tribune* took the lead in pushing the "common man" symbolism. They displayed rails with appropriate placards inside and outside their offices. Throughout the city, they reported seeing spontaneous demonstrations by party faithful "shouldering rails" and marching in "joyous triumph" through the streets. Chicago's enthusiasm for the rails was infectious, and delegates from across the North returned to their homes to create rail-splitter clubs, rail-splitter floats, and rail-splitter newspapers. H. Preston James wrote, "The 'Rail-Splitter' theme was prevalent at most Republican gatherings. Platforms, chairs, and gavels were frequently made . . . from rails supposedly split by Lincoln himself. Rail fences, fully constructed or in the process of construction, actual rail-splitters at work, and pictures of men working with rails, were customary in Republican parades." One parade sign read, "In Illinois he mauled rails and Stephen A. Douglas." Of course, Democrats countered that Lincoln was the "hair splitter" and not the rail-splitter. In Springfield, where a visit from the Prince of Wales was impending, some of the boys began calling Lincoln's oldest son, Robert Todd Lincoln, "The Prince of Rails," a nickname that stuck with him for some time.

When Oglesby returned to Decatur, he found that John Hanks had become a national hero and that the demand for "genuine" Lincoln and Hanks rails was creating a supply problem. Letters from party leaders across the nation requested Lincoln rails. Oglesby had a small supply that he intended to distribute free of charge, but when it became necessary for John Hanks to pay the property owner for additional rails, Oglesby established an account that he labeled, "Rail acct with John Hanks." The Oglesby account contains the notation: "John Has recd all the money I have had all the trouble." Since Hanks could not write, Oglesby noted that Hanks had authorized him to "make my mark to all certiffica [i.e., certificates of authenticity] of the Lincoln Rails." The records show that Oglesby handled only seventy-two such certified rails, although other enterprising persons were soon offering hundreds of "genuine Lincoln rails."

When the Democrats started the rumor that Hanks would not vote for Lincoln, Oglesby arranged for a letter published over John Hanks's name that asserted his loyalty for Lincoln. Dated July 4, 1860, the letter is in Oglesby's handwriting, and has been preserved in the Oglesby Collection. It bears Oglesby's signature and the notation, "[T]ogether we got it up and sent it forth in the Memorable campaign of A.D. 1860."

Oglesby's connection with Lincoln was not confined to the Decatur convention. Oglesby was fifteen years Lincoln's junior, but they had much in common. Both men were born in Kentucky and learned to abhor slavery from personal experience. Both migrated through Indiana to central Illinois after losing a parent at a young age (both parents, in Oglesby's case). Both were members of the Whig party and admirers of Henry Clay. Neither received more than a few months' formal schooling, but both became lawyers after having served apprenticeships in Springfield. Oglesby first heard Lincoln speak in 1840 and became an admirer. Ironically, the earliest known letter from Lincoln to Oglesby, dated September 8, 1854, is a confidential message asking Oglesby to stop referring to the alleged drinking problem of Whig congressional candidate Richard Yates. Lincoln expressed the belief that Yates, whom he was pushing for reelection, did not drink. Although Oglesby's response has not been found, Yates did have a drinking problem that eventually ruined his career and contributed to his premature death.

At the momentous 1856 Decatur "Anti-Nebraska" editors meeting, at which plans were made for the Bloomington meeting that formed the Illinois Republican Party, Oglesby identified himself as a Lincoln man. According to a newspaper account, "Mr. O. made a number of witty remarks and concluded by toasting Mr. Abram Lincoln as . . . our next candidate for the U.S. Senate." Lincoln rose and said he was in favor of that sentiment.

In 1856, a few days before the Republican Party was born in Bloomington, Oglesby took his leave and toured Europe and the Holy Land for some twenty months with the earnings from his participation in the California gold rush, but he returned in time to be nominated for Congress in 1858. Oglesby attended the Lincoln-Douglas debate in Charleston, Illinois, and staged his own impromptu "debate" with his congressional opponent, James C. Robinson, at the Coles County Courthouse that evening. Both Lincoln and Oglesby lost their bids for national office, but both were considered rising political stars.

Besides promoting the rail-splitter slogan in 1860, Oglesby was a successful candidate in that year for the Illinois Senate. At the outbreak of the Civil War, however, he resigned and accepted the command of the 8th Illinois Volunteers. After displaying outstanding leadership in the Union victory at Fort Donelson in February of 1862, Oglesby was promoted by Lincoln to brigadier general. In the battle of Corinth on October 3, 1862, Oglesby was seriously wounded, and Lincoln inquired by telegram of General Grant: "[A]m very anxious to know the condition of Gen. Oglesby, who is an intimate personal friend." Grant replied, "Genl Oglesby is shot through the breast & ball lodged in the spine. Hopes for his recovery." Oglesby mended slowly in Illinois; he was promoted to major general and returned to active duty in Tennessee in 1863, but there he found the climate injurious to his personal and political health and asked Grant to accept his resignation. Grant, however, furloughed him pending further orders of the president.

Lincoln's orders brought Oglesby to Washington to serve on court-martial duty in 1864. He became a regular caller at the White House and, with the president's acquiescence, became the Republican candidate for governor. Resigning his commission, he stumped the state for Lincoln and the Republican ticket. Oglesby was known as one of the greatest stump speakers of the period, and his contribution to the success of the Republican ticket was considerable.

The newly elected governor arrived at the White House on the fateful afternoon of April 14, 1865, for a discussion of various military and political matters. Lincoln's last interview was with his old friend. Oglesby declined an invitation to attend Ford's Theatre with Lincoln that night. He was awakened on the news of the assassination and remained at Lincoln's side until the president was pronounced dead. It was his task to make the Illinois preparations for the return of the body to Springfield. It also fell his lot to negotiate with Mary Lincoln concerning the place of burial. Oglesby and most Springfield leaders preferred the location of the present state capitol, but Mary Lincoln insisted upon a secluded site, issuing an ultimatum that she would have her way or return his body to Washington for burial. Oglesby and the Illinois committee capitulated. Oglesby was elected president of the National Lincoln Monument Association, whose members built the tomb at Oak Ridge Cemetery. When the unfinished monument was dedicated in 1874, it was Oglesby who made the major dedication speech in the presence of President Grant and the cabinet. He served as president of the association until the property was turned over to the state in 1895.

Although Oglesby repeatedly refused to write for publication about his association with the martyred president, he did express his opinion in private correspondence. Commenting to William Herndon, Lincoln's law partner and self-proclaimed biographer, Oglesby wrote, "I think Mr Lincoln at all times possessed a strong common sense but not upon all Subjects. I mean to say he sometimes seemed weak in his estimate of Men but he had an instinctive aversion to a mean man and despised a Knave he pitied a fool and laughed heartily at an ass."

Oglesby's letters and testimony of his close acquaintances reveal an individual and a career that deserve to be studied independently of the "Lincoln Connection."

Orphaned at age eight in Oldham County, Kentucky, Oglesby became an abolitionist when the family's only slave, "Uncle Tim," was up for sale as part of the estate. This is Oglesby's account: "Tim was sold on the auction block, and I stood by and saw the sale, it grieved me deeply and intensely; the tears ran out of his eyes, poor fellow, as he stood there and he asked my uncle to buy him, but he wasn't able to buy him. I was very indignant and I told him I would buy him and set him free . . . and he took me up in his arms, as he had often done, and said, no child, you can't buy Uncle Tim. . . . Some Mrs. Bradshaw bid Tim in, but he was treated very unkindly. . . . Afterwards in 1849 I went to California . . . went to mining, speculating, and finally came back with some money. . . . When I got to Decatur there was an advertisement sent me by my brother-in-law from Kentucky that . . . Uncle Tim was to be sold at Westport, Kentucky. I sent my brother-in-law [the money, and he] bought him, then I went in there and set him free." I was able to check the story in the courthouse records of Oldham County, Kentucky, and Oglesby's version appears to be essentially sustained.

After migrating to Decatur to live with an uncle, Oglesby enlisted in an Illinois regiment for the Mexican War. By out-wrestling, out-running, and out-talking his fellow volunteers, he was elected lieutenant of his company. In early 1847 he led his company on a 450-mile march from the border to Tampico, Mexico. He wrote to his sisters, "I walked every step of the way in twenty days. Tis true that my feet often wore into blood blisters, and the skin came off in pieces as large as half-dollars, but I had to go it. I knew well that it would not do to despair whilst there were so many of the men looking anxiously for my example in that respect."

Two years later he was on the march again—traveling 1,940 miles overland in the California gold rush with some Decatur business partners. The leadership problem was solved when Oglesby suggested that each person serve as rotating "Emperor for a Day." Each day, the emperor would determine when to start, how fast to go, and where to camp. From that day they traveled to Sacramento City "with never a cross word to a single dispute," according to Oglesby's account. Oglesby returned to Decatur in 1851 with $5,000 in gold dust, and through speculation in town lots, he quickly became one of the city's richest men. The main Decatur streets of Cerro Gordo and Eldorado are named for his Mexico and California experiences. With his fortune he was able to begin a twenty-month tour over three continents. He traveled through England, France, Prussia, and Russia, where he witnessed the coronation of Tzar Alexander II. He then set off to Alexandria, Egypt, traversed six hundred miles up the Nile to Thebes, rode a camel across the desert to the Holy Land, and recited the Ten Commandments on Mt. Sinai. Oglesby seems to have gained polish and confidence in his oratorical abilities as a result of the unusual trip. His Holy Land lecture was in great demand for the next thirty years. Lincoln heard the speech in Bloomington and commented favorably upon it.

Soon after the beginning of the Civil War, William Howard Russell, the American correspondent of the *London Times*, observed Oglesby at an army camp in Cairo. Russell described Oglesby as a "tall, portly, good-humored old man . . . [who] with excellent tact and good sense, dished up in the Buncombe style" a speech to the volunteer soldiers. Oglesby's "Buncombe" style also served him well in 1864. Robert G. Ingersoll, considered the finest stump speaker in the West, characterized one of Oglesby's speeches as the best political speech he had ever heard. It had "every element of greatness— reason, humor, wit, pathos, imagination and perfect naturalness," he wrote.

The correspondence of Robert G. Ingersoll, later known as the "Great Agnostic," was one of the unexpected discoveries in the Historical Library's

Oglesby Collection. Ingersoll's definition of the two political parties, which he wrote to Oglesby in 1867, is worth quoting: "[T]imes are getting hard—money getting scarce and consequently our [Republican] party getting a little *shaky*. . . . Men will never act good unless the times are good. When a man has his pocket full of money he feels like a gentleman, and when a man feels like a gentleman he votes our ticket. But when his pocket is empty, and his shirt tail out he naturally slides over to the democracy [Democratic party]."

Oglesby was elected governor for the second time in 1872, but he served only a few days before resigning to accept a seat in the United States Senate. The first Adlai E. Stevenson, who knew and liked Oglesby despite the fact that they were members of opposing political parties, thought Oglesby's skills were better suited to the Illinois scene than to the formality of the United States Senate. In his book *Something of the Men I Have Known*, Stevenson related how in the 1872 campaign Oglesby had been challenged to comment upon the Democrats' policies. Oglesby retorted, "These Democrats undertake to discuss the financial question. They oughtn't to do that. They can't possibly understand it. The Lord's truth is, fellow citizens, *it is about all we Republicans can do to understand that question!*"

Oglesby was not reelected to the Senate when his term expired in 1879. For the moment, he was content to enjoy his family in Decatur while living in a home that had been designed in part by the famous architect William LeBaron Jenney. The demand for his speeches continued, however. On May 31, 1881, Decoration Day, for example, he noted tersely in his diary, "I delivered the oration . . . in the cemetary to 2000 people. Spoke one hour and sweat profusely."

In 1882 Oglesby moved to Lincoln, Illinois. Although the reason for the move was more financial than symbolic, his candidacy for his third election as governor was not hurt by his new address. To make himself "available" without seeming to be a candidate, he began making his famous Holy Land lectures once again. Requests for his appearances poured in, but perhaps none was more unusual than the request that came from an old friend, Henry T. Noble, of Dixon, Illinois: "We believe the only complaint ever made against you . . . even by the Democrats is that you are, when terribly in earnest, liable to *swear*. While we believe that a man can swear at Democrats and still rank as a Christian, yet we thought that in delivering your lecture on the 'Holy Land' it is just possible, as you found no Democrats there, you could squeeze through without swearing." Oglesby's "nonpolitical" campaign netted him the Republican gubernatorial nomination in

1884. He was elected to his third term exactly twenty years after his first election as governor.

Oglesby's nomination vaulted him into consideration as a dark-horse candidate for president. Former vice president Schuyler Colfax wrote to Oglesby: "You may smile at the idea; but as I look at the field, I think your chance of being 'the dark horse' quite as good to-day as any . . . [if] some one acceptable to the soldier element as a fighter in the field should be wanted, one who had Congressional experience, and a Western man to boot, you see that lightning might strike dangerously near you." Oglesby replied that he preferred to stay in Illinois "where I can discharge the not very perplexing duties [as governor] with reasonable equanimity. . . . [T]hank you . . . for your . . . kindly thoughts upon the subject of the Black Horse [but I] assure you that I have not so much as a silent wish to ride that animal."

Oglesby was wrong to assume that serving as governor would require of him only "not very perplexing duties." Soon after his election, the famous Haymarket Square bombing occurred in Chicago. After all other legal remedies had been exhausted, including an unprecedented appeal to the United States Supreme Court, Oglesby had to decide whether to exercise his power of pardon to prevent the hanging of the Haymarket anarchists. His task was made more difficult by the refusal of the principals to ask for clemency. August Spies wrote, "If legal murder there must be, let one, let mine suffice!" Louis Lingg made it clear that he was not asking for commutation. "Give me liberty or give me death," he challenged, and Oglesby did not feel he could give him liberty. The governor allowed the extreme sentence to stand in the case of five of the anarchists, but he reduced the sentence of the two men who had signed statements of contrition.

Oglesby was politically active in at least three distinct eras of American history. The politics of the Civil War, Reconstruction, and the Gilded Age all offered different hazards, and Oglesby recognized that fame might be fleeting. That recognition comes through in a letter dated March 23, 1885, that was written in response to a gentleman who wished to name his son for Oglesby. The governor wrote, "I wish to say to you that you take a great risk naming your child after any living man. It seems to me that there are plenty of dead heros from which to select a good name. . . . There is no telling what may become of a living man."

Oglesby retired from public office for the last time when his term ended in 1889, with his name still held in high repute. He retired to Oglehurst on Elkhart Hill overlooking the cornfields that he actively managed. In retirement, however, his reputation as an impromptu speaker was further enhanced by his classic tribute to corn, delivered at the Fellowship Club in Chicago in 1894. According to an account given by a club member, each speaker was to propose a toast under the theme, "What I Know about Farming." Oglesby, "seemingly waiting for an inspiration," spotted the harvest decorations in the room and focused upon the corn. He began: "*The corn, the corn, the corn.* . . . Look on its ripening waving field. See how it wears a crown, prouder than Monarch ever wore. . . . Aye, the corn, the Royal corn, within whose yellow heart there is of health and strength for all the nations." Oglesby concluded: "Oh that I had the voice of song or skill to translate into tones the harmonies, the symphonies and the oratorios that roll across my soul, when standing . . . upon the borders of this verdant sea, I note a world of promise, and then before one-half the year is gone I view its full fruition and see its heap-ed gold await the need of man. Majestic, fruitful, wondorous plant. Thou greatest among the manifestations of the wisdom and love of God, that may be seen in all the fields or upon the hillsides or in the valleys."

In 1899, a few days before his death at the age of seventy-five, Oglesby wrote to an old friend, William H. Piatt of Monticello, "We of course, have had our day and time, and in the regular course of nature we have to give way to the big procession for living on behind us. I cannot understand why, when the Lord has a good set of old fellows, he cant let them alone, and let them live as long as they may care to. . . . We kept things in pretty good order for 50 years. We have done our part. Now let the world take care of itself."

14.

LINCOLN'S INTIMATE FRIEND
Leonard Swett

Robert S. Eckley

Journal of the Illinois State Historical Society
vol. 92, no. 3, A Lincoln Issue (Autumn 1999)

Leonard Swett's life intersected with a number of events and stages in the life of Abraham Lincoln. Becoming a lawyer, he rode with Lincoln on the Eighth Judicial Circuit. Swett had an important role in Lincoln's two efforts to become a United States senator, as well as in his campaigns for president in 1860 and 1864. Lincoln sought Swett's advice in his selection of cabinet members. During the Civil War, he assisted Lincoln in significant ways. Issues for professional historians are addressed.

When the journalist and aspiring Lincoln biographer Josiah Holland asked David Davis, the administrator of Lincoln's estate less than three months after the assassination, who should be contacted for information, Davis wrote back: "Mssrs. Herndon and Swett were his intimate personal and political friends and can ... give you more detailed information concerning the past fifteen years of his life than perhaps any other parties." Holland spent a couple of days in Springfield talking with Herndon, but there is no indication that he ever reached Swett. Years later, when Herndon published his own famous life of Lincoln, he chose to quote at length "two devoted and trusted friends," Joshua Speed and Leonard Swett. Shortly after, Henry Clay Whitney published his *Life on the Circuit with Lincoln* and wrote that "the great triumvirate" of the circuit "consisted of Davis, Lincoln, and Swett: and their social consequence was in the order named." What happened to Leonard Swett?

Swett was often mentioned in the reminiscence literature on Lincoln until around 1900, and less frequently thereafter. No full-scale biography of him has been written. Harry Pratt, onetime head of the Abraham Lincoln Association and later Illinois state historian, wrote two articles on Swett, one on his loss to John Paul Stuart in their 1862 Congressional race and the second a collection of letters home to a sister in Maine during his early years on the Eighth Judicial Circuit. Had it not been for Pratt's untimely death, he might have been Swett's biographer, just as he was the first biographer of David Davis. Three scholarly articles were written about the New Almaden quicksilver mine debacle in California—one by a historian and Lincoln scholar, the second by an economic historian, and the third by a legal practitioner and scholar—all disparaging the role played by Swett, except for Willard King's biography of David Davis, where he is dealt with as a collateral figure.

Swett was born in 1825 and grew up on a Maine farm—ten years younger than Davis and sixteen years Lincoln's junior. Early on it was decided that his older brother should inherit the family farm and Leonard should receive a college education. After three years at what is now Colby College, he read law for two years in a Portland firm and then set out to sell books in the lower twenty-eight states that existed in 1847. He did not sell many. Somehow, he took passage on a sailing vessel in Philadelphia bound for New Orleans, and after a few weeks there, he worked his way up the Mississippi and Ohio Rivers to Madison, Indiana. There he chose the seemingly better alternative of joining the 5th Indiana Infantry, which, with amazing speed for the time, joined General Winfield Scott's forces on the line from Veracruz to Mexico City in the waning days of the Mexican War.

In Mexico Swett soon contracted a malaria-like fever and spent several weeks in a makeshift hospital in the Veracruz cathedral. He was shipped back to New Orleans with other sick soldiers, a third of whom died en route. Swett was mustered out at Jefferson Barracks in St. Louis—elapsed time in the army, four months! From there, he headed for home, but the fever recurred in Peoria, where he was advised to get away from the river. So he stumbled into Bloomington, sick, with 126 pounds on his 6-foot, 2-inch frame in July of 1848.

There he was befriended by George Washington Minier, then a schoolmaster and later a Disciples of Christ minister. Within a year he had regained his health, resumed reading the law, was admitted to the Illinois bar, and met David Davis, the new judge of the Illinois Eighth Judicial Circuit, then consisting of fourteen counties in an arc sweeping from Springfield to Danville. On Judge Davis's second tour of the circuit in the fall of 1849 he introduced Swett to Lincoln, who was returning to the circuit after his disappointing experience in the thirtieth Congress. A warm and lifelong friendship developed among the three.

Lincoln's term in Congress roughly bisected his twenty-four years of law practice, and the second half of his itinerant practice on the circuit was shared with Swett. Every year from September through December and again from March to June, they were together on the circuit, which, with population growth and increasing caseload, shrank to eight counties in 1853 and to only five in 1857. As the number of cases in each county increased, fewer of the attorneys traveled the circuit, and in 1860 Swett wrote to a friend that "for perhaps five years Lincoln and myself have been the ones who have habitually passed over the whole circuit." Later, he said, "in the allotment between him (Lincoln) and the large Judge Davis, in the scanty provision of those times, as a rule, I slept with him." Early in the relationship, on a journey between Clinton and Champaign, Swett got Lincoln to tell him about his life, which Swett published many years later and has become a source for frequent retelling of the Lincoln story.

The two practiced together on many cases, sometimes on the same side, sometimes in opposition. In a famous murder case tried in Bloomington in 1857, Swett, as counsel for the defendant, bested Lincoln, who was acting as prosecutor. This was an early case involving the insanity defense, for which Swett prepared himself by visiting the superintendent of the Mclean Asylum for the Insane in Boston. The result led Lincoln to refer a similar case in Shawneetown to Swett a few months later, which he also helped win. In a civil case, which Swett appealed to the Illinois Supreme Court in 1860, the court reversed the judgment to one against Lincoln's client and remanded the case. According to Whitney, "in a jury case, Lincoln preferred association with him to any other lawyer in the State." Respect flowed both ways and is supported by the fact that they were associated together in a significant portion of their practice outside their home counties.

Political association also started early in their friendship, Swett volunteered to assist Lincoln in both of the U.S. Senate campaigns. In 1854 he wrote Lincoln to "use me in any way" as preparations for the contest in the legislature began to take shape. He then made an extended swing through northern Illinois to sound out support for Lincoln. Similarly, in 1858 Swett spoke extensively for Lincoln's candidacy and ran for and was elected to the legislature in order to support Lincoln there. Early in the canvass, both Lincoln and Swett spoke at the Mclean County Republican Convention on September 3, which nominated Swett, and the following day Swett introduced Lincoln for one of his major speeches in the Lincoln-Douglas campaign. Little more than a year later, Swett was one of those who met with Lincoln in the last week of January 1860 and helped make the fateful decision that Lincoln should seek the Republican nomination for the presidency.

His role is unmistakable as David Davis's lieutenant, in securing Lincoln's nomination in the Republican Convention at the Wigwam in Chicago. Whitney wrote that although "Swett contributed as much to the nomination of Lincoln as Davis did, he made no claim at all, but always gave the entire credit to Davis." Whitney however did not particularly like Davis. A reading of the record would recognize Davis's leadership, for Swett was neither the strategic thinker that Lincoln was nor did he display Davis's organizing skill. We are indebted to him for a candid description of how the nomination was orchestrated. Knowing that each of the leading candidates faced major impediments to nomination, they adopted a strategy of securing second ballot pledges for Lincoln from delegates committed to the leaders while obviously gaining as many outright supporters as possible. They almost gained too much first-ballot strength, but the strategy worked. Davis detailed various Eighth Circuit supporters to work the state delegations where they might have influence—Swett to Maine, for example. And he used Browning and Swett, who were effective speakers, to appear before entire state caucuses. Swett's colorful description of the convention's enthusiasm for Lincoln, written to a college friend from Maine only nine days after the nomination, is widely quoted in the Lincoln literature: "No language can describe it. A thousand steam whistles, ten acres of hotel gongs, a tribe of Comanches headed by a choice vanguard."

In addition to his advisory role to Lincoln regarding Republican leaders he had dealt with at the Wigwam Convention, Swett canvassed southern Illinois on behalf of Lincoln for three weeks and later traveled to Terre Haute to meet with Indiana Republican leaders.

Cabinet-making started almost immediately following the convention and lasted until inauguration day. Swett played a major role along with a half dozen others. Within nine days of the nomination, he had written four letters to Lincoln and accompanied Thurlow Weed, Seward's manager, on a visit to Lincoln. Swett wrote Lincoln twenty more letters prior to the inauguration, giving him reports on various aspects of the campaign and cabinet discussions. Weed visited Davis and Swett again in early December and was accompanied by them on a second visit to see Lincoln. Both Davis and Swett played principal roles in Lincoln's most vexing cabinet choices, Simon Cameron and Caleb Smith. Both were the targets of unsubstantiated allegations by Cameron's opponents, that they had made promises to him contrary to Lincoln's assertions. They also opposed Norman Judd for the cabinet, in concert with Jesse Fell, probably because of his conservative views, based on his Democratic background.

Lincoln dispatched Swett to Washington to assess the political scene there in late December with stops along the way to see Cameron in Pennsylvania and Governor Hicks and Winter Davis in Baltimore. Swett conferred with various Congressional members and officials in Washington for three weeks. He tried to understand the political turmoil and confusion. "Our party here is like a stream with a thousand currents and counter currents. . . . The South out manages us because their policy is well conceived by a few men . . . Jeff Davis and a few men meet privately and dictate action." Swett received a Massachusetts delegation and sought to balance Charles Frances Adam's backing against that of Gideon Welles for the cabinet, he consoled Cameron after he received Lincoln's withdrawal of the offer of a cabinet post, and he sat for hours with Seward to search for a possible compromise with a Virginia group. En route home, he became seriously ill and stayed in Pittsburgh for three weeks, where Lincoln met with him on his way to Washington. Swett spent at least fifty-three days on this endeavor—all at his own expense.

The question has been frequently asked, why was Swett not appointed by Lincoln to some position in his administration? Swett obviously wanted to be placed and expected to be, but he never complained publicly that it did not happen. When asked why he was not appointed, Swett later gave several similar but different answers, one of which was, "Some of Mr. Lincoln's friends insisted that he lacked the strong attributes of personal affection which he ought to have exhibited. I think this is a mistake. Lincoln had too much justice to run a great government for a few favorites, and the complaints against him in this regard when properly digested amount to this, and no more: that he would not abuse the privileges of his situation." Lincoln solicited what he might want when he saw him in Pittsburgh, and Swett responded to him in a letter from Bloomington on inauguration day without being specific. Actually, Lincoln offered him three different positions—colonel in the regular army, assistant adjutant general to General Eleazar A. Paine, and commissioner of Peruvian claims—all of which Swett declined. Four other positions were discussed within the executive mansion, most with Lincoln involved, without resulting in any action. Besieged as he was by mobilization problems and by office seekers, Lincoln was clearly in no position to find a slot for a friend to whom he remained loyal and devoted. During sixty months from Lincoln's nomination to his assassination, Swett was either visiting Lincoln or engaged in some assignment in more than half of the months. He also was involved in influencing the appointments of many others, including Davis Dickey, former judge of an adjoining circuit who had fallen out with Lincoln in 1858, and Orme, Swett's law partner. After visiting with Lincoln regarding the appointment of Davis to the Supreme Court in 1861, Swett wrote, "[I]f you can honor him I'll consider it as for me. . . ."

Swett spent much of August 1861 in Washington, discussing this and other appointments, and returned again in October. He was there when Lincoln sent him on a mission to deliver orders removing General Fremont from command of the western forces. Fremont had issued a proclamation on August 30 freeing slaves, confiscating property, and declaring martial law in Missouri, including ordering that anyone "taken with arms . . . shall be tried by court martial, and if found guilty will be shot." Lincoln requested that he modify the order, which Fremont declined to do unless ordered to do so. Lincoln obliged. A series of officials were sent to investigate the situation, who found many complaints of corruption and ineptitude. After cabinet discussions reviewing reports, Lincoln sent Swett off on October 24 with orders for Fremont's removal. Swett delivered the orders to General Samuel Curtis in St. Louis, and the two decided that since Fremont might refuse to receive the orders, a subterfuge was necessary. The New York papers had published the impending removal, and Swett had been seen on the train by St. Louis people who knew him. Two young captains were chosen to attempt delivery separately. The one, who got through first, with some difficulty because of Fremont's obstruction, was dressed as a farmer, who described the successful delivery to Lincoln in a November 9 letter, which is corroborated by the captain's later autobiography.

Few Americans have heard of the New Almaden mine in California, and even fewer Lincoln scholars are familiar with this minor footnote to Civil War history. New Almaden was the first mine in California (1842) and produced quicksilver used in reducing gold or silver ore. In March 1863 the

U.S. Supreme Court held that the New Almaden Company operating the mine did not hold valid title from the prior Mexican government and that it was on the U.S. government roster. General Charles Halleck had been a former superintendent of the mine and represented the owner in the lower courts, five former U.S. attorneys general represented one side or the other, including Edwin Stanton, and one former Treasury Secretary and a former U.S. Supreme Court justice were involved. Into this complicated situation Lincoln sent Swett to claim the mine on behalf of the U.S. government, with the input and backing of Attorney General Bates and Interior Secretary Usher. Before he left, however, Swett went to New York and arranged to receive a $10,000 fee from the new company, Quicksilver Mining, to which the government intended to lease the mine on completion of the recovery. So equipped, he sailed from New York with wife, child, and nurse, traversed either Panama or Nicaragua, and arrived in San Francisco in early July. He immediately obtained a cavalry company from a nearby army post, rode to the mine just south of San Jose, and presented the claim. Those in possession resisted, and he did not press the claim. While he contemplated the next step, within days Lincoln received telegrams from seven prominent Californians objecting to the seizure. These included the Republican gubernatorial candidate with the election pending in two months, the chief justice of Nevada, and former chief justice of California who was Lincoln's new U.S. Supreme Court appointee. Local opponents represented the U.S. action as a threat to all private mining interests. Although Lincoln denied this, Bates may in fact have had it in mind, judging from a new case he brought before the Supreme Court the following year which he argued himself, and lost. Lincoln quickly read the political signals and canceled the writ. Swett stayed on for seven weeks at Usher's request and purchased the mine for the Quicksilver Mining Company. He was back in Washington in time to accompany the Lincoln party on the train to Gettysburg in mid-November for the cemetery dedication.

Because of his political prominence in Illinois, Swett was called on from time to time to aid the war effort. One such urgent call occurred in late May of 1862 when Governor Yates requested two hundred to three hundred men to replace the guard at Camp Butler in Springfield, which was being moved to assist in Virginia as McClellan's peninsular campaign moved forward. Accordingly, Swett had the Mclean County courthouse bell rung at midnight May 25, and within three days he had three companies enrolled, transported to Springfield, and organized for duty.

Lacking a formal role, Swett did assist Lincoln in a number of other significant ways during his presidency. Many Lincoln associates tried to claim a crucial or key part in the origin of the Emancipation Proclamation. Swett never did. Because of the respect Lincoln held for him, his part was nonetheless real, albeit entirely passive. Swett often told how he was asked to visit him and spend an entire morning as Lincoln presented various arguments for and against emancipation, reading from letters or documents, and then dismissed him without a question.

That summer during some of the darkest days of the war, following McClellan's failure on the Peninsula, Swett appeared on the platform with Lincoln and several others in front of the Capitol building in what was called the Union or Great War Meeting, held on August 6, 1862, the last of their nine joint speaking appearances. It dealt with men and money to build enthusiasm in the call for six hundred thousand additional men and the determination to carry on to victory and peace. Swett said in his penultimate paragraph, "It is the duty of the sailors, in the storm, to stand by the ropes and man the yards, not to quarrel with the Captain about the conduct of the ship. Let Father Abraham man the helm, and let us obey."

In the fall of 1862 Swett ran for Congress against John Todd Stuart, ironically Lincoln's first mentor and law partner, and lost, primarily as a result of the unpopularity of emancipation in parts of the district and the absence of soldiers, who were heavily Republican. An astute observer, David Davis's law partner, wrote, "[O]ut of those counties there were at least 12,000 soldiers, 8,000 of whom were voters. Five thousand of these at least did and would have voted the Union ticket." It was a bitter defeat for Swett, and effectively ended his elective political career.

In the spring of 1864 the tempers of Union soldiers on furlough in Charleston, Illinois, and ardent Democrats exploded into bloodshed on the courthouse square, and nine men were killed, six of them soldiers. Governor Yates wrote to Lincoln on June 10 regarding the frequency of such incidents and asking that a district commander be appointed. It appears that Swett carried the letter to Lincoln, who endorsed it ten days later, asking Swett "to have a talk with the Sec. of War in this case."

Again, in the disappointing days in the summer of 1864, Swett served as a sustaining influence for the Lincoln administration. He was one of the few devoted supporters at the 1860 convention active at Baltimore four years later. Lincoln left the choice to fate while the ambitions of Chase and Fremont played out their intrigues. If Lincoln had a choice for vice president other than a Southern Unionist, no telling evidence has been found. Swett went to the convention supporting Joseph Holt for vice president, a judge advocate general from Kentucky and former Buchanan cabinet member who was a friend of David Davis but quickly acquiesced in the selection of Andrew Johnson when Hay pointed out that two on the ticket from Kentucky would be inappropriate. As the summer progressed with Grant bogged down in Virginia and Sherman inching toward Atlanta, the Republican radicals and the Democratic copperheads became more shrill, and it began to look like Lincoln could not be reelected. Swett discussed the political situation with Lincoln and acted as intermediary in bringing the leadership of the Republican National Committee to the White House. He wrote to his wife, "Raymond, the chairman . . . not only gave up, but would do nothing. . . . There was not a man doing anything except mischief." He added that he had "raised and provided one hundred thousand dollars for the canvas" and explained why it was necessary. This dismal outlook led Raymond to propose the sending of a peace commission to Jefferson Davis, a suggestion he attributed to Swett. Lincoln's sealed letter of August 23, 1864, saying "it seems exceedingly probable that this Administration will not be reelected," reflects the seriousness of the plight. The conference between Lincoln, Raymond, and others arranged by Swett occurred, and the peace plan was rejected. The timely fall of Atlanta changed the picture dramatically.

Swett performed one other important and unrecognized service for his friend, for which a strong case can be made but no proof is possible. General Winfield Scott sent Swett to see his inspector general, Colonel Charles Stone, when he was in Washington in January 1861. Stone alerted Swett to several conspiracy efforts, which Swett communicated to Lincoln, both by letter and orally when they met in Pittsburg. Credit for informing Lincoln of the Baltimore plot is customarily given to Pinkerton and Judd. Later, in the summer of 1862, Swett and William Hanna, an attorney from Bloomington, became concerned after a visit to Lincoln at the Soldier's Home that Lincoln was unduly exposed there and on his carriage rides to and from the White House. They discussed it with Ward Hill Lamon, Lincoln's informal bodyguard and marshal of Washington, and after gaining Lincoln's assent, they went to Stanton, who established a guard of twenty-five to thirty cavalry in September 1862. But for Swett's actions, the assassination might have occurred much earlier, possibly before the first inauguration.

Lincoln and Swett invested heavily in their sixteen-year friendship. Why have historians not done so? Swett closed his memorial on Davis before the

Illinois State Bar Association in 1887 with the following words: "I thank God and thank him again that in the mysteries of providence He placed the lines of my life between two such great men as David Davis and Abraham Lincoln, and permitted me, in the hours of my own weakness, to 'lean on their great arms for support.'"

15.

I FOR ONE AM READY
TO DO MY PART

The Initial Motivations That Inspired Men from Northern Illinois to Enlist in the U.S. Army, 1861–1862

Wayne N. Duerkes

Journal of the Illinois State Historical Society
vol. 105, no. 4 (Winter 2012)

With the beginning of the Civil War, Lincoln called for volunteers in the Northern states to enlist in the United States Army to put down the insurrection. Duerkes reports that Illinois governor Richard Yates was "besieged by hordes of men willing to do their part." The author examines the motivations to join the war effort in rural northern Illinois in the period 1861–62. His findings—based on articles, histories, reports, letters, and diaries—appear to be similar to earlier studies. The author also addresses the role and support of women.

Illinoisans! Look at the issue and do not falter. Your all is at stake. What are your beautiful prairies, comfortable mansions and rich harvests?—What is even life worth, if your government is lost? Your all and your children's all—all that is worth living or dying for, is at stake. Then rally once again for the old flag, for our country, union and liberty.

—Richard Yates, August 5, 1862

In April 1861, in response to the firing on Fort Sumter, President Abraham Lincoln called for seventy-five thousand volunteers to fill the ranks of the U.S. Army. The response was immediate and overwhelming. Men residing in the Northern states enlisted in such numbers that thousands had to be turned away, many then joining units from other states. During the first two years of the war, Illinois mustered over eighty thousand men into Federal service. Of these men, seventeen thousand or 21 percent came from the fourteen northernmost counties of the state, excluding Cook County. During the first two years of the war, more than one-quarter of all military-age males from northern Illinois enlisted. Scholars have devoted considerable effort to determining who enlisted in the Union army and to understanding their motivation for doing so. But their research is heavily focused on the eastern states. Historians have neglected to undertake a study of motivations for enlisting in the rural Midwest. Rural northern Illinois, a region that excludes Cook County and Chicago, provides an excellent place to determine whether the motivations that historians have identified as important also inspired ordinary Midwesterners to enlist.

James McPherson, in his *For Cause and Comrades*, examines a representative cross section of the volunteer forces to determine why men fought in the Civil War. His analysis shows preservation of the union, patriotism, and concerns about masculine identity as key to understanding the motivations of early volunteers. McPherson borrows from John A. Lynn a nomenclature useful for understanding volunteers' motivations for enlisting and fighting in wars. Lynn's nomenclature breaks into three useful categories the motivation of fighting men: initial, sustaining, and combat. Initial motivation refers to forces that drove volunteers to leave family and friends and to prepare for war. Sustaining motivation explains why men stayed in the military during wartime. The hardships of camp life and the potential for combat, death, and disease ensured that not all who volunteered remained in the fight. Finally, combat motivation seeks to determine why men fought. During the Civil War, large numbers of men "faced the elephant"—military slang for confronting actual combat—and Lynn uses combat motivation to explain why volunteers fought despite "the overwhelming presence of fear."

A desire to preserve the Union accounted for the initial motivation of significant numbers of volunteers from northern Illinois who enlisted in the army. That desire was nurtured in an atmosphere of patriotic fervor. The fervor owed to their understanding of national history, which they used to cast themselves as the heirs of the revolutionary generation and as the protectors of liberty and freedom. The Southern states' refusal to accept the popular election of Lincoln and their insistence on the right to secede challenged Northern views of the national union and the meaning of the election of 1860. Starting in April 1861 men in northern Illinois were presented with the opportunity to act upon those beliefs. Defense of their nation was not the only issue that dwelled on the hearts and minds of the volunteers. Volunteers also approached things more pragmatically. Men saw an opportunity to advance themselves in life through military service. Financial gains, upward mobility in social status, and, in some cases, just a simple break from the boredom prevalent in youth all presented tantalizing opportunities to elevate themselves or their families beyond what they had known prior to the conflict.

After weeks of building tension, the government of the Confederate States of America demanded U.S. major Robert Anderson stationed at Fort Sumter in South Carolina to officially evacuate the fort on April 11, 1861. Negotiations failed to appease both sides on a timeline for removal of Federal forces, and, on April 12, 1861, artillery batteries under the command of General Pierre Gustave Toutant Beauregard opened fire on Fort Sumter, which surrendered the following day. Civil War had begun.

Lincoln Declares Insurrection

On April 15, 1861, Lincoln declared an insurrection, which by law authorized him to call up militia in the various states to suppress hostilities. He initially called for seventy-five thousand men for three months of service. In his carefully worded proclamation, Lincoln appealed to "all loyal citizens to favor, facilitate and aid this effort to maintain the honor, the integrity, and the existence of our National Union, and perpetuity of popular government; and to redress wrongs already long enough endured." Well aware of the need for public approval to suppress the rebellious states, Lincoln rested his appeal on defense of the Union and his popularly elected government. The phrase "wrongs already long enough endured" was calculated to appeal to all Northerners, even Democrats, who had long felt subjugated to the demands and threats of the Southern states.

That night, Secretary of War Simon Cameron sent a message to the governor of Illinois, Richard Yates, requesting six regiments of militia. Specifically, the secretary of war requested that the state detach from the militia 4,683 officers and men. According to regulations sent forth by the secretary of

war, each regiment mandated a total of 780 officers and men. With a total
of six regiments requested, the quota per regulations would account for
4,680, only three shy of the initial request. In 1860 Illinois had a total white
male population of 898,952, of which 297,557 were men between twenty and
thirty-nine years of age. Yates's first call required only 1.6 percent of Illinois
males of fighting age to answer it. A man of fighting age had roughly a one
in a hundred chance of making the first call up.

Governor Yates had already prepared for just such an eventuality. Hours
before receiving the message from the secretary of war, he issued General
Order #1. It stated that commanders of all militia units "in view of the present
dangers . . . and the probability of an immediate call . . . for troops" should
take steps to prepare their men for service. In an official proclamation, issued
on April 23, Yates announced that Illinois would render assistance to the
government "in preserving the Union, enforcing the laws, and protecting the
property and rights of the people." Within ten days of Lincoln's proclamation,
over ten thousand men, more than twice as many as needed, responded to the
call, and a force had been sent to the most strategic point in the state, Cairo.

The response was overwhelming. In a special session of Congress on the
Fourth of July 1861, Lincoln declared, "The call was made; and the response
. . . was most gratifying; surpassing . . . the most sanguine expectation."
Harper's Weekly reported that "[n]o one who has seen the recent manifestations of the popular sentiment of the North can doubt that the Northern
blood is up, and that they will listen no more to talk of compromise, truce,
or treaty, until they are fairly beaten." Indeed, three months after the firing
on Fort Sumter, Governor Yates remained besieged by hordes of men willing to do their part. Initially, many men had to be turned away. Thomas S.
Mather, Illinois adjutant general, reported that "among the most touching
and painful incidents, indicating the patriotic fervor of our people at that
time, noticed in the preparation of these troops for the field, was the reject-
ing from their companies these surplus volunteers." He further noted that
"strong men, who had left their homes at an hour's notice to enter the service
of their country, wept at the disappointment of being refused admission to
their companies on muster day."

Most citizens, North and South, had figured the war to last only a few
months. The need for legions of men was considered unnecessary. Men were
left desperate to get into any company. To make matters worse, the War
Department only authorized 780 men per regiment, whereas the Illinois
militia had mustered 937 men per regiment, causing officials and officers

to thin the ranks even further. In a letter to his wife, Onley Andrus shared the frustration with the thinking process. He learned "the story that they were culling so close that a great many were being thrown out. The hopes & fears of many were worked up to fever heat in a very short space of time." Andrus was not a victim of military downsizing. Some companies resorted to drawing lots for positions, while others pulled out married men. Reports exist of men paying others up to fifty dollars for the opportunity to take their place.

Yates, by the middle of May, aware that the war was no ninety-day affair, called on each of the nine congressional districts to provide an additional regiment. The men initially culled from militia units who remained in Springfield formed the nucleus of the tenth additional regiment. Most of these men hailed from Cook, DeKalb, LaSalle, and Will counties. On August 12, 1861, Yates impressed upon the War Department the need for these men. "Additional regiments having been filled up, and the people of the State, as one man, humiliated at the disastrous defeat at Bull Run, on the 21st of July, were pressing upon me for acceptance." The war had changed and the need for men grew rapidly. By December 3, 1861, Illinois had forwarded to the War Department fifty-eight infantry regiments, plus cavalry and artillery. At this point, Yates was ordered by Washington to cease all recruiting.

Patriotism and Preservation of the Union

Preservation of the Union was the most predominant sentiment expressed by men who signed up for service. With their sense of nationalism attacked by the Southern states, communities across northern Illinois became hotbeds of patriotism and Union upon receiving news of the firing on Fort Sumter. The national standard and other patriotic banners appeared suddenly at every house and business. The flag became the symbol of patriotism and the rallying point to which men were called. From all levels of government, politicians cried for the preservation of the Union and for men to "protect the flag." In Illinois, party lines disintegrated. On April 25, 1861, prominent Illinois Democrat Stephen A. Douglas made an impassioned speech to the state legislature that helped solidify a united cause: "Now that all else has failed, there is but one course left, and that is to rally, as one man, under the flag of Washington, Jefferson, Hamilton, Madison, and Franklin." Evoking the unity of the founding fathers, Douglas cautioned his fellow Democrats so recently vanquished in the presidential election that "you will be false and unworthy of your principles if you allow political defeat to convert you into traitors to your national land. Gentlemen, it is our duty to defend our Constitution and protect our flag."

The strength of the sentiment toward Union, popularly elected government, and the flag permeates the letters of the men who answered the call to duty. "[We] at once signed our names . . . and [I] considered it my duty to help defend the flag," wrote Henry Eby to his family in Mendota in LaSalle County. Eby knew that others shared his sentiments. Among his compatriots, "Patriotism ran high . . . the government should be defended at all hazards." Silas Dexter Wesson, a farmer from Victor Township in DeKalb County, enlisted in 1861 and served the entire war. He displayed his love of country by signing his letters, "yours for the union." After enlisting, Luther Lee Hiatt from Wheaton later described his reason for joining as "defense of one of the best governments on earth." The patriotic feelings not only encouraged men to join but also entrapped them in the moment. William H. L. Wallace, a brigadier general from Ottawa in LaSalle County who was later mortally wounded at Shiloh, wrote to his wife "that the step I have taken is not only right, but [one] I could not avoid. The country demands the services of her citizens in the field." Some men were more romantic in their sentiments for love of country. Throughout the war, Albert O. Marshall from Mokena in Will County kept a journal. In an early entry he states, "If I have not my loved country to live in, I have nothing to live for. If this is to be its end, let it also be mine."

In many cases the feeling of love of country grew substantially as time went on. Despite the hardships of camp life coupled with the death and destruction witnessed by the men throughout the war, men drew a close and personal bond with the thought of Union. Men who had once thought of the old Union that they inherited from their forefathers began to describe themselves as defenders of their country they were destined to hand off to their children. Early in his service, George W. Pepoon wrote home, "Life to me is sweet, but I fear not death in the service of his country. And [if] I should fall I feel certain that my children and friends will tell with pride, to coming generations that I died in the defense of the best Government the sun ever shone upon."

The feelings of patriotism were fed by means other than patriotic and political speeches. Sermons, poetry, and music played significant roles in motivating men to action. Sermons were powerfully effective tools of persuasion. The direction to which sermons were focused can be extracted from their titles. "The Madness of the Southern Rebellion and the Duty of the Patriot" and "The Nation's Peril and the Citizen's Duty" are examples of sermons given in April 1861 that were designed to influence men's decisions. On April 18, 1861, Dr. Nahum E. Ballou addressed the members of the Methodist church in Sandwich with a stirring speech on patriotism and duty. His extraordinary oration was published in that week's edition of the *Sandwich Gazette* so that the entire community could be roused by his orders to "Strike for your country, God, and your native land!" His sermon inspired Daniel Ballou, his younger brother, to join the Union cause.

Clergymen had great influence over prospective volunteers. The religious beliefs and convictions instilled in the men by their religious leaders were displayed in their correspondence. Francis Bowman from St. Charles in Kane County wrote to his wife, "The future is in the hands of the Great Giver of all good, and let his will be done." Bowman was initially so motivated that he sold his half of a prosperous hardware business and moved his wife and two children in with relatives to accept the captaincy of the St. Charles Light Guard he had helped organize in 1854. Silas Wesson recalled that he and his fellow enlistees had sworn to serve the government by exclaiming "SO HELP YOU GOD!" and George Pepoon clearly summarized the marriage of God and country in a letter to a friend, "I religiously believe in . . . our cause."

Speeches and sermons were supported by music and poetry to surround men with a constant barrage of patriotic appeals. Numerous examples exist of town hall meetings breaking out into patriotic songs or the delivery of a poem between honored speakers. On April 21, 1861, Orville Hickman Browning, who was appointed by Governor Yates to fill the U.S. Senate seat left open by the death of Stephen Douglas, noted in his diary that at a meeting "the 'Star Spangled Banner' was sung [with] five or six thousand joining the Chorus." "The Star Spangled Banner" was not the only patriotic song on the lips of rural Illinoisans at the time. In 1862 George F. Root wrote the song "The Battle Cry of Freedom," which asked the boys to "rally round the flag." On April 30, 1861, famed poet Bayard Taylor penned a poem, "To the American People" that also combined God and country. The poem found its way into publications across the Northern states:

> *Throughout the land there goes a cry;*
> *A sudden splendor fills the sky;*
> *From every hill the banner burst,*
> *Like buds by April breezes nurst;*

In every hamlet, home and mart,
The firebeat of a single heart
Keeps time to strains whose pulses mix
Our blood with that of Seventy-Six!

The shot whereby the old flag fell
From Sumter's battered citadel,
Struck down the lines of party creed,
And made ye One in soul and deed,—
One mighty people, stern and strong,
To crush the consummated wrong;
Indignant with the wrath whose rod
Smites as the awful sword of God!

Songs and poems, like political speeches, immersed local men in an atmosphere of patriotic action.

Slavery Opposed

"They bring with them their unconquered prejudices in favor of freedom," the May 1861 issue of *Atlantic Magazine* described the people of Illinois. Illinois was a free state and most people in the northern counties felt slavery was evil and wicked. The antipathy felt toward the plantation South had brewed for decades in the North. Since the constitutional debates, the South had virtually held white and black men hostage to further their desire to maintain peculiar Southern social and economic values. Consequently, the outbreak of hostilities seemed to the people of the North a call for universal freedom. Most memoirs and regimental histories written after the war proudly expounded on the cause of Union and fighting for the freedom of the slaves. But, by and large, contemporary accounts of 1861 ignored the defense of black liberty as a reason for war or enlistment. Instead, rural northern Illinois men focused on the oppression that the South had forced onto the country.

The most overt linkage between volunteering and freeing slaves came from religious leaders of academic institutions. Jonathan Blanchard of Wheaton College wrote to his wife after Fort Sumter indicating "slavery over this country would be a worse calamity than Civil War." His students, who published the *Beltionian Review,* had long been incensed at the peculiar institution and declared they would "be zealous advocate[s] of all reforms both Social, Religious, and Political." The students defended their ideology with action. In the book of graduating seniors at Wheaton College for the year of 1861, President Blanchard entered, "Commencement not held. The College sent 67 young men into the U.S. Army." One of those students, George F. Cram noted in his diary, "Let America set this example before the world and the time will soon come when freedom to all men of every race and color shall be universal, the long oppressed will find rest to their weary souls."

Conversely, during the autumn of 1862, Onley Andrus from Nunda in McHenry County wrote home to his wife, "I certainly hope that they . . . keep the Niggers where they belong. Which is in Slavery & the more I see of them the more I think so." Despite his attitudes toward slaves and their emancipation on January 1, 1863, Andrus continued to fight hard. For his action at Vicksburg in July 1863, Andrus was promoted.

For men in northern Illinois, freedom for blacks may not have been a direct draw to fight, but neither was it a major hindrance. George Pepoon was representative of men from northern Illinois who, as their service took them farther south, came face to face with slavery. Reviewing his letters over the course of the war, a transition occurred in his justification for volunteering. The development of his views on slavery and the war are unmistakable. His initial letters were full of patriotism. Gradually, he began to supplement his letters with his belief that "slavery should fall." Toward the end of his service, his words are much more direct and bold. He came to consider the South "a land cursed and blighted by that hideous Demon Slavery. It is the Pandora box whence all our troubles come. Thank God its days are numbered." Patriotic fervor, a sentiment sufficient to rouse men to enlist, was replaced by the reality of the war's importance, a decisive understanding that sustained men's motivation to serve and fight.

Personal Motivations to Enlist

While patriotic fervor and concerns about slavery moved men from northern Illinois to enlist, they also enlisted for intensely personal reasons. Masculinity, reputation, and personal affections moved men to volunteer. Proving one's masculinity forms a pivotal moment in a young man's life. Maintaining his right to be called a man determines how others judge him. Therefore, whether a rural, northern Illinoisan considered a neighbor, family member, or a female companion, the desire to be thought of as a man was very personal. The fear of being labeled a coward within a man's community had graver consequences than death. Just prior to the invasion at Fort Henry in February 1862, Luther Cowan noted in his diary that his men from Warren in Jo Daviess County were concerned about showing themselves as men. He revealed his concern about reputation above all other qualities when he prayed, "I believe the boys are all ready to go in. God grant that we shall show ourselves men." Francis Bowman wrote to his contemplated resigning in early March 1862. A few days later, fearing the shame resignation would bring to the family, he rapidly sent another letter warning his wife not to share with anyone about his thought of resigning. In early April 1862, Bowman valiantly held his ground during the Battle of Shiloh and survived the engagement. Twelve days later, after proving that he was no coward, Bowman resigned his commission. Almost a month later, during his return trip home, he still worried about how his wife viewed him: "Wouldn't you advise me to return to the Army?" Bowman never returned to the Army. He had joined and stayed long enough to avoid the label "coward."

Many men wrote home chastising those who did not display Bowman's bravery. "All such who shout union and loyalty but take very good care to keep out of the way of the Rebels . . . are to [too] Cowardly to come down here and fight," John Norton from Galena wrote to his mother. Men noted that they wished only to join leaders who cried "come boys" from in front of their troops and who thereby demonstrated the manly characteristics of leadership and bravery on the battlefield. The men came to despise those who sat at home and pushed from relative safety to "go boys." A. Levi Wells from Kaneville in Kane County named some of the cowards: "But I am sorry to say that there are some in your midst whose patriotism don't amount to much. Such men as W L Perry, P Flanders, D Nard, and others." Robert Hale Strong shared similar sentiments, "I remember the public meetings . . . how G.F. and his father blew the fife and beat the drum and exhorted the men to rally 'round the flag.' I remember, too, how G.F. and his father did not do any 'rallying' themselves." The bitterness that volunteers felt toward these men became public. Commenting on which class of men he wished to be associated with, Luther Lee Hiatt said, "The boys that are now at home they are called cowards and everything else of the kind. I don't think I should like to go by that name."

To compound the issue, once the word circulated that the government might institute a draft, other men decided to join to avoid the stigma of becoming a draftee. Little delineation was made between a draftee and a coward. Only around 1.5 percent of the men from Illinois who served were drafted. William Coultrip, a farmer from Somonauk in DeKalb County, was reassigned to the 10th Illinois in 1864 after three years with his beloved 36th Illinois Infantry. He was reassigned at the same time that several dozen men were drafted into the 10th. Because of the unit's association with draftees, his family later reported that Coultrip never recognized or talked about his time in the 10th. Additionally, some communities appealed to men to volunteer to avoid becoming drafted, in an effort to show a rival town which community had more loyalty and true, brave men.

Over 25 percent of the men in the northern part of Illinois were foreign born, and of all in the region, foreign-born men perhaps felt the most need to prove to the members of their community that they were loyal Americans worthy of citizenship. William Coultrip became a naturalized citizen in 1860 and felt it was his duty to prove himself worthy of that title. The distinct ethnic groups recruited amongst their own to fill the ranks, such as the Turner Society in Ottawa, which busied itself with "getting their comrades to enlist." The men of foreign birth went on to show their patriotism and loyalty by enlisting in droves. Years later, a captain from Princeton in LaSalle County delivered a speech describing their commitment: "There resided in Illinois . . . men of alien birth. These men were Unionists." He added, "The foreign born citizens of Illinois . . . were as ready to share the perils of the moment as were their native-born neighbors."

Enlisting to serve one's country also served as a way to promote or maintain independent manhood within one's family. Hundreds of young men were off to engage in the first real adventure of their lives. Their families knew that holding them back would undermine their chance to prove themselves. At first, Robert Hale Strong's father held him back. But his son was concerned that the war would be over before he could enlist, and he feared he would not "get a chance to win any glory." Once released to serve, he wrote, "I walked straightway to Naperville and wrote my name as big as any man—I was going on nineteen—on the page among the other hero[e]s." Edward E. Ayers from rural McHenry County, who had just prior to the outbreak of hostilities left his parents' store to find glory in the west, was concerned about his future status in his community upon his return, as well as with his parents' opinions of him: "It was my duty to participate in the fullest extent, and another very important reason was that it would be difficult for me to maintain my self-respect in all the years after the war if

I did not participate." Even more, Ayers feared that "I wouldn't dare to go home and face my Father and Mother if I had neglected the first opportunity of giving the Government my services."

War has always offered successful soldiers who survive an opportunity to further themselves within their society. Ayers was astute enough to see this, as were others. William Wallace, a successful lawyer in Ottawa whose political star was on the rise, knew well the implications and possibilities that the war presented. Wallace explained to his wife, "[H]aving the opportunity of going into the service for the war, we would justly and doubtless receive censure of all loyal people should we decline." Like most men of vision, he defined his character by adding that "the impulses of patriotism and the desire for distinction in the war—the two great incentives to a soldier's calling." Luther Cowan presented his devotion to his manhood directly to his wife: "[I]f we see battle, you will never be ashamed of the way I behave in it." In March 1862, shortly after he survived the battles of Fort Henry and Fort Donelson, he told his wife, "I would rather die and lie unburied here in the woods or ditches than for the report ever to go home that I was a coward or afraid to die for need be in defence of my country." Men also saw the war as a chance to redeem themselves in the eyes of their families. Having failed to live up to the expectations of his family prior to the war, Onley Andrus felt the pressure to make something of his life. "You know I have been accused of being unsteady," he wrote his wife, "and by those pretty near related to me too. Well as it is I am making money and with it we can begin to live."

As Andrus hinted, money was a motivator to enlist. Private soldiers were paid thirteen dollars a month, but the wage could be just the tip of the iceberg. Sign-up bonuses, bounties, and family support funds were distributed to volunteers. For some of the volunteers, especially the young men just leaving home, the monthly salary was in and of itself an enticement. Bounty money, which could be paid in a lump sum or broken down over a few months to insure the men stayed with their company, was an extremely attractive bonus. Usually a percentage was paid upon enlistment and the remainder sometime after, depending on the entity that offered the bounty. Counties, townships, and communities all produced a separate bounty, and a young enlistee could receive numerous payouts as they helped local governments meet enlistment quotas set by the governor. Governments in the northernmost counties in Illinois contributed over $13.7 million in bounty money during the Civil War, which accounted for over 37 percent of the entire amount of bounty money raised in the state.

For some men their motivation for joining was less influenced by civic duty or masculinity and more by money. With a steady income, men saw the opportunity to provide a better life for their family; other family men felt the obligation to provide for the present as well as for the future. Luther Cowan informed his family of better days to come: "I had also resolved to change the course of my life in a measure; I am now as far as possible, after my duty to my family looking out for number one, trying to make money." He added that his wife should not worry about the future, as he had the foresight to purchase a life insurance policy.

The Support of Women

The desire to appeal to female companions and friends was as strong a personal motivator for men to enlist as money. The participation and influence of women on men's decisions was both direct and indirect. Young women's presence at recruiting drives was deliberate and beneficial to achieve enlistment quotas. A chorus of young ladies singing songs with refrains like "I Am Bound to Be a Soldier's Wife or Die an Old Maid" could propel young men to fight for the chance to sign the muster rolls. Newspapers encouraged female participation and promoted preferential treatment for volunteers, and editors instructed women to give their all to the men. "Whether father, husband, or brother, be ready and willing," the *Sandwich Gazette* pronounced.

Women gathered in hundreds of communities to provide aid for the men. "There was a meeting of the ladies called upon to prepare clothing for the soldiers. I hear the hall now fills with ladies and ten sewing machines," one woman proudly informed her brother. Recruiting officials were aware that a uniform issued by the army would not have the same effect as one presented by the ladies of the men's hometown. With the double distinction of a patriotic uniform made and presented by a local sweetheart, they hoped men would be enticed to enlist. The impact that the uniforms had on the men was electrifying: "[T]he men were universally . . . proud at the change from jeans and satinets to the garb of soldiers of the United States of America."

In lavish presentation ceremonies, women also made and presented military companies with national and regimental colors. The pride felt by the men at these ceremonies was almost universally recounted in memoirs and journals. Flags bearing embroidered mottos such as, "Retaliation—no mercy to traitors!" displayed the resolve the women felt for the cause. In an address by Miss Ellen Fisher, she announced to a crowd of young men, "Beloved soldiers:

We present you this banner. It is the flag of our native land. It represents our dearest hopes for country, home and life. Our hands have made it, yours must defend it; and if needed for that purpose, the choicest blood in your veins, we doubt not, will be freely poured out." She continued, "Our best wishes attend you. Our prayers will follow you; and if you fall in your country's cause, we promise that your names shall be often spoken with tender pride, so long as we shall live. See to it that this flag is never insulted with impunity."

After local townswomen presented colors in Galena, rounds of cheers answered Colonel John Eugene Smith when he responded that his command "promised that they should never trail [the flag] in the dust or be tainted with dishonor." The women then prepared large feasts for the men once they were formed into companies. Wilson E. Chapel from Malta in DeKalb County noted in his journal, "Our company 'F' had, that day, been recipients of a grand dinner by the patriotic ladies . . . for which they received our heart felt thanks." Such attention to the volunteer's welfare not only helped maintain morale of the new enlistees but was also witnessed by the other men in the area. The atmosphere of patriotic action completely enveloped the communities, which made avoidance of the excitement impossible, and volunteers were continually confronted on all fronts by the barrage of influence and encouragement to serve the country faithfully.

Abundant stories exist of the first wave of men leaving their hometowns to the cheers of their neighbors. Other men, who failed to join in the first wave of recruits, were awed by the power of the moment. "The show and pomp of war is fine and it is a fine thing to be stared at in wonder," Luther Cowan described his departure in 1862. Henry Eby described an all too familiar scene in the earliest days of the war: "People came flocking into town from all the surrounding country and villages, with flags flying, to see the soldiers start off for the war."

Enlistees also desired personal support from female family members. Many of the men would also come to grips with being away from these loved ones for the first time in their life. The men were mustered into companies at local camps scattered around northern Illinois, and camps transformed empty pastures or vacant fairgrounds into bustling little cities overnight. From these camps, men were shuffled to places like Camp Douglas in Chicago. In the process, they were introduced to the basics of army life and began drilling as units.

During their induction, men wrote constantly asking of news from home and from their families. They requested more letters to be sent to them. The rapidity of recruitment denied some men a chance to explain their decision or to receive a response. The initial letters from family received at these camps were the first opportunity to examine the reaction. Ann Wallace wrote to her husband William that "my knowledge of you and of our cause told me this would surely be the result. It does not surprise me." She ended her letter by showing her support: "I will try to be a true soldier's wife and bear my part in this work bravely." Mary Quaid from Polo in Ogle County wrote to show her support to her brother, Oscar Samis. She attempted to conceal her grief when consoling her brother by using words he had used to console her: "[I] feel very bad that you have to rough it so and go dirty and lousy some of the time but as you say it is all for the union." As time passed and new enlistees poured into the camps, the support and encouragement continued. "I am proud to say that the blood of my kindred has already flowed freely in this horrid war and I hope that none that belong to me will ever turn their backs on the glorious old flag," Eldridge Skinner of Sandwich learned from his aunt. She went on to remind him to "[t]hink of those dark days when Washington with his veteran soldiers with unshod and bleeding feet amid the frosts and snows of winter retreated before a victorious army, those were times 'that tried men's souls' that shook the courage of the firmest. But remember what grand results followed."

The atmosphere of patriotic action along with a myriad of personal reasons caused thousands of men from northern Illinois to set behind all they had to join the adventure of a lifetime. The momentum behind these first waves of volunteers catapulted further volunteer enlistments at home despite the human toll paid on the battlefield. As the war wore on, many men who had at first decided to sit out the hostilities gained courage from the example set by their neighbors. Personal pride, peer pressure, and money caused the latecomers to follow in the footsteps of the first few waves of patriotic fighters. And when called upon, the volunteers did fight. As an unknown soldier who began his march south late in the war wrote to his mother, "I for one am ready whenever called for to do my part."

RELATED READING

Stephen Buck, "'A contest in which blood must flow like water': DuPage County and the Civil War," *Illinois Historical Journal* vol. 87, no. 1 (Spring 1994).

16.

ILLINOIS SOLDIERS AND THE EMANCIPATION PROCLAMATION

David Wallace Adams

Journal of the Illinois State Historical Society
vol. 67, no. 4 (September 1974)

The research for this article tested the hypothesis that the 1862 Republican defeat resulted from Lincoln's announced intention to issue the Emancipation Proclamation. The author gathered data primarily from letters written by Northern soldiers. These showed great dissatisfaction with the progress of the war and the restrictions on civil liberties. Despite what the Democratic press was saying, Illinois soldiers supported emancipation, and the Republican losses in the 1862 election stemmed from restrictions in Illinois laws on voting outside one's home district.

It is axiomatic in national politics that the party in power loses support in off-year elections. Even in 1862, when the North might have been expected to support the party of the president, eight of the fourteen Illinois congressional seats went to Democrats.

Historians have interpreted the results in Illinois as proof of popular dissatisfaction with Lincoln's announcement, in September 1862, of the Emancipation Proclamation, in which he declared his intention to free all slaves in the states still in rebellion on January 1, 1863. The Democratic Party opposed the plan and argued that Illinois would become a haven for liberated slaves. Failures in the battlefield, the unpopularity of wartime measures

Illinois' Civil War governor, Richard Yates, the first graduate of Illinois College in Jacksonville, a school founded
by New England abolitionists. *Library of Congress.*

restricting civil liberties, and the disorganized state of the Republican Party
also contributed to the Democratic victory.

Throughout the congressional campaign of 1862, letters from Illinois soldiers were widely printed in Illinois newspapers. Letters published by the
Republican press reveal the soldiers' growing dissatisfaction with the progress
of the war. They believed that a harsher policy against the South—specifically,
confiscation of Confederate property and emancipation of the slaves—would
hasten the end of the war. According to Jerry C. Perry, serving at Camp
Montgomery, the war was not being fought "for the purpose of destroying or
preserving slavery, but for the preservation of the Republic." If slavery stood
in the way of that objective, Perry said, "[s]trike it down with a remorseless
hand." Another soldier claimed that the North would never "be free from
trouble" until slavery was "annihilated." An Illinois volunteer wrote from

Stevenson, Alabama, that there was "such dissatisfaction arising among our troops as will yet cause trouble, if there is not soon a different policy pursued."

A soldier in the 8th Illinois Cavalry saw the announcement of the emancipation plan as evidence of Lincoln's "thorough knowledge of the wishes of his soldiers." According to a volunteer who signed himself "B.L.E.," "The sentiment of the army is 'God bless Abraham.' Hitherto, the great trouble has been just here: the president has been governed by the sentiment of the people at home, in a great measure disregarding the sentiments, feelings, and suggestions of the army. On this question the army has been far in advance of the people."

Surgeon George Lucas of the 47th Illinois Infantry wrote that the soldiers had not become "abolitionized" but they did believe that "the freedom of the negroes is a military necessity." William Calkins claimed that Lincoln's proclamation "was hailed with delight by the whole army, and they regard it as having done more to end the war than all the battles we have fought." An underlying assumption of the argument that emancipation would, in one soldier's words, "wind this war up in a short time" was the belief that slavery was a major source of strength for the Confederacy. As one soldier explained, "Why not reach their very vitals? Strike at the root of the evil. Unless this is done we never can expect peace in the land." "Free the slaves," wrote another soldier, "and you cut the heart out of the rebellion."

In July one soldier had complained that "the negroes of Mississippi are fighting us now more to the purpose than any white man in the field; and if you don't believe it come and see the vast fields of corn they are tilling." Another letter defined the unwilling role played by slaves, who

> raise the corn and wheat and grind the same and convey it to the rebel army. The women and children are carding, spinning, weaving and coloring the butternut jeans and other clothing so universally worn in the rebel army and by the citizens of the South. The slaves are making most of the wagons used by the rebel army, and in fact [are] employed on nearly every kind of labor which support not only the Rebel army but the families of the soldiers left at home and are worked upon forts, field works and camp drudgery generally.

An unnamed major in the Illinois 23rd Infantry was reported as having said that "every able-bodied slave counts as an armed rebel." In the Union Army the soldiers did all the hard work as well as all the hard fighting, but in the Confederate Army blacks did one and whites did the other.

It was thus concluded that the blacks were "part of the effective force of the rebellion."

It is not surprising that many Union soldiers were opposed to the policy of refusing sanctuary to runaway slaves. The *Herald* of Lincoln, Illinois, reported the receipt of several letters from soldiers who complained about protecting "the property of Secessionists, and especially of being forced to protect the rebels in the enjoyment of their slaves."

Other troops did everything they could to aid contrabands. At Shelbyville, Kentucky, for instance, as the 104th Illinois was marching through town, a group of slaveholders gathered in force,

> hoping to snatch from our protection the contrabands who had taken refuge with us. Someone, anticipating some such move, had passed the word down the ranks of the 104th to march the contrabands in the ranks. The army was marching by the flank. One or two in some of the front brigades, were gobbled up and run off before anyone seemed fully awake. . . . Finally the tug came with the 104th. Men in citizens clothes grabbed a contraband marching in the rear of Co. A. Sergeant Woolley, Co. B. spoiled his musket over the head of Mr. Secesh, causing him to let go on the double run. Very queer, again the command ran down the ranks in quick strong voice, from captain to captain, "Fix Bayonets." The bayonets of the entire 104th went on the double "double quick." Never on drill had the men gone through the same operation a[t] double the time. The [fake] "Union citizens" were vanquished, and no more open attempts have been made to force men from our ranks.

Confiscation and emancipation were looked upon as moral measures by troops who had experienced at first hand the harsh character of slavery and were appalled at what they saw. Adjutant William T. Frohock of the 45th Regiment wrote home that "within 100 rods of this camp lies a slave girl chained to a floor; for five years she has been a raving maniac from the effects of blows given by her master, now in the rebel service." The *Carroll County Mirror* reported "men and women, as white as you and I, bought and sold into bondage. Masters deal in their own blood! We only heard of this, before. Now we see it, and *know* it! If that won't change politics, what will?" To the *Ottawa Republic,* William Scofield wrote that the common sight of a well-dressed slaveholder "riding up to headquarters and petitioning for the privilege of hunting through the camp for stray negroes, excites the most intense indignation and disgust in my bosom." To the *Carroll County Mirror* an unidentified soldier wrote, "You can't show me a soldier but what utters a solemn oath to knock slavery at his first opportunity. We have seen too much, and must, for humanity's sake, interfere."

Other soldiers thought that freed blacks should be used as laborers who would free Union troops from camp drudgery. Soldiers in the field were tired of seeing "their men die of hard work while plenty of men belonging to Secesh are anxious to do the work for their freedom." By the fall of 1862 many regiments were already relying heavily on confiscated slaves. The *Chicago Tribune* was informed by a Major Wallace of the Illinois Calvary that when Union forces under General Samuel R. Curtis reached Helena, Arkansas, they were accompanied by four to six thousand slaves, "marching in the rear." The slaves "proved invaluable in hunting up and bringing in food, acting as scouts and guides, and in clearing the roads of rebel barricades erected everywhere along the route. . . . The prejudice which might have existed in the army against the employment of men of color . . . [has] entirely disappeared; and . . . soldiers who were the most rantankerous [*sic*] of Democrats when they started from home have become practical Abolitionists, to whom the work of liberation is now a positive delight."

One volunteer reported the sentiments of many others when he wrote that the army was "abolition up to the hilt; [and it is] no more [a] party issue among us. . . . It is laughable to hear some of my democratic friends . . . talk among themselves, and swear 'tis hard to give up on our old principles, but we must give over." Another soldier, referring to the argument of Northern Democrats that abolition was not the goal of the war, stated that if any of his "treat-em [Confederates] kindly" friends were to "come down and stay in this army as a soldier three months, I'll bet my commission he'll . . . [go] back as a negro confiscations [*sic*]." In September a third volunteer wrote that he had come to the conclusion that the war would go on forever if slavery was not "exterminated." He claimed that his opinion was held by "all who are engaged in the rebellion" and that the convictions grew in part from the experiences of war: "We feel it and suffer the results: eking out a miserable life, contracting pulmonary diseases, deaths in our hospitals, no kindred near to hear the last words of a departing brother, the crimson blood flowing from the veins of many a noble son of the North; and for what?" A fourth volunteer recommended that civilians opposed to the president's emancipation plan should be brought into the field with the army and "compelled to carry the equipment of a soldier on a forced march of three days, and it would result in making an *abolitionist* of every man of them." A fifth volunteer, who signed himself "A Douglas Democrat," wrote on the same subject: "There are not forty men in our regiment opposed to the president's policy. You have no idea of the change salt pork, hard crackers, burnt coffee and long marches have made in the political opinions of your La Salle county soldiers. They would make an abolitionist of the most inveterate Democrat that ever lived."

The soldiers' support of emancipation did not necessarily imply acceptance of the idea of racial equality. It was not unusual for a soldier to favor emancipation and simultaneously express anti-Negro sentiments. George L. Lucas noted that it was the belief of most soldiers that after the war the former slaves should be "sent to Central America," or colonized in South Carolina, Georgia, or Florida. "Soldiers do not feel afraid but what we can find a way to dispose of the African race when the war is over," Lucas wrote. Illinois volunteer Jasper Barney, in a letter to his brother, expressed similar views. Barney favored emancipation but emphasized that he was not "in favor of freeing the negroes and leaving them to run free and mingle among us." He was also sure the president was of like opinion and that the ex-slaves would be colonized soon after the conclusion of the war.

A letter to the *Lincoln Herald* shows how soldiers could simultaneously hold anti-Negro and pro-emancipation beliefs:

> We want the slaves set free where they are, we don't want them up North to compete with us when we return. Set them all free where they are and they will remain; let them slip off as is now being done and they will be compelled to move up North. There is no danger of their moving up North if they are ALL set free WHERE THEY ARE. . . . I am more bitterly opposed to Negro emigration North now than ever.

That kind of logic could have particular appeal to Illinois soldiers because they knew that the black-exclusion laws would prohibit the freed slaves from settling in Illinois. Soldiers could thus embrace two seemingly contradictory beliefs: abolitionism and racism.

Because the emancipation question was the major issue of the 1862 congressional campaign, the Republican press went to great lengths to show that Illinois soldiers supported the administration. To counter Republican claims, the Democratic press tried to prove that Illinois soldiers were opposed to emancipation. Democratic newspapers produced far fewer letters in support of their position than did Republican newspapers.

Austin T. Rugg of the 16th Illinois Regiment wrote from Corinth, Mississippi, to the Democratic *Quincy Herald* that "if the abolitionists wish the 'nigger' free, they will have to fight for it, for the Democrats will not." Another Illinois volunteer wrote from the field that "the great mass" of the army of the Southwest were "astonished and chagrined" by the president's announcement; there was, he said, a great deal of anti-Negro sentiment in the army occasioned by the "hordes of negroes who are strutting the streets in Memphis, many of them wearing the uniform of a soldier of the United States." William H. Ross of the 40th Illinois wrote from Memphis: "The soldiers are swaring [*sic*] that they will stack their arms, desert, or go to the confederate army or anything before they will fight to free the negroes and I suppose they are all to bee [*sic*] free by the first of January."

A letter published in the *Chicago Times* indicated that the 109th Illinois was "democratic to a man, from its excellent Colonel to the shortest private in the ranks." A soldier from the "Lead Mine Regiment" claimed that even "with those that were republicans, the democratic principles have been almost unanimously adopted."

In all, fifty-eight soldier letters expressing opinions about emancipation were found. Forty-eight of those express sentiments in favor of the administration on the confiscation and emancipation measures. Of the forty-eight, nineteen claim that either the writer or the army in general had been converted while in the field to the Republican cause. The examination of soldier letters confirms that Republican assertion that the soldier vote was in support of the president and was essentially Republican.

Claims of the Republicans that they lost the 1862 election because of the soldiers' absence appear to have been genuine, and not, as Gray charged, public face-saving gestures.

David Davis wrote Lincoln in mid-October that Republicans were in danger of losing the state partly because of "the large number of Republican voters, who have gone to the war under the last call." Party worker Lewis Ellsworth wrote Governor Richard Yates that he regretted that "so many of our troops were necessarily sent out of the State before the election." Soon after the election, Governor Oliver P. Morton of Indiana wrote Yates that the results had not been surprising to him because Illinois had "70,000 voters out of the State, two thirds of whom were Republicans, and nine tenths of the remainder would have voted the Union ticket."

In assessing the reasons for the defeat of Republican candidate Leonard Swett in the Eighth District, Clifton H. Moore, a friend and supporter, wrote to William W. Orme, Swett's law partner,

I presume you were much surprised at the result of our election. Swett was beaten by about 1500. When we take the figures of 1860 they show conclusively that he had no chance at the start. In the counties composing this district, Lincoln in 1860 had only 800 majority over all opposition. Then take the fact that out of these counties there were at least 12,000 soldiers, 8,000 of whom were voters. Five thousand of these at least did and would have voted the Union ticket."

The evidence indicates that the conclusions advanced by John Moses, Oliver Dickerson, and Harry Pratt were correct. Illinois volunteers supported the Republican Party and Lincoln's Emancipation Proclamation; they demonstrated their loyalty in letters published in the Illinois press between June and November. Their absence from the polls in November was a blow to Republican candidates and denied the party a considerable source of support.

RELATED READING

Bruce S. Allardice, "'Illinois Is Rotten with Traitors!' The Republican Defeat in the 1862 State Elections," *Journal of the Illinois State Historical Society* vol. 104, nos. 1–2, Civil War Sesquicentennial Issue (Spring–Summer 2011).

17.

THE CIVIL WAR
COMES TO "EGYPT"

Jasper W. Cross

Journal of the Illinois State Historical Society
vol. 44, no. 2 (Summer 1951)

On the eve of the Civil War, southern Illinois, or "Egypt," shared considerable family, commercial, political, and racial attitudes with the secessionist Southern states. The author asserts that the Northern press exaggerated the extent of opposition to the war and the extent of sympathy for the Southern cause, thus giving a misleading impression of the true state of public opinion in southern Illinois as it shifted to support the Union cause. He presents evidence that the level of volunteering for the Union army was as strong in the southern part of the state as elsewhere.

Just as southern Illinois in modern days prides herself on being unlike the remainder of the state, so in the era of the Civil War was she different. Possessed of a personal heritage which was at variance with upstate Illinois, located in a geographic situation unlike that of her northern neighbors, with a political and social background which was a contrast to central and northern Illinois, her reaction to the coming of the war might be expected to be significantly different from the reaction of Illinois as a whole.

The inverted triangle which is "Egypt" rests with its peak at Cairo and its base running from Chester to Carmi. Included in this area in 1860 were sixteen counties, predominantly rural, populated by Southerners by birth or extraction, and overwhelmingly Democratic in their political sentiments.

General John A. Logan, with his wife, Mary, and two of their children, Manning Alexander Logan and Mary Elizabeth "Dollie" Logan. Logan is credited with helping dissuade Southern sympathizers in "Egypt" from supporting the Confederacy during the early days of the Civil War. Once a staunch Democrat, he became a loyal Lincoln Republican and a U.S. senator from Illinois, and once ran for president. *Library of Congress.*

Although slavery could not exist legally in Illinois, evidence indicates that the institution existed openly or secretly in southern Illinois for much of the first half of the nineteenth century. Certainly, it had the approval of many southern Illinoisans, as shown by the efforts of representatives of the region to legalize slavery, their activity in enacting the Black Code of 1818, and the unsuccessful attempt in 1823–24 to secure the calling of a constitutional convention to legitimize slavery.

The Southern background and the pro-slavery sentiments of the area combined to make Egypt a political stronghold of the Democratic Party. It was under the influence of Stephen A. Douglas, leader of Illinois Democracy, and Egypt supported the "Little Giant" faithfully for the Democratic nomination at the 1856 and 1860 conventions, and returned him a plurality over his three opponents in every county save one in the 1860 election. Similarly, in congressional elections, southern Illinois' Ninth (and later Thirteenth) District placed its faith in Democrats, electing, in 1858, John A. Logan, and in 1860 reelecting him by an overwhelming majority. County and local offices followed this general pattern as Douglas and Logan led the Democrats of Egypt through the late 1850s.

Economically, southern Illinois faced two ways. By virtue of its position between the Ohio and Mississippi Rivers, its commerce was with both North and South. Cairo was still an important waystation for water-borne traffic, although railroad building was draining away much of its early prestige. Trade, however, still flowed both ways through Egypt, and the economic loyalties of the population were divided.

With this brief background, it is not difficult to foresee the reaction of southern Illinois to the outbreak of the war. With hostilities imminent, meetings, which were held in several towns, produced resolutions highly critical of the anticipated Lincoln policy toward the South, declaring the South to be the aggrieved party, opposing the expected use of troops against the South, and declaring it to be the duty of Egypt to leave the Union if such actions were taken. Whether these resolutions were drawn up by the Democrats to embarrass the Republican administrations of Lincoln and Illinois governor Richard Yates, drafted with a hope of keeping Illinois influenced toward neutrality in the coming conflict, or whether they represented a strongly pro-Southern sentiment in southern Illinois cannot be determined, and a case for each of the three views can be developed.

The authorship of these highly critical resolutions has never been fixed. Probably most of them were joint efforts by assembled Democratic leaders. In one case, however, the Williamson County resolutions emanating from Marion, an attempt has been made to place credit with William Joshua "Josh" Allen, a former law partner of John A. Logan, later to succeed him in the House of Representatives (1861–65) and to become one of the small but vociferous "Copperhead" group. No proof exists of Allen's responsibility, although he would undoubtedly have subscribed to the sentiments therein.

Along with these more or less formal expressions of sentiment in Egypt were many informal indications of lack of sympathy with the administration and with the war. Newspapers expressed their sympathy with the rebels and their joy over the fall of Fort Sumter, United States flags were torn down, Jefferson Davis was cheered and Abraham Lincoln reviled, and many other petty incidents were recorded by the press. These events, while they undoubtedly occurred, were possibly only isolated acts of irresponsible individuals. Certainly, they were magnified by the Republican press, notably the *Chicago Tribune*, which never failed to point out evidences of "Democratic disloyalty" in southern Illinois.

As supporting evidence of the indications of disloyalty mentioned, one might adduce the letters of "loyal" people in southern Illinois to their Northern correspondents. The letter files of such pro-Union leaders as Governor Yates and Senator Lyman Trumbull contain correspondence from southern Illinoisans eager to point out their own loyalty and denounce the disloyalty of many of their fellows. However, the political angle must again be noted. Most correspondents of Yates and Trumbull might logically be Republicans, who would not be averse to boosting their own qualifications at the expense of their Democratic neighbors.

Also of interest is the position of the figure most notably identified with Egyptian politics—Congressman (later General) John Alexander Logan. Logan's later career as a Civil War leader, as a Radical Republican, and as a vice-presidential candidate is well known. Less popularized has been his pre–Civil War activity as a staunch Douglas Democrat and opponent of Lincoln policies. No small part of the "mystery" of Logan's maneuvering in late 1860 and early 1861 has been due to the unavailability and probable censoring of the Logan papers.

Through February 1861 there is no confusion in Logan's thought. A thoroughgoing Democrat, he condemned all of the Republican doctrines and candidates and clung to the extreme Southern view that slavery could be carried into all the territories of the United States. Lincoln he regarded as "a strictly sectional candidate," and he feared "the happiness and prosperity [of the country] . . . is about to be buried in the infamous grave dug by the hand of the sectional fanaticism." This same note runs through a Logan speech in Congress on February 5, 1861, but with the blame for the existing strained situation divided between abolition extremists and radical extremists from the South, to whom he denied explicitly the right of secession. However, he decried the use of any force against the South and felt compromise efforts had not yet been exhausted. The line of this speech is quite similar to that of the Peace Democrats of later years.

This was Logan's only speech between the election and the opening of the war, and no personal record remains to show his thoughts in that period. One bit of information on Logan's position may be found in a letter of Charles H. Lanphier, editor of the *Illinois State Register* of Springfield, virtually the official Democratic newspaper of downstate Illinois. Lanphier declared Logan's attitude was well known and so dangerous to Illinois' support of the war that he (Lanphier) urged Senator Douglas to come to Springfield where Logan was attempting to influence the special session of the legislature against war support. Douglas, who had declared his support of the administration and of the war, managed to swing Democracy to his position despite accusations by Logan of "selling out" the party. After his failure at Springfield, Logan returned to Egypt, said Lanphier, and endeavored unsuccessfully to prevent the organization of a regiment in that area. Only after he found the current swinging against him did he reverse his course to go with the tide becoming an administration man, raise a regiment, and denounce his former associates.

Unfortunately Lanphier's letter must be discounted somewhat. While no date appears on it, internal evidence shows it to have been written after the war and at a time when Logan was up for reelection to the U.S. Senate, probably 1877. Since Logan was, by then, bitterly anti-Democratic in his sentiments, it seems possible that Lanphier may have been moved by a desire to discredit Logan. Logan himself declared he had been in "substantial accord" with Douglas and the administration from the first. However, since this declaration did not come until 1886, after Logan had been a Republican for twenty-five years, it, too, may be discounted.

By early summer Logan's mind was made up, and on June 18, 1861, he wrote the *Illinois State Register*, denying any implication in a southern Illinois secessionist movement. The following day came his passionate defense of the Union before Ulysses S. Grant's troops at Camp Yates, Springfield. Grant declared his reluctance to let Logan speak to men whose formal muster into service was not yet accomplished, fearing, from Logan's reputation, he might influence them not to accept service. However, said Grant, Logan's speech "breathed a loyalty and devotion to the Union."

Shortly following this, Logan resigned from Congress and returned to southern Illinois to raise a regiment for the Union cause and begin his rise to military renown.

One more of the disloyalty episodes in southern Illinois history was to involve Congressman Logan before his entrance into the administration fold. This occurrence is the only well-agreed-upon instance of an organized group leaving Egypt to fight for the Confederacy. While minor details are subject to some disagreement, accounts concur that a group of at least thirty men was recruited by one Thorndike Brooks in Williamson County. After a rendezvous south of Marion, they proceeded on foot toward Paducah, crossed the Ohio River at Mayfield, Kentucky, and joined Company G of the 115th Tennessee Volunteers.

While agreement is general that Brooks was the organizer of the company, a variance exists as to the persons responsible for stirring up feeling for such an organization. Commonly listed were political leaders A. P. Corder, John M. Cunningham, James D. Pully, W. J. Allen, and Logan.

Logan denied explicitly any part in the formation or inspiration of the company and declared he had never encouraged any to "go South." Two members of the company also later denied that Logan had any part in encouraging them or anyone else to join the company. However, the value of these corroborations must be slightly minimized since they first appeared in print in a Logan campaign biography and since one of the defenders, Hilbert B. Cunningham, was Logan's brother-in-law. However, it is possible Logan's denial is valid, since Milo Erwin's *The History of Williamson County*, usually reliable, specifically exempts both Logan and Allen from any activity in promoting the Brooks company.

Still another charge laid frequently at the door of southern Illinois was that of being overrun with the allegedly seditious Knights of the Golden Circle. This secret organization, about which little of an exact nature is known, was said to be highly active in the downstate counties. While no thorough "exposé" appeared until the *Chicago Tribune*'s lengthy attack of August 26, 1862, shorter items had reported individual cases of membership and organized councils in Union, Williamson, Franklin, Hamilton, and other counties and a possible downstate membership of ten thousand. These groups opposed the war and were presumably in communication with and gave aid to the Confederacy. Again, a note of caution in accepting these reports must be interjected. The descriptions of the K.G.C. activity came only in the Republication press and the correspondence of Republican leaders, hence the possibility of political motivation must again be considered.

From these "evidences" of disloyalty, which were magnified by the Republican press and politicians of northern Illinois into a general condition rampant throughout the lower end of the state, let us now look at the other side of the ledger. From what has gone before, one might expect to find no loyal activity in Egypt. This expectation would be far from accurate. Only one look at the most important aspect of wartime loyalty is necessary.

Participation by southern Illinoisans in the armed services was, at the outset of the war, excellent. The initial response to the creation by the Illinois legislature on May 2, 1861, of ten infantry regiments was highly creditable. On May 16 the 18th Illinois Volunteer Infantry rendezvoused at Anna and was mobilized May 28 under command of Colonel Michael K. Lawler, a vigorous Irishman with some Mexican War experience. The customary method of recruiting was used, that of individuals gathering volunteers to about the number of one hundred and offering this company to the regimental commander, usually reserving the captaincies for themselves. The eight companies of the 18th were nearly all from Egypt, while two companies of the 9th, one of the 10th, and two of the 22nd were nearly all Egyptians. This early and enthusiastic response to the call for troops surprised and delighted the northern Illinois press.

In May, June, and July 1861, Secretary of War Cameron authorized additional regiments to be raised in Illinois, but only five companies were made up largely of southern Illinoisans, since no commanders were from the area. After Bull Run, however, Cameron approved additional troops from Illinois, and two more infantry regiments—the 29th, under Colonel James S. Reardon, and the 31st, under Colonel John A. Logan—and one cavalry regiment, the 6th, under Colonel Thomas H. Cavanaugh, were raised almost entirely from Egypt. As usual, companies in other regiments came from southern Illinois. Two more regiments—the 56th (Colonel Robert Kirkham) and the 60th (Colonel Silas C. Toler)—were raised in southern Illinois in the fall of 1861, and the year of 1862 saw additions to this list of regiments.

All of this, however, is mere statistical data unless it is related to other information. On August 23, 1862, the adjutant general of Illinois ordered an enrollment made of all males between the ages of eighteen and forty-five. In southern Illinois, a total of 30,346 men were in this age group. Of these, nearly 40 percent, 12,206, were already in service in the Union Army. Hamilton County, where disloyalty had been prevalent according to the rumors of the day, led the state in this percentage with 48.3. Franklin County, with 46.6 percent, ranked fourth in the state, and Williamson County, already mentioned repeatedly and unfavorably by Northern critics, had 46.1 percent of her enrolled men already in uniform. Clearly, southern Illinois furnished her quota and more in the first twenty months of the war.

When one compares this record with that of the state as a whole, it is seen that Egypt had done easily more than her share thus far. In the remainder of the state, 102,917 men, or approximately 28 percent of the age group mentioned, had entered service. It should be noted, too, that these men were volunteers, presumably entering armed service willingly and out of patriotic motives, which had not generally been attributed to southern Illinois.

This response of southern Illinois to the actual need that was most important—men for the army—is the best yardstick for measuring her patriotism. It was the volunteer soldier who fought the Civil War and it was he who risked most for the Union. To be sure, if he were from Egypt, he had not elected the Republican administration of Abraham Lincoln which directed the war, he had not approved its theories or its policies as he understood them, he had not wanted to invade the South where his antecedents lay. Yet, once he became convinced the war was to save the Union—and the conviction must have come rather rapidly—his reaction was prompt and overwhelming. When the real struggle came, Egypt's lack of verbal enthusiasm for the war was exceeded by her military enthusiasm.

What, then, was southern Illinois' position on the war? Since most of her population was Southern in origin, it naturally was not interested in a crusade to exterminate slavery or in an apparently offensive war against the South. With her economic interests divided North and South, pocketbooks would logically dictate a desire to remain in commercial contact with both areas. Had she desired to disrupt Illinois and join the Confederacy, she would undoubtedly have faced great difficulty and been coerced into line. Equally certain, however, she could have caused the Union no little difficulty. An area, overwhelmingly and actively Confederate, situated astride the Illinois Central Railroad and controlling the Ohio–Mississippi Rivers junction area, would have required a large force to occupy it and a tremendous police garrison to keep it from harassing the Union rear in the river campaigns. Further, southern Illinois was not remote from areas sympathetic to the Southern cause. A unified pro-Confederate southern Illinois, southeast Missouri, and western Kentucky was not impossible to conceive.

Why, in view of the evidence offered, was southern Illinois loyal? Actually, as has been suggested, much of the "evidence" is invalid. Partisan politics, personal ambitions and jealousies, unfounded rumors all had their part in building up the "disloyal Egypt" myth. To the Union she had been and was loyal. Deploring efforts North and South, abolitionist and "fire-eater," to break the Union, she finally came to the conclusion that the Confederacy constituted a real threat to the Union and steered her course accordingly. A minority of individuals continued to be Confederate in their sympathies, and activities and criticism of individual governmental policies flourished throughout the war, but Egypt as a whole had decided to help preserve the Union.

PART IV

CHICAGO AND BEYOND IN THE LATE NINETEENTH CENTURY

18.

DID THE COW DO IT?
A New Look at the Cause of the Great Chicago Fire

Richard F. Bales

Illinois Historical Journal vol. 90, no. 1 (Spring 1997)

Mrs. O'Leary and her cow remain in the public mind as the cause of the Great Chicago Fire on October 8, 1871. Richard Bales has conducted an extensive search of available materials, including a transcript of testimony presented to a police and fire commission. Detailed evidence suggests that a neighbor, "Peg Leg" Sullivan, may have in fact been responsible rather than Mrs. O'Leary. Had firefighters not been delayed in getting to the scene, it might have been just another fire that could have been put out.

At about 8:45 P.M. on the evening of Sunday, October 8, 1871, fire broke out in the barn of Patrick and Catherine O'Leary. The fire spread quickly, and while it ironically spared the O'Leary house, located on Chicago's West Side at 137 De Koven Street, much of the rest of the city was not fortunate. Before dying out in the early morning of Tuesday, October 10, the fire had cut a swath through Chicago approximately three and one-third square miles in size. Property valued at $192 million was destroyed, one hundred thousand people were left homeless, and three hundred people lost their lives.

Even as the fire raged, Mrs. O'Leary and her cow were being blamed for causing the fire that destroyed the heart of Chicago. That theory appears to have had its origin in an October 9 extra of the *Chicago Evening Journal*:

View looking north on Clark Street from Cook County Courthouse and City Hall after the Great Chicago Fire, which destroyed the city on October 8, 1871. *Photo courtesy Chicago History Museum.*

"The fire broke out on the corner of De Koven and Twelfth streets, at about 9 o'clock on Sunday evening being caused by a cow kicking over a lamp in a stable in which a woman was milking."

Mrs. O'Leary steadfastly denied causing the fire. Both she and her husband maintained that they were in bed at the time that the fire broke out. That was confirmed by a neighbor, Daniel Sullivan, who stated, "I stood by Leary's house and they were in bed. A man by the name of Regan came along. I was hollering and shoving in the door when Leary came out. He had nothing on but his pants and his shirt, and this is the way he done. He put up his hands and scratched his head same's he had a foot of lice in it. He went in and called his wife and she came out and just clapped her hands together."

Nonetheless, the story of the cow and the lantern spread with the same intensity as the fire. The embers had barely cooled before publishing houses began churning out a storm of books and pamphlets about the fire. Those works helped to insure the immortality of Mrs. O'Leary. For example,

Alfred L. Sewell's *"The Great Calamity!"*—the first post-fire history—merely repeated the story of the cow: "At 9 o'clock on Sunday evening, October 8th, the fire-alarm was sounded for the De Koven-street, in the West Subdivision, near the scene of the previous night's fire, filled with shanties. There, as is alleged, an Irish woman had been milking a cow in a small stable, having a kerosene lamp standing on the straw at her side. The cow kicked over the lamp, which exploded and set fire to the straw, and speedily the stable was on fire." Other authors, however, greatly embellished the original *Evening Journal* account. Elias Colbert and Everett Chamberlin, for example, solemnly affirmed that "the great fire of the 9th October is attributed by the Fire Department of the city to the upsetting of a kerosene-lamp in a barn."

The fire department, however, made no such determination. From November 23 through December 4, the Board of Police and Fire Commissioners held an inquiry, the purpose of which was to determine, among other things, the cause of the fire. Despite interviewing fifty people, including the O'Learys and Daniel Sullivan, the board failed to ascertain the fire's cause: "Whether it originated from a spark blown from a chimney on that windy night, or was set on fire by human agency, we are unable to determine."

Were Mrs. O'Leary and her cow the cause of the fire, or is that merely an enduring fragment of nineteenth-century Chicago folklore? While not conclusive, an analysis of the original transcripts of the inquiry, 1871 Chicago real estate records, and other period source materials provide powerful evidence for a more plausible theory as to the fire's cause.

Of all the fire histories, Harry Albert Musham's monograph "The Great Chicago Fire, October 8–10, 1871" (1941) is probably the most exhaustive in its conclusion that Mrs. O'Leary was responsible for the blaze: "When all the evidence in the case is fairly considered, there can be but one conclusion and that is: That the Great Chicago Fire of October 8–9, 1871 was started in the barn of Mr. and Mrs. Patrick O'Leary, 137 De Koven Street, by one of their cows kicking over a lighted kerosene lamp between 8:30 and 9:00 P.M. on Sunday, October 8; that it was brought about by an accident; and that Mrs. O'Leary was in the barn at the time." Musham supports his statement by claiming that shortly after the fire started, Mrs. O'Leary admitted starting it. Unfortunately, Musham, in his otherwise excellent treatise, relies completely on hearsay in order to reach that conclusion. Mrs. O'Leary's alleged confession is in direct contradiction to her later testimony at the inquiry hearings, during which she claimed no involvement in the fire's cause. Musham blithely brushes off her denials. In graphic detail he writes of how she must have noticed "the ever-widening wave of fire rolling relentlessly over the city" from her unburned cottage on Sunday night. He similarly describes her likely view the following morning as "the vast clouds of smoke that marked the destruction of the business district and the North side." Finally, he paints a picture of what she must have seen on Monday evening, "the flames still burning along Lincoln Park, about four miles from her home." Musham asserts that the O'Learys, fearing retribution for having caused those horrors, "closed up like clams" when questioned about it.

As proof of Mrs. O'Leary's involvement, Musham offers up the story noted above that on the morning of October 9, while Chicago still burned, she admitted causing the fire. Using Musham's own reasoning—that fearing punishment, she later stated at the hearings that she was not responsible—the story seems apocryphal. By October 9 she would have realized the enormity of the fire. If she were predisposed to lie about causing it, she would have done so, even at that time. She would not have waited until November 24, the day of her testimony.

Musham's conclusions may be further flawed because he fails to consider that under ordinary circumstances the fire would have been extinguished easily at its inception. There were twenty-eight significant fires in Chicago during the first week of October 1871. That was due, at least in part, to an unusual summer with above-average temperatures and below-average precipitation. Nonetheless, had it not been for an unlikely series of events, the fire of October 8 would have been remembered as merely fire number twenty-nine, and nothing more.

There are seven factors that transformed an ordinary barn fire into what Fire Marshal Robert A. Williams called a "hurricane of fire and cinders."

First, the firemen were exhausted from fighting a fire the night before at the Lull & Holmes planing mill, located on Canal Street on the city's West Side. The fire had started at about eleven o'clock on Saturday evening and burned through Sunday afternoon. Many of them had not eaten and had virtually no sleep before being called out to the O'Leary barn.

Second, as a result of the Saturday-night fire, the equipment, including the fire hose, was not in the best of condition. Furthermore, the hose that was available was in short supply.

Third, Mathias Schafer was the fire department watchman stationed in the cupola in the courthouse tower. His job was to scan the city for fires. Upon sighting one, he would, via a voice tube, give the location of the fire to the telegraph operator in the third-floor central fire alarm telegraph office.

The operator would then strike the appropriate fire alarm box, which would ring the courthouse bell and bells in the various fire department company houses located throughout the city. On the evening of October 8, Schafer noticed a light in the southwest. He called down to William J. Brown, the night operator, and told him to strike box 342, which was located on the corner of Canalport Avenue and Halsted Street, about one mile southwest of the O'Leary barn. As Schafer examined the growing blaze from his location in the courthouse tower, he realized that he had made a mistake. Such an error was understandable, as smoke from burning coal piles ignited by the fire of Saturday night, together with the autumn haze, obscured Schafer's vision, blurring the outlines of the landmarks that he would normally use in determining the location of fires. Furthermore, the night was dark, with no moon. He called back down to strike box 319, which was located at Johnson and Twelfth Streets, closer to the fire but still seven and a half blocks away. Incredibly, Brown refused to do so, stating that he "could not alter it now." He apparently believed that since box 342 was in the line of fire, the approaching fireman would see the flames anyway, and he did not want to confuse the fireman by striking a different alarm box. As a result, engine companies that would otherwise have immediately answered the alarm were delayed. Many of the firemen later maintained that had the alarm been given correctly, the fire could have been extinguished relatively quickly.

Fourth, Brown may have seen the fire as much as a half hour before Schafer called down to him. Brown, however, inexplicably failed to sound the alarm, choosing instead to wait for Schafer to confirm the fire's existence. This also caused a delay in the fire department's arrival at the scene of the fire.

Fifth, William Lee lived two houses east of the O'Learys at 133 De Koven Street, a house owned by Walter Forbes. Upon seeing the fire, Lee ran southeast approximately three and a half blocks to Bruno Henry Goll's drugstore, located at the northwest corner of Canal and Twelfth Streets. Fire alarm box number 296 was located at the store. Lee later claimed that not only did Goll refuse to turn in an alarm but he also prevented Lee from doing so. Goll, on the other hand, stated in an affidavit that upon requests of two men he turned in not one but two alarms, which may or may not have been the case. Regardless, neither alarm registered at the central office in the courthouse. As a result, the firemen were delayed in arriving at the O'Leary barn.

Sixth, fire alarm box number 295 was located only about two and a half blocks northwest of the O'Leary barn, at the corner of Des Plaines and Taylor Streets. Thus, that alarm box was even closer to the fire than the alarm at Goll's drugstore. Despite its close proximity, the O'Learys and their neighbors apparently did not attempt to turn in an alarm at that location. Consequently, firemen were delayed again in responding to the fire.

Seventh, Chicago Engine No. 5 was one of the first engines to appear at the scene of the fire, having responded to the call for box 342. Shortly after arriving at the fire, however, the engine broke down. Even though it was repaired minutes later, albeit temporarily, the damage was done. In that short interim, the fire crossed Taylor Street, and the fire was out of control. Echoing the belief of numerous firemen, Fire Marshal Williams stated, "After the fire had crossed Taylor Street, and had found lodgment among the wooden buildings which filled that block, the destroying element became the master, and nothing could hold it back."

Fireman William Musham stated that at first the blaze "was a nasty fire, but not a particularly bad one, and with the help of two more engines we could have knocked it cold." Thus, when fire broke out in the O'Learys' barn, there would have been no reason to think that the fire would be of any more consequence than any of the other previous twenty-eight fires of that first week of October. Unfortunately, as fireman Leo Ry noted, "From the beginning of that fatal fire everything went wrong," and the above factors melded together to become a seven-act comedy.

Mrs. O'Leary ran a milk business in her neighborhood. In her barn were five cows, a calf, and a horse. The barn also contained at least two tons of hay, and two tons of coal were stored in an adjoining shed south of the barn. A new wagon stood nearby in the alley. The O'Leary property was not insured. Had Mrs. O'Leary been in the barn when the fire broke out, it seems unlikely that she would have run back into the house in order to feign surprise, fearful of being blamed for starting the fire that destroyed Chicago. Rather, she would have cried for help and attempted to extinguish the fire and save the barn and its contents. Musham does not recognize that fact. Instead of evaluating Mrs. O'Leary's behavior from an October 8, 1871, perspective, he comments on her reaction to the fire with post-fire hindsight acquired years after her barn burned its way into Chicago history. In his zeal to bring Mrs. O'Leary to justice, he ignores the above attendant circumstances, and thus he fails to consider the possibility that the story of her cow kicking over the lantern was merely the product of the overimaginative mind of an unknown and long-forgotten newspaper reporter—a harbinger of the sensationalism that would immediately characterize many of the newspaper accounts and much of the literature of the fire.

Much of the sensationalism was directed toward the unfortunate Mrs. O'Leary. While it seems a certainty that she and her cow were not responsible for the fire, she remained a hapless target of the vitriolic press of the day. The October 18, 1871, issue of the *Chicago Times*, for example, described her as an "old hag," about seventy years of age, and "bent almost double with the weight of many years of toil, and trouble, and privation." The article went on to imply that she deliberately set her barn afire because she was taken off the welfare rolls. On the other hand, the December 3 issue of the same newspaper inconsistently described her appearance at the inquiry hearings as "a tall, stout, Irish woman, with no intelligence." The article stated that she appeared before the board carrying a baby and that "during her testimony the infant kicked its bare legs around and drew nourishment from immense reservoirs."

So why such invectiveness, if in all likelihood Mrs. O'Leary did not cause the fire? It has been suggested that she suffered the vituperative pen of the fourth estate not so much because of any culpability as to the fire but, rather, because of the prejudices and stereotypes of the native born. On one level, the legend of Mrs. O'Leary and her cow is merely the quintessential urban legend. But the legend also represents a means by which middle- and upper-class Chicagoans could blame conflagration, chaos, and calamity on not only an important constituent of the urban working poor but also on a member of the "dangerous classes."

But O'Leary was not the sole focal point. Contrary to popular opinion, many possible causes—not just Mrs. O'Leary's cow—have been theorized in the years following the fire. Indeed, several were widely discussed, even in the first few weeks after October 8. People smoking in the barn, spontaneous combustion of green hay, incendiaries, people from a party seeking milk for punch or oyster stew, oil-impregnated building stone, and even a comet have all been hypothesized since the fire. Nonetheless, the cause of the Great Chicago Fire has never been conclusively determined. While most of those theories can be easily dismissed, one possible cause, based on the testimony of Daniel Sullivan at the Board of Police and Fire Commissioners investigation, cannot be brushed aside so simply.

Daniel "Peg Leg" Sullivan—so nicknamed because he had a wooden leg—lived across the street from the O'Learys at 134 De Koven Street on a parcel of land owned by his mother, Catherine Sullivan. He testified before the board on November 25, 1871. When he was asked if he knew "anything about the origin of the fire Sunday night October 8 that was back of Leary's," he replied,

I went across the street over to Leary's and went in there. When I got into Leary's house both him and his wife and three young ones was in bed. The youngest one and the oldest one was up. I asked what was the reason they went to bed so soon, and the old woman said she didn't feel very well. I stayed there as near as I could think of it very near an hour and maybe more. . . . I went out of [the] house, went across the street on the other side of the street where I lived myself—one lot east of me—and stayed there a little while. There was a little house belonging to Leary that was in the front. There was a party there, and I stayed there as long as from about twenty minutes past nine to twenty five minutes past nine. Said I, it is time for me to go in and go to bed. Just as I turned around I saw a fire in Leary's barn. I got up and ran across the street and kept hollering fire, fire, fire. I couldn't run very quick. I could holler loud enough but could not run. At the time I passed Leary's house there was nobody stirring in Leary's house. I made right straight in the barn thinking when I could get the cows loose they would go out of the fire. I knew a horse could not be got out of the fire unless he be blinded, but I didn't know but cows could. I turned to the left hand side. I knew there was four cows tied in that end. I made at the cows and loosened them as quick as I could. I got two of them loose but the place was too hot. I had to run when I saw the cows were not getting out. The boards were wet, my legs slipped out from under me and I went down. I stood up again and I was so close to the wall I could hold on to something and made for the door.

Later in this testimony, Sullivan clarified his location, stating that he was sitting against a fence "at the head of White's house or head of his lot." William White owned a tract of land east of the O'Leary property, but across the street, on the south side of De Koven Street. That land was indeed east of Sullivan's property. The fence that Sullivan claimed he sat against was probably located along the front line between De Koven Street and White's property.

Sullivan testified that he left the O'Leary house around nine o'clock, walked across the street, and walked east, *past his own house*, to White's house. Twenty to twenty five minutes later he saw the fire. The obvious question is why did Sullivan do that?

The O'Leary property consisted of two small houses built close together. Patrick and Catherine McLaughlin lived in the front house; the O'Learys occupied the rear building. The party that Sullivan mentioned was in honor of Mrs. McLaughlin's "green horn" brother, who was visiting from Ireland. It has been suggested that Sullivan sat in front of White's house in order to enjoy the music of Mr. McLaughlin's fiddle. McLaughlin, however, played only two times, just long enough for Catherine McLaughlin's brother to dance a polka. Mrs. McLaughlin testified at the inquiry that the fire started half an hour after her husband finished playing. Thus, Sullivan could not have been sitting in front of White's house in order to listen to the music.

One might think that Sullivan sat there in order to enjoy the sounds of merrymaking at the McLaughlin's party. But, if Sullivan had wanted to do this, he probably would have sat directly in front of the McLaughlin house or in front of his own house. He would not have crossed the street, walked past his own property and sat down in front of a neighbor's house.

The commissioner never asked Sullivan why he chose to sit at that particular location. That seems strange, especially since Mrs. McLaughlin was the second person to testify on November 25; Sullivan was the fourth. One would think that after hearing Mrs. McLaughlin's testimony about her party, the commissioners would have extensively asked Sullivan about what he might have seen or heard that night. Instead, their questions were perfunctory at best.

Further analysis of Sullivan's testimony produces several conclusions. Sullivan could not have seen the fire from his position in front of White's house because at least one neighboring house blocked his view. Sullivan testified that while in front of White's house, he saw "a fire in Leary's barn." That would have been impossible. Regardless of where Sullivan sat along the front line of White's property, his view of the barn would have been completely blocked by the house of James Dalton, located immediately east of O'Leary house. It is also possible that Walter Forbes's house, which was east of Dalton's, would have obstructed his view. Furthermore, an eight-foot-high fence ran from Dalton's house to his shed at the rear of his property. That also may have blocked Sullivan's view of the barn.

Had the fire started in the hayloft of the barn, and thus first broken through the roof, which was fourteen feet high, one might argue that perhaps Sullivan saw the fire above Dalton's house. At first, that theory seems to be somewhat buttressed by Sullivan's statement in an affidavit published in the October 20, 1871, *Chicago Tribune* that when he went into the O'Leary barn, "he found the hay in the loft on fire." A few weeks later when Sullivan testified at the inquiry, however, he completely reversed himself. First of all, he stated that when he entered the barn, the fire had not yet broken through the roof. He added that the fire was not in the loft but in the east end of its "lower portion." Finally, he said that he did not know *what* was on fire. Incredibly, the board never questioned him about the inconsistencies between his earlier published affidavit and his testimony.

It is almost certain that Sullivan could not have seen the fire above Dalton's house. His affidavit is silent as to whether or not the fire had broken through the roof when he entered the barn. At least concerning that matter, there are no inconsistencies between Sullivan's affidavit and his later testimony. Furthermore, Dalton's house was at least two stories high, and it was very likely taller than the O'Leary barn.

Dalton's house was one of the first destroyed by the fire. It is possible that Forbes's house also burned down. One might be tempted to excuse the commissioners from failing to address the incongruity of Sullivan's testimony, arguing that any buildings that blocked Sullivan's line of sight were not in existence at the time of the inquiry. Thus, his claims as to seeing the fire from across the street could not be verified or challenged.

It is quite likely that on November 25—the day that Sullivan testified— debris from the burned buildings still littered the area where the houses were, and thus the original locations of the buildings were probably still discernible. It is more convincing that throughout much of the investigation— indeed, especially throughout Sullivan's testimony—the commissioners utilized detailed diagrams that indicated not only the location of destroyed buildings in the area but also possibly such minutiae as the location of the doors of those buildings. Consequently, there appears to be no explanation for the failure of the board to question Sullivan's testimony.

One might suggest that the location and height of those buildings is irrelevant, that Sullivan saw the smoke of the burning barn rising above Dalton's house. Such a possibility seems doubtful. On October 8 the sun set at 5:31 P.M., followed by a moonless autumn evening. Thus, at the time the fire started, there would have been no light by which Sullivan could have seen the smoke. Furthermore, it is possible that the smoke from Saturday night's fire—the Lull & Holmes planing mill was only about ten blocks away—together with the autumn haze, would have made it difficult, if not impossible, for Sullivan to discern the smoke of the burning O'Leary barn. Most important, Sullivan did not testify that he saw smoke. He specifically stated at the inquiry that he "saw a fire in Leary's barn." Accordingly, any hypothesis that Sullivan spotted the smoke from his position in front of White's house seems to have little merit.

In his attempt to extinguish the fire and rescue the animals, it is highly unlikely that Sullivan would have had time to run across the street to the barn without being injured by the flames. He testified that as he ran across the street, he "made right straight in the barn." There was a small alleyway that ran along the east side of the O'Leary property back to the rear yard. It seems reasonable to assume that Sullivan ran through that alleyway to get to the barn. Chicago real estate records reveal that the distance from the front of the barn, south through the alleyway to the street, was approximately 84.5 feet. The width of De Koven Street, as widened, was sixty feet. The distance from Sullivan's initial position in front of White's house, due west to a point directly opposite the alleyway, was about ninety feet. The estimated total distance that Sullivan claimed he ran can be determined as 192.67 feet.

The barn door that Sullivan claimed that he entered was located on the south wall of the barn. As the door was located on the east, or right, side of that wall, it is reasonable to conclude that the door was nearly opposite the alleyway. Since one must assume that Sullivan did not continually run in a straight line toward the rear of the O'Leary property but eventually at an angle to the left toward the door of the barn, it would not be inappropriate to round off the distance to 193 feet.

By his own admission, Sullivan could not run very fast with his wooden leg. Furthermore, the street was unevenly paved. It does not seem possible that Sullivan would be able to hobble 193 feet into a burning barn that was full of hay and wood shavings, struggle with animals, fall down, but still ultimately free a calf without being injured. In his *History of Chicago*, Alfred Theodore Andreas writes of how the fire burned Dalton's house so quickly that Mary O'Rorke—Dalton's mother-in-law—who was in the house at the time, was barely able to escape the house before two sides of the building crashed in. On the other hand, Sullivan, who was not even in the barn when the fire started, was allegedly able to run to it and enter and exit unscathed. Consequently, Sullivan's testimony appears to be somewhat implausible, but the commissioners did not question it.

It is doubtful that Sullivan yelled "fire" as he ran to the barn. He stated that he yelled "fire, fire, fire" as he ran. Indeed, during the inquiry he even bragged of his "hollering" prowess. Despite his claim, neither Catherine McLaughlin nor the O'Learys, nor even Sullivan's mother, said anything during the inquiry about hearing his cries as he ran to the barn. By 4:00 p.m. on October 8, the temperature had climbed to seventy-nine degrees. Because of the unseasonably high temperatures that day, the windows of the homes along De Koven Street surely would have been open that evening. One would think that if Sullivan had cried out, someone would have heard it. The commissioners never commented on that incongruity.

Consider, then, a possible explanation for all of those inconsistencies: After Sullivan left the O'Leary home, he never went across the street to sit in front of White's house. That statement was merely a convenient alibi to explain where he was when the fire started. Instead, he went directly to the O'Leary barn, where he started the fire.

Sullivan stated that while he was never in the O'Leary barn on Sunday, October 8, he "used to go in there every evening because my mother keeps a cow herself and I used to go in there and bring feed. I knew where the cows were. I have been there in Leary's barn hundreds of times." Perhaps he went to the barn that evening to bring feed to his mother's cow, to relax and enjoy the night air, perhaps even to listen to the sounds of the McLaughlin party. While there, he dropped a match, a pipe, or possibly even a lantern in some hay or wood shavings. He immediately attempted to extinguish the blaze, but the fire spread quickly. Realizing that his efforts were of no avail, he abandoned those measures and turned instead to rescuing the trapped animals. He was only able to untie two of them before the flames forced him to flee for safety. While attempting to leave, he slipped on the floorboards and fell. Quickly getting up, he exited the barn and ran to the O'Learys' house in order to warn them of the fire. The neighborhood began to stir, even though only a few moments had passed since the fire started. That shorter and more realistic elapsed time is a distinctive difference between Sullivan's testimony and this new theory.

Two days later the fire was extinguished, but Sullivan needed only a fraction of that time to realize that he was responsible for the leveling of much of Chicago. For obvious reasons he was reluctant to admit his culpability. Therefore, he needed an alibi as to where he was from the time that he left the O'Leary home to the time that the fire broke out in their barn. Sitting "at the head of White's house" was the perfect explanation. As Sullivan lived nearby, his presence in the immediate vicinity would arouse no suspicion. He could not state that he was closer, in front of his own house or the McLaughlins', since anyone present at the McLaughlin party could possibly contradict him, stating that he was never seen in the area that evening. Mrs. McLaughlin's front porch overlooked De Koven Street. It would not be unreasonable during the course of the festivities for someone to step outside onto the porch for some fresh air, perhaps even walk onto the sidewalk or street. Indeed, Mrs.

McLaughlin stated at the inquiry that three men left during the party. Sullivan could not risk one of those men challenging his alibi.

Sullivan claimed that he was sitting against White's fence. People living along the south side of De Koven Street would not be able to question that, as they would not be able to see him. Sitting in front of the fence, he would be hidden from view. Finally, since he was outside and in close proximity to the O'Leary barn, he would be able to claim that he noticed the fire from the beginning.

Sullivan's statements at the inquiry must have been convincing since he was never charged with causing the fire. Nonetheless, in many respects his testimony does not seem plausible. The commissioners never asked him why he walked past his own house and sat down. Despite having diagrams of the location of the buildings in the neighborhood, they never asked him how he was able to see the barn from his position in front of White's house. The commissioners never asked him to explain the marked inconsistencies between his published affidavit and his testimony. They never questioned the time element, how Sullivan was able to run approximately 193 feet into a burning barn full of hay and wood shavings, struggle with animals, fall down, and eventually exit without being injured. Sullivan stated that he yelled "fire, fire, fire" as he ran to the barn. The neighbors who testified, including his own mother, said nothing about hearing those cries. The commissioners never questioned that either,

It has been suggested that Dennis Regan, who lived at 112 De Koven Street, might have been at least partially responsible for starting the fire. Regan also testified at the inquiry. When asked if he knew anything about the "origin and commencement" of the fire, he replied,

> All I know I was into Mrs. Leary's at half past eight and I was talking to the man that was in bed and his wife. I asked his wife what was the reason she went to bed. She told me she had a sore foot. I went away, so as the man was in bed. I went home. A short while after 9 o'clock I heard one of the neighbors say Leary's barn was on fire. I jumped out of bed and went up there and the barn was on fire, and all the neighbors around it. I ran through the alleyway, but could not go near it. I went to work there to throw water on the house because the house was not insured or nothing. That is all I know about it.

Regan was one of the first people to arrive at the O'Leary property after the barn caught fire. In two affidavits published in the October 20, 1871,

Chicago Tribune, the O'Learys and Sullivan all stated that it was Regan who alarmed the O'Learys. Interestingly, several weeks later at the inquiry, both Mr. and Mrs. O'Leary testified that it was Sullivan who alerted them. Similarly, when Regan testified, he never mentioned anything about alarming the O'Learys. The commissioners did not comment on the inconsistency. Sullivan, though, did state at the inquiry that while he was attempting to alert the O'Learys, "a man by the name of Regan came along." When Mrs. O'Leary was asked if she knew how the fire started, she replied, "I could not tell anything of the fire only that two men came by the door." Based on Sullivan's statement and on the aforementioned affidavits, it is reasonable to presume that those two men were Sullivan and Regan. It is also reasonable to conclude that any inconsistency as to who alerted the O'Learys—Sullivan or Regan—is insignificant at best, since it appears that both men were outside of the O'Leary house during the very early stages of the fire.

Regan lived a block east of the O'Learys on the opposite side of De Koven Street. He testified that while in bed he heard a neighbor say that the O'Leary barn was on fire. In order to give credence to his testimony, that neighbor would have had to learn about the fire before the O'Learys did. That seems highly unlikely. Unfortunately, the commissioners never asked Regan who the neighbor was.

The possible shortcomings of the commissioner's interrogative techniques became insignificant, however, when one considers the distinctive and crucial difference between Regan's and Sullivan's testimony. Sullivan testified that he sat against a fence in front of White's house, and at twenty to twenty-five minutes past nine o'clock, he saw the fire. He was silent, however, as to whether or not there was anyone outside at that time—someone that the board could have interviewed in order to determine the veracity of Sullivan's statements. Regan's testimony, however, includes such references to third parties, and thus his statements, unlike Sullivan's, could have been confirmed by the commissioners. They could have asked Regan to identify the neighbor who alerted him, and that neighbor could have been questioned. Regan testified that neighbors were near the O'Leary barn when he arrived there, and the commissioners could have asked Regan who they were and then interviewed them all as well in order to determine if they had seen Regan running from his house, down the street, to the barn—probably through the same alleyway that Sullivan claimed to have run through. One would think that if Regan had indeed caused the fire, he, like Sullivan, would have given the board an alibi that the commissioners would have been unable to verify by the questioning of other parties.

The four-volume inquiry transcripts total more than eleven hundred pages. Regan's testimony consists of only four and a half pages. It is unfortunate that the board did not interview him more thoroughly, and since there really is no other evidence, circumstantial or otherwise, that links Regan to the fire, any conclusion that Regan was even partially responsible for the fire seems at least somewhat tenuous.

The evidence that most exonerates Mrs. O'Leary is in the final analysis the most damning to Sullivan. As noted earlier, at the time that the fire broke out, there was no reason for anyone to believe that it would be of any more consequence than the previous fires of that first week in October. Therefore, the person responsible for the fire would most likely attempt to extinguish it—that Sullivan did. Failing that, the person would try to save the animals and then alert the neighborhood—that Sullivan also did. Failing that, the person would try to save the animals and then alert the neighborhood—that Sullivan also did. Because of his incriminating behavior and because of his equally incriminating testimony, it seems reasonable to theorize that Daniel "Peg Leg" Sullivan, and not Mrs. O'Leary and her cow, may have been responsible for the Great Chicago Fire.

Although contemporary research appears to vindicate Mrs. O'Leary, she remains vilified by history. A writer for the *Chicago Evening Journal* wrote the following in 1871, and more than 125 years later the words are just as timely:

> The story told that night, and before anyone had the least idea that the great conflagration was in store, was caught up by the electric wires the next morning and flashed wherever telegraphy extends. Even if it were an absurd rumor, forty miles wide of the truth, it would be useless to attempt to alter "the verdict of history." Mrs. Leary has made a sworn statement in refutation of the charge, and it is backed by other affidavits; but to little purpose. She is in for it, and no mistake. Fame has seized her and appropriated her, name, barn, cows and all.

19.

CLASSICAL MUSIC IN CHICAGO
AND THE FOUNDING OF
THE SYMPHONY, 1850–1905

Robert McColley

Illinois Historical Journal vol. 78, no. 4 (Winter 1985)

Although the life and work of Theodore Thomas is the overall focus of this article, the author describes the work of a number of significant musicians and groups in Chicago during the second half of the nineteenth century. There were choral societies and church musicians, and the piano was a central feature in the home of the well-to-do.

As conductor of the Chicago Orchestra, Thomas was dissatisfied with the Auditorium Theatre as the venue of the orchestra and worked with Daniel Burnham in the design of Orchestra Hall, which opened shortly before Thomas's death in 1905.

T his essay has two important points to make. The first is that, contrary to a legend that Maestro Theodore Thomas himself helped create, the founding of the Chicago Orchestra in 1891 was not the beginning of the serious performance of classical music in the city but rather climaxed forty years of musical growth—quite apace with that of other leading musical centers in the United States and Europe. The second point is that the permanent home of the ensemble, Orchestra Hall, exists *because* of the determined will of that same Christian Friedrich Theodore Thomas and not, as the charismatic architect Frank Lloyd Wright would have us believe, because of the machinations of another Chicago architect, Daniel

Theodore Thomas and the Chicago Symphony Orchestra at the Auditorium Theatre, Chicago, Illinois, circa 1897. *Photo courtesy Chicago History Museum.*

Hudson Burnham. In the course of discussing these topics, one necessarily encounters several colorful characters besides the three already mentioned, as well as some interesting questions about the place of the fine arts in American civilization.

It may be useful, at the outset, to clarify the name of Chicago's most famous musical institution: As created by the Orchestral Association in 1891, its official title was The Chicago Orchestra, and that is what it is called throughout most of this paper. The trustees changed the name to The Theodore Thomas Orchestra in 1905, to honor the memory of its great conductor after his death on January 4 of that year. Finally, in 1913 the association changed to the present name, The Chicago Symphony Orchestra, adding as part of its official title, "Founded by Theodore Thomas."

It may also be useful to define with some precision what is here meant by "classical music." In one important sense, any piece of music is classic that endures beyond its own time and place—"Greensleeves" and "Deep River" as much as Bach's *Mass in B Minor* or Verdi's *Otello*. But today we commonly call classical music those works of considerable elaboration and difficulty, all of whose notes are written out in score, and which are playable to good effect only by expert musicians, and even then only after careful study and rehearsal. Such music requires, by common consent, the full attention of its audience, both to follow the elaborate invention of the composer and the skill in execution as well as nuance of interpretation supplied by the performer. Anyone who has looked into the history of Western music knows that impressive scores survive from the late Middle Ages onward; but the public concert, open to anyone with the price of a ticket, reflects modern industrial and commercial society, with its specialization, its educated and cultured middle and upper classes, and its vast capacity for absorbing entertainment. The modern musical scene was, in fact, developing at the same time that Chicago was growing from a village to the second largest city in the United States.

From 1850 to 1890 classical music in Chicago consisted of two quite different, though sometimes overlapping, spheres. On the one hand, Chicago had a growing group of professional, amateur, and student musicians among the permanent residents. On the other hand, Chicago was becoming an increasingly attractive place for touring "stars" and opera companies to visit. The world concert circuit is, historically speaking, a very recent invention. The child prodigy Mozart was a pioneer of it in the later eighteenth century. Jenny Lind, the Swedish Nightingale, and Ole Bull, the Norwegian violinist, were among the first professional musicians to grow rich on American tours. Thousands have followed, with varying degrees of success. The rapid improvement in steam transportation, both transoceanic and transcontinental, made such touring both possible and potentially profitable. Although there were occasional exceptions, it is generally true that any famous musicians who toured the United States in the second half of the nineteenth century performed in Chicago, including such legendary people as Adelina Patti, Jean de Reszké, Ignace Jan Paderewski, and Colonel James Henry Mapleson's traveling opera company.

But Chicago might more properly be remembered for her resident musicians, beginning with the immigrant Julius Dyhrenfurth, whose Philharmonic Society offered a series of eight concerts of light classics in the fall of 1850. After a few seasons that group disappeared, but in 1860 a new, larger, and musically more ambitious Philharmonic Society performed under the leadership of another immigrant, Hans Balatka. Balatka had already achieved national recognition by organizing a musical society in Milwaukee.

The year 1867 was memorable for music in Chicago because of the arrival of the German Florenz Ziegfeld Sr. and a Yankee organist from New

Hampshire, William Smythe Babcock Mathews. Ziegfeld opened his Chicago Musical College in the splendid Crosby Opera House. When the building perished in the Great Fire of 1871, Ziegfeld occupied an even larger structure, the Central Music Hall, and was so successful that his classes—chiefly instrumental and vocal—soon spilled over into other properties. Mathews was not only an accomplished church musician but a musical journalist, scholar, and teacher of teachers. He wrote dozens of articles and many books in a forty-five-year career. From 1891 to 1902 he edited an excellent monthly magazine, *Music*, published in Chicago. His large and comprehensive book, *A Hundred Years of Music in America*, was the first full-scale history of music in this country, and remains useful today.

Another extraordinary year was 1869, at least in retrospect. The Blumenfeld family, originally from Silesia, moved from Appleton, Wisconsin, to Chicago, where they tried their hands in the dry goods business. But six-year-old Fannie was already playing the piano. By 1885, as Fannie Bloomfield Zeisler, she was Chicago's first world-famous virtuoso of the piano, and remained so until her death in 1927. From nearby Peru and Aurora came the first internationally renowned concert violinist from the United States, Maud Powell. She was born in Peru and moved to Aurora in 1870, when her father became superintendent of schools there. At the age of nine she was traveling alone to Chicago every Saturday for music lessons. At twelve she left for Europe, at fifteen she was touring England, and at seventeen she made her debut with the Berlin Philharmonic. Mary Garden, the world-famous soprano, was born in Aberdeen, Scotland, but her family came to America in 1881 and moved to Chicago in 1888, when Mary was ten. She studied voice in Chicago for several years and appeared in many recitals and concerts before leaving for Paris in 1897. She returned to Chicago for performances more often than to any other American City and managed the Chicago Opera Association for two years in the 1920s.

Choral societies were an important feature of musical life in the nineteenth century—especially in Central Europe, the United Kingdom, and the United States. Chicago's German community had several male choruses, and Hans Balatka organized choral concerts as well as orchestral ones and grand opera. Carl Wolfsohn moved from Philadelphia to Chicago in 1873 to lead the newly formed Beethoven Society, a large mixed chorus for the performance of large-scale works with orchestral accompaniment. An especially important group, the Apollo Music Society, started up in 1872. As Mathews reminisced, "It was a neat little male chorus they had, about thirty voices, singing part songs, and holding Bohemian rehearsals with a little singing, a very little serious study and a great deal of *Gemutlichkeit*, duly washed down by a quarter-keg of the liquid which to a German throat is the only universal solvent known to art." By 1874 the Apollo Music Society had grown in size, given up beer (at least during rehearsals), and enrolled women. It soon surpassed the Beethoven Society in the presentation of oratorios, including many we are still familiar with today—Handel's *Messiah* and Mendelssohn's *Elijah*, for instance—and some that are long forgotten: Max Bruch's *Fair Ellen* and Sir Arthur Sullivan's *On Sea and Shore.*

As Chicago grew in population (well beyond one million in 1890, and still growing) and in wealth, her churches provided increasingly good employment for trained musicians, who in turn educated their choristers and congregations in the possibilities of serious music. While the world-famous church of Dwight L. Moody specialized in the expert performance of popular religious music, the large and increasingly prosperous Protestant denominations hired professional organists, choir directors, and often added a paid quartet of soloists. The late nineteenth and early twentieth century also represented the historic high point of that remarkable instrument, the pianoforte, or, in rural Midwestese, the "pie-anna." Led by the pathbreaking merchandisers of the House of Kimball and the bargain-pushing House of Cable, Chicago achieved a preeminence in the manufacture and distribution of pianos comparable to its preeminence in making and selling hams and sausages. The piano enjoyed its reign mainly because it was the central instrument for popular music, a position it later yielded to the family of electric guitars. But as the incomparable historian of the piano Arthur Loesser has reminded us, it became a dominant fashion for middle-class families to require their daughters to count piano playing among their "maidenly accomplishments." It became unthinkable for the wealthy to furnish their homes without a grand piano in the parlor.

Four people who contributed in various important ways to the musical life of Chicago were members of the same family: children of the Reverend Charles Fay, raised in Massachusetts and a graduate of Harvard College, and Charlotte Emily Fay, one of the thirteen children of John Henry Hopkins, first Episcopal bishop of Vermont, and Melusina Muller. Among their other highly accomplished children was John Henry Hopkins Jr., who wrote the words and music to "We Three Kings of Orient Are." Charles Fay was an accomplished scholar and Charlotte Fay was a pianist of great skill and wide musical sympathies. All their children acquired a full liberal education at home, with special emphasis on music. Melusina Fay (1836–1923) completed her education in Cambridge, Massachusetts, and joined the Boston-Cambridge group that at that time enjoyed the most advanced musical life in North America. She married the brilliant and eccentric philosopher Charles Sanders Peirce in 1862, but left him in 1876. She lived for several years in Chicago, where she wrote music criticism for the *Herald* and made part of her home available to the fastidious Theodore Thomas during his orchestra's Chicago summer concerts in 1883. From that time forward, the Fays seem to have been among the conductor's most intimate friends.

Amy Fay (1844–1929) completed her education at Cambridge and lived with the Peirces for several years; among her music teachers was John Knowles Paine, composer and soon to be Harvard's first professor of music. She studied piano in Europe for six years, from 1869 to 1875. Franz Liszt was sufficiently impressed with Amy Fay to name her among his ablest students. But Amy returned to the United States convinced that Herr Ludwig Deppe of Berlin had been her most effective teacher. She was the first member of the family to meet Theodore Thomas, appearing as soloist with his orchestra in Sanders Theatre at Harvard and at the Worcester Music Festival. She moved to Chicago in 1878, dividing her time among the related pursuits of teaching, giving concerts, and writing articles about music for newspapers and magazines. Chicago's A. C. McClurg published Amy Fay's *Music-Study in Germany* in 1880. The book was so popular that it went through twenty-five editions, including foreign ones. It consisted of the letters that Amy had written home during her six years abroad. Legend, no doubt aided by McClurg and the Fays, has emphasized that the poet Longfellow arranged for the publication by Melusina, or "Zina" as her brothers and sisters called her. Among Amy Fay's piano students in Chicago was a young man who would become an internationally recognized composer in the early twentieth century, John Alden Carpenter.

Charles Norman Fay (1848–1944) graduated from Harvard in 1869 and moved west to Marquette, Michigan. At first he worked for a bank, but he soon moved into the telephone business. He has described his place in music perhaps better than anyone else could:

> In August, 1877, I was unexpectedly called to Chicago to protect business interests involved in a failure precipitated by the railway strike and riots of that year. I do not know when I started that I could even enter the town, and gentlemen from the country were supposed to

take their lives in their hands in the mob-ridden streets of what had once been called "the Garden City."

I got there safely, however, and found as quiet a burg as ever seemed to drowse, and very hot. That evening, wandering out for a breath of air, I came upon the old Exposition Building, down on the Lake front, and from its open doors and windows floated, instead of shots and battle cries, the divinest music. Theodore Thomas was giving there his first Chicago season of Summer Garden Concerts, and for the first time I heard a great orchestra.

I moved to Chicago that autumn, and he came again for Summer Garden Concerts in 1880, and every year thereafter, except 1884, until 1891, when he brought his Orchestra to Chicago for good—for exceeding great good—and played there until he died in 1905.

I became personally acquainted with Mr. Thomas in 1881, and the acquaintance ripened into intimacy. One day in 1889 I met him on Fifth Avenue [in New York City], and we turned in to the old Delmonico's. He looked worn and worried, and I asked him why. There were reasons enough. There was mortal illness in his home [Minna Rhodes Thomas, the conductor's wife of twenty-five years, would die in the spring of that year]; the American Opera Company, that short and melancholy chapter of good music and bad management, had swept away his savings; and almost worst of all, he had been obliged to give up his own permanent Orchestra. To use his own words, "I have had to stop engaging my men by the year, and now I play with scratch orchestras. In order to keep my old Orchestra together I have always had to travel constantly, winter and summer, the year round, and year after year. Now I am fifty-three, too old to stand the traveling. New York alone cannot support my Orchestra, so it has had perforce to be disbanded."

For a moment, so bitter was his tone, I had nothing to reply, but finally I said: "Is there no one, no rich and generous man, to do here in New York as Major [Henry Lee] Higginson has done in Boston—keep your Orchestra going and pay the deficit?

"No one," he answered. "I have told them often, those who say they are my friends, that for good work there must be a permanent Orchestra; and for a permanent Orchestra, which will not pay, there must be a subsidy. My work is known. I am old now, and have no ax to grind. But they do not care. They think I have always kept the body and soul together somehow, and that I always will—that I have nowhere else to go. They treat me as a music merchant, a commercial proposition, subject to the laws of supply and demand."

My thoughts went back to those ten years of Summer Garden Concerts, and to some powerful devoted friends of Mr. Thomas and his music at home, and I asked, "Would you come to Chicago if we could give you a permanent Orchestra?" The answer, grim and sincere, and entirely destitute of humor, came back like a flash: "I would go to hell if they gave me a permanent Orchestra."

Charles Norman Fay then set to work. He created the Chicago Orchestral Association. Through which he recruited fifty wealthy benefactors, each of whom promised to guarantee $1,000 each year. Although he never held the office of president of that association, Fay was its guiding spirit for several years. No doubt the prospect of a world's fair contributed to the enthusiasm that Chicago's leaders then showed for Theodore Thomas and his orchestra. In any case, massive investment in high culture seemed to be infectious, for Chicago had an art museum, two major private universities, and seven music conservatories.

We should recall that Charles Norman Fay had, with the rest of his family, a long experience in the enjoyment of good music before he became a wealthy businessman, While civic pride undoubtedly ranked high among the motives of the sponsors he secured for the Chicago Orchestra, no great prestige has yet accrued to either cities or social classes for supporting virtuoso orchestras. Therefore the frequently voiced observation of high culture—that the nouveaux riches purchased in Europe, or from the East, for prestige that it would give them—is a gross distortion of the facts. Good music, painting, sculpture, and even grand opera gained far more in prestige from the patronage of social leaders than those leaders gained from lending their patronage.

It remains to mention Rose Fay (1852–1929). She does not tell us when she came to live in Chicago, but she was there in the summer of 1883 when Theodore Thomas was boarding with her sister Melusina, and exchanged letters with him during the next several years. Theodore Thomas had lost his wife and given up his own orchestra in 1889; his spirits were naturally at a low ebb. "All his thoughts and interests now centered around his family," Rose later recalled "and, as the time passed, he became, also, more and more dependent on me. One beautiful evening, May 7, 1890, we were married, and a few days later went to Cincinnati for the Festival." Rose Fay Thomas supposed that the creation of the Chicago Orchestra "was perhaps, facilitated by our marriage," which drew Theodore Thomas and Charles Norman Fay still closer together.

Like her brother and sisters, Rose Fay Thomas had literary as well as musical talent. Her first book, *Our Mountain Garden* (1904), celebrated the fun and healthfulness of doing real work outdoors while giving brief glimpse of the celebrated conductor in and around their retreat in the mountains of New Hampshire. Her *Memoirs of Theodore Thomas* (1911) has the reputation of being less accurate than George Upton's edition of *The Autobiography of Theodore Thomas*. Rose's biography is very much in the informal "life and letters" style so widely used in that era. Yet it is, quite simply, the one thorough account of Theodore Thomas that brings him fully to life. The chief fault of the work, if it may be considered one, is that Rose Fay Thomas says so little about herself and her remarkable family.

Anyway, we may be certain that Theodore Thomas did not move to Chicago solely because he desired to live there with his new wife and in-laws. During their first year of marriage the newlyweds divided their time between Thomas's New York home and his summer home in Fairhaven, Massachusetts. They moved to Chicago in the fall of 1891 for the first season of the Chicago Orchestra. It should be mentioned that Thomas was by no means forced to leave New York. He was, more than ever, generally considered the finest conductor in the United States. A certain rivalry with Walter Damrosch, however he may have felt about it, rather heightened interest in classical concerts; moreover, the conductorship of the venerable New York Philharmonic was still his for the asking. But as he had explained in the conversation recorded by Charles Norman Fay, he no longer had the stamina to keep touring with his own orchestra, and unless he toured he could not find enough work to keep his musicians together. He could always earn enough to live on by conducting established orchestras in New York and other cities. But he was no longer willing to make what he considered artistic compromises: these were not, and could not be, his orchestra.

As we have seen, Chicago had an increasingly rich and varied musical life from about 1850 onward. What Theodore Thomas established in 1891 was a permanent virtuoso orchestra, requiring revolutionary changes in leadership, financing, and repertoire. The sort of programs played by the Dyhrenfurth Orchestra, and most often by Thomas's own touring orchestra, were what we today call "pops" concerts. The closet thing we have to them today are the programs of the Boston Pops Orchestra and its various imitators. Six to twelve numbers would appear on the program, all of them short and melodious. Featured prominently among them would be dances and marches; and interspersed among the purely orchestral works would be songs, choruses, arias from popular operas, and instrumental solos. Gradually more demanding works—for players as well as for audiences—began appearing in orchestral concerts in such centers of high musical culture as Boston, New York, and Cincinnati. Hans Balatka and his Philharmonic Society were playing as weighty programs as any orchestra in the world in the 1860s. But no permanent orchestra had succeeded in playing only entire symphonies, concertos, and the new "symphonic poems" without playing even more of what Sir Thomas Beecham called "Lollipops," until the Boston idealist Henry Lee Higginson staked his private fortune on the Boston Symphony Orchestra in 1881. Even there Higginson felt his audience had to be led gradually to programs of only superior music.

Theodore Thomas, who arrived in the United States at the age of ten in 1845, belonged to the first generation of "star" conductors and was unique among them in winning his fame entirely by leading orchestras in the United States. The goal of the star conductor was to have complete control of a superb orchestra. By means of unlimited rehearsals and excellent personnel, he could guarantee performances of transcendent quality. By control of repertoire he could substitute his informed and superior taste for the rather fickle and traditional preferences of a more or less untutored public. Theodore Thomas agreed to settle in Chicago because our barons of beef, pork, flour, railroads, and telegraphy were willing to guarantee money by hundreds of thousands to pay for the best players available and thereby make the Chicago Orchestra, unlike its predecessors, relatively independent of public taste. After paying their thousands to subsidize the orchestra, the rich benefactors were then expected to pay for season tickets and attend the concerts made possible by their benevolence.

Having secured financial support and the beginnings of an audience from his wealthy patrons, Thomas then confronted the issue of personnel. The orchestras that dominated American and European music making in the democratic nineteenth century were, in most cases, self-governing associations of local musicians, joined in a society for whatever pleasure or profit they could gain from it. Such was the oldest continuously existing orchestra in the United States, the New York Philharmonic Society, which began in 1841 with three concerts. Such orchestras were made up of musicians who, whether amateur or professional, had to hold other jobs to secure their livings. Conductors were drawn from among the more talented members of these associations; whatever discipline existed in them was a convention agreed upon by all members. An orchestra might dismiss a conductor and elect another, but a conductor could not dismiss a member of his orchestra.

A fledgling musician's union existed in the 1890s; it tried to establish the rule that orchestras should draw their players entirely from the pool of musicians available in their own cities. Theodore Thomas brought the staggering number of sixty players to Chicago with him—exactly the number of his famous touring orchestra of the previous quarter century; he then hired thirty Chicagoans to fill out the ranks. As in Higginson's Boston Symphony, the members of the Chicago Orchestra were not to hold any other jobs that might prevent them from attending scheduled rehearsals and concerts. In exchange, management would contract to pay them a living wage—something previously unknown to orchestral players in the United States, and rare enough in Europe. As other cities imitated the Boston and Chicago methods, it happened that America's best orchestral players became a sort of professional proletariat, losing control of their jobs at the same time that they were making unprecedented wages. Unlike such European cities as Vienna, Dresden, or Prague (but not exactly like Boston), Chicago would continue to draw its players from an international pool of talent rather than from the local pool, large as it was. One is reminded of the way William Rainey Harper ranged all over the civilized world to attract the best possible faculty to the new University of Chicago.

When the Chicago Orchestra began its first season, it played in the largest permanent concert hall in the United States, the vast and costly Auditorium, designed by Dankmar Adler and Louis Sullivan and encapsulated in an enormous building that also contained a hotel and a block of offices. The seating capacity of the Auditorium was over forty-two hundred. Frank Lloyd Wright—who had gone to work for the firm of Adler and Sullivan at the age of eighteen in 1887—labored for over two years as Sullivan's assistant on the project and contributed mightily to the legend that the Auditorium was the best hall ever built for both orchestral concerts and for grand opera. Here are Wright's recollections and remarks, as recorded by radio station WFMT in 1957 and transcribed by them for *Chicago* magazine; he is discussing how Theodore Thomas was somehow forced out of the Auditorium and into Orchestra Hall:

I heard [Theodore Thomas] say in the room next to mine in a wail that was sort of a broken man's voice, "Sullivan, nothing comes back, nothing comes back. I can't play in that place." That's your Orchestra Hall.

You see, Chicago Gold Coasters wanted a Diamond Horseshoe like New York, like the Metropolitan. Socially ambitious, I imagine. Or what was it? Uncle Dan Burnham was a great salesman and he sold them the present Orchestra Hall, which is totally unfit for music, and here's the Auditorium languishing—a magnificent thing.

In the first edition of his *Autobiography* (1933), Wright shows a floor plan of the offices of Adler and Sullivan at the height of the firm's prosperity. They were occupying the top floor of the large tower Sullivan had designed for the Auditorium Building. And sure enough, there was Wright's office right next to Sullivan's. But Wright left the firm in 1893, eleven years before the building of Orchestra Hall.

Theodore Thomas expressed the following misgivings about the Auditorium:

> The only hall in which our concerts could be given was the Auditorium—an immense theatre, with a seating capacity of four or five thousand, which had been erected a few years previously for opera festivals, political conventions, and other large popular gatherings. The great size of this standing of this theatre called for the largest possible orchestra, but even then it was often ineffective, notwithstanding the remarkable acoustic properties of the building. It also contained so many seats that people felt under no obligation to buy season tickets to our concerts, knowing full well they could always find good places at the box-office at the last minute, whenever they desired to attend a performance. . . . Our season was also interrupted several times a year by the other engagements for which the building was rented, such as the opera season, flower show, balls, and the like.

The stage of the Auditorium projected sound outward very well, but the hall was so large and the reverberation period so long, that a musician could not depend on hall echo to tell him how loud his ensemble was playing: hence Thomas's complaint "Nothing comes back."

Wright's recollection, some sixty-five years after the event, may very well be accurate except in one important detail: Theodore Thomas was protesting to the great architect Louis Sullivan not about Orchestra Hall but about the Auditorium itself.

Far from being a powerful and rich man who exploited Theodore Thomas for reasons concerning social status and salesmanship, the architect Daniel H. Burnham was friend, sponsor, and loyal supporter of the aging conductor and his orchestra. The two became friends while planning for the World's Fair of 1893; besides coordinating all the designs for the fair, Burnham personally supervised the construction of the entire White City and its landscaping, which included three different concert halls for popular and classical music. As director of music for the fair, Thomas (trusting too much in the elevation of taste since 1876) repeated his gargantuan errors of the Philadelphia Exposition—booking far too many classical concerts—and he resigned his post on August 12, 1893, just before the visiting Bohemian, Anton Dvorak, picked up a baton and led Thomas's superbly trained Festival Orchestra in his lovely G-major symphony. Another reason for Thomas's resignation was the rhubarb caused by his bringing in Paderewski's Steinway piano for a concert, even though Steinway had declined to exhibit at the fair (not trusting a panel of judges that included a director of Kimball!), and the other piano manufacturers undertook to enforce a rule that pianos not exhibited could not be played.

In the remaining years of his life, Theodore Thomas had the sense to avoid world's fairs and, indeed, pretty well restricted his activities to his splendid Chicago Orchestra and the biennial Cincinnati May Festival— organizations that met his high standards and somehow managed to avoid the conflicts to which great artists seem especially vulnerable. Meanwhile, the architect Burnham joined the directors of the Orchestral Association, contributed to its operating fund, and encouraged Thomas to elaborate his own interest in acoustic design. The collaboration of the two men is clearly explained in Philo A. Otis's history of the Chicago Symphony. An early member of the Apollo Music Society, an original trustee of the Chicago Orchestra, and a pillar of the First Presbyterian Church, Otis may be accepted as an eyewitness. He writes:

> Orchestra Hall, as we know it today, with its commodious arrangements for orchestra and chorus, is the joint creation of Theodore Thomas and Daniel H. Burnham. Thomas had his first opportunity to try out the new hall Tuesday morning, 6 December 1904. He led his orchestra in Wagner's "Overture to Tannhauser," and turned to

two of the trustees in their box seats and shouted triumphantly, "Your Hall is a success, gentlemen, a great success."

The next day he wired Burnham, who was exercising his arts as a city planner in Manila: "Hall a complete success. Quality exceeds all expectations." Finally at age seventy, Theodore Thomas had everything he required to serve his musical ideals: a splendid orchestra under his own benevolent and high-minded dictatorship, complete financial security, and a hall designed to his own specifications and entirely under his own control. Unlike Moses, Theodore Thomas actually entered his Promised Land, but not for long. After conducting five concerts in Orchestra Hall, he contracted pneumonia and died on January 4, 1905.

Louis Sullivan argued eloquently in his literary testament, *The Autobiography of an Idea,* that Daniel H. Burnham—for all his talent and good intentions—had corrupted art and indeed the very soul of America by cooperating with eastern architects to establish a uniform classicism in the White City of the Chicago's World Fair of 1893, and through its immense influence in the classical revival that followed. The argument was accepted by Frank Lloyd Wright and has entered into the mainstream of American cultural history through Wright's eloquence and that of the gifted historian of American architecture Hugh Morrison. It seems never to have occurred to those talented and industrious men that their arguments and charges were peculiarly self-serving and far-fetched.

Sullivan and Wright, then, have proved very misleading guides to the character and motives of the founders of the Chicago Orchestra. But they were great architects, and, happily, Sullivan's Auditorium has been restored and is now in regular use, though not by the Chicago Symphony Orchestra or the Chicago Lyric Opera, each of which has its own building. It is perhaps worth mentioning that there are still plenty of experts today who claim that Orchestra Hall has terrible acoustics while those of the Auditorium are miraculous, but experts disagree on these matters as on others.

Such esthetic disputes cannot be settled, but a historical point can be affirmed: Theodore Thomas was fundamentally responsible for the creation of Orchestra Hall, just as he had earlier been responsible for bringing a virtuoso symphony orchestra to Chicago. If anyone had an autocratic spirit, it was he, for he never supposed that great orchestras were built by committees or great programs chosen by election. Nevertheless, Thomas had his own sort of faith in the people: he supposed that, if sufficiently exposed to proper (which means virtually perfect) performances of the world's greatest classical music, they would develop a taste for it. The historian can also note that the elite Chicago Symphony Orchestra has by no means stifled the musical societies of the Chicago area: it continues to be extraordinary for both home-grown and visiting musicians. And while symphony orchestras ought not to be ranked exactly, as if they were teams competing in an athletic league, probably no other great musical city of the United States would reject Chicago's claim to have enjoyed one of the two best orchestras in the United States in 1891 and one of the three or four best in 1986.

20.

POLITICS AND PARKS
Businessmen and the Recreation Movement

Michael P. McCarthy

Journal of the Illinois State Historical Society
vol. 65, no. 2 (Summer 1972)

Developing recreational parks was a phase of the progressive movement and supported by settlement workers to benefit families living in slum and crowded conditions. Businessmen, including those on the boards of existing park districts, were among the leaders in developing small parks.

Machine politics explains the initial opposition of the West Chicago Park Commissioners to developing small parks. With the appointment of a new group of businessmen and professionals to that board, progressive reform took over. Finally the author introduces the topic of Cook County–wide park planning.

Once depicted as implacable foes of municipal reform, businessmen of the early 1900s are now gaining recognition as important contributors to the reshaping of local government in an emerging industrial society. While primarily involved in tax and charter modernization, businessmen were also instrumental in the recreation movement that swept America during the Progressive era. Chicago, in particular, was widely praised for its development of new parks and playgrounds, a project that owed much of its success to prominent businessmen.

By 1890 Chicago already had an impressive system of large parks. Stretched in a broad arc around the city, from Lincoln Park at the north, to

Garfield Park at the west, and Jackson Park at the south, and connected in several districts by tree-lined boulevards, these parks had been the pride of the city since their establishment in the 1860s and 1870s.

There was little interest in developing the parks, however, and between 1880 and 1895 the city's park acreage remained virtually unchanged despite the enormous rise in population, especially in the industrial districts. By 1892, for example, thirty thousand Poles clustered in a few blocks around the Church of St. Stanislaus Kostka on the West Side. Nearby, some seventy thousand immigrants of all nationalities inhabited approximately one square mile in the vicinity of Hull House. These people and others in the wards along the branches of the Chicago River, in the stockyards area, and in manufacturing districts of Calumet had no park facilities. Charles Zueblin, a University of Chicago sociologist who analyzed the inequitable distribution of park acreage among the city's neighborhoods, estimated that in the eleven wards where the bulk of the parks and boulevards were located there were 234 persons to each acre of parks space; in the rest of the city, the ratio was 4,720 persons per acre. "If we were to compare, however, the eleven favored wards with eleven wards along the river," he continued, "we should find the proportion even more startling." Of the city's approximately two million residents, Zueblin said, between six and seven hundred thousand lived more than a mile from a large park. Furthermore, if one of these thousands did journey to an existing park, he could do little more than admire the scenery, for there were few recreational facilities.

By the 1890s the notion of parks as playgrounds was beginning to gain general acceptance. Recreation and play had long been known to be important in a child's natural development, but the determination to provide public play areas was a new concept. Settlement workers were the first to call attention to the need for playgrounds. Reports like the following by Agnes Sinclair Holbrook, a resident social worker at Hull House, were typical:

> Rear tenements and alleys form the core of the district, and it is there that the densest crowds of the most wretched and destitute congregate. Little idea can be given of the filthy and rotten tenements, the dingy courts and tumble-down sheds, the foul stables and dilapidated outhouses, the broken sewer-pipes, the piles of garbage fairly alive with diseased odors, and of the numbers of children filling every nook, working and playing in every room, eating and sleeping in every window-sill, pouring in and out of every door, and seeming literally to pave every scrap of "yard."

Finally, in 1894 William Kent, a young businessman of inherited wealth, provided three-quarters of an acre of land to be used by Hull House as a playground. A sand pile, swings, and building blocks provided fun for youngsters. A similar but somewhat larger park was established by the Northwestern University Settlement in 1896. Then, in June of 1898, the University of Chicago opened a third play area of this type in Chicago.

Except for Kent and a few other wealthy philanthropists who contributed funds for these first playgrounds, the people involved in the small-park movement were primarily settlement workers. Only when Jane Adams, Zueblin, and concerned journalists publicized the correlation between crime and congestion and disease was the base of support broadened. One civic group that gave early support to the movement was the Municipal Science Club, a small group of business and professional men organized in 1898. Its members included Zueblin and the young architect Dwight Heald Perkins, who were sympathetic to a proposal by George E. Hooker, a resident worker at Hull House, that the club survey the playground and recreational facilities in the city. The proposal was accepted, and as a result of the survey the club adopted a set of resolutions calling for a commission to deal with the problem. These recommendations were submitted to the Chicago City Council in the fall of 1899 by Alderman William Jackson. The council approved the resolutions in November and then, in the following month, Mayor Carter H. Harrison appointed a Special Park Commission, with Jackson as chairman, to examine and meet the city's playground needs in a systematic manner. The commission consisted of nine aldermen, three each from the North, West, and South Sides, and one representative from each of the three existing park boards—Lincoln, West, and South. In addition, the city council requested that the mayor appoint to the commission six citizens who did not hold "official positions," including one lawyer, one civil engineer, one landscape gardener or architect, one physician or sanitary engineer, "who shall be of recognized ability in their profession." Thus businessmen and professionals constituted a significant portion of the new agency's membership.

The commission had been formed only as an advisory group, and its funds were limited. It was therefore unable to purchase the necessary real estate for developing a comprehensive system of small parks. It consequently turned for funds to the city's park boards, which had the legal authority to float bond issues. The commission also worked to amend the Illinois law that restricted park acquisitions to property adjacent to existing facilities. The legislative acts of 1901 and 1903 that empowered the boards to buy and maintain play sites in neighborhoods where the need existed were major victories for the commission.

The South Park Board of Commissioners was the first to implement commission recommendations; it purchased a number of sites for parks around the stockyards and in the manufacturing districts of Englewood and Calumet. By the end of 1904, fourteen new parks, totaling almost 682 acres, had been opened. Six years later seventeen small parks under the jurisdiction of the South Park Board were in full operation, with two more parks partially improved. The most significant feature of nearly a dozen of these new parks was the spacious and attractive fieldhouse. Each fieldhouse had a cafeteria, an auditorium, and meeting rooms as well as gymnasium and bathing facilities, thus making it possible to have year-round recreational activities, meetings, lectures, and entertainment. The fieldhouse concept was largely the idea of J. Frank Foster, a highly regarded administrator who had been general superintendent of the South Park District since the 1880s. Daniel H. Burnham, the architect prominent in the planning of the World's Columbian Exposition in Jackson Park in 1893, supervised construction of the fieldhouses, and the noted firm of Olmsted Brothers landscaped the grounds. Using this kind of talent, the South Park commissioners insured that its community centers would be distinctive additions to dreary industrial neighborhoods.

The project soon attracted national attention. In 1907 the newly organized Playground and Recreation Association of America selected Chicago as the site of its first convention. President Theodore Roosevelt delighted board members by urging delegates from other cities to attend the gathering in order "to see the magnificent system that Chicago has erected in its South Park district, one of the most notable civic achievements of any American City."

The prompt and enthusiastic response of the South Park Board to the need for small parks reflected not only the district's financial strength—the downtown Loop area was on its tax rolls—but also the degree to which board members were influenced by the leadership of their president, Henry G. Foreman. A wealthy realtor and member of a prominent South Side banking family, Foreman first became interested in the recreation movement by observing the playground at Hull House. Later, as president of the Cook County Board of Commissioners, he supervised the county hospital, jail, and insane asylum. Subsequently, "his observation of the human wreckage which floats into corrective and curative institutions led him to consider what could be accomplished through the parks to catch the tide at its source."

In a speech at suburban Morgan Park in 1904, Foreman outlined his philosophy of government. "In progressive countries," he remarked, "all men have certain equal rights, but Nature, always capricious, has made no two men equal. As an inevitable result, some men surpass others because they are more intelligent, more industrious, more saving, more daring, more prudent, and more temperate." Local government therefore has the responsibility, he argued, to aid those "blinded by environment"; "useful parks," in particular, meet the working man's needs, he said. "This population that by heredity requires recreation. By tradition, as well as by instinct, pleasant occupation out of working and sleeping hours is necessary for its physical and moral health, for its happiness and for its contentment."

Residents of the fashionable neighborhoods along Lake Michigan may or may not have accepted Foreman's theories of progressive uplift, but, in either case, they still had to contend with his practical arguments for more parks. Well-equipped facilities in working-class areas were a sound investment, Foreman assured anxious taxpayers, for by helping resolve the problems of "repressed ambition" and "discontent," the parks "would be a benefit to the entire city,"

Foreman faced opposition from the Chicago Real Estate Board, which was concerned about rising taxes in the South Park area. In 1905 the real estate men initiated a special investigation of the board's policies and expenditures, but soon dropped the issue. In the testimony taken during the investigation is a statement from Mary McDowell, director of the University of Chicago Settlement in Packingtown, a neighborhood behind the stockyards. Her testimony may have helped assure the realtors and other businessmen as well of the wisdom of spending public money on parks for the poor:

All thinking people agree we must humanize these communities of mixed peoples, we must raise the standard of living among them, and they must become more rational in their thinking and acting, to make them good and safe citizens. If we can do this, we will make our city more desirable for the home-seeker, and a safer place for business enterprise and development. . . . One finds that muscle exercised on a punching bag, or a swinging club, or a turning pole or in a swimming pool, is not apt to be used to bully fellow-workers and lead to struggles against law and order.

Such faith in parks as a safety valve for discontent was reinforced by a study conducted by Allen T. Burns, dean of the Chicago School of Civics and Philanthropy, for the Russell Sage Foundation in 1908. Burns discovered that during the period under study, delinquency in Chicago as a whole had increased 11 percent, while in the stockyards district it had actually decreased by 44 percent.

The West Park Board remained a Republican stronghold where patronage generally took precedence over progressive reform. Small parks and playgrounds offered little opportunity for handsome construction or maintenance fees, and the few employees needed by such parks were expected to come from the ranks of the settlement workers rather than the normal patronage pool. The West Park Board also had financial problems. It lost more than $300,000 in deposits in 1897 when the mortgage bank of its treasurer, E. S. Dryer, went bankrupt in connection with the failure of the National Bank of Illinois. This, coupled with the high cost of real estate in the congested district where almost no undeveloped land existed, gave the board the excuses it needed for ignoring the small-park issue.

The one action the West Park Board did take was a token gesture only. In 1903 it gained legislative approval for a $250,000 issue. The only bidder for the bonds, Home Savings Bank, withdrew its offer on the advice of its attorney, who pointed out that special legislation for a specific agency was unconstitutional. Members of the Special Park Commission were irate when they learned that during the legislative session the West Park Board had been warned that the bill was illegal.

Finally, in 1905, the reform-conscious Republican Charles S. Deneen became governor and reorganized the West Park Board, appointing prominent businessmen and professionals to all seven positions. Bernard Albert Eckhart, founder of a milling firm and director of several Chicago banks, was elected president. A member of the board of trustees of the Chicago Sanitary District from 1891 to 1900, Eckhart was no political novice. Keenly aware of the formidable problems in operating the parks of the West Park Board, he offered to donate $25,000 to any charity suggested by Deneen if the governor would look for another candidate for the post. Once committed, however, Eckhart worked to provide the West Side park system with the same efficient operation that characterized the other systems. "What the west parks need," he commented shortly after his appointment, "is a man like Foster of the south side system. We want men who know a great deal about parks and nothing about politics."

One of Eckhart's first actions was to name Jens Jensen superintendent for the entire West Side park system. Jensen, a highly regarded landscape designer who had served as consultant to the Special Park Commission and designed a park system for Racine, Wisconsin, had been fired in 1900 as superintendent of Humboldt Park by the previous West Park Board for exposing a coal supply swindle. His diverse experience made him acutely aware of the district's long overdue need for reform.

Like Foreman and the other businessmen, Eckhart believed in the value of play and the far-reaching influence of parks. He thought young people who used the parks came to know "with remarkable readiness, the value of cleanliness, and to feel the stimulating sense of self respect that results from the manly contests of skill and strength." Moreover, Eckhart noted, "they carry to their homes these new ideas, and a new spirit, which are bound, in the long run, to make their parents, as well as themselves, better citizens of the commonwealth."

In addition to advocating a small-park system, the Special Park Commission urged that recreational plans be made on a regional Chicago-area basis. The city of Boston had incorporated regional planning in its metropolitan system in 1892, and as early as 1897 Chicago's West Park Board recommended the purchase of "from five hundred to two thousand acres of natural timber land . . . along the banks of the Des Plaines River, which, for a comparatively small outlay of money, might be made accessible and enjoyable to our citizens." This area would have constituted part of a comprehensive outer belt of parks not within the jurisdiction of any existing city park board. In 1904 Jens Jensen and Dwight Perkins, an early advocate of parks who established a national reputation in school architecture, developed a detailed proposal for such a system for the Special Park Commission. Their proposal called for parks in four zones, two within the city and two outside. One of the outside zones was to include twenty-eight sites stretching from Skokie Valley on the north to 111th Street on the south. The second outside zone would include thousands of acres along the Des Plaines River–Mount Forest area, Salt Creek, Flag Creek, Calumet River, and the shores of Calumet Lake. The Special Park Commission urged prompt acceptance of the plan while land was still reasonable and free of commercial and suburban development. The proposed parks were not to be playgrounds or ornamental parks with play facilities. Instead, forest and waterfront lands were to be preserved in their virgin state for public use. In presenting the case for forest parks, Jensen pointed in particular to the working man who had "access to no other grounds for recreation or summer outings."

Foreman shared Jensen's concern and in 1903 convinced his fellow members on the County Board of Commissioners to create an Outer Belt Park Commission, designed to supervise the city-suburban project. Foreman became president of the new commission and promoted the forest preserves as a necessary supplement to the city's parks. Citing statistics showing that 70 percent of Chicagoans lived in congested neighborhoods, Foreman emphasized again the high rates of crime, mortality, political radicalism, and physical and mental illness found in these areas. "The true refreshment for the working man, the clerk, the small shopkeeper, the professional man," he continued, "is to be found by contact with nature in the forest, by the streamside and in the meadow, away from the city with its grime and noise." For those uninterested in ecology or conservation, Foreman argued that forest parks would enhance real estate for miles around, more than offsetting the cost of their purchase and maintenance.

The Outer Belt Park Commission pressed for implementation of the Special Park Commission proposals, and in May of 1905 the legislature authorized the creation, subject to referendum, of the Forest Park District of Cook County, which had the power to issue $4 million in bonds for initial land purchases. The district was to be supervised by a six-member board appointed by the governor.

Although the concept of a forest preserve had met with general approval, the specific legislation faced a considerable amount of organized opposition. The Civic Federation and Citizens' Association, for example, viewed with dismay the formation of yet another independent agency. Even the Special Park Commission refused to endorse the measure because it failed to create a single regulatory agency for both the forest preserves and the small parks. Chicago teachers also voiced dissent, arguing that there was but one tax pie and an additional taxing body would mean a loss of funds for the schools. Prominent businessmen and bankers such as Franklin MacVeagh and John J. Mitchell came out in favor of the bill. Labor leaders were the only major group to object to the idea of forest parks. They scoffed at Foreman's vision of the parks as country playfields for the masses, pointing out that many of the proposed sites were accessible only by automobile, a luxury few laborers enjoyed in the early 1900s. The Chicago Federation of Labor urged its members to vote against picnic grounds for the residents of Prairie Avenue and passed a resolution criticizing Foreman and the South Park Board for their "pandering to the taste of the idle and nonproductive class."

At the November election the measure was defeated; passage required a majority of the total votes cast in the election, and the vote on the referendum was approximately six thousand short (there was, however, a favorable majority of votes cast on the proposition itself). Foreman and the other planners, although unsuccessful, had created interest in the issue, and county parks were finally authorized by referendum in 1914.

Tax-supported recreation programs were still considered by many as a radical innovation in the early twentieth century. The movement nevertheless drew substantial support from individual businessmen, who played important roles on the Special Park Commission, the city's park boards, and the Outer Belt Park Commission. Influenced by the ideal of efficiency so popular in the Progressive era, these men were attempting to create a functional environment in a sprawling, polyglot metropolis that had long resisted systematic planning. They were also exercising their business judgment, for they knew that the unhealthy worker is not productive, that a high incidence of crime discourages investors, and that parks and playgrounds boost land values. The large number of realtors involved in park planning underscored the fact that reform activity was for many businessmen a natural extension of their business activities.

The wide interest of the business community in the park program was also indicative of an important shift in attitudes toward labor. The belief in using organized recreation as a means of controlling labor was one of many changes from earlier attempts to control labor by lockouts, strike-breakers, Pinkerton guards, and even the militia. In seeking to order the metropolis through providing parks for recreation, the businessmen of Chicago reflected an outlook that was consistent with the progressive spirit.

RELATED READING

Allen F. Davis, "Jane Addams vs. the Ward Boss," *Journal of the Illinois State Historical Society* vol. 53, no. 3 (Autumn 1960).

Addams lost her fight to oust Alderman Johnny Powers, but it taught her lessons in other ways to advance the cause of social justice. According to the author, "The picture of Jane Addams as a kindly social worker and gentle pacifist should be altered to include Jane Addams as the realistic reformer who battled Johnny Powers . . . and who knew when to stop."

21.

THE SANITATION REVOLUTION
IN ILLINOIS, 1870–1900

F. Garvin Davenport

Journal of the Illinois State Historical Society
vol. 66, no. 3 (Autumn 1973)

The author describes the variety of sanitation problems in downstate rural areas as well as in middle-sized cities such as Rockford
and Decatur in the later third of the nineteenth century. School
toilet faculties were woefully unsanitary, and water filtration
or treatment was slow to be adopted. Some sanitation issues
merged into environmental ones. The author focuses most of
his attention on Chicago, where problems were greater due to
extensive crowding of people and the effects of industry and its
by-products, such as that from the operations of slaughterhouses.

A landmark engineering feat was the opening of the Chicago
Sanitary and Ship Canal in 1901. The author describes the many
ways progress was made in sanitation practices.

From the sanitary point of view the history of mankind is a dirty story.
Even Western civilization, despite its remarkable political and cultural
contribution, paid little attention to personal hygiene, sewage disposal, clean
food, or pure water until the nineteenth century. After 1850 the situation
began to improve, and by the end of the century the West had undergone
a sanitation revolution comparable to the great developments then being
made in medicine. The two movements, in fact, were closely related, each
being stimulated by the development of bacteriology. England took the lead

246

in the crusade for pure water, clean streets, and sewage disposal, and Sir Edwin Chadwick of that country became known as the greatest sanitarian of the nineteenth century. Not only did he write some of the most important books on the subject, he was also responsible for the introduction of glazed earthenware pipes for drains and water systems. But sanitary engineering reached its fullest development in the United States, not, however, without the usual period of quackery, trial and error, and experimentation. Sanitary science involved not only simple hygiene but hygiene from a chemical point of view. In a city like Chicago it involved, besides the ordinary problems of garbage disposal, the extraordinary problems that arise when people crowd together in congested areas and are endangered by poor ventilation and the by-products of industry. Reformers, philanthropists, and starry-eyed, public-spirited citizens were all necessary if sanitary programs were going to be undertaken; but in sanitary engineering, as in other professions, a little knowledge was sometimes a dangerous thing. The sanitary expert needed a thorough knowledge of chemistry and physics. He also needed to know something about geology and meteorology, or at least to have enough sense to seek the advice of experts in those fields. The public was slow to fully appreciate the fine points of specialization involved in a sanitary program.

The need for sanitation was obvious in a densely populated city like Chicago, but many improvements were also needed in small towns, farm homes, dairy barns, milk houses, and schools. In the early 1870s most of the public school buildings in Illinois were "ancient and unsuitable," dirty, poorly ventilated, heated with makeshift equipment, and served by outside toilets that were cesspools of infection. Under those conditions pupils sometimes developed fevers or suffered from nausea and faintness. In some schools improper ventilation caused such restlessness and irritability in the children that teaching was almost impossible. In Wayne County some of the old log schoolhouses of frontier times were still being used as late as 1872. Even newer and more expensive school buildings in the state were often poorly heated and inadequately ventilated. Proper toilet facilities and inside plumbing were almost nonexistent.

The inside toilet did not become standard equipment in Illinois until the twentieth century, and where it was installed, as in the new statehouse in Springfield, the plumbing was so primitive that sewer gas was a frequent irritation to the occupants of the buildings. Inside water closets were dependent upon sewers and running water, which most communities did not have. Towns like Rockford and Galesburg were just beginning their sewer systems in the 1880s. Galesburg, with a population of twelve thousand, had about two thousand privies, six hundred of which were usually rated as "foul" by health authorities. Decatur, with a smaller population, seemed to have more privies per capita than Galesburg had, but several hundred of them were defective and a danger to nearby wells. Unsanitary conditions existed throughout Illinois, especially in railroad stations where dirty and neglected water closets and privies were commonplace.

In Champaign, in the shadow of the University of Illinois where scientific studies of sanitary problems were being made, most of the population of about ten thousand were still using outside toilets in 1895. During the next three years the city constructed twenty-four miles of sewers, but in 1899 only about four hundred connections were on record. This number included some hotels, restaurants, and university buildings; only a small percentage of homes in the city had sewer connections at the turn of the century. A similar situation existed in neighboring Urbana.

Champaign-Urbana was one of the few communities in downstate Illinois that had installed a scientific sewage disposal plant by the turn of the century. All the larger towns in the state were at least paying lip service to the new vogue of sanitation, but what was considered sanitary for one town might result in unsanitary conditions for another town, especially if the latter happened to be downstream from a city that dumped all of its waste products into a river. Seepage from a privy into well water could be even more deadly than the organic matter in a river that supplied a city's water.

The idea of filtering water or treating it with chemicals was slow to be accepted. The Decatur waterworks was built in 1871 with the Sangamon River as the source of supply. Apparently no one paid any attention to the organic purity of the water, although many people complained about the mud and silt in it. Consequently, when a filtering system was installed, its purpose was to give the water a more pleasant appearance and taste. So long as the water looked good, the customers did not seem to be concerned about whether or not it contained bacteria.

The Rock Island waterworks, built in 1871–72, pumped water directly from the Mississippi River into the city mains. Not until 1891 was a filtering plant installed, and it proved to be too small to be effective. In 1892 the system was enlarged so that it could easily filter 1.64 million gallons of water a day with a maximum capacity of more than 2 million gallons a day if necessary. The Rock Island plant was one of the most modern and efficient of the mechanical filters available at the time. In addition to pumping machinery, the system had four gravity filter tanks that contained crushed quartz thirty inches deep. The tanks were cleaned every night with back pressure from the mains, but no chemicals were used either in cleaning the tanks or in preparing the water for human consumption. The filtering plants in some towns used chemicals, especially aluminum sulphate, called "potash alum" by the engineers. Lake Forest and Quincy used alum regularly, but Belleville used it only when the water was "bad." As a coagulant this chemical was both cheap and reasonably effective; a year's supply at Quincy, for example, cost under two hundred dollars. In Springfield water was being pumped from the Sangamon River, but purification remained a problem. In 1903 the digging of wells was undertaken as a solution for anticipated water shortages.

The sanitary problems of downstate towns were dwarfed by those of Chicago, which was rapidly becoming one of the great industrial centers of the world. The Chicago water system was started in 1861, and by 1877 the city was supplied with one hundred million gallons of lake water every twenty-four hours. The water, drawn through a tunnel that extended out into Lake Michigan two miles from shore, was distributed through 416 miles of pipe to every section of the city. Normally, the lake water was quite clean, averaging 0.0688 grains of organic material per gallon at the source and about 0.1377 grains at the faucet. One reason for the purity of the lake water was that the Chicago River—Chicago's open drainage ditch—had been reversed in its course by deepening the Illinois and Michigan Canal at a cost of $5 million. The Chicago River was supposed to carry away from the lake and down the Illinois River the sewage from 266 miles of sewers and all the refuse from the city's industrial plants.

This system was far from perfect, and as Chicago grew, the river became a stinking ditch unable to perform its sanitary duty. After a heavy rain the river sometimes reverted to its original course and emptied its filthy contents into the lake. This happened in 1877, and for several days the river emptied sewage and putrid waste from the slaughterhouses into the source of the city's water supply. During this period the water that came from city faucets was wine colored, and when it was left uncovered, it became offensive to smell and nauseating to drink. Chemical analysis showed 5.8548 grains of organic matter per gallon.

The problem of purifying the city's water supply was not resolved until the turn of the century. In the meantime the Chicago River was converted into an elongated cesspool containing sewage mixed with waste products from slaughterhouses, glue factories, and breweries. The stench from the dirty water, so thick at times that it was almost solid, was described as "simply horrible." The situation was particularly bad in the spring of the year after the ice melted and the accumulation of chemicals, offal, sewage, and partially decomposed cats and dogs was exposed to the sun. Appleblossom time in Chicago was not a season of carefree happiness for those who lived near the river or had to pass it on their way to work.

The city fathers recognized the nuisance (it would not easily be ignored!) and passed various resolutions and ordinances from year to year. The fact that the unsanitary condition of the river was a perennial topic of debate indicates that the problem was not handled realistically and that only temporary relief was achieved until 1892. Before then, the history of drainage and sewage disposal in Chicago was to a great extent a story of costly errors and poor judgment. It took thirty years of rotting offal and public complaint to convince authorities that only a carefully planned comprehensive engineering project costing millions of dollars could bring permanent relief.

The final phase of the movement began in 1880 when the Citizens' Association of Chicago recommended that a canal or "new river" be dug to the headwaters of the Illinois in order to increase the current in the stagnant Chicago River. This recommendation won wide acceptance in 1885, and Mayor Carter H. Harrison Sr., replying to an aroused public, appointed a Drainage and Water Supply Commission, which proposed a plan quite similar to the one already suggested by the citizens' committee. Legal and administrative problems were eased considerably when the state legislature created the Sanitary District of Chicago by an act of May 29, 1889. The district embraced "all of the city north of Eighty-seventh street, and some 43 square miles of Cook County outside the city limits." In the same year the first board of trustees of the Sanitary District was elected, and this body appointed Lyman E. Cooley as chief engineer of the drainage project.

The selection of the canal route should not have been difficult, for the only logical route through the watershed between Lake Michigan and the Mississippi Valley was the trough made by a prehistoric river. Cooley was fully aware of the magnitude of the proposed engineering project, and he conducted his survey carefully and thoroughly. His calculations, he said, were made "upon the most comprehensive scale and by the most exact methods." It was his opinion that careful, detailed planning in the beginning would lower the cost by millions of dollars. He thought also that the drainage system ditch should be incorporated with a lakes-to-gulf waterway that would have an important bearing on the economic development of the Midwest.

The Chicago Sanitary and Ship Canal, which opened in 1900, attracted the attention of scientists and engineers throughout the United States. The huge ditch was 28 miles long, with an average width on the bottom of about 150 feet, and a low water depth of 22 feet from Chicago to Lockport. During construction, forty million cubic yards of soil and rock were excavated, and almost every type of steam shovel and digging apparatus known to American contractors was brought into use. According to Charles Shattuck Hill, associate editor of *Engineering News*, "nowhere at any time in the history of the world have so many novel and different machines for excavating and removing earth and rock been in operation in so small a territory."

The mechanism that controlled the flow of water through the canal was located at the western terminus near Lockport. The main feature of the works was a bear trap dam, 160 feet wide with a vertical play of 17 feet, and 7 sluice gates, each 30 feet wide and having a vertical play of 20 feet. The dam was the largest of its type ever constructed and provided an efficient means of controlling the flow of water through the canal. The dam went into operation at 11:05 A.M., January 17, 1900, and the great drainage ditch, which had been filling with lake water since January 2, began to flow. The canal was not entirely completed, however, and dredging and widening went on for years. In 1905 it was estimated that the big ditch and its accessories had cost $40,873,629.71.

During the period when Chicago was hoping and planning for the central drainage canal, more routine problems of sanitation had to be met every day of every year. Streets had to be cleaned, garbage collected, manure removed from sidewalks and yards, sewers flushed, and tenement houses inspected. To cope with these problems, a special sanitary committee, headed by a superintendent, was created in 1867. The city was divided into sanitary districts, each of which was patrolled by inspectors and sanitary police. The effectiveness of the inspectors depended on their conscientiousness, intelligence, and industry. The committee recommended that the inspectors take "special interest in all sanitary questions, and keep themselves informed of what is being done at home and abroad relative to the causes which affect health or disease; thus they will contribute their share to the accumulation of knowledge which is destined to . . . establish sanitary science on the most permanent foundation."

There is no evidence that the sanitary police ever followed those suggestions or that they ever regarded themselves as men of destiny. But they did attempt to clean up some of the dirtiest sections of Chicago. Their task permitted little time for idealistic planning but called, instead, for a steady hand and a strong digestive system. The second district, on the near South Side, was one of the city's dirtiest. There the streets were generally littered with trash, and the alleys were filthy from "being used as a common receptacle for manure and garbage of all sorts." The fourth district, on the South Side, was in a similar condition. There the stables, houses, and privies had been neglected, and the yards were "oozy with filth of all types." Garbage was scattered everywhere, sewers were obstructed, and some of the streets were impassable to a team and wagon. In the fifth district, on the far South Side, about twelve hundred hogs added to the unsanitary condition of streets and yards. The hogs were fed on kitchen slops, distillery swill, and rotten meat from the slaughterhouses, and "were allowed to wander around free, along with poultry and dogs."

Sometimes it seemed easier to try to disinfect the filth rather than remove it. Between 1865 and 1900 almost every known disinfectant was used by the sanitary police and health officers. Quicklime, an old standby, was sprinkled on damp alleys and dirty gutters or used as a whitewash on the walls of stables and privies. Gypsum was sometimes used instead of lime if a whitewash was not wanted. Charcoal powder was combined with dry lime and gypsum to absorb "putrid gases," and chloride of lime was sprinkled over offal piles to stop putrefaction. Copperas, another popular disinfectant and deodorizer, was used to purify privies, urinals, catch basins, and sewer drains. It was usually mixed at the rate of ten pounds to a pail of water, and sanitary officials claimed that about twenty pounds (or two pails of the mixture) was needed to disinfect a privy six feet in diameter and twelve feet deep. Other disinfectants in use were carbolic acid, creosote, and permanganate of potassium. Mercuric bichloride became popular about 1890, and city employees used watering cans with fine sprinklers to spread it over yards, cellars, and gutters.

Problems related to street cleaning and garbage and sewage disposal were considered the legitimate business of city government, but when health officials began to talk about inspecting factories, houses, and tenements on the *inside*, many people thought sanitation reform was being carried to extremes. Dr. Oscar Coleman De Wolf, Chicago's progressive health commissioner, knew that proper sanitation in a building depended upon good plumbing, and he suspected that much of the city's plumbing would never pass inspection. Before 1880 whole blocks of houses, even in the better residential sections, were without proper waste and soil pipes, and most of the sinks were not equipped with traps. In the Criminal Court Building the plumbing was so primitive that on one occasion a judge was almost overcome by sewer gas. Conditions in factories and tenements were even worse. Almost every lower-class home had a deathtrap "in the nature of a kitchen sink which discharges into a foul grease-basin, or privy-vault, through an untrapped waste pipe." Less than 3 percent of families in slum areas had bathroom facilities. The factories and packinghouses that employed many of these people had inadequate and unclean facilities; even the better stores failed to provide clean toilets or lunchrooms for their clerks.

In 1877 De Wolf began limited sanitation inspections of Chicago buildings on the pretext that he was looking for cases of contagious diseases. Only four of the several hundred buildings examined met the minimum sanitary standards De Wolf employed. Encouraged by public interests in the reports, he was able to get the city council to adopt a revised health code in 1880. With a special appropriation, he hired six competent inspectors and began (for the first time in the United States) the legal inspection and regulation of tenements and factories. In 1881 he received additional encouragement from the state legislature, which set up minimum plumbing and sanitation standards for tenements and factories. Hundreds of office buildings, factories, furniture shops, railroad buildings, tenements, bakeries, breweries, and slaughterhouses were inspected within a year. As a result, several thousand improvements, repairs, and alterations were made in plumbing systems. Under the 1881 law, plumbing plans for every new building had to be approved by the city health department before contractors and carpenters could start construction.

Although considerable progress was made by 1900, there were still many tenement houses and cheap hotels with inadequate or nonexistent plumbing. Greedy landlords, especially the owner of the "old rookeries and shells" on Clark Street and similar slum areas, were the most persistent violators of sanitary regulations. But dirty as the tenements were, they could not compare with the flophouses. These institutions, supported by bums, drunks, dope addicts, and the most poorly paid laborers, were described as foul pestholes. Sanitary officers eventually found these filthy buildings and gave orders to clean up the bedrooms, eliminate the vermin, and repair the plumbing. Some improvements were made, but not enough to make the flophouses sanitary.

Mattresses, pillows, and sheets were brought in, and straw-filled ticks were stored away for a time, only to reappear when the "heat was off." Little was done about the dirt, the bugs nesting in the walls, and the inefficient toilets.

Disposal of city garbage and the refuse from rendering plants and slaughterhouses was another difficult problem that came within the jurisdiction of the health department. In 1898 the daily output of garbage alone was estimated at four hundred tons. In spite of the installation of a garbage furnace, patterned after one in use in Montreal, the end of the century found Chicago without any satisfactory solution to the garbage problem. Waste from slaughterhouses and packing plants reached staggering quantities after 1870. Between five and six million hogs, cattle, and sheep were slaughtered annually. This left the packers with about 150 million pounds of blood, bones, intestines, and scraps to dispose of. Before 1878 most of the waste went to the rendering and fertilizer plants, but after that time the packinghouses began to install dryers and other machinery to take care of their waste. As a result, the rendering plants had to go out of the city and even out of the state for the scraps and bones on which they depended. Ohio, Michigan, Indiana, Wisconsin, Missouri, Kansas, and Colorado shipped thousands of tons of fetid material each month to the Chicago plants. Chicago not only was the hog butcher of the world but the offal center as well.

Most of the animal refuse was dried and converted into fertilizer. In 1878 by actual count there were within the city limits 292 rendering tanks, each with a capacity of eight tons, and only eleven were constructed in such a way as to minimize air pollution. In most cases the blood, bones, and scraps were thrown into the tanks and subjected to a steam pressure of forty pounds per square inch; pungent gases generated by the heat were allowed to pass directly into the air. Some plants had conduits that carried the gas either over or under the furnace fire, but combustion was so imperfect that most of the gas escaped through the chimney. After cooking for eight to twelve hours, the steamed mess of offal was drawn off at the bottom of the tank. The fat was skimmed off, the water drained out, and the residue, or "tankings," was transferred to the dryers.

Some industrial managers and owners recognized the dangers of pollution and were apologetic but made no real effort to improve the situation. Others were entirely selfish and resented what they called interference with free enterprise. These businessmen, according to De Wolf, "were oblivious to every appeal ... and ... could no more be brought to an acknowledgment of the great wrong they were inflicting upon the people ... than can the Jaguar be made amenable to the influences of Christianity." They had become "entirely indifferent to the teasing attacks of sanitary authorities." Recourse to the courts brought only embarrassment to the health department. Several cases were tried in 1877, but in each instance the jury, instead of finding the manufacturer guilty, censored the health officer for interfering with a legitimate business. Grand juries were also adamant, especially since only police testimony was available.

Obviously a more stringent law was needed. This was secured in the summer of 1877, when the city council passed an ordinance regulating the slaughtering, packing, rendering, and fertilizer businesses. Under the new law all persons or companies that slaughtered or packed cattle or hogs, made fertilizer, or manufactured glue were required to be licensed by the city at a cost of one hundred dollars per year. The mayor could issue the license on application and revoke it if the company violated any ordinance of the city council or any statute of the state in Illinois. A firm operating without a license could be fined up to one hundred dollars a day until it complied. Health authorities were given legal right to enter and inspect any plant at any time, day or night. The ordinance also applied to concerns within one mile of the city limits. The Chicago Packing and Provision Company, located outside the city limits, immediately challenged the law in a test case that was carried rapidly through the lower courts to the Supreme Court of Illinois, which upheld the validity of the ordinance.

After this decision, industries associated with the packing business bought modern equipment and machinery in an attempt to meet sanitary regulations. A process called "Turner's apparatus" was adopted by the rendering plants to correct the gas problem. This machine forced gas from the rendering tank through an iron conductor into a large iron coil immersed in cold water. After the condensation and separation of the watery vapor, the dry gas passed through another tank partially filled with gasoline. The gas, now charged with gasoline vapor, passed from this tank over the burning coal bed of the furnace. The combustion was complete, and the process was economical because it produced extra heat. Other methods were soon introduced to either destroy or deodorize the gases. Some of the processes were dependent upon chemical decomposition, but one utilized a hydrogen flame of intense heat in a small separate furnace through which the gases were forced.

In 1880 De Wolf was able to report that the once intolerable stenches from the packinghouse district were under control. Actually, there was to be a never-ending struggle between the city and industry to keep odors, smoke, and gases out of the air. All smoke was considered a nuisance, but the chemists at the city health department were especially worried about the fumes of metals, such as antimony from type works, and the fumes of arsenical compounds from copper works. Carbon dioxide, which reduced the amount of oxygen in the air, was considered highly objectionable; carbon monoxide, sulphurous oxide, and nitrous oxide were also dangerous to the health of the community. Carbon compounds were regarded as irritants to the throat and lungs. Although Chicago had a smoke ordinance in effect after May 1, 1881, it proved very difficult to enforce.

The sanitation revolution in Illinois had become a major movement by 1900. There is no doubt that the movement was spearheaded by the scientific discoveries of the late nineteenth century. New technology, especially the development of refrigeration, also contributed to the revolution, as did the growing acceptance of the germ theory of disease. The refinement and more widespread use of microscopy gave physicians and other scientists indisputable data that was used to convince legislators, food dealers, sanitation engineers, and the general public that an unsanitary environment was an unhealthy environment. Public health officials now received stronger support from certain newspapers, like *Prairie Farmer*, and from organizations and institutions such as the Illinois Agricultural Experiment Station, the Illinois Farmers' Institute, the State Board of Livestock Commissioners, and the United States Department of Agriculture.

Sanitarians had by 1900 made a positive impression on the people of Illinois. The movement to produce clean food and pure water, which was conducive to a longer life, was considered desirable by a majority of the people. But the movement also met some negative reaction. In the nineties the mission of the sanitarian was to control disease and lengthen life by providing a clean environment and pure food. But was this enough? Was this an adequate aim of human endeavor? Some sociologists thought otherwise. The sociologist was beginning to develop theories pertaining to environment and crime and home life and delinquency. Viewed sociologically there was no point in merely lengthening life unless that life was to be happy and productive. It took more than giant sewers, a better water closet, unadulterated beef extract, and sterile ice to produce the ideal society. "The sound body is of little use," said Marion Talbot of the University of Chicago, "save as it can help in the manifestation of sound mental and spiritual activities. The house which is sanitarily perfect has a small function in the economy of life unless it contributes to the upbuilding of men with perfect minds and souls."

Sanitation alone was not enough. In the mind of the sociologist, science for science's sake was as barren as art for art's sake. This school of thought attracted some interesting and important people, including Shailer Mathews, Jane Addams, and John Dewey. There was much in this doctrine that was sensible and realistic, and it was to bear fruit later on in the twentieth century. In the meantime, the people seemed to enjoy what they called "the improved sanitation" without worrying very much about the moral or intellectual condition of society.

The sanitation revolution cleaned up the milk shed and the meat market and condemned the outside toilet, but it failed to produce the lasting results called for by the sociologists. The politicians, health officials, and private citizens associated with sanitation reform were more concerned with the immediate attainment of pure food and clean homes than with the preservation and purification of the total biological environment. At least half a century went by before man realized that pollution and unsanitary conditions were evils that went far beyond his personal life.

22.

JOLIET'S ENTERPRISING UNIVERSALISTS
The Church and the City in Late Nineteenth-Century Illinois

Timothy Dean Draper

Journal of the Illinois State Historical Society
vol. 92, no. 1 (Spring 1999)

The Universalist church of Joliet had long planned for a new and larger building, and finally in 1892 it opened the Auditorium Block. Among the building's purposes was to aid in the commercial development of the downtown area and to provide more space for civic and cultural events. By renting the space for such use, the church was able to improve and stabilize its own finances. Its leaders were men of prominence in commerce and industrial life of the Joliet area; many were civic leaders. This article won a Pratt Award in 1999.

The Nature and Character of Nineteenth-Century Joliet Universalism

Universalist history in Joliet was very much bound up in the material and cultural development of the city during the nineteenth century. From its humble beginnings as a prairie settlement in 1831, Joliet quickly separated itself from similar communities by [the time of] the Civil War largely because of its fortunate location, which enabled Illinois capitalists to centralize transportation, commerce, and manufacturing in the locale. During the three decades between 1860 and 1890, population in the city increased threefold from around seventy-one hundred to over twenty-three thousand inhabitants, with the area east of the Des Plaines River becoming the city center because of the availability of rail transport, financial institutions, industries, and other infrastructure. Joliet became known as the "City of Steel and Stone" because of ore processing and extraction, but other entrepreneurial and corporate endeavors included breweries, real estate, agricultural commodity exchange, farm implement manufacturing, bottling, and retail sales. Due to accelerating demographics and enterprise, building construction in Joliet very much reflected the expansiveness of the modern age. The *Joliet Daily News* noted that "[n]ew buildings since 1885 have sprung up more rapidly in proportion than the population." A week later the same publication noted that the city's prosperity was very evident in the razing of old city landmarks and the construction in their place of new business blocks. One of these would be the Auditorium Block, reflecting the consonance between Universalists and Joliet history.

The Universalists were among the earliest settlers in the area that would become Joliet, but that early beginning did not ensure the success of the congregation as it faced formidable challenges throughout much of the nineteenth century. As early as 1836 Universalists first convened in the three-year-old settlement then known as Juliet. Originally meeting in local public and commercial buildings, Joliet Universalists initially began raising subscriptions to construct a church building in 1838 but quit the project after raising only $240. Two years later they raised funds sufficient to build a small, wooden frame meetinghouse at a cost of only $1,800 on the corner of Chicago and Clinton Streets, located in the business district east of the Des Plaines River. The low cost of the structure was partly attributable to its modest design and partly to the fact that congregants volunteered their own labor and some of the tools and material for the project. By 1844 the congregation incorporated itself as the First Universalist Society of Joliet and ratified its first constitution. Eleven years later the society sold the wooden frame building (which was then moved to another location by the purchaser) and erected an elegant stone church costing $22,000. This 1856 Gothic-style edifice showed that the Universalists were both affluent enough to undertake a major construction project and conscious of making a suitable aesthetic appearance in the developing downtown area.

Unfortunately, the Universalists' commitment to the new building and an attractive downtown location failed to bequeath congregants a future free of hardships. From 1836 until 1878 the Universalists struggled to maintain a permanent pastorate, often resorting to guest ministers or supplying the pulpit from within the congregation. This lack of ministerial continuity may have been symptomatic of worsening financial prospects, which, in turn, contributed to the congregation's inability to ensure a stable ministry. Problems such as chronic indebtedness and at least one lawsuit plagued the congregation during the post–Civil War years and, at one point, nearly convinced society members to sell their property to the Roman Catholic Diocese, which had lost a parish church in a fire. At this critical juncture, activist congregants led by J. D. Paige took control of the church and restructured finances so successfully that the society not only quickly repaid all of its debt but was able to update its facilities by purchasing the first pipe organ in Joliet. Most importantly, this newfound financial stability allowed the congregation to recruit a young minister, A. H. Laing, who would remain in the Joliet pulpit for the next three decades.

When the Reverend A. H. Laing assumed the pastorate of the First Universalist Society of Joliet in 1878, he provided the congregation with the stability it needed, although his tenure was not without some troubled times. In the forty-two years of Joliet Universalism before Laing, thirteen clergymen had ministered to the congregation on a relatively full-time basis, although intermittent periods totaling nearly a decade saw the congregation without a regular pastor. Laing, a Civil War veteran, began his pastorate in Joliet on September 1, 1878, and remained with the Universalist congregation until his retirement in 1908. Under his leadership, Joliet Universalists reorganized the congregation, updated the church finances, played an increasingly visible role in municipal affairs, and built the Auditorium Block. Times were not always salubrious for Laing, however, and on several occasions he tendered his resignation. But each time the congregational leadership found the financial wherewithal to retain one loved "for his sterling qualities as a man and a minister of the gospel." What perhaps so endeared Laing to his congregation and the Joliet religious community was his ability to synthesize secular and sacred topics, which, of course, attested to this Universalist theology. A perusal of Laing's sermon subjects in the early 1890s, when the Universalists had undertaken their great building project, shows that the minister used the heroes of the Civil War—Lee and Jackson, Sherman and Porter—to teach great moral lessons. He conceptualized "Gospel Temperance" not as pharisaic moralizing but as a device for uplifting humanity. And, in perhaps one of his finest efforts, Laing addressed the controversy over having the Chicago Columbian Exposition of 1893 open on Sunday by arguing that the opening of an art gallery and similar venues nurturing mankind were not inconsistent with the Sabbath. It should not be surprising, then, that a minister comfortable with a pragmatic and syncretic approach to faith would also be comfortable with enterprising lay leaders who envisioned a bold new program for their local church.

The fact that civil and commercial leaders had long exerted profound leadership over the Joliet Universalists made the congregation both especially sensitive to the economic development of downtown Joliet and eventually willing to craft a solution to church needs that combined congregational, commercial, and civic impulses. Among the earliest Universalists were Charles Sayler, Benjamin Richardson, N. H. Cutter, Uri Osgood, H. D. Higinbotham, and Abijah Cagwin. These men's economic endeavors ranged from the service sector to manufacturing, banking, and agriculture. Yet their interests did not just pertain to economic development in antebellum Joliet. For example, Cutter, a farmer, served as alderman, justice of the peace, assessor, and school director; Osgood, one of Joliet's first attorneys, served in the state Senate; and Abijah Cagwin, an 1835 settler active in commodity investment, manufacturing, and finance, served in various political capacities, including justice of the peace, county judge, and city treasurer. The legacy of community activism by such early Universalists set a precedent for the postwar period, especially when reinvigorated by the teachings of a dynamic, young pastor.

And it was the postwar generation of Joliet Universalists that sought to reconcile liberal religion with modern, urban reality in Joliet. Profiles of five prominent Joliet Universalist leaders—all strong supporters of the Auditorium Block—testify to the intimate relationship between spiritual and secular concerns. L. E. Ingalls, who served on the board of trustees in the 1880s, ran a lumber company in Joliet before investing in real estate and serving as general superintendent of the Agricultural and Mechanical Association, which sponsored an annual local fair. John F. Wilson, clerk of the church board during construction of the Auditorium Block, was well connected with the local manufacturing establishment, having helped supervise finances for the Joliet Iron and Steel Works. George M. Campbell was, like Wilson, well acquainted with the industrial side of Joliet, since he was an equal partner and secretary treasurer of the Joliet Stone Company. Like Campbell, George J. Munroe served as a church board member in the 1880s and then on the building committee in the early 1890s. Munroe, at one time Campbell's partner with the Joliet Stone Company, was a highly successful attorney and financier, which made him the ideal person to supervise the financial affairs of the Auditorium Block. Munroe, also involved in civic affairs, served on the board of directors for the Joliet Public Library.

Among the enterprising measures undertaken by society members, Paige included organization of the First National Bank, modernization of police and fire departments, formation of the waterworks and first telephone company, enforcement of saloon regulations, and various other projects both civic and commercial. It was this industrious temperament among church members—especially in consideration of recent congregational challenges and new commercial opportunities downtown—that convinced the Joliet Universalists that it was both desirable and possible to link spiritual and material interests in constructing a new church edifice.

Economics, then, help explain why the church leadership persuaded Joliet Universalists to conceive of a new church building as more than a house of worship, but also influencing the project was the fundamental faith of the age in the unity of progress. From Abijah Cagwin and Henry Higinbotham to George Munroe and J. D. Paige, Universalists witnessed the fairly rapid and intensive urbanization and industrialization of their city. From its humble beginnings as a collection of farms and mills along the Des Plaines River, Joliet had become one of the state's principal industrial centers by the final years of the nineteenth century. The Illinois and Michigan Canal and several railroads made the downtown area east of the Des Plaines River the thriving center of commerce, thereby increasing the value of the Universalist property. Along with transportation systems, Joliet's economy included breweries, iron and steel manufacturing, production of agricultural implements, limestone extraction, flour mills, a state prison facility, and much more. Such economic activity attracted workers who swelled the population of the city, thus creating myriad opportunities for those in the financial, service, and professional sectors. And this was good. Or so believed the citizenry of late nineteenth-century Joliet. For at least one modern observer, such faith in progress reflected the worldview of nineteenth-century Americans. Richard D. Brown argues that for

> nineteenth-century people [like the Joliet Universalists] the drama of modernization of thrift, self-discipline, and improvement for the sake of future rewards, was underwritten by religious faith for Protestants, Catholics, and Jews. Modernization was endowed with moral purpose, as mankind would be raised from ignorance, superstition, filth, and

degradation so as to become enlightened, cosmopolitan, rational, and productive. Experience merged with secular and religious aspirations to legitimate modernization.

Economics, *zeitgeist* (the spirit of the age), and religious conviction, then, animated the designs of Universalist leaders as they sought to utilize their downtown facility more efficaciously, but, as events would demonstrate, vision and implementation were two very different things.

The Universalists' Auditorium Block and the Commitment to Progress

The decision to raze the old church building in the name of progress met some initial hesitancy on the part of society members. Because of previous financial problems, church leaders by the late 1880s desired to improve the society's finances and, as a first step, appraised the value of the Chicago Street property, which assessors found to be worth in excess of $29,000. For the next two years church leaders discussed the possibility of using this valuable downtown property to increase church income and, in 1888, proposed to "borrow a sum not to exceed six thousand dollars . . . to be used to build a block of one story brick stores" along Chicago Street. The congregation at first opposed church involvement in such secular matters as rent collection and soundly defeated the measure by nearly a two-to-one margin, voting instead for a new subscription drive to erase the monthly deficit of fifty dollars. Apparently, this solution did not ameliorate the financial situation, for at the annual meeting in November 1889 the congregation approved a special ways and means committee to "examine the financial condition . . . and report . . . with plans, ways, and means for conducting the matters for the following year."

The selection of a special ways and means committee proved decisive in committing Joliet Universalists to a new, radical course despite the previous rebuff. At a special congregational meeting on December 9, 1889, the ways and means committee presented its report, calling for a comprehensive, long-term solution. The committee report states that

> it is advisable to lease the [present church] property for ninety-nine (99) years and take the lease to raise the money to build the church elsewhere or move the present church to the east side of the lot, and lease 90 feet in depth of the Chicago Street front, and use receipts from the lease to meet necessary expenses.

This proposal passed with overwhelming support from the congregation, yet not without some heavy politicking and ruffled feathers. There was an almost cabalistic intercourse between the church board and the ways and means committee, both led by prominent capitalists such as Paige and Munroe, who supported the project. To their credit, however, church leaders tried to soothe opposition in the congregation by nominating two opponents of the plan, M. Brunson and L. Hyde, as trustees; however, the two men refused to serve and continued to oppose the plan for the new building, although in vain. The machinations behind securing approval for a multipurpose facility evidenced the key leadership role played by businessmen in restructuring the nature of Joliet Universalism.

The newly installed church board and a special building committee formulated plans for the new building in early 1890. As the board and building committee began work, however, Reverend Laing, disappointed over the congregation's failure to raise his salary as expected, tendered his resignation. Board members comprehended that the popular minister's resignation could derail their ambitious new project; therefore, while publicly mulling over a replacement for Laing, church leaders privately worked out a plan to increase his compensation and thereby persuade the minister to withdraw his resignation. With the pastorate now firmly settled for the foreseeable future, work proceeded on the new building project. After considering diverse plans, the building committee settled upon a combination commercial and church building, selecting a design submitted by Joliet architect and church member G. Julian Barnes. On April 3, 1890, the congregation first received the general building plans as well as guidelines for securing a $45,000 loan to pay construction costs, and, by a vote of twenty-four to three, overwhelmingly accepted the joint proposal.

The Universalists' planned construction of the Auditorium Block represented a significant commitment to religious modernization, but it was only the first—albeit most important—step in the process. Church leaders also pressed for a reorganization of the society that had been defeated four years earlier. On August 4, 1890, during a specially convened meeting, the congregation adopted several reorganization schemes. First, the official name of the congregation changed from the First Universalist Society of Joliet to St. John's Universalist Church, a name that apparently had been in informal use for some time. Second, the congregation reincorporated under the provisions of the General Act of 1872 for church corporations. Third, a new constitution, replacing the original one of 1844, substantially

changed the method of electing board members. Later that year, the congregation replaced the 1844 bylaws with a set that was in accordance with
the new constitution. Most of these changes were not extremely drastic.
However, the reincorporation of the church under the 1872 General Act
and the reorganization of church offices—considered along with the plans
for the new multipurpose church facility—exemplified Universalist desires
to modernize the association along the lines of the more highly organized
American secular society of the age.

In addition to congregational governance, church leaders addressed new
financial challenges occasioned by their building project. Methodically, Reverend Laing and board members dealt with disparate concerns. Since church
facilities were unavailable during the construction project, the church board
rented space in the Grocer's Block for Sunday Services and laid off choir
members in order to reduce expenditures. Church leaders approved plans
for selling salvageable materials and unneeded furnishings, and Reverend
Laing directed efforts to move and store musical instruments and furniture that would be used in the new building. Most notably, Reverend Laing
and others convinced congregants to replace the time-honored method of
funding the church through pew rentals with a more systematized plan to
canvass church members for pledges. Through the autumn of 1891, these
efforts raised over $2,000, resulted in a cash surplus of $228.26, and reem-
phasized the commitment of church leaders to a more commercially viable
system of church finance.

Finally, in the spring of 1892, with these various material concerns settled, the congregants of St. John's Universalist Church opened their new Auditorium Block. The structure itself reflected both the architectural impulse
of the age and the Universalists' contemporary tastes. Designer G. Julian
Barnes readily applied the Romanesque revival style of H. H. Richardson
then so popular in American church construction. On Monday, March
21, 1892, doors opened to the general public for a gala secular concert that
overflowed the huge auditorium and necessitated additional seating in the
Sunday school room and the foyer. The Universalists opened the Auditorium Building with this secular concert as a celebratory salute to the larger
municipal community, especially since the building was to provide, in part,
a venue for more serious types of entertainment and culture than were generally offered in the city. Two months later the Universalists dedicated the
specifically religious facilities of the building. Three different services held
throughout the day attracted large, generous crowds to listen to prominent

area Universalist ministers and contribute financially to the completed project. One local newspaper reported that

> [i]n all nearly 300 people assisted in what was practically the clearing up of the church indebtedness, and their giving to Joliet another beautiful building that may with pride be reckoned among our best possessions. It is in truth a Universalist church; and as the auditorium is designed for the giving of lectures and concerts, the holding of religious or charitable conventions . . . , as well as holding public worship, the entire city may share in the pleasure of those who have so zealously labored in the uprearing thereof.

Both the public opening and the later dedication services exhibited the enthusiasm of Joliet residents and Universalists for the building project. To church leaders, who had for so long insisted on the merging of congregational, commercial, and civic interests, the successful debut of the Auditorium Block predicted the future survivability of liberal religion in Joliet.

And Joliet Universalism *did* survive in large part because of the financial farsightedness of church leaders. Admittedly, the financial exigencies of the construction project proved greater than initially imagined, and, as late as the First World War, St. John's Universalist Church negotiated extensions to the original loan. Yet the new rental income promised Joliet Universalists a financial security previously unknown. The building opened for commercial use by the end of 1891 and enjoyed almost full occupancy from the beginning. In October 1894, for example, reporting as agent to both the congregation and the creditor, George H. Munroe declared

> all of the property is occupied and rented. Most of the store rooms are rented for a number of years, and the offices until next Spring. The rentals of the store property being at the same rate as we received in 1892, when times were prosperous. Rentals are generally much lower, but the value of the church property is increased owing to its practically becoming the center of business.

Church financial records bear out nearly continuously full occupancy even during the Panic of 1893 alluded to above. Retailers such as the Grand Union Tea Company, Stillman Pharmacy, Rene Christens, E. E. Henry & Co., and Drew Inman held lengthy leases during the 1890s. Businessmen such as J. D. Paige, George Campbell, and George Woodruff rented office space, while attorneys, physicians, dentists, and other professionals practiced in the building. The Auditorium Block also housed at various times a music college, telephone companies, and a local lodge of the International Order of Odd Fellows. In 1891 the annual rent of commercial properties amounted to nearly $7,000, and, even during the severely depressed mid-1890s, rentals amounted to well over $6,000. These rentals even further cemented the relationship between church and commerce as congregational leaders became responsible for renovating the property to suit new tenants, negotiating leases, and employing maintenance personnel.

Not just financial gain made the Auditorium Block a success, for the building also served as an attractive cultural venue for Joliet. A perusal of local newspapers during the quarter century following the building's dedication shows a wide range of activities, including meetings of fraternal organizations, lectures, and concerts, held in the structure. Typical of these events was a 1902 recital by a well-known contralto, Myrtle Wilkins, who accompanied by local and Chicago instrumentalists performed, among other numbers, the *Habanera* from Bizet's *Carmen*. Some of these musical presentations represented more than simple cultural edification. For example, on May 5, 1917, the local Business Women's Club sponsored Madame Labadie, a touring singer and dramatist, in an Auditorium Block concert for the benefit of the Hannah Harwood Home for Working Girls. Perhaps the most memorable event hosted in the building was a festive evening banquet held in honor of visiting president Theodore Roosevelt on May 12, 1905. These types of programs well reflected the Universalists' faith in the merging of secular and spiritual interests.

RELATED READING

Stephen Freedman, "Organizing the Workers in a Steel Company Town: The Union Movement in Joliet, Illinois, 1870–1920," *Illinois Historical Journal* vol. 79, no. 1 (Spring 1986).

PART V

THE EXPOSITION
THROUGH THE 1920S

23.

ILLINOIS AND THE FOUR PROGRESSIVE-ERA AMENDMENTS TO THE UNITED STATES CONSTITUTION

John D. Buenker

Illinois Historical Journal vol. 80, no. 4 (Winter 1987)

The Progressive Era amendments created a national income tax (the Sixteenth), authorized the direct popular election of senators (the Seventeenth), established a national policy of Prohibition (the Eighteenth), and extended the vote to women (the Nineteenth).

The author identifies the attitudes, groups, and politicians in support or opposition to each one. He includes the history of each amendment in Illinois and nationally, noting that income tax was an issue as far back as the Civil War. The amendment passed early and easily in Illinois. The activities of the colorful and corrupt Republican Party boss William Lorimer had a major impact on the Illinois General Assembly's approving the direct election of senators. The conflict over the Prohibition amendment more than any other reflected the traditional antagonism between Chicago and downstate. This amendment had in terms of support some linkage with the women's suffrage amendment. The approval of the suffrage amendment in Illinois had a major impact on its approval nationally.

John D. Buenker

The primary purpose of this paper is to examine Illinois' role, both positive and negative, in generating the climate of opinion that suffused the proposal and ratification of the four Progressive Era amendments, as well as the later Twenty-First Amendment. Second, it will delineate the sources of support for and opposition to each amendment, especially within the halls of the Illinois General Assembly.

The Progressive Era reformist impulse, in Illinois and elsewhere, was essentially the response of people from a variety of ethnocultural, socio-economic, and geographical backgrounds to the emergence of the United States as a modern, urban-industrial, multicultural world power. Galvanized by rapid and massive alterations in their life situations, large numbers of Illinoisans in similar circumstances banded together to advance their mutually perceived self-interest and to promote their common conception of the general welfare. Initially, that organizational revolution spawned a bewildering variety of voluntary associations, including business and professional organizations, labor unions, farmer cooperatives, settlement house federations, women's clubs, fraternal and benevolent societies, social gospel institutions, and altruistic reformist groups. Eventually, however, nearly everyone acquiesced in the necessity to engage in political activities by campaigning for compatible candidates and lobbying for desired legislation. The surest road to political success was to build a series of shifting, issue-oriented coalitions whose members were at best compatible and at worst mutually contradictory. Nevertheless, they agreed on a common candidate, party, program, or law. As issues changed, allies of one coalition often found themselves adversaries, and vice versa. Coalitions that supported and opposed the four Progressive Era constitutional amendments in Illinois were each *sui generis*, generated by the internal logic of the specific issues involved rather than by some consistent disposition either for or against "reform" or "progress."

The situation was further complicated by the continual factionalism that plagued both major parties and by the enduring antipathy between Chicago and the rest of the state. The Republican Party was divided into as many as five factions, all primarily centered in Chicago, with allies downstate. First was the "federal bunch" headed by such national office holders as Joseph Cannon, Shelby Cullom, and Charles Dawes. Second was the "machine" faction led by William Lorimer and his allies Fred "Poor-Swede" Lundin and William "Big Bill" Thompson. Next was the "reform" faction led by major Chicago newspaper publishers—Victor Lawson of the *Chicago Daily News*,

Herman Kohlsaat of the *Inter-Ocean*, and the Medills, Pattersons, and Mc-Cormicks of the *Chicago Tribune*. Sometimes allied with the publishers and sometimes not were the "insurgents" led by Harold Ickes, Raymond Robins, and Charles Merriam of the Windy City and Frank Funk of Bloomington; these men eventually formed the nucleus of the Progressive Party in 1912. Finally there were the followers of Governor and United States senator Charles Deneen, who fluctuated between alliances with Lorimerites and reformers.

Democrats were split at least three ways, with each faction again deriving its leadership and primary constituency from Chicago. First were the followers of former mayor John P. Hopkins and his ally Roger C. Sullivan. Next were the supporters of five-time mayor Carter Henry Harrison II, who sometimes cooperated with reform elements of the Republican Party and sometimes with various Democratic ward bosses who wielded the real power within party councils. Finally there were the "radical" Bryan-Altgeld Democrats led by Chicago mayor and Illinois governor Edward F. Dunne. Each faction was willing to support reformers or ward bosses in order to achieve and retain power; they often made bipartisan deals that involved "knifing" candidates of their own party.

Superimposed upon this pattern of intraparty warfare was the ongoing rivalry between Chicago and downstate Illinois. For the most part, factionalism and geographical rivalry tended to protect the status quo against "reform," but that was not always the case so far as the four amendments were concerned. The absence of an integrated, statewide Republican organization, for example, clearly enhanced the chances for ratification of the Sixteenth and Seventeenth Amendments. By the same token, antipathy toward Chicago was a unifying force in the debates over Prohibition, while factionalism allowed suffragists and prohibitionists to divide and conquer.

Federal Income Tax Amendment

The early and relatively easy Illinois ratification of the income tax amendment in 1910 was especially significant because it so thoroughly confounded the assumptions of proponents and adversaries alike. Based upon the experience of the Civil War and 1894 federal income taxes and the machinations that attended the proposal of the Sixteenth Amendment, it was almost universally assumed that the most effective opposition would come from heavily industrialized states with significant concentrations of high-income earners and strong Republican organizations. The former condition was especially crucial because it was almost universally assumed that any income tax levied under the power conferred by the amendment would affect, at most, the upper 5 percent of income receivers. During the Civil War, Illinois residents had ranked fifth in the amount of tax paid, behind only New York, Pennsylvania, Massachusetts, and Ohio. Residents of those five states—along with California, New Jersey, and Maryland—had paid nearly 80 percent of the Civil War tax. When the income tax finally went into effect in 1913, inhabitants of those same eight states paid about three-fourths of the tax levied. Beyond those states, there were only eight others that accounted for more than 1 percent of the national total. The 2.9 percent of Illinois' 1913 income receivers who took in over $5,000 a year accounted for 16.3 percent of its income. The 0.9 percent over $10,000 received 10.1 percent of the total. Fourteen residents took in over $1 million a year, while another five hundred or so took in over $100,000 a year. The state ranked third in the number of millionaires, behind only New York and Pennsylvania, while those three states, along with Massachusetts and Ohio, accounted for three-fourths of those who earned over $100,000 annually.

Although Illinois clearly fit the socioeconomic profile of a state opposed to income tax, that condition was largely obviated by geographical rivalry and Republican factionalism. Because nearly all of those who earned over $100,000 a year were Chicago-based industrialists, financiers, and professionals, the amendment benefited from the traditional antipathy of the downstate area toward the Windy City. By the same token, it also profited from the influential populism of the Bryan-Altgeld Democrats who had rallied behind Mayor Dunne's unsuccessful but exciting campaign for municipal ownership of the transit system from 1905 to 1907. Any hopes of Republican solidarity were quickly dashed by Governor Deneen when he endorsed ratification in early 1910, even though he qualified his position by opining that it "is a disputed question whether or not such a tax should be imposed by the nation in ordinary times." Significantly, the spokesman of another reformist Republican faction, the *Chicago Tribune,* not only favored ratification but also challenged other major industrial states to follow suit lest they be considered selfish and unpatriotic.

Significantly, the ratification resolutions in the respective houses of the legislature were introduced by two downstate lawmakers in bipartisan operation. In the Senate, ratification forces were led by Charles Hurburgh of Galesburg, a Deneen Republican. In the House the forces were headed by Democrat Martin J. Dillon of Galena. The vote in the upper chamber was 41–0, with twelve of the thirteen Democrats and twenty-nine of the thirty-eight Republicans voting for ratification. Significantly, nine of the ten senators who were absent or abstained were Republicans, but their number included Frank Funk, who was to be the Progressive Party's gubernatorial candidate in 1912. In the lower house, the tally was 83–8, with sixty-two members either absent or abstaining. Of the eight nay votes, two were cast by downstate Democrats and six by Republicans, including Speaker Edward D. Shurtleff of Marengo, whose loyalties were usually with either Lorimer or the federal bunch. On the Democratic side, such prominent Sullivanites as Anton Cermak and John H. McLaughlin were not recorded, but Robert E. "Bathroom Bob" Wilson, another Sullivan loyalist, voted for ratification. The large number of those not recorded consisted mostly of regular Republicans and Sullivan Democrats who presumably were unwilling either to declare openly against an obviously popular measure or to antagonize the state's affluent citizens by voting for ratification.

Illinois' early and easy ratification gave great heart to income tax proponents in other major industrial states. Illinois was the fourth state to ratify; it followed southern states with little income concentration at the top. At the end of 1910, the ratification score read nine victories and seven losses, with all the other supporting states being southern; such industrial states as New York, Massachusetts, and Rhode Island had rejected the measure. Not until 1911 did another major industrial state join Illinois in the ratifying ranks. Eventually, all such states, except Rhode Island, Connecticut, and Pennsylvania, followed Illinois' example. The importance of that model was acknowledged by the *Philadelphia Evening Bulletin*, an income tax advocate, when it chided Pennsylvania's regular Republican organization:

> Notwithstanding the fact that only two more states are needed and that they will be found among the ten states that have not acted make it idle for Pennsylvania to say "aye" or "nay" to the proposition, and that such states as Illinois, New York, and Ohio which share with Pennsylvania and Massachusetts the great bulk of the tax, have approved it, yet your committee has recommended that the legislature, as a matter of principle, shall refuse to ratify the amendment.

Direct Election of Senators

Far less positive was Illinois' role in creating the climate of opinion that led to the adoption of the Seventeenth Amendment—direct election of senators—

despite the fact that Illinois was probably the first state to experiment with some form of popular expression on that reform. In 1858 the state Democratic convention endorsed Stephen A. Douglas's position on Kansas while the Republican convention proclaimed Abraham Lincoln "our first and only choice for U.S. Senator," thus making the legislative election, in effect, a senatorial race as well. In 1890 voters in the Democratic primary declared for the right to express their senatorial preference and gave a plurality of thirty thousand votes to John M. Palmer. All told, the majority of Democratic voters in 90 of the state's 102 counties favored the proposition, including Cook County, which contained nearly 25 percent of the state's registered voters. Although the legislature was deadlocked for several weeks, it eventually selected Palmer, and he responded by introducing an unsuccessful resolution proposing direct popular election of senators. In 1902 the general assembly permitted a referendum on the subject, which passed by a margin of nearly six to one. It then memorialized Congress in favor of a constitutional amendment to that effect, one of twenty-seven states to do so. The Illinois congressional delegation regularly supported the proposal of a constitutional amendment, voting 15–1 with six abstentions in 1900. After 1905, Illinois candidates for United States senator could appear on the primary ballot by presenting a petition signed by five thousand legal voters, but that election was "for the sole purpose of ascertaining the sentiment of the voters in the respective parties." That was as close as Illinois voters came to direct election before the Seventeenth Amendment, but clearly there was much popular sentiment for the innovation.

Illinois' greatest gift to the cause was to serve as a concrete illustration of the evils of election by state legislatures between 1909 and 1913. "Perhaps the one thing that forced consideration of the resolution," George E. Mowry concluded, "was the so-called Lorimer affair." Less sweepingly, George H. Haynes, considered the leading Progressive Era authority on the U.S. Senate, pronounced the Lorimer case and the three-month deadlock over the selection of two Illinois senators in 1913 as two of a dozen or so illustrations of the worst features of legislative election that occurred during the last five years before the adoption of the Seventeenth Amendment. Whether considered separately or as part of a pattern, there can be little doubt that the Lorimer case and the fortunes of the Seventeenth Amendment were inextricably intertwined between 1909 and 1912. From January to mid-May of 1909, the Illinois General Assembly was deadlocked over the selection of a senator; the two leading Republican candidates refused to compromise. It was not until May 13 that Lorimer, who had not been a candidate during the 1908 preferential primary, received his first votes. The very next day, Lorimer, the Republican "Blond Boss," was elected with a total of 108 votes on the joint ballot, including 53 Democrats. A subsequent investigation revealed that Lorimer's election had been greatly aided by a slush fund of $100,000 raised by large Chicago corporations and that the votes of at least seven legislators had been secured by bribery. Four of the seven confessed in open court that they had accepted bribes.

In the United States Senate, a coalition of Insurgent Republicans and Progressive Democrats led the interconnected fight to unseat Lorimer and enact a direct election resolution. The former were headed by William E. Borah of Idaho and Coe Crawford of South Dakota, and the latter by Robert Owen of Oklahoma and Jeff Davis of Arkansas. In an extended January 1911 speech, Senator Owen concluded,

> I believe if Mr. Lorimer should retain his seat under these painful circumstances it would lower the United States Senate in the esteem of the American people. I believe the time has come when the American people will approve stern measures in dealing with bribery and with corrupt conduct in public affairs, and I think it better for all the people that there should be an end made to the election of Senators by the sinister commercial forces of the Republic.
>
> Mr. President, I submit to the Senate that the time has come for the adoption of a constitutional amendment for the election of Senators by the direct vote of the people, under the safeguard of an honest and thoroughgoing corrupt-practices act and publicity pamphlet such as Oregon has adopted, which gives an equal chance to the rich man and the poor man and strictly limits the use of money in the election of Senators.
>
> In view of the fact that many seats in the United States Senate are about to be determined in various legislatures, it is of the highest importance that the Senate of the United States should give the country to understand that the election of Senators shall be absolutely free from bribery or corrupt practice.
>
> In my opinion Mr. Lorimer was not the choice of the legislature of Illinois nor of the people of Illinois, and his election, so called, is entirely vitiated by the corrupt practices of his supporters, was illegal and void ab initio, and does not merit present recognition.

It is no longer William Lorimer on trial, but the Senate itself is on trial before the bar of the American people.

A few days later, Senator Davis expanded on the same theme by insisting that "if the Senators were elected by the direct vote of the people the country would not witness the nauseating spectacle that the Senate itself presents to the country today in an effort to purge itself of corrupt and improper practice in the selection of one of its Members." Waxing rhetorical, Davis asked, "Why compel men to pass through the season of humiliation and shame through which the sitting member in Illinois is passing if he is guiltless? Why make it possible for men thus to come here if guilty? It is a system vicious and out of date, prepared for a different age and under different conditions than that in which we live. The times demand a different system, a different mechanism for selecting the members of the great body."

As the case against Lorimer built, former president Theodore Roosevelt, courting Insurgent support for 1912, refused to sit with Lorimer at a Hamilton Club banquet. President Taft, who initially cautioned against prejudging Lorimer, later wrote to Roosevelt that the Illinois election "should be stamped with disapproval." Despite that fact, the Senate establishment managed to prevent both Lorimer's unseating and the Seventeenth Amendment on consecutive days. To make direct election unpalatable to southern Democrats, regular Republicans attached an amendment to the resolution that gave Congress the power to alter state election laws. Accordingly, the two groups combined to defeat the resolution 54–33, with Lorimer, in a new definition of *chutzpah*, voting in the negative. The following day the Senate voted 46–40 to retain Lorimer, accepting the argument of regular Republicans that only seven of Lorimer's fourteen-vote margin were secured by bribery. As Mowry correctly noted, "The Senate's defeat of the direct election measure and its retention of Lorimer led to a fusillade of criticism. The *Kansas City Star* even suggested that the Senate be abolished if it failed to reverse the twin travesty."

Just two months later, Insurgent Robert La Follette of Wisconsin succeeded in getting the Senate to reopen the Lorimer case by appointing an eight-man subcommittee of the Committee on Privileges and Elections. After nearly a year of investigation, the majority members of the subcommittee concluded that the Senate had acted in a judicial capacity in 1910 and that the doctrine of *res adjudicata* protected Lorimer from further action. They also found that his election was "the logical result of existing political conditions in Illinois, and was free from any corrupt practice." The three minority members, however, offered a counterresolution declaring that Lorimer's election was invalid. Galvanized by public pressure, the Senate adopted the minority resolution 55–28 on July 13, 1912. It was the only instance in the Senate's history, according to Haynes, when the doctrine of *res adjudicata* did not prevent reopening of an election case once the member's right to sit had been affirmed. Just a few days after La Follette's resolution was adopted, the Senate had voted in favor of submitting the Seventeenth Amendment to the states by a vote of 64–24–3. Consistent to the end, Lorimer joined eight southern Democrats and fifteen other regular Republicans in opposition.

So powerful was public sentiment energized in favor of the Seventeenth Amendment that it was ratified by the necessary number of states in less than thirteen months. Whatever additional impetus it may have needed was largely supplied by another Illinois fiasco. Faced with the task of electing not only Lorimer's short-term successor but a full-term senator as well, the general assembly consumed nearly three months of its 1913 session before compromising on short-term Republican Lawrence Y. Sherman and long-term Democrat James Hamilton Lewis. The deal was finally consummated on March 26, just two months before the final triumph of the amendment, and the attendant critical publicity certainly did the measure's chances no harm. Haynes called it "an appropriate ringing down of the curtain upon the election of Senators by state legislatures."

Seeking to salvage its tarnished reputation, the Illinois General Assembly moved quickly to ratify the amendment, but only after Lorimer Republicans tried unsuccessfully to stall. Failing to defeat Chicago Democrat John P. Denvir's motion to submit the amendment to the favorably disposed Committee on Constitutional Amendments, Senate Republicans acquiesced in a unanimous vote. In the lower house, only downstate Democrat Lee O'Neil Browne, one of the Democrats for Lorimer in 1909, voted in the negative against 146 positive tallies. Governor Dunne, an avid supporter of direct election, hailed ratification as "the greatest victory for popular government in fifty years."

Prohibition Amendment

If anything, Illinois' role in the adoption and repeal of nationwide Prohibition via the Eighteenth and Twenty-First amendments was even more negative. More precisely, it was Chicago—along with New York, Boston, Cincinnati, Milwaukee, St. Louis, and a handful of other metropolises—that were

John D. Buenker

chief targets of Prohibition and the worst-case examples that embellished the texts of both Prohibitionists during the Progressive Era and advocates of repeal during the 1920s. "With their simplifying techniques," Andrew Sinclair argued, "the spokesmen of the prohibitionists equated the worst type of Chicago saloon with all liquor." Although historians still debate whether the conflict over Prohibition was primarily urban-rural, ethnoreligious, or socioeconomic in nature, it seems certain that it contained all of these elements in interconnected fashion and that Chicago and similar cities embodied all the evils that Prohibitionists sought to eradicate. "The vices of the cities," Purley Baker of the Anti-Saloon League charged in 1914, "have been the undoing of past empires and civilizations." Prohibition sentiment was clearly strongest in rural areas, among the native-stock middle class of village and suburb, and in such evangelical Protestant churches as the Methodist, Baptist, Presbyterian, Congregational, Disciples of Christ, Mormon, and Christian Science. In the eyes of Prohibitionists, great metropolises like Chicago were primarily the habitats of foreigners, Catholics, Jews, corrupt machine politicians, radicals, charity cases, and purveyors of vice and gambling.

For Prohibitionists, the urban saloon was the quintessential symbol of the dangers that all of the above posed to the American way of life. Only its total annihilation could save American institutions and values from destruction or corruption. "Great cities were the enemies of the evangelical Protestant churches of America," Sinclair argued. "They fostered liberals and agnostics, saloons and Roman Catholics." Prohibitionists, he insisted, "carefully attacked alcohol in its urban foreign form—beer and rum. They did not crusade with any vigor against country liquor—hard cider and corn whiskey. They represented the cities as full of foreigners making evil profits out of poisonous drink." As dry editor Alva Hopkins put it in 1908, "Besodden Europe, worse bescourged than by war, famine, and pestilence, sends her drink-makers, her drunkard makers, and her drunkards, or her more temperate but habitual drinkers, with all their un-American and anti-American ideas of morality and government." In his 1914 article, Purley Baker also charged that "already some of our cities are well-nigh submerged with this unpatriotic element, which is manipulated by the still baser element engaged in the un-American drink traffic and by the kind of politicians the saloon creates." Writing of the early twentieth century from a post-Prohibition perspective, George Ade, author of *The Old Time Saloon*, estimated that "over half the population of Boston and Chicago paid a daily visit to the saloon. Chicago under Capone was a paradise compared to Chicago at this time." Such an outlook was buttressed by the findings of the Chicago Vice Commission of 1910–11 that "the most conspicuous element, next to the house of prostitution itself, was the saloon, and the most important financial interest, next to the business of prostitution, was the liquor interest." To Prohibitionists and vice crusaders, according to Herbert Asbury in *The Great Illusion,* that saloon was "the Devil's Headquarters on Earth." The view of Chicago as a "wide-open city" was also captured in Ade's observation that "when a drink parlor was opened anywhere in the Loop, the proprietor went over and threw the key in the lake." In Chicago and other large cities, Sinclair concluded, "the most obvious symbol of evil and corruption was the urban saloon, where immigrants and Roman Catholics drank and provided the bought votes that supported the unholy Congresses in Washington."

That the urban saloon, as the embodiment of all these evils, was the prime target of Prohibition is also apparent from its chronological/geographic progression. For many years before the adoption of the Eighteenth Amendment, Prohibitionists enjoyed significant success in drying up the country through statewide or county prohibition of local option. By 1917, there were twenty-six totally dry states, nearly all in the south and west, and over half the national population on four-fifths of its land mass was dry. In his *Era of Excess,* Sinclair graphically illustrated that the remaining wet areas were heavily urban, predominantly foreign stock, and largely Catholic. By 1919, there were only twelve states without statewide Prohibition: California, Louisiana, Wisconsin, Minnesota, Missouri, New York, Pennsylvania, Rhode Island, Massachusetts, New Jersey, and Illinois. Even in Illinois there were twenty-six dry counties by 1917 and, thanks to the 1907 law that provided for precinct option, nearly two-thirds of Chicago was legally dry. The remaining saloons were crammed into the slums, working-class neighborhoods, and the Loop, representing what Perry R. Duis has aptly styled "the triumph of moral geography." The dry vote, as Harold F. Gosnell observed, was "found in the higher rental areas where the native white of native parentage predominated."

Still, the vast majority of Chicagoans clearly voted wet, as the success of Anton Cermak's United Societies for Local Self-Government, a multiethnic organization claiming two hundred thousand members dedicated to "personal liberty," starkly demonstrated. "Almost no known dry has been elected mayor, prosecuting attorney or sheriff of Chicago or Cook County," Charles E. Merriam once observed, "and many campaigns have turned chiefly upon the problem of comparative wetness." Outside of Chicago, the remaining wet areas were usually in downstate cities with significant foreign-stock and/ or Catholic populations. Rockford, the state's second largest city and a predominantly Yankee-Scandinavian population, went dry in 1914. Thus it was apparent to Prohibitionists in Illinois and in the rest of the nation that only a constitutional amendment could dry up the great metropolitan centers.

The same ethnoreligious and geographical divisions prevailed in the Illinois General Assembly as it wrestled with statewide Prohibition in 1917 and with the Eighteenth Amendment in 1919. The former passed the Senate 31–18 only to fail in the House by an 81–67 count. In the upper chamber, the largest Prohibitionist bloc consisted of twenty-one downstate Republicans, all of old-stock protestant heritage. The opposition was led by ten foreign-stock Catholic Democrats. Five of Chicago's nine Republican senators voted in the affirmative; they were all old-stock Protestants, one a Baptist minister. Two Chicago Republican senators, representatives of black districts, voted nay, while two others, one Jewish, abstained. The other six negative votes were equally divided between downstate Republicans and Democrats. The three Republicans were an Irish Catholic from Peoria and two German-Americans from East St. Louis and Madison County. One of the three Democrats was an Irish-Catholic from La Salle, while the other two were of old-stock derivation, as were the five downstate Democrats who supported Prohibition. The same pattern prevailed in the lower house where the entire twenty-seven-man Chicago Democratic delegation led the opposition, joined by eighteen of the city's thirty Republican representatives. The twelve Prohibitionist Republicans were all old-stock Protestants while the thirteen in opposition were either black, Irish, German, Swedish, Norwegian, or Jewish. Downstate, all of the fifteen Democrats and thirty-nine of the forty Republicans who supported Prohibition were old-stock Protestants. Of the twenty-three Democrats and twelve Republicans from downstate who opposed the measure, seventeen were Roman Catholic, fifteen were of Irish extraction, and ten were of German descent.

Much the same pattern characterized the vote on the ratification of the Eighteenth Amendment, which passed the Senate 30–13 and the House 84–66. Once again, the entire Chicago Democratic delegation, all foreign-stock Catholics, voted no, as did three Windy City Republicans (one Irish, one German, and one Jew). Five of the city's old-stock Republican senators supported ratification, while the other abstained. Downstate, the Senate vote was nearly identical to that of 1917 except that two dry Republicans had replaced wet senators from La Salle and East St. Louis. The same five old-stock Democrats voted yes, while the same two Democrats were the only old-stock senators to vote in the negative. In the lower house, dry gains in the 1918 elections facilitated the triumph of ratification, but the voting pattern was almost identical to that of 1917. Once again the entire Chicago Democratic delegation (eighteen Irish, three Jews, one Czech, two Italians, one German Catholic, and one Pole) declared against prohibition. They were joined by fifteen Chicago Republicans (two blacks, two Jews, three Irish, three Germans, one Norwegian, one Swede, one Pole, and one Yankee). By contrast, all but four of those Chicago Republicans who supported ratification were old-stock Protestants. The largest single bloc of downstate lawmakers who favored Prohibition consisted of fifty-seven Republicans, all old-stock Protestants except for one Irish Catholic from Lockport. They were joined by twenty-two downstate Democrats, all but one of whom were old-stock Protestants. Of the fourteen Democrats in opposition, nine were of Irish or German extraction, while the rest generally represented Chicago suburbs or East St. Louis. Eight of the eleven dissenting downstate Republicans were of Irish, German, or Swedish descent, while the other three represented Peoria, Belleville, and suburban Chicago. Perhaps the division in the legislature and in the state as a whole was best summarized in a debate between Chicago Democrat John Boehm, a Czech Catholic, who denounced the Eighteenth Amendment as part of a larger design to take away "his religion and his God" and Oak Park Republican Henry Austin, a Son of the American Revolution, who replied that his religion taught him that liquor was evil and that therefore he had never tasted it.

Given Chicago's role in the enactment of nationwide Prohibition, it is ironic, but not particularly surprising, that the city quickly came to occupy a similar and even more prominent place in the lexicon of those advocating repeal. Historian Larry Englemann has referred to Chicago as the "city upon a still," whereas social commentator Herbert Asbury, an avid critic of the Eighteenth Amendment, sarcastically dubbed the Windy City "prohibition's finest flower." Nowhere else, he added, did gangs attain such power as "all the evils of prohibition came to a head." The Research Department of the Board of Temperance, Prohibition, and Public Morals studied Chicago in 1922 in order "to uncover prohibition at its worst." As early as November 1921, the *Chicago Tribune* reported that there were at least four thousand saloons operating in the city, all "selling some kind of beer, some sort of whiskey, and some unbranded wine." Reform Democratic mayor William E. Dever declared in 1923 that the city's more than six thousand "soft-drink parlors" were really fronts for saloons. Two years later he testified before a congressional committee that "no man knows whether there are five thousand or eight thousand or ten thousand or twenty thousand stills in Chicago." While Police Chief Charles C. Fitzmorris ordered policemen to "rivet the lid down until it squeaks" and promised to "make Chicago so dry that a sponge can be wiped across it without picking up a drop of liquor," Mayor "Big Bill" Thompson pledged to make the city "as wet as the Atlantic Ocean" and to break any policeman who enforced Prohibition too vigorously.

While New York probably deserved the title of the nation's wettest city, several others claimed it. According to John Kobler, "In the public mind the depredations of Chicago gangsterism under Al Capone together with the permissiveness of its corrupt, clownish Mayor William 'Big Bill' Thompson came to symbolize the bootleg era." At 12:01 A.M. on the day that the Volstead Act took effect, there were three simultaneous liquor thefts in the city. Eleven days later, Chicago was the scene of the first raid by federal Prohibition agents, and by June of 1920 there were already over five hundred indictments for Volstead Act violations. The federal Prohibition administrator for Illinois estimated that physicians had already issued three hundred thousand suspicious liquor prescriptions by June of 1920 and that fifteen thousand physicians and fifty-seven thousand retail druggists had applied for licenses to dispense intoxicants. Nearly three thousand new wholesale drug houses sprang up in the first five months of Prohibition. Chief of Police Morgan Collins estimated payoffs to state and federal agents at $1 million annually, while the chief investigator for the state's attorney's office claimed that "a one-legged prohibition agent on a bicycle could stop the beer in the Loop in one day if he was honest." Clearly, the nation's most ambitious experiment in joint federal-state law enforcement failed miserably in Chicago, largely due to the bribery of underpaid officials of both jurisdictions.

Sinclair has placed the number of murders during the Capone era at 350 to 400 per year and the number of bombings at 100. Astonishingly, by the end of 1921, the Board of Temperance, Prohibition, and Public Morals claimed that Prohibition had actually lowered the death rate, improved the prosperity of the city, and decreased the number of murders, burglaries, and robberies. Even though rapping the city for nonenforcement, the board concluded that "prohibition has worked wonders in the city." Such views, however, were extremely rare. By 1930, four of the city's five newspapers, most of them former advocates of Prohibition, were clamoring for repeal. John Landesco concluded in his highly regarded study of Chicago crime that if it were not for newspapers, gangdom and political henchmen and protectors would have stolen the town. Although other cities may have rivaled Chicago in the frequency with which advocates of repeal cited it as a case study of the failure of Prohibition, it is certain that none surpassed it.

Women's Suffrage Amendment

By contrast, nothing could have been more positive than the contribution that Illinois made to the adoption of the woman suffrage amendment. Prior to the enactment of its Presidential and Municipal Suffrage Law of 1913, female enfranchisement had enjoyed almost no significant success east of the Mississippi River. It was generally conceded by proponents and opponents alike that major urban-industrial states contained powerful forces arrayed against woman suffrage: (1) industrialists and financiers who exploited female and child labor; (2) machine politicians who manipulated male voters by methods that might not be effective with female electors; (3) liquor and brewing interests who feared that voting women would inevitably engender Prohibition; and (4) foreign-stock males with a narrow "kinder, kirche, kuchen" mentality concerning women's place in society. Those perceptions were exacerbated by the frequency with which leading suffragists linked Prohibition and woman suffrage and contrasted putative, honest, intelligent, independent female voters with ignorant, corrupt, controlled, foreign-stock male electors.

Not until settlement-house workers and others within the suffrage movement who worked regularly with ethnic working-class men and women, labor leaders, and politicians succeeded in moderating the movement's prohibitionist/nativist bent did the movement make significant gains in urban-industrial states. As late as 1912, an advisory vote on woman suffrage lost heavily in Cook County as Lorimer Republicans joined Sullivan and Harrison Democrats in opposition. Despite that, the state Democratic convention of that year endorsed limited suffrage at the behest of Edward F. Dunne, its successful gubernatorial candidate. Dunne assured suffrage leaders that he would not support a constitutional amendment necessary to achieve full suffrage because he was committed to securing initiative and referendum by that route, and the constitution permitted only one amendment per legislative session. Consequently, Dunne convinced suffragists to introduce a proposed statute permitting suffrage in elections where the state constitution did not specify male electors.

Employing new militant, politically astute tactics, suffrage lobbyists led by Grace Wilbur Trout and Elizabeth K. Booth pressured individual lawmakers and organized pro-suffrage forces into units, complete with captains responsible for turning out the vote. When Speaker William McKinley asked suffragists for a demonstration of support to counter the powerful pressures that he was receiving from the liquor interests and fellow Chicago Democrats, they responded with an avalanche of letters, telegrams, and telephone calls that gave the Speaker the necessary mandate. In a dramatic five-hour climax, suffrage leaders guarded the doors of the legislature against antisuffrage lobbyists as the Senate passed the measure 29–15 and the House 83–58. Nine of the ten Chicago Democrats in the upper house and twenty-two of the twenty-six in the lower chamber formed the most appreciable opposition. They were joined by several Lorimer and federal-bunch Republicans and by lawmakers from foreign-stock districts heavily opposed to Prohibition. The victory was clearly a triumph engineered by the native-stock middle class, aided by a handful of radical Democrats. Dunne quickly signed the measure, although later he reported that he had been "importuned in many directions to use my veto power." Although he did not say so openly, it is clear that most of the pressure came from fellow Chicago Democrats. The Progressive Party delegation in both houses unanimously endorsed the legislation.

The impact of the Illinois victory on the suffrage cause was electrifying. No less a person than Carrie Chapman Catt, president of the National American Woman Suffrage Association (NAWSA), later insisted that neither the 1917 triumph of suffrage in New York nor the Nineteenth Amendment two years later would have been possible without the Illinois victory in 1913 and that "the work in Illinois was fundamental and as vitally important to the women of the whole nation as it was to the women of Illinois." Historians Andrew Scott and Anne Firor Scott have concluded that the victory in Illinois, along with those in Washington and California, were the three breakthroughs that brought the movement out of a long period of stagnation. "For the first time in a state east of the Mississippi (and a large populous state at that)," they wrote, "women would be able to vote in presidential elections. Morale rose again." Catt and Nettie Rogers Shuler referred to Illinois as a "turning point" and claimed that "the effect of this victory upon the nation was astounding" and that "suffrage sentiment doubled overnight." According to the *Literary Digest*, the national press referred to the Illinois victory as "important," "notable," "substantial," and "amazing." The *New York World* called it "the first victory in enemy country," while the *Philadelphia Record* proclaimed that suffrage had "crossed the Rubicon." The *Telegraph* of New York warned that no presidential candidate in 1916 could afford to oppose suffrage because Illinois had twenty-nine electoral votes. In the NAWSA history of woman suffrage, Ida Husted Harper opined that "the Illinois legislature led the way and within a few years bills of a similar nature had been passed by those of fourteen other states."

Although enactment of the 1913 presidential and municipal statute was unquestionably the apex of Illinois' contribution to the suffrage cause, the state continued to play a significant role over the next six years. The national press reported that over 250,000 Chicago women voted in the April 1914 municipal elections and that over 15,000 women marched in a suffrage parade down Michigan Avenue on May 2 of that year. On June 14, 1914, the *New York Times* reported that the 1913 suffrage statute had been upheld by the Illinois Supreme Court in a suit brought by a Chicago citizen with the backing of Cermak's United Societies. The court rejected the plaintiff's argument that the statute was, in effect, a constitutional amendment and that by voting on advisory policy questions women were participating in the amendment process. Also in June 1914 the national convention of the General Federation of Women's Clubs met in Chicago and for the first time declared in favor of "political equality regardless of sex." In April 1915 women voters played a key role in the outcome of municipal elections, especially in Chicago, where as Graham Taylor reported in *The Survey*—there were 217,614 women registered, compared to 455,283 men. In the primaries, 73 percent of registered women voted, compared to 72 percent of men. Taylor claimed that women voted overwhelmingly for aldermanic candidates endorsed by the Municipal Voters League, and he credited them with electing at least "seven of the better candidates and with wielding their power either to defeat or lessen the majorities of many more undesirable candidates." Significantly, Taylor estimated that 65 percent of downstate women voting on Prohibition voted dry but admitted that "in some places, as at Springfield, women's votes helped swell the majority for the saloon."

Writing in the *American Magazine*, Hugh S. Fullerton credited women with securing the nomination of Robert M. Sweitzer over Carter Harrison in the Democratic primary and of "Big Bill" Thompson over Harry Olson in the Republican contest. In the general election, an estimated 61 percent of women voted for Thompson in an election that turned heavily on Sweitzer's Catholicism and on his alleged wetness. Ironically, Thompson got the majority of the women's vote as a champion of Prohibition and public schools. Writing in *Harper's Weekly*, William L. Chenery concluded that "Chicago women are not always on the side of 'angels,' but they have shown that they are always interested and powerful in the effort to make their city a more human home." Writing in the same periodical, Katharine Buell lauded the Windy City's women voters and insisted that "what happens in Chicago is probably more typical of the country as a whole than what happens in some of the more cosmopolitan Eastern cities." It was in Chicago that the 1916 Republican convention endorsed suffrage on a state-by-state basis, while its presidential candidate Charles Evans Hughes favored a federal constitutional amendment. Significantly, the *New York Times*, which called Illinois "the greatest of the suffrage states," reported that Illinois women "had voted for Wilson and Hughes generally in the same ratio as the men" and "appeared to be actuated by the same wishes and motives."

In the main, Illinois' actual experience with woman suffrage between 1914 and 1919 convinced many politicians and male voters in Illinois and elsewhere of two very important propositions: (1) that women, while somewhat more susceptible to reformist appeals and women's issues, tended to vote along ethnocultural, partisan, and socioeconomic lines similar to those of men; and (2) that women were not monolithically in favor of Prohibition. Both of these perceptions, along with the efforts of social feminists and labor-oriented suffragists, did much to break down the opposition of ethnic voters and politicians to woman suffrage. The enactment of nationwide Prohibition, ironically, removed one of the major reasons for denying women the vote, as the ultimate horror had come to pass without full woman suffrage.

As a result, most of the overt, effective opposition to woman suffrage had evaporated by the time the legislature considered the Nineteenth Amendment in June 1919. Even Roger Sullivan and Governor Frank Lowden, an erstwhile Lorimer Republican, declared openly for ratification. So irresistible was suffrage momentum in Illinois that it was the first state in the Union to ratify the amendment, by votes of 135–3 and 46–0. The negative votes were cast by recalcitrant Sullivan Democrats. Because of a minor mistake in Illinois' certificate of transmittal, Wisconsin claimed the honor of being the first to ratify, but the United States secretary of state ruled that Illinois deserved that designation. NAWSA's official history of the movement, edited by Ida Husted Harper, concluded that "Illinois, the first State east of the Mississippi River to grant suffrage to its women, was the first to ratify the Federal Suffrage Amendment."

RELATED READING

Suellen Hoy, "Chicago Working Women's Struggle for a Shorter Day, 1908–1911," *Journal of the Illinois State Historical Society* vol. 107, no. 1 (Spring 2014).

The article received the Pratt Award for 2014. It identified the groups in favor of and opposed to a shorter day and their tactics both in Chicago and the Illinois General Assembly.

24.

HEGEMONY AND RESISTANCE AT THE WORLD'S COLUMBIAN EXPOSITION
Simon Pokagon and the Red Man's Rebuke

Lisa Cushing Davis

Journal of the Illinois State Historical Society
vol. 108, no. 1 (Spring 2015)

Of Potawatomi heritage, Simon Pokagon played a prominent part at the Columbian Exposition of 1893 in presenting there both a conciliatory and condemning message toward the white audience.

Born in 1839 in an Indian village in Michigan, Simon learned from his father the history of the Potawatomi—notably, the signing of the 1833 treaty ceding Potawatomi land on which Chicago was built and the 1812 Fort Dearborn massacre. He saw himself as standing between whites and his race. He was an object lesson "in the possibilities of adaptation rather than total assimilation and cultural persistence rather than extinction."

Simon Pokagon was the special invited guest of Mayor Carter Harrison to the Chicago Day celebration of the World's Columbian Exposition in October 1893. Pokagon, whose father signed the 1833 treaty ceding Potawatomi lands on which Chicago was built, was scheduled to participate in a reenactment of the treaty signing and join in the ringing of the Columbian Bell of Liberty in recognition of the sixtieth anniversary of the land cession.

Later, in the parade of floats depicting Chicago history, he was the central figure on the float depicting the events of 1812, including the Fort Dearborn Massacre, in which some Potawatomi participated. Addressing the crowd during the festivities, Pokagon delivered a call for forgiveness of past wrongs and an appeal for the future of his race.

At the time of his address, however, a very different judgment was circulating among the fairgoers, authored by Pokagon and printed on spiritually significant birch bark leaves. It was more condemning than conciliatory:

> On behalf of my people, the American Indians, I hereby declare to you, the pale faced race that has usurped our lands and homes, that we have no spirit to celebrate with you the great Columbian Fair now being held in this Chicago city, the wonder of the world. No; sooner would we hold a high joy-day over the grave of our departed fathers, than to celebrate our own funeral, the discovery of America.

Statue of the Republic overlooking the Grand Basin and the Court of Honor at the World's Columbian Exposition, Chicago, Illinois, 1893. *Photo courtesy Chicago History Museum.*

The explanation for this disparity is a subtext of power, agency, and resistance, underlying the celebration of Chicago Day at the World's Columbian Exposition. Simon Pokagon's engagement with the non-Native community throughout his life, but specifically at the exposition in Chicago, illustrates the complexities of defining an Indian identity in an era in which programs of civilization and assimilation reached their zenith, but during which memories of the "savage" Indian continued to dominate public imagination.

Simon Pokagon was born in 1839 in an Indian village on Pokagon Creek, about one mile from the St. Joseph River on what became Berrien County, Michigan. He was the third son of the Potawatomi chief Leopold Pokagon. Within his tribe, the elder chief was second in rank only to Potawatomi chief Topinabe. Leopold Pokagon signed a number of important treaties with the United States, including the 1833 Treaty of Chicago, which sold and ceded to the United States the territory on which the city of Chicago was built. From all appearances, devoutly Catholic after years of tutelage by the Jesuits (which earned them the distinctive moniker "The Catholic Potawatomi"), Pokagon's band was described as "the farthest advanced in civilization of all their race in the St. Joseph valley." In the press, the Pokagon were portrayed as exemplary Indians to be extolled and imitated. Leopold's reputation with Euro-Americans as a "noble red man," along with the civilizing effect of their Catholicism, persuaded the United States government to allow his people to remain on a small portion of their original land base when other Indian tribes, and all other Potawatomi bands of Michigan, Ohio, and Indiana, suffered the trauma of removal. On this land in southwestern Michigan, Simon spent the early years of his life.

Simon himself relates that he returned to his village in 1850, marrying and settling into the quiet life of a family man, farming, hunting, and spending his evenings in quiet contemplation of his beloved Greek texts. Upon the deaths of his brothers, he became the head of the Pokagon Business Committee, although, because of what came to be seen as his own self-promotion, he later became a controversial figure within the community. In their attempts to collect the annuities due from the 1833 sale of Chicago and the surrounding country, Pokagon was a junior member of the delegation that twice visited with President Abraham Lincoln, as well as [the delegation that visited] with President Ulysses S. Grant. By 1893 Simon Pokagon and his band of Potawatomi were viewed by white society as exemplary models of the level of civilization which could be attained by Native Americans; through the public persona created by Simon

Pokagon, the Pokagon Potawatomi became poster children, if you will, for the success of the assimilationist policies of the United States government in their efforts to eradicate the "savage" Potawatomi, first encountered at Fort Dearborn.

Birth of a City

If his father's tales of the events at Fort Dearborn lingered at the fore of Simon's memory, so it was with the citizens of Chicago, as well. At the time of the World's Columbian Exhibition in 1892–93, Fort Dearborn remained an important touchstone in the collective memory of Chicagoans, particularly the memories of the violence that occurred near the site in August 1812. At that time, the military outpost was little more than a trading post. Built on land acquired from the Potawatomi in the 1795 Treaty of Greenville, it housed a small group of traders, soldiers, and their families. A peaceful relationship with the local Indians was maintained from the signing of the treaty until 1812, when, in the wake of the impending war between the United States and Great Britain, tensions erupted between the Native inhabitants and their Euro-American neighbors. With the declaration of war on August 7, 1812, Indian tribes, including some Potawatomi, allied with the British in hopes of reclaiming their homelands from the Americans.

As the British moved south from their territory in Canada, the fort at Mackinaw fell to the British and the Indians. Detroit was threatened. Under these circumstances, Captain Nathan Heald, the commander of the Chicago outpost, received orders from General William Hull, commander in chief of the Northwest Territory, to evacuate Fort Dearborn with all due haste, bringing soldiers and civilians alike to Fort Wayne. Additionally, Heald was instructed to transport only those stores necessary for their journey and to distribute what remained to the local Indians.

Captain Heald held council with the local Indians, announcing the evacuation and informing them of his intention to distribute among them the surplus provisions, including firearms, ammunition, and whiskey, before their departure. The date for the evacuation was set: August 15, 1812. However, two events of August 14 perhaps presaged the violence that would occur the following day: the destruction of a portion of the promised supplies (including guns and alcohol), and the arrival of a detachment of soldiers from Fort Wayne led by an officer that the Indians despised, Captain William Wells.

On the morning of August 15 the evacuation began, with Captain Wells leading the party south along the shore of Lake Michigan. As they approached the point at which sandhills divided the prairie from the beach, their Potawatomi escort proceeded up onto the prairie instead of following along the beach with the Americans. A short mile and a half further down the trail, Wells's group was confronted by a war party of Potawatomi, and the attack began. In the melee, over two-thirds of the Fort Dearborn garrison were killed or badly wounded.

Over the intervening years, the story of the incident at Fort Dearborn would be told and retold, becoming a sort of creation story for the city of Chicago. Its interpretation became a matter of very public disagreement over eighty-one years later, piqued by one man's memories of the massacre and competing public displays of the "civilized" and the "savage" at the Word's Columbian Exposition of 1893.

The Centrality of Fort Dearborn

The World's Columbian Exposition was conceived as a celebration of the four hundredth anniversary of Christopher Columbus's arrival in the Americas in 1492. Planners intended the event to showcase "the resources of the United States of America, their development, and . . . the progress of civilization in the new world." The United States Congress approved the World's Fair bill in April 1890, with a proposed budget of over $2 million to fund "Uncle Sam's Exhibit." Almost immediately, various federal departments began planning their exhibitions for the fair. The Bureau of Indian Affairs was no exception. To bureau commissioner Thomas Morgan, nothing seemed more appropriate than to showcase the bureau's progress in the "civilization" of the "savage" Indian.

Officials for the city of Chicago were also keen to showcase both progress and civilization. They envisioned the exposition as an announcement to the world that their city, a mere Indian trading post in 1812 and devastated by fire in 1871, had risen from the ashes to become a world-class metropolis. Chicago was advertised internationally as "the most progressive of American cities . . . as well as one of the most prosperous on the face of the globe." Chicago Day, Monday, October 8, 1893, would be a celebration of the city's accomplishments. To effectively demonstrate the progress made, however, organizers deemed it necessary to emphasize the events of the past, including the massacre of "peaceful" white settlers by "savage" Indians at

Fort Dearborn. Conflict between these competing visions, of progress and the past was perhaps inevitable.

Securing the honor of hosting the World's Columbian Exposition was a great coup for Chicago. City fathers took pains to ensure that the "Great Columbian Display" at Chicago was nothing short of a "magnificent success." The site chosen for the exposition, a large portion of the south side park system, offered both an expansive, little-used space for development and a spectacular panorama of the city and Lake Michigan. A referendum approved by voters issued $5 million in bonds to fund the exposition, with an additional $3 million guaranteed by private subscription. Beyond their wishes for the fair's overall success, however, the city's World's Fair Committee planned the Chicago Day Celebration to be the "greatest event in the history of the Exposition."

In line with the theme of four centuries of progress, the day's events reviewed the history of Chicago from its beginnings. As such, the focus necessarily fell on the settlers' most famous early encounters with Native Americans: the signing of the Treaty of 1833 and the massacre at Fort Dearborn. Among the pivotal events in the city's history, the brutality of the events of August 1812 continued to capture the imagination of Chicago's residents, the fort an enduring symbol of tragedy overcome.

At the celebration itself, images of the fort were unavoidable. Tickets printed expressly for the Chicago Day event reproduced an image of Fort Dearborn on their obverse. Ceremonies throughout the day referenced the fort and the massacre. The culmination of the day's events, a spectacular parade scheduled for just after dusk, was calculated to outshine even the Mardi Gras and featured "four floats . . . representing the four greatest events in [Chicago's] history." The most spectacular of the lot, "Chicago in 1812," dealt entirely with the fort and the massacre and was described as "the most noticeable of the entire number in the pageant, [of] purely historical . . . design." The audience was assured that it dealt "exclusively with events that have deep significance in the past of this great town." The *Tribune* concluded that the float, with its historic design, was "sure to be followed with eager attention." Subsequent entries from various civic organizations of the city paid tribute to the development of Chicago and the civilization of the Americas, without further representation of the Indians. In the view of most Americans, progress did not include Native Americans, who were consigned to the past, along with the other obstacles overcome along the path of progress. Popular representations at the fair validated this point of view. Romanticizing the "vanishing red men," tragically, but clearly, defeated in the modern America presented at Chicago Day, there was no future for the first Americans.

Thomas Morgan disagreed with that assessment. The Bureau of Indian Affairs commissioner recognized the potential for major governmental presentation of the Bureau's successful assimilation program at the Columbian Fair. Morgan recognized that the popularity of William "Buffalo Bill" Cody's Wild West shows guaranteed that Indians would be represented at the fair. Refusing to cede primacy to what he considered "a display of savage and repulsive features of [past] Indian life," Morgan was determined that the Bureau's program be the centerpiece of any Indian presence at the fair.

Initial plans for the Bureau's display were based on an expectation that Congress would appropriate funding sufficient to cover several aspects of the assimilation program, as Morgan remained committed to the comparative framework employed at Philadelphia. "The new and the old can be sharply contrasted," he stated, "and though the old may attract popular attention by its picturesqueness the new will impress the thoughtful with the hopefulness of the outlook and the wisdom, as well as fairness, of extending to the weaker the helpful hand of the stronger race." He envisioned an exhibit that, despite sizeable components of traditional Indian culture, would "show conclusively that the effort of the government to educate and civilize these people is being made a triumphant success." Morgan hoped to show that the promise on display at Philadelphia had been fulfilled and that the government was succeeding at making "United States citizens out of American savages."

Unfortunately, when the final budget was approved, Morgan found that Congress had appropriated a meager $25,000 for the bureau's entire exhibit. In view of such budget constraints, Morgan elected to focus exclusively on education, planning to establish a model Indian school capable of housing thirty students and providing exposition visitors with a "complete idea of the educational work that is being done by the government."

As opening day approached, the presence of Indians at the fair became a major topic with the local press. Newspaper accounts initially focused equal attention on the displays of traditional Indian culture, as well as the "progress" made in "civilization." Feature articles described in detail plans for the model school building, its inhabitants, and the curriculum in which the students would be engaged. Unfortunately, because of various delays, the bureau's educational exhibit was not completed in time for opening day at the exhibition; the two hundred thousand visitors that crowded the fairgrounds that May Day saw only representations of the Indian past. One of those visitors was Simon Pokagon.

The Red Man's Rebuke

Simon Pokagon witnessed this mix of memory (which included Native Americans) and modernity (which decidedly excluded the same), on Opening Day. Pokagon, like Bureau of Indian Affairs commissioner Morgan, was a strong proponent of Indian education. Pokagon's disappointment at the delay in the opening of the model Indian school at the exposition was genuine. A product of Euro-American schooling himself (whatever its duration), Pokagon had long advocated for the transformative power of such an education and its importance for the survival of his people. Indeed, his children and grandchildren enrolled in the Indian boarding school in Lawrence, Kansas, over the previous decades. His articulated belief was that "government schools were conceived by the Great Spirit."

At the time, Pokagon's views were celebrated within the non-Native population. Indeed, it was his personal adoption of American-style clothing, his Roman Catholicism, and his emphasis on Western-style education that earned him the respect of white citizens. However, within Native communities—on the reservations and in the homes of Indian families where the harsh realities of government assimilation programs were felt—Simon's message was not necessarily well received. While many Indians agreed with his assessment that only through education would the next generation of Indian children live successfully in the white man's world, many more viewed these schools as reeducation camps, stripping Native children as young as five years old of their language, their culture, and their very identity. Within his own community, Simon Pokagon was viewed as a pawn of wealthy white Americans or, worse, as a self-aggrandizing satrap. While he was not able to completely reconcile his opinions and actions with those of other tribal members, he nonetheless remained a passionate spokesperson for the preservation of Native cultural practices. And, despite his perception of the necessity for change, Pokagon also remained an impassioned advocate for the rights of Indian people.

As Pokagon saw it, Native American communities had evolved just as had white society; while maintaining their distinctive cultural identities, many indigenous people of America were successfully acculturating themselves to Euro-American fashions, agricultural practices, laws, and educational standards. It greatly disturbed Pokagon to see them excluded from the representations of progress or, worse, depicted as somehow frozen in time; to see them depicted as anthropological specimens, as somehow less than human. He later described what he saw that day, "with a critic's eye"; the "aliens and strangers from every land [seated] on the great platform in the shadow of the gilded dome of the Administration building," while he and "a few others of [his] race, the only true Americans stood in the background, unnoticed and un-provided for." As he stood watching the opening festivities, a young Native girl stepped quietly up to him and, seemingly in pity, handed him a small bouquet of wildflowers. In his autobiography Pokagon recalled, "I cannot fully explain . . . why it was, but on receiving the flowers I could not refrain from tears; and even now as I think of it the same tearful feeling creeps through my soul."

What Indians he saw that day did nothing to alleviate his distress. On the Midway Plaisance, the war whoops and battle dances of the Sioux and the "rude . . . dwelling places" of the Navajo and Zuni, without the mitigating influence of the Indian school, belied the progress that Native Americans had struggled to achieve. Public perception being easily swayed, Pokagon feared that in the wake of such dramatics, efforts to promote the successes of Indian advancement would fall on deaf ears. This was the frame of mind in which he wrote *The Red Man's Rebuke*; these were the emotions that inspired such fervent condemnation of the Chicago Fair.

In *The Red Man's Rebuke* Pokagon voiced his resistance to the dominance of Western civilization over his Native culture. Understanding the need for education was one thing; wholesale abandonment of the rich cultural patrimony of his people was a decidedly different matter altogether. At the exposition, and throughout his life, Pokagon attempted to make white Americans better understand his own people and to appreciate the value in many traditional Indian cultural practices. In his later writings, Simon attempted to reconcile his belief that Native peoples would cease to exist with his fervent hopes for their survival; with his belief that Native practices must be abandoned with his conviction in the value of Native skills. In every case, his writings introduced or prolonged the public debate on issues central to the future of Native Americans.

In "The Future of the Red Man," Pokagon offers his dark assessment of the inevitability of Indian "amalgamation with the dominant race." He reviews interactions between Natives and non-Natives—invaders, conquerors, warriors and priests—a brief history to counter defamatory charges of

"Indian treachery and cruelty" which have "always been published to the world by the dominant race." However, while concluding that "the blood of our people . . . will be forever lost in the dominant race," he insists that his audience, that same dominant race, acknowledge the historical exigencies which sometimes forced "vindictive and cruel acts." *"Cruelty and revenge are the offspring of war, not of race,"* he insists, "and . . . nature has placed no impassable gulf between [Indians] and civilization," a conviction he elaborates in two articles written for the *Chautaquan* following his appearance at the World's Columbian Exposition.

In both articles, Pokagon trumpets the value of traditional Potawatomi material culture. "Indian Native Skills" describes not only the artistic talents of Indian women but the craftsmanship of Indian men as well. "Our Indian Women," details the talents and virtues of Native women in contrast to those of their "white sisters." In each, Pokagon extols the expertise of Native women in crafting utilitarian articles from birch bark, their "fancy work" with porcupine quills, and especially their black ash splint basketry. His motivation is not that of a "boastful heart" but the realization that "unless the natural ability of my people is recognized by the dominant race they cannot rise to that station for which the God of Nature intends them." In other words, without recognition of the inherent abilities of the Indians, they could not achieve the "civilization" demanded by that same dominant race.

Some scholars have speculated that Simon's motivation in writing these articles was the increasing demand by museums and tourists alike for Indian handicrafts, thereby promoting the economic interests (and survival) of the Michigan Potawatomi. However, at least one historian places Simon in the vanguard of the discussion of the "social context of contemporary Indian art in America," with material culture a source of ethnic pride and identity. His writings in the 1890s thus presaged discussions held by the Society of American Indians in the first quarter of the twentieth century as well as regulations established "to promote the development of Indian arts and crafts" by passage of the Indian Arts and Crafts Act in 1935.

Simon Pokagon found himself in the difficult position of being caught between two worlds, as did many of his Indian contemporaries. Because of his education and his apparent support for acculturative practices, Pokagon was not fully accepted by his people as Indian; because of his Indian heritage, he often found himself excluded from the very "civilization" he seemingly promoted. Perhaps his writings are best regarded as promoting reconciliation between two races rather than continued efforts to "civilize" Indians

Group of Eskimos in the Eskimo village at the World's Columbian Exposition, 1893. *Photo courtesy Chicago History Museum.*

out of existence. *The Red Man's Rebuke*, the earliest of his published works,
was dedicated to the memory of William Penn and others who promoted
justice for Native Americans, recognized them as brothers, and defended the
race. Written in a spirit of righteous indignation, Pokagon gave voice to the
lamentations of his people, a powerful admonition yet free of vindictiveness.

Pokagon's motivation in writing *The Red Man's Rebuke* was twofold. Not
only did he genuinely resent the exclusion of his people from the opening
ceremonies of the exposition but he recognized the danger to all Native
Americans posed by the prominence of the ethnological exhibits and Indian
villages. He knew that public perception was easily swayed, and the romantic
image of the "savage" Indian was already well established in the American
psyche. Pokagon's fear was that such displays might jeopardize the programs
he believed were crucial to the very survival of the Indian by overshadowing
the very real progress Native Americans had made in their lives.

His fears were soon realized. Public attention shifted from the model
Indian school to the demonstrations of traditional Indian dance, which
shocked many fairgoers and provoked public indignation. An August 20,

1893, editorial called for the World's Fair manager to "Stop the Horrid Torture Dances," which were described in vivid detail. The dance itself, perhaps derivative of the Lakota Sun Dance, involved the piercing of the dancers' skin and was indeed shocking when taken out of context, with no explanation offered as to its origins or its meaning to the dancers. The fact that this dance, so obviously in conflict with the values of the fair-going public, might well have been intended to provoke such a reaction, an overt act of resistance against hegemonic authority, was lost on a crowd that expected to find slightly less exotic entertainment on the Midway Plaisance.

The sentiment expressed in *The Red Man's Rebuke* caught the attention of Mayor Carter Harrison and secured Pokagon's invitation to attend the Chicago Day celebrations as the guest of the mayor. Here Pokagon intended to work directly to counter the misperceptions of both fairgoers and the larger American public. Joining forces with the Department of Indian Affairs in the World's Fair Auxiliary, Pokagon lobbied for a congress of educated Indians to discuss the problems of their race, the most pressing of which was, "Can the North American Indian be civilized or is he incapable of being assimilated in [to] national life and [the] body politic, and consequently doomed to destruction by the conflicting forces that surround him?"

The idea for such a conference was not original to Pokagon or the World's Columbian Exposition organizers. At the time, a group calling themselves the "Friends of the Indians" was meeting annually to discuss strategies to improve living conditions of many Native Americans, which they believed were compounded by failed United States Indian policies. Composed of leading white reform advocates, the group first met in 1883 at Lake Mohonk, New York, and would continue to do so into the twentieth century.

Although he failed in his efforts to secure an Indian congress at the Fair, Pokagon did not fail to make the most of the opportunity to promote both his continued frustration at the exclusion of the Indians as well as his continued belief in the wisdom of adopting at least some of the white man's ways. Addressing the Women's Auxiliary on the eve of Chicago Day, Pokagon expressed his gratitude:

> I am glad that you are making an effort, at last, to have the educated people of my race take part in the great celebration. That will be much better for the good of our people in the hearts of the dominant race, than [the displays] on Midway Plaisance. It will encourage our friends, and encourage us. . . . Tomorrow will make the sixtieth year that has

passed since my father sold for his tribe over one million acres of land, including the site of this city and the grounds on which the Exposition now stands. . . . We wish to rejoice with you, and . . . accept your invitation with gratitude.

On the morning of Chicago Day, nearly seventy-five thousand people crowded Terminal Plaza on the fairgrounds to participate in the opening chorus, to hear the ringing of the Columbian Bell of Liberty, and to witness the ceremonial reenactment of the 1833 transfer of Indian land upon which the City of Chicago was built. Mayor Carter Harrison accepted a parchment duplicate of the title deed for over one million acres from Simon Pokagon, standing in for his father, Leopold, who signed the original treaty. Following the ceremonial presentation, Pokagon addressed the crowd. Published accounts describe him as "quiet, dignified and self-possessed," with a "look of sadness in his face showing . . . the weight of years . . . pressed into a moment of time." His words urged both change and conciliation:

What can be done for the best good of . . . our race? Our children must learn that they owe allegiance to no clan or power on earth except these United States . . . [they] must be educated and learn the . . . trades of the white men . . . [and then] they will be able to compete with the dominant race.

However, even as he called for Native Americans to give up many of their traditional ways and adopt those of the "white man," he continued to support his people's strategic resistance to the cruelty so often experienced at the hands of that "dominant race," reminding his audience that "the red man is your brother, and God is the Father of all."

I was pained to learn that some who should have been interested in our people discouraged our coming to the Fair, claiming openly that we are heartless, soulless, and Godless. Now let us all as one pray . . . that [the Great Spirit] will open the eyes of their understanding and teach them to know that we are humans as well as they.

Simon Pokagon's experiences at the World's Columbian Exhibition inspired a late career as an author. Between 1893 and his death in 1899 he wrote nearly one dozen articles for some of the most prestigious magazines of his time, delivered numerous public addresses, and authored his autobiography. Near the end of his life, Pokagon wrote,

I have stood all my life between the white people and my own people. Without gun or bow I have stood between the two contending armies, receiving a thousand wounds from your people and my own. And I have said to my people, when they were bitterly wronged, and felt mortally offended, "Wait and pray for justice; the warpath will but lead you to the grave."

Thus was the wisdom and quiet dignity of Simon Pokagon, indeed a consummate example of the "civilized" Indian throughout his life, but never more so than at the World's Columbian Exposition. However, Pokagon's was also an object lesson in the possibility of adaptation rather than total assimilation and cultural persistence rather than extinction. Navigating the perilous road between two cultures, Pokagon's was the voice that announced to the world that his people were not desiccated relics of a distant past but remained very much in the present. His was a stance of courage and resistance in the face of a dominant culture determined to relegate the Pokagon Potawatomi, and Native Americans generally, to the dustbin of history. Never doubting the validity and value of his own uniquely Indian identity, until his death Pokagon fought to ensure that all Native peoples would be afforded that same dignity.

RELATED READING

David Silkenat, "Workers in the White City: Working Class Culture at the World's Columbian Exposition of 1893," *Journal of the Illinois State Historical Society* vol. 4, no. 4 (Winter 2011).

David Silkenat focuses on the twenty-five thousand workers, whose jobs included carpentry and other labor, who constructed the buildings and the guards, guides, waiters, janitors, ticket takers and others who kept the exposition's day-to-day operations going. Whether hobos or college students, these workers were primarily young, white, native-born, and highly mobile males. The author provides many case studies of the frustration of finding and keeping their jobs. Grievances over working conditions led some groups of workers to collective action.

Gayle Gullett, "'Our Great Opportunity': Organized Women Advance Women's Work at the World's Columbian Exposition of 1893," *Illinois Historical Journal* vol. 87, no. 4 (Winter 1994).

This article focuses on the development and operation of a complex organizational structure to bring together women's groups and their leaders at the 1893 exposition to promote the advancement of women in the many settings of women's work. While unity was the official position, the author points out the realities of hierarchies of race and class. There was much concern with the oppressive condition of work performed by women in factories, and socialist positions were voiced by some women. Yet working-class women had little involvement with the Board of Lady Managers and representation in the Women's Building.

25.

"HOW I HATE THIS HATEFUL WAR!"
An Illinois Farm Woman Faces World War I

Virginia R. Boynton

Journal of the Illinois State Historical Society
vol. 93, no. 3 (Autumn 2000)

Drawing on a diary faithfully kept for many years, the author relates the activities and thoughts of a western Illinois farm woman, Martha Treadway. World War I was a matter of great interest and worry, as her two sons served in the army in Europe. Her entries also show concern with agricultural issues affecting the family farm. Treadway's diary reveals her vote in 1916 and 1920 as she eagerly took advantage of newly acquired women's suffrage.

L ittle is known of the impact of World War I on the lives of rural Illinois women. Even less is known about their attitudes toward this initially unpopular European conflict. Historians have only begun to investigate the ways in which women found their lives challenged, enhanced, or disrupted by the war. We can begin to illuminate this hidden corner of twentieth-century history by examining the life of Martha Treadway, an Illinois farm woman who lived during the first half of the twentieth century. Martha Treadway might seem at first to be an unlikely subject for historical study. She was not a great statesman; neither was she a leader of the woman suffrage movement. Additionally, although this article focuses on her experiences during World War I, she was neither a worker in a war industry nor an army nurse. She was, in fact, in many ways a perfectly ordinary farm wife of rural west central Illinois, a woman whose life revolved primarily around her family and her domestic responsibilities.

Yet, in another sense, she was quite extraordinary. In 1908 Martha Treadway's oldest son gave her a blank recordkeeping book, and for the next thirty-three years she kept a daily record of her activities and, even more extraordinarily, her thoughts. It is because of this diary that we know of her life, her fears, her hopes, her joys, her sorrows. She was a high-school-educated woman who raised a family of teachers and one school superintendent (all attended "the Normal" in nearby Macomb, Illinois—the future Western Illinois University). So she is perhaps more articulate in her diary than many women might have been. Indeed, the very fact that she recorded her thoughts and deeds at all makes her unusual among rural women of the early twentieth century. However, in many ways, as we shall see, her diary opens up for us a rare window into the personal and private world of mid-western farm women's inner lives, one we would profit by peering through.

Martha Treadway was born Martha Ann Hinchcliff in 1864. In 1886, at the age of twenty-two, she married twenty-seven-year-old John Treadway. After their marriage in Virginia, Illinois, the young couple farmed in Nebraska for eight years, where their four oldest children were born, before moving back home to rural west central Illinois, where two years later they purchased a farm in Chalmers Township, south of Macomb and near Colchester, in McDonough County. Here their last child was born. They farmed in Chalmers Township for thirty-eight years, before retiring to Macomb in the midst of the Great Depression in 1934.

What manner of woman was Martha Treadway? Although she had the self-awareness to keep a diary, she seems to have had no inflated sense of self-importance. This is apparent in one of her diary entries in the early postwar era. In October 1919 she recorded an unexpected visit from her Sunday school class.

My S.S. class and their husbands and families come to spend the evening had a lunch they brought along at midnight and then they gave me a dandy teacher's Bible Nice of them. I sure appreciated it as it was just what I needed. I never suspected it & wondered why they had come . . . never once suspected a present of any kind. never thought of it being just for me alone. I sure was surprised.

Although Martha Treadway dedicated much of her life to the service of others—Sunday school class, family members, friends, and neighbors—she always seems to have been surprised when they noticed and appreciated her efforts.

It is also clear that she did not see herself as having a significant public identity; her perspective was, instead, that of a farm wife. This is evident from one of the many clippings that she saved from the newspaper and pasted into the scrapbook of clippings and pictures that she kept along with her diary. This World War I era clipping, a joke entitled "Milker and Militant," pokes fun at the female public figure who is so absorbed in world events that she fails to consider the everyday necessities of farm life. In this story, "an English militant crusader," presumably a suffragette, "strolled into a barn where a young man was milking a cow" during World War I. "With a snort she asked, 'How is it that you are not at the front, young man?' 'Because, ma'am,' answered the milker, 'there ain't no milk at that end!'" Thus, even though her scrapbook is filled with color magazine illustrations of far-off people and places (from *National Geographic*), her primary allegiance was to her home and family. Indeed, her interest in such places was most likely due at least partly (if not primarily) to her two sons' World War I experiences in Europe.

Throughout the prewar, wartime, and early postwar years, Martha Treadway's life reflected many of the concerns typical of Illinois farm women. Her diary entries regularly reported on a wide range of matters pertaining to her role as wife and mother and help to illuminate those aspects of early twentieth-century rural women's lives. She faithfully recorded the arrivals and departures of her husband, her children, and, eventually, her grandchildren from the farmstead, as well as saving newspaper clippings about their accomplishments. In December 1917 she confided to her diary, "I am lonely for my Kiddies wish I could see all of them." She did not often have such opportunities, however, for as she noted the following month, well before the disruptions brought by the war, her family was "badly scattered" from the Chicago area in the east to Omaha, Nebraska, in the west, with "just Pa and I here alone" in McDonough County. She also recorded the births, illnesses, injuries, and deaths of family members, neighbors, and friends and kept an extensive collection of related newspaper clippings. She detailed her domestic responsibilities, including laundry days, canning days, and time spent processing and preserving the by-products of the farm's seasonal butchering. Her entries also reflect her concern with variations in her own physical health, and she faithfully reports on the state of her spiritual life as well, recording her own attendance (or absence from) Sunday school, together with the number of others present that week.

Martha Treadway's life as a farm woman, however, was also dominated by agricultural concerns, as was common for farm women of her generation in Illinois and elsewhere. Hence, while she comments only sporadically on the state of her husband's and son's corn and potato crops, she is clearly aware of the overriding significance of weather for farmers, as is evident from her frequent references to rainstorms, frosts, and heat waves. She also reports frequently on the state of the family's various livestock, including horses, cows, pigs, and chickens. She records not only the periodic slaughtering of and sale prices received for the livestock, but also births and unplanned deaths among the animals due to illness, injury, or weather. Winter freezes, for example, could take a ferocious toll on the henhouse, which was her responsibility. During the frigid early months of 1918 she noted in middle January that "I took 8 frozen chickens out of the hen house this A.M." A week later, she observed that the toll had risen to eleven, and by the end of February, it was up to sixteen chickens, "froze to death, this winter."

Some of the rest of the livestock was also of particular concern to her because it was her responsibility as well. Her diary includes references in 1916 to "my heifer," "my little black calf," and "my 1st calf" and proudly notes the day in the spring of 1918 when "my little red calf come into the world." In the spring of 1920 she reports that "my cow was gone this A.M. Pa [her husband] found her up at J. McGann's place with a little calf." This was her cow's fourth calf; she had sold the first two and noted that "I have two here." Husband and wife each had their own livestock; she noted in the winter of 1920 that "Pa sold my calf & his. I got $49.50 for mine." Martha Treadway's language—"I," "my," and "mine"—may well reflect her pride in her ownership of this livestock.

Of much greater importance to her, however, were the fragile occupants of her henhouse. Each spring she regularly recorded the number of hens, "chix," and eggs she had, as for example when she reported in the spring of 1918 that she had "181 little chix [sic] from 17 hens." Tending the chickens could be time-consuming work; several times she notes that she "worked all day with chickens," and in the fall she "caught my young chickens & put them in the hen house." However difficult it might be, the work was profitable. In spring 1916 she sold her eggs in the nearby town of Colchester and with the proceeds bought two shirts for her youngest son, as well as wallpaper and curtains for the sitting room and kitchen of her home. Her egg business also allowed her to help out her grown children's families. In spring 1918 she gave the proceeds from her egg sales to her son Willie's family, observing that "they need it . . . worse than I." The next year, she noted, "I gave Laura [her younger daughter, recently married] 15 little chix and loaned her a Mother hen."

That this farm wife was also responsible for maintaining the lawn and garden is apparent from her reference in 1916 to "my lawn mower," which needed fixing and sharpening. Her diary also contains numerous references to the bulbs, geraniums, hollyhocks, and dahlias that she planted, tended, and appreciated. Her appreciation of the beauty that nature brought into her work-dominated life is evident in a diary entry for early fall 1918: "Sunday. Glorious day. Leaves all green red yellow. [T]he time of the year I like."

Although like most farm women she was primarily occupied with family and farm affairs, Martha Treadway was nonetheless eager to exercise her new political rights after Illinois enacted a law in 1913 giving women the right to vote in presidential and municipal elections. In both 1916 and 1917 she notes that "Pa and I went over to vote" in the April elections. However, it was the presidential election in fall 1916—her first—which most engaged her. Two days before the election, enjoying her newly acquired electoral power, she accompanied her husband, son, and daughter (who was also preparing to vote in her first presidential election) to the "big Republican rally" in Macomb. Then on Election Day she proudly recorded that "I went to the Polls and cast my first vote for President," voting for the Republican candidate Charles Evans Hughes. The occasion was further celebrated that night when a neighbor couple "come down to spend the evening and hear the election news. Had lots of fun over it." The evening would perhaps have been less joyous had they known then what they learned three days later—that Hughes had lost the election to President Woodrow Wilson. Treadway does not seem to have been intensely partisan in her politics, however, because she had allowed a neighbor to use her phone several days before the election to make arrangements to attend the "big Democratic meeting" that night. Also, her husband was nominated the following spring by local Democrats for the position of "road Supervisor," although he declined.

In the 1920 presidential election Martha Treadway joined women across the nation when she "went over to vote this afternoon" in the first presidential election since the newly ratified Nineteenth Amendment granted all

American women the right to vote. She rejoiced in the outcome of the voting that day and reflected rural midwestern isolationism when she noted in her diary, "Election all Republican. The Nation wants no League of Nations." Her opposition to the League was also apparent in her decision to give pride of place in the front of her scrapbook to a newspaper column titled "The League of Damnation"; the author of this column ardently opposed the participation of the United States in the League of Nations because such participation would lead the nation to once again "shed good American blood" to assist European monarchies. Martha Treadway's views on this matter were no doubt influenced by her own family's experience with the war which had just ended.

In all these areas of life—her private domestic responsibilities, her economic contributions to her family's welfare, and her new public role as voter—Martha Treadway's life proceeded largely uninterrupted and unaffected by World War I. In other ways, however, wartime brought considerable change into her life. It also proved to be the greatest test of her normally stoic approach to life, generating periodic emotional outbursts not otherwise observable in her more than three decades of diary-keeping as an adult. In large measures, this was because her two oldest sons served overseas in the American Expeditionary Force during World War I.

As the war began for America, Martha Treadway pasted into her scrapbook a poem clipped from the newspaper, a verse she clearly found meaningful in terms of her own wartime experience on the home front. This poem nicely summed up, in a humorous way, the emphasis on conservation during World War I:

> My Tuesdays are meatless,
> My Wednesdays are sweetless,
> I am getting more eatless each day.
> My home, it is heatless,
> My bed, it is sheetless,
> They're all sent to the Y.M.C.A.
> The bar rooms are treatless,
> My coffee is sweetless,
> Each day I get poorer and wiser.
> My stockings are feetless,
> My trousers are seatless,
> Oh! How I do hate the Kaiser.

Martha Treadway's own experience with the wartime home front mir-rored this poet's in several ways. In January 1918 she reported that when her daughter Mary went to Macomb for groceries, she could "only get 88 cts [*sic*] worth of sugar" because that was "all they will sell to one person . . . during this war time." On the other hand, war could bring profit to those with scarce resources, and the farm wife noted that the previous fall her husband had been able to sell one of his brood sows at a very good price, causing her to confide to her diary that it was "some price! But that is the fashion [*sic*] these war times." These experiences were reflected throughout Illinois in women's efforts, spearheaded by the Woman's Committee of the State Council of Defense, to encourage Illinois women to produce and con-serve more food during wartime.

As a family, the Treadways contributed to the war effort on the home front in numerous ways. Both parents took their youngest daughter, Laura, to a movie being shown in nearby Macomb to benefit the Red Cross in May 1918, and they also purchased liberty bonds. When Macomb's "soldier boys" came home from Fort Dodge, Iowa, for a holiday before shipping out, the Treadways contributed money to help pay for a "big dinner" for them. In addition, the war separated Martha Treadway from her youngest daugh-ter, Laura, who married Ted Perkins in June 1918 and immediately moved to Rock Island, where Ted had a "war-work" job. "I wish they could have gone to housekeeping near home," the bride's mother mused to herself, "but maybe they can when the War is over" (which, indeed, they did).

By far the greatest impact of the war for Martha Treadway, however, was the enlistment of her sons in the U.S. Army. As a result of this per-sonal relationship to overseas events, she developed an intense interest in and well-articulated views on United States participation in World War I. As soon as war was declared on Germany by Congress, she began to feel apprehensive, well before her own sons' involvement. On April 7, 1917, she recorded in her diary that "war was declared on Germany yesterday. I do dread the result." Her normally neat handwriting was noticeably shaky for that one entry, and she circled the date, which was not her usual practice. Clearly, she understood the significance of overseas war and was worried about her sons' future. This concern reappears several months later, when she noted on June 5 that "today is registration [day, for the draft]. how I hate it." She reflected the attitudes of many rural Americans that day, in her conclusion that America "should have kept out of this European trouble." She also shared the hostility toward German-Americans that was common during World War I when she worried about the local county extension agent, who was of German descent. She was "afraid of him" she wrote in the privacy of her own diary, for "fear he was a spy." As 1917 approached its close, her pleas that "I wish the war would cease" became almost a litany.

Meanwhile, her sons prepared for the inevitable. On New Year's Eve 1917, Osie, her eldest, who had already been drafted, finished splitting enough wood for his parents to last two winters. His mother noted that Osie "wants to get enough to do me until he gets back from France." She concluded, "I hope he never has to go." She had cause to expand on that sentiment at the end of January 1918, when her second son, Johnnie, was approved for service. "This war gives me the heartache," she lamented, expressing her forlorn hope that Osie and Johnnie, her two oldest sons, both already drafted, would never cross the Atlantic. A week later, when the notification of Johnnie's medical examination date arrived, she cried out in the privacy of her diary, "How I hate this hateful war!"

As the bureaucracy of the war ground on over the next few months, Martha Treadway faithfully recorded every step in her two older sons' shift from civilian to military life. Finally, on June 26, 1918, Osie left for Camp Grant in Rockford, Illinois, from Richmond (northwest of Chicago), where he had been working as a school superintendent. On the very same day, the elder Treadways took their son Johnnie to Macomb, where he and 174 other young McDonough County men took the train to Camp Wheeler in Macon, Georgia. "No body knows how I hated to see the boys go to war," Treadway mourned privately, "but it seems there is no other way and no help for it. How it makes my heart ache, but they seemed anxious to go." Her pain is palpable and she writes that it "seems terriabelly [sic] lonely this evening. Daddy [her husband] feels bad over it. All our children are gone for good now."

The days that followed were dominated by thoughts of her sons, with every letter received from them carefully noted in her diary and their identification numbers and changing stateside addresses recorded for future reference. As she noted in late June 1918, "Have been thinking of them all day." Before long, her worries increased significantly, as word came that her daughter Mary's husband, Howard Gray, had reached Europe, and Osie wrote that he "thinks he will soon cross over" the Atlantic. When both her sons reported receiving the olive drab wool suits that they would wear for the Atlantic crossing, she got "scared to death for fear" of losing her two oldest boys. Intensely aware of the carnage caused by trench warfare during the first four years of the European war, she cried out that "I can't bear to have them in that dreadful battle." When, later in August, she learned that Osie was in New York, his point of departure for Europe, she feared that "that means Good bye to my boy."

The wheels of America's military machine ground slowly for the Treadway brothers, however, and they were destined to be in New York awhile longer. Nonetheless, their mother, separated from them by half a continent and unsure of their futures, continued to be plagued by worry. For Martha Treadway, late August 1918 was dominated by the fear that Osie and Johnnie would ship out at any moment and she would never see them again. "It seems to [*sic*] terrible to be true. Seems hard to bear," the terrified mother exclaimed upon hearing from Osie that he expected to be on the high seas by the time she received his letter. "I am sick because Osie is going to war," she noted in August. (And, indeed, she was physically ill much of the time that her sons were gone.) Delays in shipping out, however, meant that the two Treadway brothers were actually able to spend a few evenings together at Camp Mills, on Long Island, in September, before Osie finally left for the battlefields of Europe on the fifteenth of the month, with Johnnie following a few days later.

In the following weeks, Martha Treadway's fears escalated daily as she waited anxiously to hear of the safe arrival of her sons in Europe. Even though they were "somewhere on the Ocean," she wrote to them, noting in her diary that "I can hardly wait to hear from them" because she was "uneasy all of the time for fear of Submarines." She also realized that while "it is a dreadful to think of them on the sea, in the [midst of] storms and submarines, . . . it will be not much better over there, among airplanes and zepalins [*sic*]." Knowing that her two oldest sons were on their way to battle "makes my heart ache," she painfully noted yet again in late September 1918.

On September 26 Martha Treadway again had cause to draw a circle around the date in her diary; however, this time her reason was great joy and not great sorrow as it had been when the war began for the United States. On the twenty-sixth of September, she received a card notifying her that Osie had arrived safely in England, which, she noted, was "the best news of all. I was so glad, had to take a cry over it" (not a common reaction for this normally stoic rural woman). She remained on pins and needles about Johnnie's safety, however, making careful note of how long it had taken Osie to make the Atlantic crossing and keeping close track of how long it had been since Johnnie had left New York. Finally, on October 21, she joyfully noted that she had finally received letters from both Johnnie and Osie, who were now in France. "We were sure happy to get them," she wrote about those precious missives. "Both like the look of the old country," which they wrote was "beautiful," while Johnnie commented that "the Atlantic was some big pond!"

Her sons' trip across "the big pond" was to be only the beginning of Martha Treadway's worries, however. She followed closely all reports on the war, complaining at one point that there was "not much good war news today." Then, like others on the home front, her hopes alternately soared and crashed as conflicting reports about the prospects for peace made their way to rural McDonough County. On October 6, 1918, she reported that they "got word last night that the war is over. The noise in town woke us up at 11," as people celebrated the new German government's willingness to end the war. "Cannons were booming and whistles blowing. We were awake until 2 and the cannons kept going all night. We got up to find out what was doing and I knew it was good news of the war." Alas, however, the news was not good enough, and the next day she reported that "the word received was all a lie"—the war was not yet over. Still more reports later that month raised her hopes up again, as she dwelled on what mattered most to her: "I hope the fighting ceases real soon," before her two sons became involved. The seesaw continued in November, as she recorded the celebration on November 7 in response to what turned out to be yet another cruelly false report of peace. "War is over," she wrote. "Sure glad." And then she got to the heart of her interest in the issue as she worried, "Have had only one letter from Osie" since his arrival in Europe, so she was "afraid something is wrong." Nonetheless, the world celebrated the good news that Germany was on the verge of surrender: "Bells all ringing & whistles blowing in Col[chester] & Macomb. . . . The passenger train blew the whistle all the way from Col. to Macomb. Everybody happy." But the next day, she had to once more record that "the report was all a lie again. they did all stop fighting on part of the line, until the messengers [the German armistice commission] crossed to [Marshall] Foches [sic] [the Allied commander's] headquarters." And once again, this mother's diary entry concludes with what mattered most to her: "Are still fighting today." On November 10 she reported, "Germans in big revolution," and noted, with great anticipation, "Kaiser abdicated."

Finally, November 11, 1918, was, for Martha Treadway as for the world, literally a red-letter day, as she switched to red pen to cheer in her diary, "the war is over!" After underlining her exclamation point three times in red pen, she continued in black: "Signed the armistice this morning . . . fighting ceased." Once again, McDonough County residents celebrated. "Macomb & Col. simply wild," she reported. "Commenced to blow whistles and ring bells at 2 O'clock this morning . . . had a parade before daylight in Macomb. Pa went up . . . staid all day. . . . The band was playing and the whistles blew all afternoon and the Bells kept busy. Will have a big parade tonight." And this time, she noted, "I would like to be there" as part of the "big crowd in town" that her daughter-in-law phoned to tell her about. She wanted to share in the general joyousness that she recorded in her diary. "Everybody is very glad and happy. The bills are all ringing. . . . Sound pretty. The whistles has [sic] stopped. . . . The cannons are firing, sound like thunder. Everybody will be relieved." But for Martha Treadway, as for all parents, the war was not truly over, because she did not yet know the fate of her sons. So she celebrated the armistice in her own way: "I am writing the boys tonight."

Her worries were not over yet, because of the delays in mail delivery from Europe. Even though this anxious mother received letters from both Osie and Johnnie the day after the armistice was signed ("good things all coming at once," she rejoiced), she knew that both had been written before the fighting stopped. Osie, the erstwhile school superintendent, reported making use of his spare time in France to study French, but his mother still worried. Her anxiety sharpened when Johnnie wrote that he had heard from Osie, who was "where he could hear the sound of war" and "could hear the guns," Johnny reported. "I hope he didn't get in the battle," his mother worried, "as there was 7 days yet of war" at the time of Osie's letter to Johnnie. Johnnie, on the other hand, was busy building barracks "far from the battlefront." He wrote that he was "somewhere in France," but not anywhere dangerous. Osie, however, his frantic mother was to learn later, "was at the front on the firing line. In a dugout."

Although the elder Treadways continued to receive, after the armistice, occasional letters written by their sons before the fighting had ended, it was not until almost Christmas 1918 that they could truly breathe a sigh of relief, having finally received letters from both boys, written since the armistice was signed and the fighting ended. In addition, her youngest son, Willie, was drafted in June 1918 (causing her to sigh "All my boys are in the draft now"), but he did not receive his orders to report for military duty until November 14, three days after the armistice. Upon receiving Willie's notice to report, his mother exclaimed, "My . . . I am glad the war is over!"

She continued to hear regularly from Osie and Johnnie, making a mark in the margin of her diary next to the date each time a letter came. Even with the fighting over, however, she could still not relax and reported being "anxious" and "uneasy" whenever she did not hear regularly from her doughboys. This was understandable, given the terrible toll that the influenza epidemic of 1918 took on American soldiers both at home and overseas. When she heard from Osie in late January 1919, after almost a month's silence, his relieved mother rejoiced. "Got a letter from Osie at last," she wrote, noting that she "was terriabely [sic] uneasy" because she "hadn't heard for so long." When, in February, she heard from Johnnie, too, who was still in France and now building railroads for the army, her reaction was to "wish he was home." On March 15 she noted that "today is Johnnie's birthday. He is 26 years old. Wish I could pat him on the back."

At long last the interminable months of anxiety and uneasiness approached an end, however, when the Treadways received a telegram from Osie on July 5, 1919, saying that he had landed in New York. The next day, more good news came, in the form of a letter from Johnnie, saying that he had landed in Virginia. "Sure a burden has fallen from us and we are happy," their grateful mother reported. "They left for France last Oct. Osie about the 15 and Johnny about the 18th as near as we could learn," she recalled. Then, in her usual understated fashion, she noted that "I'll be happy when they get home" to Illinois. At long last the blessed day came, and on July 26, 1919, she was able to write that "Osie and Johnnie both got home today." As was typical for this rural matron, the celebration of her sons' return was a family event. Although her oldest daughter Mary had returned to Idaho in May with her husband after his return from France, the Treadways' younger daughter Laura and her husband shared in the family festivities, as did the Treadways' youngest son Willie and his wife, who "all staid until midnight," long after the elder Treadways were accustomed to retiring for the night.

What does this glimpse into the life of Martha Treadway tell us? How does it enhance our understanding of Illinois history during World War I? To begin with, her regular reports of her daily life during this era illuminate the lives of other midwestern farm women, especially those of the middle class. As a middle-class woman—one whose family owned rather than rented a farm, could afford to send all the children to college, had a telephone, and even subscribed to *National Geographic*—her material life was no doubt superior in many ways to that of a tenant farmer's wife. Nonetheless, her diary emphasizes the never-ending nature of the tasks that dominated the waking hours of early twentieth-century farm women, even those of the middle class, as well as reminding us of the importance of family in the lives of most of her female contemporaries, both rural and urban, whether or not they belonged to the middle class. Where her children were, when she had heard from them last, when they were coming for their next visit, how they were faring—these issues constituted one of the dominant themes of Martha Treadway's diary.

Moreover, her life tells us something about the significance that public life could have, even for these rural women who defined themselves, as Martha Treadway did, primarily in terms of family responsibilities. Despite the predominance of family and farm matters in her diary, Martha Treadway still took the time to exercise her newly won right to vote—and to comment on it rather extensively in her diary. And although she went to the polling place with her husband, she cast her vote as an individual citizen.

Finally, because she confided in her diary her hopes and dreams, her fears and worries, we are able to understand how World War I affected this rural mother of soldiers. It seems likely that her more or less continuous anxiety about her sons, from the time they left home until the time they returned, was typical of other doughboys' mothers, knowing as they did, as soon as they received a letter, that anything could have happened in the days or weeks since it was sent. And Martha Treadway's joy when the war ended and her sons finally came home was shared by millions of people across the nation. Because Martha Treadway was so articulate in expressing her feelings, her diary makes palpable the emotional impact of this first twentieth-century war.

RELATED READING

Virginia R. Boynton, "Even in the Remotest Parts of the State: Downstate 'Woman's Committee' Activities on the Illinois Home Front during World War I," *Journal of the Illinois State Historical Society* vol. 96, no. 4 (Winter 2003/2004).

Pratt Award winner, 2004.

26.

SOCIETY ANNUAL REPORT, 1922–23

Jessie Palmer Weber

Journal of the Illinois State Historical Society
vol. 15, no. 3–4 (October 1922–January 1923)

"Society Annual Report 1922–23" was prepared by Jessie Palmer Weber, the society's secretary treasurer and first editor of the society's *Journal*. It contains an article about Lotte Holman O'Neill, the first woman member of the Illinois General Assembly. Included is a report of the Illinois Day celebrations organized by the society, which provides a view of the society in the 1920s. Among the activities were a lecture-recital of Indian music and the awarding of an essay contest prize.

Mrs. Lottie Holman O'Neill of DuPage County, First Woman Member of the Illinois General Assembly

The Fifty-Third General Assembly of Illinois, which convened January 3, 1923, will be notable in the history of the state because it counted a woman among its members, the first of her sex to hold this office. The name of Illinois' first woman legislator is Lottie Holman O'Neill, and she represents the forty-first senatorial district, and her home is at Downers Grove, DuPage County. She is a Republican. She is married, her husband being William J. O'Neill of Downers Grove.

After the election, when it was found that Mrs. O'Neill's candidacy had been successful, the people of Downers Grove held a great celebration of the event on November 18, 1922.

Jessie Palmer Weber, the first director of the Illinois State
Historical Society and the first editor of the *Journal of the
Illinois State Historical Society. Photo courtesy Abraham
Lincoln Presidential Library and Museum.*

The celebration included a torchlight procession and speeches by Mrs.
O'Neill and others. In her address Mrs. O'Neill said,

> I would rather it had been some other woman, and so would my hus-
> band. I didn't file my candidacy until two hours before closing time,
> hoping some other woman would run. But I and several staunch sup-
> porters were determined that a woman should be in Springfield to
> work for things that affect the home.

The lady from DuPage took her seat in the Fifty-Third General Assembly,
January 3, 1923. As Illinois' first woman representative, escorted by more

than a thousand women from all parts of the state, she walked down a flag-draped pathway to a seat on the aisle in the fifth row on the right hand side of the room. The quietly efficient woman in plain dark suit and blue silk hat represented a twofold milestone, a triumphal conclusion for the pioneer suffragists who lined the galleries and a significant beginning for new politicians who nodded down at her behind a mass of flowers.

Mrs. O'Neill, who is neither offensively feminine nor disturbingly masculine, removed her hat, smoothed her hair and, inconspicuously, but in the limelight, sat back, a spectator at her own induction. The reception, which the women, under the direction of the Illinois League of Women Voters, have been planning for weeks, broke forth: a high soprano scream from a woman who is an expert on the eight-hour-day legislation; three yells and a giggle from a dignified Chicago Club woman, who nearly wobbled off the chair on which she was standing; seven simultaneous songs from nine different groups; yells, individual and collective, the blowing of horns, and the enthusiastic but noncommittal hand-clapping of the men of the assembly. But through the noise and the excitement, Mrs. O'Neill, sensibly pleased, heard again and again a deep baritone voice leading the refrain, "District 41, District 41, woman's work has just begun." It was the voice of William J. O'Neill, not the "lady from DuPage's" husband, but a modern man, married to a modern woman, whose efficiency and sincerity have won for her a seat in the state legislature.

At ten minutes to one, Chief Justice Floyd Thompson administered the oath of office to the group and Mrs. O'Neill settled back in her seat ready for work.

When the women had ceased their welcoming songs and cheers, the executive body paid its homage to its first woman member. Norman G. Flagg, temporary speaker, extended a "special welcome from every man in this house to the typical example of beloved American womanhood, a typical wife and mother," and urged the women in the audience "years hence when perhaps lady members occupy 152 seats in the house and one man is present, may you grant that man the same gracious consideration."

Speaking for the Democratic side of the house, Michael L. Igoe welcomed the Republican lady, reminding her that suffrage was granted women in Illinois in 1913, during the administration of a Democratic governor, Edward F. Dunne. It was 1:30 and Mr. Flagg ordered that no demonstration delay the proceedings as Mrs. O'Neill rose to make her first speech, a brief, concise paragraph seconding the nomination of David E. Shanahan, as Speaker of the house.

In the evening a banquet was held by the Illinois League of Women Voters, Miss Julia Lathrop president of the league, presiding. Senators and representatives of the General Assembly were present.

Of her platform Mrs. O'Neill said "these women have already told you what I stand for—legislation for humanity, and I earnestly request you men to work with me for these people in this legislation—the care of mothers and babies, better teachers and schools, aid for delinquent girls, and improved industrial conditions for women."

ILLINOIS DAY CELEBRATION BY THE ILLINOIS STATE HISTORICAL SOCIETY

As the third of December, the one hundred and fourth anniversary of the Admission of the State of Illinois into the Federal Union, this year fell on Sunday, the State Historical Society held its annual observance of the day on Saturday evening, December second, in the Senate Chamber in the Capitol building at 8:15 o'clock. During the past year the Historical Society and the Illinois Daughters of the American Revolution have conducted a prize essay contest among the schoolchildren of Illinois of the eighth to twelfth grades, inclusive. The subject of the essay this year was "Pioneer Women of Illinois," and through this contest much original material has been discovered in the way of old letters, diaries, family histories and family traditions and much has been learned by interviews with old settlers.

A lecture recital by Mr. Henry Purmort Eames ably delivered and highly interesting on "The Music of the American Indian—Its Primitive and Art-Music Forms" was a specially interesting feature of the celebration. Dr. Eames illustrated his lecture on the piano with examples of the primitive music of the Red Man and then gave a brilliant recital of piano solos, the theme or inspiration for the selections, which were of his own composition, being derived wholly or in part from the music of the Indians. Dr. Eames said in his address, "The Indian rhythm is the most inspirational of all. The Indian Scale is a five-note scale. They play it downward. They sing it downward and make the climax downward, not upward. Good music comes from the soul, whether it be the composition of a Beethoven or a Mendelssohn, or not. The Indian scale is the same scale as that which the Zulus use. We are not any more advanced in rhythm than the Indians, though we are along other lines in music. The Indian is a greater musician than the white man in that he thinks little of words, but in the song itself he throws his whole soul. He seldom uses more than two words in his song."

An audience of 350 persons was present at the celebration. Over the desk of the president of the Senate were two large silk flags—one of the United States and the other the flag of Illinois, the white flag with an eagle with outspread wings in the center. Beautiful bouquets of chrysanthemums were in vases topping the lamp pedestals on either side of the desk of the secretary of the Senate.

Dr. Otto L. Schmidt, of Chicago, president of the Illinois State Historical Society, presided, and introduced the Reverend William F. Rothenburger, pastor of the First Christian Church, who offered the invocation.

Mrs. Gary Westenberger of this city then sang a group of Illinois songs, consisting of "Illinois," "Hymn to Illinois," and "Hail, Illinois."

The gold medal, the state prize given by the Illinois State Historical Society and the Illinois Society of the Daughters of the American Revolution for the best essay on "Pioneer Women of Illinois" competed for by pupils of the public schools of the state from the eighth to the twelfth grades, was then presented to the winner, Miss Julia Ann Buck, daughter of State senator Clarence F. Buck of Monmouth, by Honorable Francis G. Blair, state superintendent of public instruction, in a brief but eloquent address. At the close of the meeting President Schmidt of the Illinois State Historical Society told of the campaign to be made by the society and the Illinois Society of the Daughters of the American Revolution to preserve the great Indian mound at Cahokia, Madison County, known as the Monks Mound.

After the meeting, the Society retired to the historical rooms where refreshments were served by Mrs. I. G. Miller, Mrs. F. R. Jamison, and Mrs. John H. Piper.

27.

A TRIBUTE TO JESSIE PALMER WEBER

Evarts Boutell Greene

Journal of the Illinois State Historical Society
vol. 19, no. 3–4 (October 1926–January 1927)

As stated in the introduction to the preceding article, Jessie Palmer Weber served for many years as secretary treasurer of the Illinois State Historical Society and in 1908 was the first editor of its journal. She also carried the title of state librarian. This merging of positions was put in place very early in the society's history.

Weber's story is told in a tribute read at her memorial on Illinois Day, December 3, 1926. It was written by Professor Evarts Boutell Greene, early founder of the society. It includes a review of the early history of the State Historical Library and the Illinois State Historical Society, noting that the library was originally located in the State House but moved to the Centennial (now Howlett) Building in the early 1920s. This article also contains much information on the state's centennial, noting that Weber was the secretary treasurer of the centennial commission.

It is fitting that on this particular occasion we should think especially of Mrs. Weber in her relation to the work of the Historical Society and the state department with which it is associated. To the cause of state history as represented by these agencies she gave her best energies for twenty-eight years; and it is as fellow-workers in this cause that we are assembled today.

When Mrs. Weber became librarian in 1898, the Illinois State Historical Library was still a young and comparatively small institution, but it was fortunate in its board of trustees. The president of the board was Hiram W. Beckwith, an indefatigable student of the history of the Old Northwest, with a keen scent for out-of-the-way material and a wide range of information in his chosen field. Under his editorial direction the first volume of the *Illinois Historical Collections* was issued.

About a year after Mrs. Weber's appointment as librarian, the first steps were taken toward the formation of the State Historical Society. This organization, which had its starting point in a meeting at the University of Illinois in 1899, was incorporated in the following year and in 1903 was legally affiliated with the State Historical Library, whose trustees and librarian had been associated with the movement from the beginning. President Beckwith of the Library board was also the first president of the Society, and in 1903 Mrs. Weber became its secretary. It was in this capacity that she was probably best known to the people of the state at large. Upon her fell the chief responsibility for planning the programs of successive annual meetings; of keeping in touch, through correspondence and conferences, with individuals and local historical societies; and of issuing the Society's publications. In 1908 she founded, in addition to the annual volume of the Society's *Transactions*, the quarterly *Journal of the Illinois State Society*, which she continued to edit until the time of her death. It was to a large extent through the work of the Society and Mrs. Weber's part in it that public interest was aroused, and public support secured, for the expansion of the Library and the improvement of its publications.

My own acquaintance with Mrs. Weber began in connection with our efforts to get the Historical Society on its feet and I well remember one early meeting in Springfield in which Senator Palmer, then nearing the end of his distinguished career, made the principal address. Other striking personalities associated with the Society in its early years, and especially with its secretary, were: Dr. J. F. Snyder of Virginia, a tall impressive figure, deeply interested in the prehistoric remains as well as the history of the state, and a vigorous defender of unpopular opinions; Paul Selby, the veteran journalist, with his reminiscences of prewar politics and the slavery conflict; Judge David McCullough, the local historian of Peoria County; Clark E. Carr of Galesburg, who never tired of telling his story of the Gettysburg address. There were many others of that older generation—most of them now gone—whom Mrs. Weber brought together at the annual meetings.

It was natural that an institution which has its headquarters at Springfield should give special attention to the commemoration of Abraham Lincoln. To Mrs. Weber, more than to anyone else, was due the formation and steady enlargement of the Lincoln Collection, with its manuscripts and illustrative material of various kinds—an admirable piece of work, now happily housed in the New Centennial Building.

Before long, students of state history began to look forward to the centennial anniversary of the admission of Illinois to the Union; and in the winter of 1913, the General Assembly took the first step toward an adequate statewide celebration. A centennial commission was appointed, consisting of members of the Senate and House of Representatives, three representatives of the University of Illinois, and the president and secretary of the State Historical Society. Mrs. Weber, as the secretary of the Society, was the logical choice for the secretaryship of the commission. It was in her office that the sessions of the commission were most frequently held, and through it most of the correspondence passed. In short, she became the general executive officer of the commission, as well as of the Library and the Society. In addition, she served on several of the committees and was especially responsible for the success of the series of exercises held in Springfield.

Out of the work of the centennial commission came the six volumes of the Illinois Centennial History and the final success of the movement for the new building, which now houses the Library, the Society, and other more or less related interests. The entry of the United States into the World War made it necessary to modify the centennial program in some respects; but in the main, it was carried through as a patriotic enterprise, and the anniversary exercises held during the spring and autumn of 1918 were particularly impressive.

A natural outgrowth of Mrs. Weber's official and personal interest in the history of her native state was her active participation, in cooperation with the Daughters of the American Revolution and other patriotic organizations, in the preservation and marking of historic sites. A notable example of this is her part in the development of the State Park at Fort Massac; another is the setting up of markers at various points associated with Lincoln's career as lawyer and political speaker.

During the twenty-eight years of Mrs. Weber's service, there have been changes in the control of the state government from Republican to Democratic and from Democratic back again to Republican, not to mention those contests within parties which are often no less bitter; but there has been only one change in the personnel of the Library for any reason other than death or removal from the state. So, more and more as the years passed, Mrs. Weber came to occupy a unique position. In a sense she became the dean of the official body at the State House. Everybody knew her and her word went a long way, not only with her fellow workers but with those to whom she went on her official errands. She sat through long meetings of appropriation committees; on the busy closing nights of legislative sessions, she was a watchful sentinel, jealously guarding these items in the appropriation bills which affected one or another of the historical interests she had so much at heart. It was a service which none of her colleagues could have performed so well.

I have sometimes thought, in these days when women have begun to take a more formal part in politics, that Mrs. Weber had many of the qualities which make for success in a political career. I am sure there have been many members of our national legislature, past and present, who have shown far less insight in difficult political situations. But, in the long perspective of time, I am sure that in her chosen work she gave a service to her beloved state more important than that achieved by most men who have chosen the precarious honors of a political career.

Perhaps in this brief record of Mrs. Weber's service I may seem to have said too much about the causes for which she worked and the friends, now gone from us, with whom her work was done. I have done so deliberately, however, for I believe that it is in such familiar and friendly associations that she would like best to be remembered.

PART VI

MID-TWENTIETH CENTURY

28.

HELL AND HIGH WATER
The Flood of 1937 in Southern Illinois

Richard Lawrence Beyer

Journal of the Illinois State Historical Society
vol. 31, no. 1 (March 1938)

Beyer discusses the ominous rise in early 1937 of the Ohio River to record-breaking levels, causing widespread property damage and homelessness. He describes the evacuation of Cairo and refugees finding safety in Carbondale. Eight counties in southern Illinois were either completely or partially inundated. Help came from many sources: the Red Cross, the Works Progress Administration (WPA), and state agencies. The author recommends a number of conservation measures to limit future flooding.

"It is the Ohio only which has ever given the city of Cairo any trouble of consequence," wrote John M. Lansden twenty-seven years ago. "Even when both rivers are high at one and the same time, little or no notice is taken of the matter unless the Ohio reaches one of its very highest stages. It is the Ohio that claims for itself the right to rise and fall through a perpendicular distance of fifty feet." The observations of the learned southern Illinois judge were sound insofar as he evaluated the devastating qualities of the Ohio and Mississippi Rivers, respectively, but the floods of 1937 revealed that he missed the swelling possibilities of the Ohio by nearly ten feet.

The rampage of the Ohio River in late January and early February 1937 constituted one of the major catastrophes in the history of this state. Results of the tragedy are frightfully plain, and even at the risk of sacrificing some

Debris floating through the streets of Old Shawneetown during the flood
of 1937. *Photo courtesy Special Collections, Morris Library, Southern Illinois University Carbondale.*

of the mellowness that time and perspective afford the historian, the author
believes that the outlines of this disaster should be preserved before records
are erased and the memories of victims and relief workers are tinctured with
too many dashes of imagination and illusion.

In trying to estimate the materialistic consequences of the disaster, one
learns the proportions of the Ohio River flood. Thousands of residents of
the state were rendered homeless, and property damages estimated at $75
million resulted. In one community of less than two thousand inhabitants,
Shawneetown in Gallatin County, the losses are calculated at nearly a half
million dollars. Damage to the state highways has been placed as high as
two hundred thousand dollars and injury to county and township roads is
estimated by some to be even greater. The effects of death (from both drowning and disease), sickness, privation, disruption of industry, shattering of
home life, and rupture of morale can scarcely be measured in this, southern
Illinois's greatest trial.

Floods are not new in Egypt, and accounts of them date back into the
pre-state history of the region. Their frequent threats to life and property

and the refusal of the people to move from areas threatened by inundation amazed and irritated visitors in the Illinois country years ago.

Granting the ravages of these nineteenth-century floods, it must be indicated again that none ever reached the proportions of the swell of the Ohio in January and February 1937.

Omens suggesting floods for southern Illinois began to appear by the middle of January. The weather had been mild, but heavy rains had fallen in the entire Ohio Valley. Rivers were rising rapidly, and in many places highways were already covered. Predictions on January 20 were to the effect that within a week the Ohio would reach a fifty-two foot stage at Cairo, but this occasioned no alarm since that figure was almost a foot lower than the crest in the flood the previous year. "Protected by 60-foot sea walls, neither Cairo nor Shawneetown is in danger," an Associated Press correspondent wrote at this time.

However, by Friday, January 22, it was apparent that southern Illinois was on the verge of disaster. Thirty hours of rain in the upper Ohio Valley, coupled with sleet and a six-and-a-half-inch snowfall in Egypt, contributed to the uneasiness of those who watched the river rise. At Shawneetown it had already reached the fifty-foot mark. Disquieting, too, were the reports of the rampage of the Ohio in the eastern part of the valley. Even this early, the river had climbed to seventy feet at Cincinnati and shattered the sixty-nine-and-nine-tenths-foot mark, which had previously been the all-time "high" for that city. Observers now predicted that the greatest flood on record was imminent. Illinois read of these happenings and of the exodus of fifty thousand people from their homes in the river towns of Ohio and Indiana. To battle the impending flood in Illinois, forces of WPA workers, engineers, and boatmen were mobilized. Residents in threatened towns began to pack, while some had already left for higher ground.

With the passing of the hours, the Ohio, a churning yellow fury, continued to rise to new record heights, and danger grew as the river mounted inch by inch. The lower part of Shawneetown was filling with seepage water from the seawall and levee, and doubts were expressed as to whether the flood could be resisted. Elizabethtown, Golconda, and Rosiclare were isolated. Rescue work was started in earnest as pleas for help came from the valley towns. Naval militia boats were sent into the flood area. National Guard planes soared over Egypt to help establish communication with the isolated region and make necessary observations. The rescue work itself was hampered by wind, snow, sleet, and cold weather. Telephone and telegraph lines were injured by storm, and communication was largely confined to amateur radio stations. Waves two feet high and a powerful current made it impossible to use small boats for rescue work on the Ohio. It seemed that all Nature was in conspiracy against man on Saturday, January 23. But in the face of terrific obstacles, relief work went ahead, and in the towns on the lower river, men patrolled the levees and piled row after row of sandbags on top of seawalls.

The evacuation of the Ohio Valley began in earnest with the advent of the new week. Floodwaters had climbed beyond the fifty-seven-foot mark at Shaweetown, and future safety for the inhabitants became increasingly dubious. About five hundred refugees were taken up the river by the steamer *Patricia Barrett*, pushing a barge. Some people fled to the uplands. The Shawneetown High School, situated on a ridge outside the town, provided a haven for hundreds of people who remained jammed together there for days. By Sunday evening, apart from those engaged in rescue or defense work, only 150 persons remained in town, and they sought safety on the second and third stories of buildings. Red Cross and WPA workers were rushed in to help the people. This was merely part of a gigantic rescue-relief program that was started by the state and nation. In Washington, President Roosevelt put five federal agencies on what was described as virtually a wartime basis to help sufferers from the flood. The United States Coast Guard mobilized the greatest flood relief forces in its history when it sent eight hundred men and two hundred boats, representing practically every one of its units from Maine to Texas. Governor Henry Horner issued the statement, "I want everything necessary done to aid the flooded areas." In Illinois, the Emergency Relief Commission, the Health Department, the National Guard, and the Division of Highways swung into action to work with the regular army and with the American Red Cross.

On Monday, January 25, the river at Cairo had risen to fifty-eight-and-three-tenths feet at 7 A.M., and the evacuation of that city began. Five thousand people left by automobile and train in the first exodus. The refugees were women and children. Men were allowed to escort their families northward on condition that they would return to help bolster the defense of the city. Meanwhile the flight of the inhabitants from the other river towns, with the exception of the flood fighters, was practically completed.

The story of caring for the thousands of refugees in towns outside of the flood area is a monument to the generosity and compassion of the people of Illinois. The chronicle, to be completed, would far outstrip the limits of this article, for it was a program that directly or indirectly involved the entire state. There was hardly a town in Egypt, outside of the stricken region, but what had refugees to care for, and some communities in central and northern Illinois were also havens for the needy. Just to illustrate the type of work that was done, let me select the city of Carbondale as an example.

Refugees poured into this town by the hundreds. Some of them came by automobile and truck, but more often they were brought by railroad. Four trains, with a total of more than one hundred cars, carried about a thousand refugees and their belongings to Carbondale in one day. The victims who were financially able took rooms in hotels or with private families. However, the majority were destitute and were completely dependent on the accommodations that charity could provide for them. Some of the sufferers left their homes with no possessions other than the clothes they wore. Others managed to gather together pieces of movable property, livestock, and their pets. And speaking of pets, the devotion of human beings to their dogs, cats, and birds never has had better illustration than it did in this flood. Refugees refused to leave their pets at home and even objected to being separated temporarily from them, when assigned to relief stations. The tenacity with which one aged woman clung to a square cage containing four canaries during the trip north in a boxcar is simply one case in point.

When trains bearing victims arrived, they were met by volunteers who assisted with the unloading and escorted the refugees to registration depots and thence to their living quarters. College and high school students, as well as Boy Scouts, were prominent in this type of work. The sick were rushed to hospitals, while the able-bodied were quartered in churches, public buildings, and gymnasiums, and in Carbondale at the Teachers' College. Eventually seven hundred people were being cared for at the college. White refugees were placed in the gymnasium, while the Negroes were put in the old science building. For several weeks these victims were accommodated, and so efficiently was the project managed that not one day of school was lost.

Rows of cots were arranged in the two buildings used for relief purposes at the college. This equipment, together with pillows and blankets, was supplied by the army. Refugees were given food that was prepared in a field kitchen built on the south end of the main building of the school. Under the supervision of the National Guard, groups of WPA workers, students, and refugees quickly built this kitchen, and it was immediately put into use. Donations of food came from various parts of the state, while the remainder was purchased in the area. Heading the commissary was Leland P. Lingle, track coach at the college, who fed the refugees well and economically. Captain William McAndrew, athletic director, supervised the entire relief project at the school.

The problem of handling the refugees was rendered easy by the cooperation of many individuals and groups. The American Red Cross acted with its customary efficiency and was aided by groups of townspeople, faculty members at the college, and students. A health service was set up and refugees were given the best of medical attention. Vaccination against smallpox and inoculation against typhoid fever were provided. Refugees suffering from minor ailments were given attention in the gymnasiums, while those who developed serious symptoms were taken to the hospitals. It was this keen observation of and ready attention for the victims that did much to keep disease minimized among the worn, weakened people from the flood zone. As the relief work continued, the refugees aided in the management of affairs. Kitchen details were organized and these assisted in the serving of hundreds of people daily. At the college, special classes were organized so that refugee children would lose as little schoolwork as possible. Entertainment in the form of concerts and motion pictures was furnished for adults and children.

The behavior of the refugees themselves provided an excellent opportunity for a psychologist interested in the conduct of fellow humans in distress. No generalizations are possible beyond the statement that so quickly had disaster come to Egypt that the majority of the victims were dazed, and that they were completely grateful for the accommodations afforded. In a few cases the people were hysterical. Others were dejected as they reviewed their losses. Many were resigned to the fact that they had lost all of their property but were thankful that their lives and the lives of their associates had been spared. All of them were eager for information about their homes and were anxious to get in touch with relatives and friends from whom they had been separated. Some found consolation in prayer. They were an orderly group, anxious to help their benefactors in the relief program and resolved to cause no more trouble than was necessary. For the most part they spent their time in little huddles around their cots, talking in hushed tones. Here they were, friends and neighbors from the same town, suddenly bunched together in a queer environment. "We have our entire missionary society here," a Brookport woman said to me as she looked up from a group that was seated on and about her cot.

No thought of belittling other communities that did relief work is intended by the author in his mentioning the program at Carbondale. What was done in that place was repeated in a score of other towns. Indeed the towns of Egypt showed every disposition to share the work, and when one place became saturated with victims, it could answer a half dozen invitations to share the burden with others. Ultimately tented cities were created, and they lightened the load that the towns had borne at the outset of the disaster.

While many refugees were pouring out of the Ohio Valley, the able-bodied men remained to fight the flood. Temporary recess from the attack was given Cairo with the dynamiting of the fuse plug levee on the Missouri side. This was the old levee that followed the course of the Mississippi from the Ohio confluence to New Madrid. The blasting of this levee allowed the floodway of 131,000 acres to admit the waters and relieve the pressure on Cairo. Instead of watching the steady rise of the river, Cairo now saw a drop of two-tenths of a foot in twenty-four hours. The defenders were heartened by the information that the stage of the river would not change appreciably for two or three days. Then, when the floodway basin would be full, the waters were expected to rise again. The truce, however, was welcome, for it gave the Cairo workers more time to extend the three-foot sandbag-and-timber bulkhead they were building on top of the wall that protects the city.

"FLOOD RECEDES AT LOUISVILLE" screamed the headlines on Thursday, January 28, and the public that had been gripped by the disaster in the upper Ohio Valley now turned to watch the western part of the river. Inevitably, attention was focused on Cairo, which was waiting for its crisis. For the first time since the Civil War, Cairo had the eyes of all America riveted upon it. By the next day, Cairo's first line of defense was completed, and the *Cairo Evening Citizen* commented, "Residents of Cairo, Alexander and Pulaski counties, WPA, CCC, and other workers by the thousands have done one of the fastest jobs of bulkheading ever accomplished anywhere. Thursday, the bulkhead was being extended with such rapidity that it seemed to be walking."

One of the surprising aspects of the Cairo situation, to those of us who were high and dry, was the attitude of the people from that city. During the course of the relief work among the refugees, many times did I hear the statement, "Cairo has never had, and will never have a flood." Some of the refugees felt that their departure from the town was unnecessary and that all would be well in Cairo. The *Citizen* reflected this attitude. Here was Cairo waiting for the crest, the river was rising again, more rains were forecast, and the bulkhead was yet to be tested. One would think that, in view of the tense situation, streamer headlines would have been used to deal with the local conditions. Yet in picking up the issue of January 30, one finds "QUAKE FRIGHTENS TIPTONVILLE" as the major headline. A minor tremor in Tennessee was played up—the vital Cairo situation subordinated. Even when the river was crawling close to the fifty-nine-foot mark, a headline writer facetiously composed the following: "OLD MAN RIVER SETS A NEW ALL-TIME HIGH RECORD FOR THIS CITY."

Towns near Cairo—Mound City, Mounds, Ullin, and others—were not to be spared. High waters in the Cache River basin and backwater from the Ohio were responsible for this further disaster in Illinois. Mound City was completely deserted as the flood wrought damage that is not even yet fully repaired. The town of Mounds, earlier in the flood period, had been a refugee center; but, as the waters rose, its evacuation became necessary. Many of the victims made their escape before the road to the north was inundated and the town was completely cut off from the world. A few took refuge in a school building at the north of the town. The rapid rise of the floodwaters was one of the remarkable aspects of the situation at Mounds. According to a school-teacher who assisted with the rescue work there, the water rose from two to three feet in two hours' time. In the southern end of the town, my informant says it eventually attained a depth of fifteen feet. He estimated the property damage at Mounds, a town of about two thousand inhabitants, at $200,000.

As January ended, eight counties in southern Illinois were either completely or partly inundated, and the Red Cross estimated that the homes of 73,876 people were flooded. Almost half that number were refugees. One of the astounding phases of the disaster was the flooding of Harrisburg, a city located more than twenty miles from the Ohio. The Saline River spilled over when the Ohio backed up and water rose in Harrisburg an inch an hour. From the county seat of Saline County to the Ohio River, there was practically a continuous sheet of water. All of Harrisburg was flooded except for a downtown orbit that encircled the courthouse. National Guard boats were the means of transportation in this community, and several thousand people were hauled about in them every day. It was from Harrisburg that one of the most helpful services in the disaster came. This was the valuable work of radio station WEBQ, which devoted most of its broadcasting time to relief and rescue work, not only for Saline County but for all of southern Illinois. Thousands of Egyptians kept their radio dials constantly tuned to this station and listened for bulletins about the crisis.

Streets of Harrisburg, Illinois, thirty miles from the Ohio River but underwater for several weeks. *Photo courtesy Special Collections, Morris Library, Southern Illinois University Carbondale.*

Meanwhile, the Ohio was rising and the crest drew nearer to Cairo. By Sunday, January 31, the peak of the disaster was at Evansville, Indiana, and southern Illinois knew that it was to experience the full strength of the river's fury next. Cairo, never completely shaken in confidence in its defense, became wary. A double bulkhead was constructed at the levee near the waterworks, and elsewhere the wall of sandbags was tightened. August Bode, mayor of the city, issued the following proclamation, which was ostentatiously carried on the front page of *Sunday's Citizen.*

PROCLAMATION

The proclamation for the evacuation of the city of Cairo by all citizens except able-bodied men must be observed. All persons who have no means of transportation, other than able-bodied men, must report for transportation at once as follows:

White people at Safford School, Cross at Walnut.

Colored people at Sumner High School, 22nd and Poplar.

This must be done not later than 10 P.M., Sunday, January 31st.

The Red Cross has arranged for movement and care of all persons reporting at above places without expense. This order will be enforced by the Sheriff, police officers and the National Guard.

No persons will be permitted to enter the City of Cairo until further notice without a permit or on official business. No able-bodied men will be allowed to leave the city without a permit.

August Bode
Mayor

The above document was issued because some fifteen hundred women and children, in addition to the aged, sick, and infirm, were still within the city limits, despite potential danger and previous opportunities for evacuation. Indeed the population of the town was actually growing, due to the arrival of refugees who had returned, workers from the outside, and sight-seers who were panting with curiosity. Once again the Cairo confidence asserted itself. It was not so much danger from the roaring Ohio that warranted the evacuation, it was stated, but the possibility of a fuel shortage.

The early days of February, nonetheless, were tense ones in Cairo as the town awaited the predicted crest of the flood. The Ohio finally rose to the fifty-nine and sixty-two hundredths foot mark. On Thursday, February 4, the first slight recession was noted after the waters had come within six inches of the top of the concrete sea wall. Observers rejoiced, but continued their vigil. By Friday, Cairo was positive it was victorious, for the Ohio continued to recede and the town began to resume its normal life. Refugees, however, were not allowed to return immediately, for engineers concluded that there would be no absolute assurance of safety until the river dropped to the fifty-five foot mark. On February 10, the return of some of the people was allowed; those who were financially able to come back, and were willing to do so at their own risk, were given this permission. Scores of men who had remained in town to fight the flood now took their automobiles and went after their families who had been removed from the threatened area.

With the passing of danger, southern Illinois began the grim task of reconstruction. Many agencies contributed to this task, and conspicuous in the work were the State Department of Public Health and the National Guard. Approximately one thousand officers and men of the latter, under the command of Lieutenant Colonel Robert W. Davis, assisted in the rehabilitation program.

Also prominent in the cleanup program were the WPA and the Red Cross. The former supplied much of the labor, while the latter fed and clothed the refugees and handled the administration of the refugee camps until it was possible for the homeless to return. As late as February 19, over twenty-seven hundred refugees still had to be cared for, and four camps—located at Anna, Marion, Wolf Lake, and Pinckneyville—were still in operation. According to Walter Wesseulius, who directed the flood relief work in Egypt, the Red Cross spent $1.1 million in relief and rehabilitation work in southern Illinois, and in addition distributed approximately a half million dollars' worth of donated foodstuffs among the sufferers.

Even in late February, Shawneetown was still inundated, and observers on the twenty-fifth found that eight to ten feet of water remained in the town. The opening of the clogged sewers (two mattresses were found in one pipe) permitted a drop of an inch of water every two hours. So stricken was the community that investigators learned that only twenty houses in the entire place were fit for habitation when the waters receded.

Throughout the emergency period and during the weeks of reconstruction, another agency played an important part. It was the State Highway Department, the men of District Nine having the chief responsibility of fighting the floods that covered one thousand miles of primary and secondary roads. Keeping some of the roads open, saving others, and repairing still others constituted the job of the Highway Department, which operated efficiently throughout the crisis. Saline and Gallatin were the two counties that particularly required the work of the department.

Now that the waters have subsided and the work of rehabilitation is progressing, thoughtful people are raising the question, "What can Illinois do to prevent the recurrence of these floods?" As these disasters grow mightier with the years, the answer is one that should be evaded no longer. Indeed, it has already been postponed far too long. One thing is certain—the problem is not that of this state alone—it is a problem for all America. Illinois, at the receiving end of the Ohio Valley, cannot solve the flood question without cooperation from the upper valley and from the areas washed by the many streams that enter the Ohio.

The first step that can be taken is to make the people of Illinois and the rest of the nation highly conscious of the perennial danger of floods, and of the ruthless raping of our natural resources that has so largely contributed to creating them. Then the task will be to find remedies. To create an intelligent understanding of the subject, I suggest that volumes such as Stuart Chase's *Rich Land, Poor Land* be made required reading for our voters and taxpayers.

At least three types of artificial flood control should be studied. They are the development of immense storage reservoirs, improvements on river channels so that the capacity of flow may be increased, and finally, more levees and higher sea walls. Since the flood of 1937, a reaction has set in against the latter device. To many, the use of the levee-sea wall is a costly method that is becoming less and less satisfying. It is the opiate that lessens the pain and does not go to the origin of the malady. For two centuries, men have depended on the levee as a major protection against floods, but as Stuart Chase phrases it: "Every year it grows more preposterous. With river bottoms rising because of the piles of silt that are washed from fields, the use of the levee becomes increasingly impractical."

The only sound method of attacking the flood menace is a long-range program of planning in a cooperative manner by federal and state governments. It would have as a principal phase the introduction of a program of conservation on a scale never before attempted in this country. It would try to prevent (1) destruction of forests, (2) stripping of grass lands, and (3) improper cultivation of lands in the river valleys. An important cause of floods today is the rapid run-off of water from the watersheds. Geographers insist that our thoughtless use of natural resources has permitted water to run off the hills into the rivers at a rate three times faster than was the speed before our ruthless methods began. If mankind can be educated (or possibly legislated) into stopping its blundering tactics, if a system of reservoirs can be provided, if river channels can be deepened or widened, then it is possible that in some Utopian tomorrow, Illinois may be spared repetitions of the disaster of 1937.

29.

BISHOP JAMES A. GRIFFIN AND THE COAL MINERS' WAR

Susan Karina Dickey

Journal of the Illinois State Historical Society
vol. 101, no. 1 (Spring 2008)

In the mid-1930s, Peabody Coal Company and the United Mine Workers of America, under the leadership of John L. Lewis, both thought it was in their best interest to ask union members to approve a reduction in weekly wages. Opposition by many miners led to the formation of the Progressive Miners of America, widespread violence, and sharp criticism of Springfield bishop James A. Griffin for supporting the wage-reduction proposal. The author asserts that the objectives of the PMA echo concepts from *Rerum Novarum* issued by Pope Leo XIII in 1891, which explores the social and spiritual value of work.

In the winter of 1932–33 violence ripped across the mining towns of Illinois. Drive-by shootings, bombings of public buildings, and acts of sabotage rocked District 12 of the United Mine Workers of America (UMWA), an area contiguous with the state boundaries. A split within the union precipitated the chaos. In the summer of 1932 bituminous miners rejected a new contract with the Illinois Coal Operators Association (ICOA), and that autumn the Progressive Miners of America (PMA) came into existence. By the time the miners' war died down in 1937, hundreds of men and women had been harassed and intimidated, dozens injured, and at least twenty-one had died.

Susan Karina Dickey

More than seventy years later we continue to unravel the strands of the story. Most scholars interpret the mining war in economic terms, but economics was just one dimension. Papers from the episcopacy of Irish-American James A. Griffin, bishop of Springfield from 1924 to 1948, allow us to frame the conflict in new terms. Much of the violence took place in Griffin's diocese, and his papers, parish records, oral histories of retired miners, newspaper accounts, and various secondary sources reveal religious aspects in the dispute. Of the parties involved—the bishop, the miners, the union, and the mine owners—Griffin could draw upon a well-developed theological understanding of the affair.

He was familiar with the social encyclical *Rerum Novarum* (On the Condition of Labor) issued by Pope Leo XIII in 1891, and it shaped the bishop's opinions about the relationship between capital and labor. Briefly, the encyclical addressed the threat to human welfare posed by industrialization and socialism. Leo called upon both labor and capital to cooperate with each other so that the human dignity of each person would be respected while simultaneously promoting the common good.

Rerum Novarum explores the social and spiritual value of work. Among other things, the document outlines the rights and responsibilities of workers and of industrialists. The major points are:

— Man has the power of self-direction.
— Men have a right to found a family and a duty to care for it.
— The church is to acknowledge that inequality is inevitable and that man must suffer and endure; his final end is the hereafter.
— Yet, the human body, created by God, is to be provided for, hence the necessity of work. Furthermore, the Christian is obliged to act with charity and promote justice so as to alleviate poverty.
— There exists a natural right to private property. The state is to protect private property, regulate the conditions of work, insure a just wage, and encourage a wide distribution of property under the law.
— Voluntary organizations, e.g., labor unions, are to be encouraged.

Forty years later in 1931 the Church reiterated these points in *Quadragesimo Anno* issued by Pope Pius XI. Griffin also relied upon his firsthand experience as pastor in the mining town of Coal City in Grundy County from 1917 to 1921. Throughout his episcopacy, the bishop supported organized labor and sought to educate the faithful through his own preaching.

342

Griffin instructed the parish pastors to include labor among the topics for the diocesan-wide program for Sunday sermons. Griffin was the first bishop of the diocese to explicitly encourage the faithful to integrate religion and everyday life. Religion should inform behavior and attitudes in every sphere of action.

The affable and well-educated Griffin, who held a PhD and the STD, frequently consulted and socialized with the political and business leaders of the day. His "A" list for dinner parties at the Bishop's House included Illinois governors, newspaper editors, and the captains of industry. Griffin's role as bishop, as he understood it, required that he maintain a certain lifestyle—a lavish one in comparison to that of the miners.

Mining families typically lived a hand-to-mouth existence. Mining was seasonal, so there was no income during the layoffs that began in the spring and ended in late summer or early autumn. Few miners, nor their wives, possessed more than an elementary education. Within the diocesan boundaries, most of the miners were first- and second-generation Italians and Slovaks, but there were also numerous Croatians, Lithuanians, and Slovenians. There were Irish, Scottish, and German miners as well. Kinship networks within each group provided stability in the face of poverty and changing conditions in the coal industry.

Most parishioners were not well versed in the subtleties of Catholic social teaching. In fact, if parish annual reports are to be believed, more than a few miners were nominal Catholics who seldom attended Mass. Even those who occasionally heard about *Rerum Novarum* from the pulpit, more than likely from an Irish priest, probably could see little relevance to their own situation. Yet the understanding of the social value of labor expressed by the Progressive Miners of America was remarkably similar to that of Griffin.

Socialist influences led some of the future Progressive Miners to arrive at conclusions consistent with Catholic teaching. Even though Griffin, like Leo XIII, vigorously condemned socialism and communism as inconsistent with human dignity, church leaders and radicals alike aimed for a living wage and freedom from exploitation. One could argue that for most miners their grasp of social justice sprang from natural moral law. In the Catholic tradition this law is "written and engraved in the soul of each and every man; because it is nothing but our reason commanding us to do right and forbidding us to sin." By virtue of the natural law, individuals grasp the difference between right and wrong and behave accordingly.

343

In regard to the mining situation, a remark by Joe Ozanic Sr., a parishioner of Ascension Church, Mt. Olive, and one of the founding Progressive Miners, seems to exemplify this intuitive understanding. In his memoir, Ozanic repeatedly alluded to the Progressive's concern for the welfare of the miner, his wife, and family. Ozanic never referred to the encyclicals but nonetheless emphasized the representative nature of true unionism. Nineteenth-century miners, he noted, fought to establish the UMWA "[b]ecause it wasn't only a case of establishing a union, but to have an honest representative union through which the miners could negotiate contracts, not only merely wages, but conditions—the difference between life and death in a mine. . . ."

The UMWA came into existence to empower miners to secure fair wages and safer working conditions. By 1932 the union could claim an illustrious, if bloody, history. Knowing something about the international president John L. Lewis is critical to understanding the origins of the Miners' War. Regular observance of religion did not figure significantly in his public life, yet he could quote scripture chapter and verse when it suited his purposes. Lewis came to prominence in the UMWA, first in District 12 and then nationally. If Griffin was a Prince of the Church, Lewis was, by 1932, a King of Labor.

Both organizations employed a hierarchical model of leadership. The difference is that Church leadership was neither democratic nor representative. The UMWA structure was designed to be both. It consisted of officials elected by the rank and file. Members voted on contract proposals and in other ways participated in their own governance. Lewis's autocratic leadership, his interference in district governance, and mishandling of funds alienated tens of thousands of miners, including those in Illinois.

Lewis, who became the international president in 1920, found himself leading a kingdom in decline. Years of strikes, coupled with advances in alternative energy sources, hastened the turn to natural gas and electricity. Demand, after increasing during World War I, declined nationwide almost sixty million tons from 1920 to 1927. In Illinois the number of miners fell from a high of 103,566 in 1923 to 51,544 in 1932. Many relocated to the Calumet region of northern Indiana or Detroit. Given the grim outlook, Lewis and other UMWA leaders concluded that a contraction of the labor force was in order.

The coal operators looked to the largest mining company in the state, Peabody Coal, to set the agenda. The president, Stuyvesant (Jack) Peabody Jr., was Catholic. His Chicago-based company was the largest in the state and one of the biggest in the nation. Kincaid, Langleyville, and Tovey, all in the Springfield diocese, were company towns. Jack Peabody was a well-liked philanthropist, civic leader, and sportsman. He served on the board of Chicago Catholic Charities and the advisory board of Loyola College. Peabody embodied the Catholic version of "muscular Christianity." Griffin, also a Chicago native, knew and admired Peabody and believed that he was "willing to be fair and even generous with the men." Griffin knew several other Peabody executives and carried on a brisk correspondence with them throughout 1931 and 1932.

Peabody and other large Illinois operators began to mechanize in the late 1920s, thus displacing thousands of workers, but those who survived received the highest wages in the UMWA. Wages represented the operator's largest single expense. Labor and capital typically find themselves in opposition to each other, but Lewis and the operators discovered they had a common goal. By reducing the number of mines and miners, Lewis could build a stronger union and the operators could increase profits. They reasoned that a pay cut, from $6.10 to $5.00 a day, would drive thousands of men from the pits. This collaboration of labor leaders and management set the stage for the violence that erupted a few months later.

More than a year earlier, Griffin expressed his apprehension to Joseph Breen of Peabody Coal. Griffin wrote, "At the present time I am much concerned about the mining situation in this part of the State. We have thirty parishes in mining towns that are absolutely dependent upon the mining industry." Griffin suggested using his influence to persuade the miners to accept a pay reduction. He proposed that Governor Louis L. Emmerson, a personal friend, invite representatives for the operators and the union to a conference "in order to talk things over and see if a decision could not be reached. Possibly a neutral party might get some machinery working in order to secure a satisfactory solution." Nothing developed. No further correspondence on the subject appears in the bishop's files. Most likely Griffin's intervention would not have prevented the unsettling events yet to come. There was already too much "bad blood" between the UMWA leadership and the rank and file.

An atmosphere of gloom pervaded the 1932 negotiations. The Great Depression reached new heights of misery. The rank and file stood firm on the $6.10 wage. They categorically rejected the ICOA offer of $5.00. The contract expired and Illinois mines closed on April 1. Negotiations continued. District president John H. Walker lobbied hard for the $5.00 figure and scheduled a referendum for July 16. Two days before the vote, Griffin and Walker met by chance. Later that day the bishop wrote about the meeting to another friend at Peabody. Griffin was sympathetic with Walker and the operators who believed that $5.00 was the highest wage possible given the state of the economy. The bishop also mentioned that he was planning a series of sermons "on the reconstruction of society and the philosophy of present day economic factors. It is surprising how ignorant the average man is not only of his government but also of the conditions that operate in our social and economic life." Griffin had little confidence in the rank and file to vote in their own best interest and he was disappointed when union members defeated the $5.00 proposal by a large majority.

Soon Walker scheduled a second referendum for August 8. Griffin wrote to J. Paul Clayton, another friend at Peabody, "The union officials are now more aggressive and are endeavoring to prevent the radicals from stealing the show." The "radicals" were socialists and communists among the miners. Some of them objected not only to the wage, but advocated the eventual nationalization of the mines. "Whilst there is an element of uncertainty," the bishop continued, "still we are confident of a favorable vote."

The evening of August 8, UMWA locals forwarded the ballots to Springfield for counting. That evening, district officials locked the ballots in a bank vault. The next morning the officials retrieved the ballots which then mysteriously disappeared while in transit to the counting place. With just cause, many blamed John L. Lewis and accused him of planning the theft. UMWA leaders made no effort to obtain the duplicate ballots back at the locals. Lewis immediately declared a state of emergency in the district and authorized Walker to act on his own authority. Walker signed an emergency contract with ICOA to continue in effect until April 1, 1933.

Why did Lewis short-circuit the referendum? A new coal season was just around the corner. If the miners did not return to the pits, Illinois would lose markets. It was imperative to accept the $5.00 wage. Lewis also seized power because only working miners paid dues, money that would keep the UMWA, and Lewis, afloat.

Declaration of a state of emergency angered countless miners. Violence erupted in Franklin County. From the miners' perspective Lewis had usurped power from the rightfully elected officials and ignored the will of the miners as expressed in the democratically conducted referendum. Joe Ozanic believed that the ensuing war, "was provoked, created, planned and caused by John L. Lewis' takeover of the Illinois miner's (sic) autonomous district. If the Illinois miners could have gotten hands on John L., they'd have torn him limb from limb."

Disgruntled miners soon met in Gillespie. On September 1, 1932, they founded the Progressive Miners of America. The Preamble of the Constitution states that coal contributed to the social and industrial progress of civilization. They believed that the men in the pits seldom received the "fruits of their labor and self sacrifice." The preamble also stated their belief "that those who work in the Mines are entitled to the full social value of their Labor . . . [and that] the will of the majority of the rank and file of this organization would be final and binding on those they employ. . . ."

The PMA accepted members regardless of creed, color, or nationality. It also pledged to work for old-age pensions, workers' unemployment insurance, and health insurance, as well as to increase wages and improve working conditions. The new union endorsed a six-hour day, five-day week, the creation of a Women's Auxiliary; and the education of youth in regard to workers' rights and contributions to society. Finally, the new union vehemently condemned deceptive practices in hiring strikebreakers and the employment of private armed guards. Progressives recalled how in the past

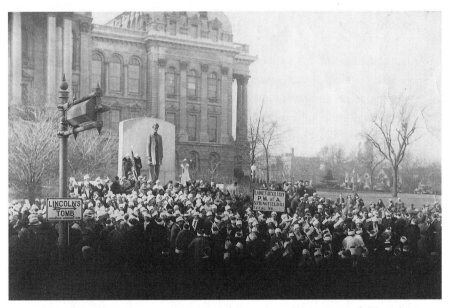

Women of the Progressive Miners of America rally in Springfield at the state capitol, circa 1933, to support better working conditions for their husbands and families. *Photo courtesy Sangamon Valley Collection, Lincoln Public Library, Springfield.*

Peabody and other operators imported unemployed miners without telling the men that they were going to be strikebreakers. Operators also frequently resorted to using armed guards to break up picket lines and demonstrations.

The objectives of the PMA echo concepts from *Rerum Novarum*. The encyclical spoke of reasonable hours and Sunday rest. It stated that "wages ought not to be insufficient to support a frugal and well-behaved wage-earner." Leo XIII wrote that workers were entitled to employ nonviolent means to "form associations among themselves so as to shake off courageously the yoke of so unrighteous and intolerable oppression."

For a while it appeared that the PMA might gain sufficient strength to overcome the opposition. Membership peaked at about thirty-five thousand in the mid-1930s. Several unmechanized small operators recognized the new union and signed contracts, but Peabody Coal refused. Bloody rioting soon broke out at Peabody mines in Christian County.

Griffin did not record his personal feelings about the actions of Peabody Coal, but within two weeks of the founding of the PMA, the bishop wrote a letter of support to District President Walker. Griffin spoke of the necessity of compromise and commended Walker for his efforts to give "generous consideration of both sides of the problem in the unhappy economic conditions of 1932." Regarding the rebel unionists, Griffin had these words:

How one could read [your statement in the *Illinois State Register*] and follow the leadership of the irresponsible element now calling themselves progressives is beyond comprehension. The insurgents are making a mess of it. The Indiana settlement [a UMWA victory] which I understand was signed Saturday should be an eye opener for the most ignorant and dumbest specimen.

Even for the outspoken Griffin, the tone was unusually strident. Did he realize that thousands of diocesan Catholics supported the Progressives? Did he consider the consequences if the letter were to be made public? A few months later, on January 7, 1933, Walker published the letter in the *Illinois Miner*, the District 12 mouthpiece.

Soon, the PMA's weekly newspaper, *The Progressive Miner*, reprinted Griffin's letter to Walker, several replies from PMA members, and Griffin's response. William Stoffels, secretary of Local 56, Pana, wrote, "Walker in our eyes is a crook, and naturally we cannot help but feel that birds of a feather flock together." Griffin replied, "I am trying to uphold his hands and to uphold the hands of union labor. I care not what you say John Walker is in your eyes. I judge a man according to my experience and I have found him a gentleman." In a pithy retort Stoffels wrote, "Apparently the horses that pull our plows shall never have the fine polish and luster of our stablehorses (sic). But think how quickly the sleekness of the latter would vanish were it not for the oats that the plow horse produces."

William Hendron of Gillespie told the bishop that two of his daughters attended Ursuline Academy, Springfield. Still, Hendron had no use for Griffin's pronouncements about the Progressives. The miner pointedly reminded the bishop about the papal interference when Charles Stewart Parnell, leader of the Irish Parliamentary Party, went broke promoting the Irish Home Rule bill. "The people of the Catholic church sent the Pope this message, 'We take our religion from Rome. All other political beliefs we reserve that right ourself (sic).'"

Mrs. M. McKeever of Tovey told the bishop that the miners were capable of counting their own ballots. She described the inhumane treatment of the law enforcement officers. "How would you like a drunken deputy to flash his light in your bedroom window three or four times a night, fire off their big guns at two or three o'clock in the morning to scare you to death. . . . They have thrown tear bombs in the streets, on the sidewalks when we would be walking, we were ordered off the streets like a dog."

Another Gillespie man, Michael Campion, also thought that Griffin had exceeded his role as bishop by getting involved in the mining dispute. Campion stated that the bishop might teach him something about the church, but that he was mistaken about the Progressives. The miner presented evidence of the deceitful and corrupt practices by Lewis and Walker. Regarding allegations that the Progressive miners were communists, Campion wrote, "Mr. Lewis would try and make you believe that we are a bunch of reds from Russia. This is a misrepresentation." But he cynically conceded, "If a man is a red or Bolshevik because he is opposed to this gangster racket, I came from Ireland, I am as red as anyone in Russia—Stalin, Trotsky, or Lenin included."

There were indeed a few socialists and communists in the PMA from its founding to 1937. Some of them held positions of influence. Gerry Allard, for example, editor of *The Progressive Miner*, was a socialist, and, in a blistering editorial, Allard called Griffin a tool of the coal operators and labor racketeers. The editor believed that Walker published the letter when he did as "another trick of the Walker-Lewis and the Peabody Coal Company to split the ranks of the Progressive Miners of America. A Bishop is imported to provoke religious strike between various elements in the organization." On the contrary, the bishop's statements did little to destabilize the Progressives. ICOA thugs and strikebreakers hired by Peabody Coal were a much greater threat.

Existence of the PMA and the escalating violence harmed the mining parishes. Several of the annual reports for 1932 and 1933 indicate that 50 to 75 percent of parishioners, many of them unemployed Progressives, received state aid. Miners who remained loyal to the UMWA were sometimes too intimidated to report for work. August Groh, who worked at a Peabody mine near Pawnee, reported that some Progressive miners with shotguns showed up in his yard to prevent him from going to work. Groh stayed away from the mine, off and on, for three months. The war compromised the ability of miners, regardless of affiliation, to support their families and their parishes.

Reverend James J. Holmes, pastor of St. James, Riverton, remarked that the violence between members of the UMWA and PMA forced Peabody to close its mines in that town and in Springfield. In the 1934 report he noted that the prolonged conflict had "effected (sic) the parish both spiritually and financially." About half the households received state relief.

The dispute affected St. Rita in Kincaid in a number of ways. Father Lydon reported,

> Spiritual side of the parish: The people come to church and frequent the Sacraments fairly well when one considers their present lamentable condition and ancestral background and training.
>
> Material aspect of the parish: The parish (and the same is true of the whole immediate locality since both are economically dependent on the mining industry) is suffering intensely by reason of the present strike among the miners. 'Tis with sorrow I say that I fear very much that the miners themselves are doing their thoughtless best to kill the goose that lays for them the golden eggs.

On a more optimistic note, Lydon commented, "There are several good, sensible people in the parish who know how to distinguish between the Catholic church and coal. Such people stand out like an oasis in the hot desert of class hatred. They are the best hope for the future of this parish and community."

At Benld the Reverend John J. Goff wrote the following in the annual report for 1933: "Feb. 15. Bomb exploded presumably by radicals on front porch of rectory. Considerable damage to front of house. After this deed radical element lost much of their following. Conditions much better last half of year." The bombing occurred just a few weeks after the exchange of letters in *The Progressive Miner*. No one was hurt. Goff, who usually slept in a bedroom at the front of the house, had that night, for no apparent reason, slept in another room.

Griffin made no public statement about the bombing. Nor did he further correspond with anyone at Peabody Coal, at least not officially. Extremists on both sides offended his sense of fair play. Given the bishop's commitment to social justice, it may seem odd that he took sides. In Griffin's mind, the deal offered by the operators and the UMWA leadership met his criteria for a fair deal. In an undated sermon on labor Griffin stated, "Three interests are to be considered in fixing wages, three needs are to be met. They are family life, condition of employer's business and public economic good." These sentiments were consistent with *Rerum Novarum* and the objectives of the Progressive Miners of America. Why, then, the estrangement?

Griffin and the Progressives shared similar views about the dignity of labor, but Griffin's friendship with coal operators, his admiration for Walker, his abhorrence of radicals, and his understanding of the economic dynamics of the coal industry colored his decision to stand with the UMWA. The rebel unionists, on the other hand, did not have Griffin's advantages when it came to education and broadness of life experience. This limited the rank and file's ability to comprehend the fragile state of the coal industry in the context of the national economy. By 1937 the ICOA and the UMWA had prevailed. The Progressives secured contracts at a few small mines, primarily in Macoupin and Madison Counties, but a majority of the remaining rejoined the UMWA. Parish finance reports indicated a gradual recovery as miners returned to work or moved on to other jobs.

The tension between the bishop and the PMA miners is a sad chapter in the history of the Catholic Church in central Illinois. To this day, in portions of Macoupin and Christian counties, there remains a residual bitterness toward Bishop Griffin among those old enough to remember the conflict. The estrangement resulting from the mining war deprived well-intentioned Progressives of an influential advocate in the state capital. Forces beyond the control of any individual, or even any single group, led to the death of twenty-one Progressives in riots, drive-by shootings, and other incidents. Most of the fatalities occurred in the winter of 1932–33. In 1936 the PMA erected a monument at the gravesite of Mother Mary Jones in the Union

Miners Cemetery, Mt. Olive. The monument remains a shrine for advocates of organized labor.

Peabody Coal weathered the war but found it necessary to close almost all of their mines in Springfield and the Midland Tract. Today, Peabody Energy, the successor corporation, continues operations in every mining region of the United States. The United Mine Workers of America had its ups and downs following the unrest of the 1930s but is no longer the powerful force that it was in the mid-twentieth century. As for the fate of the Progressives, the men who remained loyal to the union eventually lost their pensions. The small PMA simply could not maintain economic viability. Griffin fared better. His confrontation with the Progressives did not adversely affect his reputation as an advocate for organized labor. In a tribute after his death in 1948, several labor leaders paid him homage.

In the coal miners' war we see competing visions of the common good. Griffin made an effort to root his words and actions in the Gospel and in Catholic teaching. Like the American bishops of later eras, he believed that religion was not a strictly private matter but a comprehensive belief system that shapes attitudes and behavior in the public sphere.

RELATED READING

David Maxwell, "A Turning Point: The Lasting Impact of the 1898 Virden Mine Riot," *Journal of the Illinois State Historical Society* vol. 99, no. 3–4 (Fall–Winter 2006–7).

30.

A SPECIAL PLACE
Lake Forest and the Great Depression, 1929–1940

Frederick Mercer Van Sickle

Illinois Historical Journal vol. 79, no. 2 (Summer 1986)

The sprawling Chicago suburban sector has grown to the extent that it greatly exceeds Chicago in population. Van Sickle's article focuses on Lake Forest, long the home of many of the Chicago area's wealthiest citizens. The Lake Forest train station was the suburbanite's link to Chicago commerce.

The article describes a number of its prominent residents, identifying their position in the larger Chicago area and the leadership some took regionally and statewide to alleviate the effects of the Great Depression. The author notes that although Lake Forest was insulated from the worst effects of the Depression, a Lake Forest council was formed in an effort to help people get back to work. Lake Forest participated in many New Deal Programs.

L ake Forest's reputation as a special place dated back to the mid-1850s, when pioneer Chicagoans chose it as the site for a Presbyterian seminary (later to become Lake Forest College). During the next four decades, Lake Forest grew famous as a summer retreat—"the Newport of the Middle West"—comparable to Grosse Point, Michigan; Bryn Mawr, Pennsylvania; or Scarsdale, New York. Located just thirty miles north of Chicago's Loop on the shores of Lake Michigan, Lake Forest attracted many of the city's wealthiest families. It became an enclave of the elite, a community of "palatial homes, country estates, and splendid farms."

An insulated and untypical Illinois suburban community, Lake Forest was the subject of an extensive oral history project conducted by the author in 1983 and involving interviews with twenty-five longtime residents. Their recollections of the Great Depression, supplemented with contemporary newspaper accounts and other sources, present a fascinating view of the city in which, as historian Herman Dunlap Smith so aptly commented, the effect of hard times was definitely "secondary."

The years immediately preceding the Great Depression found Lake Forest flushed with ten years of substantial expansion. Arthur Meeker, a summer resident of the North Shore and chronicler of Chicago society, observed during those frenetic years, "Lake Forest has become so amazingly 'the thing' that it is almost impossible nowadays to find standing room for your household gods." The community experienced its greatest population increase in the 1920s, growing from thirty-six hundred to sixty-five hundred.

Examples of prosperity abounded. The economy was sound and growing, and Lake Foresters were confident about the future. Gerard Verbeke, a Belgian immigrant who became a gardener on the estate of Louis F. Swift, recalled, "The twenties were very good, there was plenty of work. . . . There was a building boom, everybody was working, had good jobs. You couldn't keep up with it. . . . These estates here in Lake Forest were all booming. You could get a job anywhere, just go, and that was it."

Marion Warner Hodgkins, a daughter of one of Lake Forest's founding families, spoke of the city's legendary social life during the period: "There was a tremendous amount of entertaining. People had lots and lots of servants. They could entertain at home as much as they liked. . . . There was a great deal of illegal drinking, because we supposedly had Prohibition, to which nobody paid much attention as they should—even the Presbyterians."

Upbeat activity continued through 1929. Sound pictures opened at Lake Forest's Deerpath Theatre. A private railroad car, known formally as the *Deerpath* and informally as the "Millionaires' Special," was initiated on the Chicago and North Western Railroad. Some thirty commuting businessmen, all Lake Forest residents, paid $15,000 annually for the privilege of riding the exclusive car to their Chicago offices. The *Deerpath* remained in the city throughout the workday, available as a private club.

The reality of the nation's economic circumstances became apparent with the stock market crash of October 24, 1929. According to Edward Arpee, former faculty member of Lake Forest Academy and author of the city's most comprehensive history, there was an almost immediate ramification in Lake Forest: "On October 29, 1929, workmen left the half-finished interior of the locker building [of the proposed country club at Mellody Farm] never to return. . . . The business depression had begun."

Another measure of the Depression's effect on Lake Forest can be found in construction statistics. As would be expected, many projects were underway in 1929 when building permits totaled $2,631,610. Two major buildings were initiated: a $200,000 headquarters for the First National Bank and a $250,000 city library, the gift of Helen May Shedd Reed and Laura Shedd Schweppe, daughters of Marshall Field executive John G. Shedd. The new Lake Forest Library, constructed of pink Holland brick and white stone, won the Craftsmanship Award of the Chicago Architects' Club for 1931.

In 1930 it seemed evident that Lake Foresters were seeking to challenge the Great Depression by launching an ambitious round of construction projects. In fact, the town frequently exceeded the combined total of all other construction in Lake County. The First Presbyterian Church built a $47,483 manse, and two of the town's exclusive country clubs expanded. The Knollwood Club and the Onwentsia Club each had a $30,000 project.

Just fifteen square miles in size, Lake Forest was surpassed only by Chicago and Peoria for building permits in 1931. The Lake Forest Day School built a $100,000 addition, and the Marshall Field store on Market Square was enlarged for the fourth time in three years. The grandest example of Lake Forest's affluence was the $274,000 home of Helen May Shedd Reed, widow of Kersey Coates Reed.

Construction increased to $278,066 in 1933, and growth continued gradually to $705,346 within five years. Although 180 homes were built in the 1930s, and the population increased by 242 persons, Lake Forest was a long way from its $2,631,610 construction peak in 1929.

Just as Lake Forest seemed to resist national trends in economics, it resisted the majority impulse toward Franklin D. Roosevelt and the Democratic Party. Lake Forest was traditionally Republican. Unlike most other American cities when the Depression worsened, Lake Forest remained loyal to Herbert Hoover. Two Lake Foresters were members of Hoover's administration—Robert Patterson Lamont as secretary of commerce and James Henderson Douglas Jr. as assistant secretary of the treasury.

The elite of Lake Forest were virulent in their opposition to FDR. Some argued that he wanted to pit class against class, that he was giving too much power to the federal government, and that he was turning over the country to the "unqualified."

Roosevelt was not totally without admirers in Lake Forest, however. Hermon Dunlap Smith, an officer in the Onwentsia Club and one of the North Shore's outstanding business and civic leaders, counted himself among FDR's supporters. But he acknowledged that he was in a minority in Lake Forest. "There was a great bitterness about Roosevelt," he said, "and that was more true of a prosperous community." Smith, along with the Dicks and Adlai E. Stevenson II (a frequent summer resident before his marriage), formed the liberal counterpoint to the majority.

As Roosevelt ended his first term, the *Lake Forester* accused him of attempting to "spend us back to prosperity." In the 1936 presidential election, Lake Forest returned a strong Republication majority, and the same editor concluded, "Although the outcome of this election is disappointing to the majority of voters in Lake Forest, they must agree that the country as a whole wants Mr. Roosevelt for a second term."

The Depression had carried Roosevelt into office, but in the prosperous community of Lake Forest the effects of the Depression were not as dramatic as they were elsewhere. Peter Toomey, a painting contractor, testified to that fact: "Nobody was on the corner begging," he said. Lake Foresters "knew from the paper, and what they read, that things were much worse" elsewhere. Yet not many storefronts were empty, and no one was "falling down on the street, starving."

Uri Grannis agreed that his neighbors did not suffer "drastic changes." He recalled: "[O]ur life-styles were cut to a certain extent. There wasn't a drastic change as far as our family was concerned. Certainly, individuals had a hell of a time but as a whole the limousines were still at the 6:00 train when it pulled in in Lake Forest."

Lake Foresters were acutely aware of the sad situations in nearby North Chicago and Waukegan. As Uri Grannis remembered, "There was a threat of violence during the period. I can remember Father talking about some of his friends who lived on the north side of Lake Forest who took out a kind of riot insurance because of the possibility of some kind of invasion from North Chicago, which was hard hit by the Depression. These people were afraid."

Lake Forest city government reflected the Depression's impact. Delinquent taxes threatened the community. In November 1932, payment of $283,000 worth of outstanding bonds was due from special assessment taxes. A collection campaign was waged in order to save the city's credit rating, and within a year the city clerk announced that the city had sufficient money to pay off the bonds. The expenditure per student at the township high school, located at nearby Highland Park, slipped from $272 in 1929–30 to $200 three years later. (Each of those figures, however, represented more than double the prevailing average cost per student expended throughout the rest of the state.)

Private businesses and institutions likewise felt the pinch. The Deerpath Inn was named in a foreclosure suit in 1932 and for three years was operated under receivership. The weekly *Lake Forester* changed its format, rag content, and scale in January of 1933, allowing a reduced subscription price from $2.00 to $1.50 a year. The Knollwood Club filed for bankruptcy in February of 1935, claiming a $250,000 indebtedness; the club was later reorganized and continued under the same name.

Fear of crime was a major problem of the Depression years. Burglaries in 1930 caused municipal authorities to add four patrolmen, and Police Chief Tiffany requested that door-to-door salesmen register at headquarters. Fear prompted the installation of a $69,049 street lighting system that was described as a crime deterrent.

Extortion was a constant worry to monied households, especially those with young children. Jackson Garrett Durand, son of the owner of the S. S. Durant sugar distributing company, received a $50,000 threat on the life of his two-year-old daughter. The wedding of Sophie Harrington and Jacob Bischoff was protected by armed guards because of threats made to the bride's father, George Bates Harrington, president and general manager of the Chicago, Wilmington, and Franklin Coal Company.

In 1933 Solomon Smith, president of the Northern Trust Company, was victimized three times. The first incident involved a bomb mailed to his Chicago home. The second was a demand for $4,000 coupled with a death threat. The third was a demand for $5,000 to be placed at the gate of his Lake Forest home. A dummy package was planted there, and police watched the area, but the extortionists did not appear. Robert Abbe Gardner, a Chicago stockbroker, received two extortion notes: one threatened the life of his eleven-year-old son unless $10,000 was furnished, and the other threatened to bomb his niece's debut at Chicago's Casino Club. Because of the national awareness of the Lindbergh kidnapping, there was heightened concern about the safety of Lake Forest children. June Laflin attributed the prevalence of kidnapping to "the poverty and the great difference in life-styles between life in Lake Forest and elsewhere."

The city's first attempt to ameliorate differences in lifestyles through Lake Forest occurred in October 1930, when Reverend Herbert William Prince of the Church of the Holy Spirit, the community's Episcopal Congregation, convened a meeting of representatives of the city's civic organizations and churches. Calling themselves the Lake Forest Community Council (LFCC), the volunteers provided a variety of services, including a clearinghouse for relief work. The LFCC was characterized by a distaste for the dole and a positive emphasis on self-reliance. Members persuaded the local newspaper to provide free classified advertisements for the unemployed, urged individuals to create odd jobs, and distributed relief to needy families.

One LFCC unemployment registration revealed that 105 men and 12 women were out of work in the community. The response was to arrange for forty-two jobs, but that was hardly enough to alleviate the problem. Work was created in conjunction with Lake Forest College, Lake Forest Academy, Lake Forest Day School, Ferry Hall School, and the park board. In 1931 fifty individuals found one day's work per week through the program. The LFCC spent $6,000 in 1931 and $15,000 in 1932.

By 1932 the magnitude of the council's relief burden forced it to turn over its administrative work to William O. Paape, building commissioner for the city; that action was consistent with the national pattern of transferring relief functions from the private to public sectors. By 1934 the LFCC had disbanded, and the township and the Illinois Emergency Relief Commission assumed responsibility for the needy. By fiscal year 1934–35, the Shields Township Poor Fund had doubled to $50,000. In addition, it maintained two programs for relief—making farmland available and cooperating with Fort Sheridan in hiring men to cut firewood on government lands for the needy. As Gerard Verbeke said, "You fell back to your township."

The Illinois Emergency Relief Commission, the state agency created in 1932, was administered in part by Lake Foresters. Of the seven original commissioners appointed by Governor Louis L. Emmerson, four had strong Lake Forest ties: Edward L. Ryerson Jr., Samuel Insull (until his departure), Colonel Albert Arnold Sprague, and Joseph M. Cudahy. Lake Forest by tradition had long provided strong leadership in the state and metropolis in time of need, as well as in times of prosperity. Many of Chicago's charitable institutions were headed and supported by Lake Foresters.

Jane Dick recalled the variety of noblesse oblige practiced by her father:

Well, I think his was a privilege oblige—if you were privileged, if you were lucky enough to have wherewithal more than others. It was: Why are we so privileged and other people aren't? I mean, this is a hard thing to ever figure out. If you are, you certainly, *you must* share and do what you can.

The same explanation applied to Lake Forest residents' involvement in the affairs of Chicago. Hermon Smith explained it best: "We were involved in Chicago. If the future of Chicago fell apart, Lake Forest wouldn't survive. So much of the wealth of Lake Forest came from Chicago. . . . As a practical matter, it was important for Lake Forest people that Chicago remain sound financially."

Despite its conservative politics, the community of Lake Forest wasted little time in utilizing the federal largesse of Roosevelt's much-criticized New Deal. In 1933 the city applied for a $412,000 loan from the National Recovery Administration (NRA) for expanding and improving the municipal water plant. (Six months later, however, when the Public Works Administration offered $338,000 for construction of a filtration plant and water distribution system, city officials determined the project could be built more economically with corporate financing.)

The most controversial of the New Deal Programs, the NRA had an interesting history in Lake Forest. Intended to increase private employment by helping businesses and their employees form fair competition codes based on mutually acceptable wages, prices, and work hours, the NRA initially enjoyed wide support in Lake Forest. Local businessmen joined residents in collecting signatures for creation of a local compliance board. Such institutions as the First National Bank endorsed the drive. Employers were asked to sign the code of regulations designed to create more jobs. Robert Douglas Stuart Sr., vice president of Quaker Oats Company and one of Lake Forest's most prominent citizens, was appointed head of the NRA national industrial advisory committee.

The Works Progress Administration enabled another long-held dream, construction of a new and separate high school for Lake Forest and its affluent neighbor, Lake Bluff. (Secondary school students attended the township high school located at Highland Park.) In January 1934, a $275,000 bond issue was approved by a vote of 1,999 to 1,037. The new structure showed few signs of Depression scrimping. Three stories high and built of brick and stone, it opened in 1935 for approximately 420 students. A Federal Writers'

Project reporter described it as "luxurious in detail" and "the last word in modernity." Among the amenities were a spacious auditorium equipped with a motion picture screen, up-to-date chemistry and biology laboratories, and a large gymnasium, complete with pool. Perhaps most surprising, the entire building was air conditioned.

Civil Works Administration projects in Lake Forest exceeded $45,000 in 1933, and the *Lake Forester* proudly noted that "practically all of the men on the local emergency relief rolls" were at work. In all, some sixty jobs were created, from paving streets to painting City Hall. Federal Emergency funds extended part-time employment to twenty-nine students from Lake Forest College, allowing them to remain enrolled.

The First National Bank of Lake Forest—along with other financial institutions across the nation—took part in the bank holiday declared by President Roosevelt immediately after his inauguration in March 1933. The First National remained open during the holiday and provided "permissible services," including making change, accepting payments, and conducting trust business. Fortuitously the bank had been examined the previous month and was found to be sound. After eleven days the Federal Reserve System authorized it to resume full service on March 15, the day following the reopening of major Chicago banks.

Philip L. Speidel, an officer of the bank who was otherwise critical of most of Roosevelt's programs, allowed that the Federal Home Owners Loan Corporation (HOLC) had an extremely beneficial effect on the community. "The purpose of that corporation was to help a man keep his home," he recalled. At least twenty families, he said, "would have lost their homes without government help."

Much of the First National's strength must be attributed to its board of directors. Its members included A. B. Dick Jr., Thomas E. Donnelley, Charles F. Glore, D. R. McLennan, John T. Pirie, and Robert J. Thorne. In fact, within only four months of the bank holiday, buoyed by such stability, the First National increased its deposits by almost a half million dollars, a sure sign of confidence in the institution. By 1936 deposits had increased by $2 million.

Before 1929, twenty-five banks were operating in Lake County, but by the end of the 1930s only ten survived. The First National Bank retained the confidence of its depositors because, according to Speidel, "When the chips were down in 1933 there were men on our board who personally could have underwritten the assets of our bank." In fact, the First National was the only "unrestricted" bank between Racine, Wisconsin, and Evanston. Deposits came from as far away as Kenosha, Wisconsin. Business flourished. By and large, Lake Forest fared very well. Elsewhere in Lake County, there were two-block lines at some Waukegan banks. The bank in Highwood closed permanently; the capital stock of the bank in Highland Park was reduced by one-half; and the First National Bank of Waukegan was liquidated. Such instability allowed the First National Bank of Lake Forest to acquire considerable new business.

Thus, while the Great Depression did not devastate Lake Forest institutions, it did contribute greatly to the irreversible alteration of the old lifestyles. Peter Toomey summed up the change: "After the Depression the big estates . . . started breaking up. Even before World War II, they never did come back in full force, Swifts and McCormicks. They never went back to these big homes—they were so large. The costs were so much . . . they couldn't get the employees."

In 1920 a total of eighty persons were employed on the three McCormick estates. By 1936 the number had shrunk to six or eight, according to the *Lake Forester*. The writer concluded that "[t]he day of large estates" was clearly over. Such changes had been brought by a multiplicity of factors: changed tax laws, new employment opportunities for the servant class, and the general return of prosperity.

There was indeed a Depression in Lake Forest, as in the nation, yet it was not generally a time of widespread pain. The Depression was recognized and in some ways hit home; but, as Hermon Dunlap Smith so astutely observed, its impact proved "secondary." Lake Forest's sizeable upper class insulated the community from the overwhelming pain felt elsewhere during the Great Depression. Lake Forest was a special place.

RELATED READING

Carl Abbott, "Necessary Adjuncts to Its Growth: The Railroad Suburbs of Chicago, 1854–1875," *Journal of the Illinois State Historical Society* vol. 73, no. 2 (Summer 1980).

31

A REINTERPRETATION OF BLACK STRATEGIES FOR CHANGE AT THE CHICAGO WORLD'S FAIR, 1933–1934

Christopher Robert Reed

Illinois Historical Journal vol. 81, no. 1 (Spring 1988)

The sponsors of the Chicago World's Fair—called the Century of Progress—wanted to show the great scientific and material advancements in the hundred years since 1833, the year of Chicago's founding. But for Chicago blacks, progress was measured in terms of combating discrimination in employment, restaurant service, and even in fair exhibits.

With new information, this article revises an earlier *Journal* article that focused on the strategy of protest in achieving these ends. Reed finds, however, that conciliation was the dominant strategy of blacks when interacting with white Fair managers. That was made possible by an accommodating attitude of the managers, who "were supportive of justice from the onset." The biracial Urban League represented this approach as blacks worked to define their place at the fair and in society in general.

A Century of Progress, the Chicago World's Fair of 1933 and 1934, generated a surge of black assertiveness for justice and equal rights. Three decades later, the fair also inspired August Meier and Elliott M. Rudwick to write a pacesetting study on the character of that racial advocacy. Primarily based on research of the black press, "Negro Protest at the Chicago

World's Fair, 1933–1934," published in this journal, concluded that protest was the primary means used by blacks to combat discrimination in exhibits, restaurants, and employment:

> If the fair was any index to the nation's progress in race relations, it simply indicated that Negroes were still largely "invisible men" and that the race would have to fight for recognition of even the most elementary rights. . . . The Chicago fair of 1933 indicated that white America had made very little progress in its treatment of colored Americans. But the experiences of those who fought its discriminatory policies indicated that militant use of political action was to be an important strategy for achieving progress toward recognition of the Negro's citizenship rights in the future.

Shortly after Meier and Rudwick's article was published, the official papers of A Century of Progress were donated to the University of Illinois at Chicago, and by 1971 the collection was opened for examination. The papers presented a new well of information that contrasted dramatically with the impressions gleaned from the contemporary black press relied upon by Meier and Rudwick. The Century of Progress records, by revealing the official interaction of blacks with the white managers of the fair, suggest that conciliation—rather than protest—was the dominant strategy.

By the late 1920s there was a well-defined black civic structure in Chicago. In order to promote their interests at the world's fair, the city's blacks planned and implemented a complex organizational effort. Sometimes resembling a movement, the effort effectively bonded both civic and political organizations in behalf of race advancement. The social class supporting the endeavor was primarily, but not exclusively, the black middle class—a group with resources and influence far exceeding its size.

Promoters of A Century of Progress envisioned it as a financially profitable demonstration of how far humankind had progressed in both material and scientific terms since 1833, the year Chicago was founded. "The keynote of the coming exposition is 'Science in Action,'" the managers proclaimed. "The design is principally to show the world how the physical sciences have made their contributions to human advancement." The success of the endeavor was measurable at turnstiles, as almost 38.6 million persons visited the fair's marvels and attractions between 1933 and 1934.

Chicago blacks, in contrast, measured progress in fundamentally different terms. They set three objectives: representation in the fair's exhibits that would portray fully and accurately their race's heritage and contributions to the world; full enjoyment of their rights as citizens; and, in the middle of the Great Depression, an equal share in employment opportunities generated by the fair. The *Chicago Defender* stated, "The real 'Chicago spirit' is unalterably opposed to the surrendering of civil and legal rights." The paper challenged fair organizers instead to show "advancement over sinister and insidious propensities to the point where [Chicago] can recognize in mankind character, fitness, and ability as the only essential elements of real progress." As planning for the fair continued, there were disparate perceptions of purpose and even the nature of progress. In addition, there were controversies whenever the fair's pecuniary and scientific interests clashed with black racial concerns.

Race ideology had undergone considerable change in the twentieth century. Racial strategies for advancement were far from unified. An important issue was how blacks would define their places specifically in the world's fair and generally in American society. In his 1903 classic *The Souls of Black Folks*, W. E. B. Du Bois had described the anxiety that resulted when persons of African descent found themselves psychologically facing the competing influences of nationality and race. There was, he said, a "two-ness,—an American, a Negro; two souls, two thoughts, two unreconciled strivings."

During Chicago's first world's fair—the Columbian Exposition of 1893—the conflict between racial identity and nationality had been debated and, to a certain degree, settled in favor of nationality. Frederick Douglass's misgivings about the Exposition's Colored American Day can be seen in his address, in which he "began by questioning the motives of the Exposition people in giving the colored people a day and intimated that he doubted the advisability of returning any thanks for the honor conferred."

A second problem involved the relative importance of conciliation and protest. In Chicago, especially during the fair, conciliation assumed a level of importance equal to protest. Also, as the two strategies were manifested in activities aimed at achieving the black version of progress, they moved correspondingly through the stages of prevention, confrontation, and remedy. At various times, both conciliation and protest were promoted through a sizable civic and political structure that included the Chicago Urban League, the *Chicago Defender*, the Chicago branch of the National Association for the Advancement of Colored People, and black Republican politicians at the local, state, and national levels, as well as affiliated black groups and organizations.

Within the black community, middle-class concerns encompassed civil rights, racial image, and employment. Blacks had supported the *Chicago Whip*'s "Don't Spend Your Money Where You Can't Work" campaign of 1930, which for the first time involved the use of the picket line and boycott by Chicago blacks. By 1933 those concerns had also developed into a well-established pattern that included resistance to housing restrictions, school segregation, and racially exclusionary politics.

The efficacy of conciliation was rooted in the relationship that existed between the Century of Progress management and black middle-class leaders. From 1928, when the fair corporation conceived its operating plan, black business leaders such as Jesse Binga and Robert Sengstacke Abbott were invited to participate. Binga was the founder and president of the Binga State Bank, which along with the city's Douglass National Bank owned by Anthony Overton controlled one-third of all banking resources held by blacks nationally. Abbott, who had accumulated considerable wealth by the 1920s, was the founder, owner, and publisher of the *Chicago Defender*, perhaps the leading black newspaper in the nation. Century of Progress records indicate that Abbott was solicited to join the founding circle of members but declined, although he did send the $1,000 membership fee.

Century of Progress records show an amicable relationship between other black leaders and the fair's managers. Members of the duSable Club, the Men's Division of the Chicago Urban League, were described as "young and progressive professional and business Negroes." The league itself was considered "an organization of the better class of colored people of Chicago," as well as "an outstanding organization." These descriptions were unusual given the racism of the period.

The Chicago Urban League, whose leadership was biracial, best represented middle-class interests in utilizing the strategy of conciliatory tactics at the fair. The Chicago branch of the NAACP was the organizational choice for protest. With its all-black leadership, the organization became increasingly militant during the Depression. Through both direct and indirect leadership, the league led the movement to insure parity in jobs, exhibits, and the enjoyment of recreational facilities. By 1932 the league had petitioned for and won recognition of its leadership role in all matters pertaining to blacks and the fair. Concomitantly, the league organized the Colored Citizens World's Fair Council (CCWFC), an organization representing forty organizations. The council not only served as a clearinghouse but also monitored civil rights and encouraged the upkeep and protection of the South Side neighborhoods affected by visitors and the criminal element attending the fair. Monthly meetings of the council averaged one hundred persons.

The prestige of the Urban League was enhanced in 1928, when the group petitioned for a memorial to the city's first permanent settler, Jean Baptiste Point Du Sable, a black man. Significantly, the Du Sable campaign avoided any tone of racial advocacy. That deliberate strategy strengthened the case in an often hostile environment. The crusade was led by Dr. Arthur G. Falls, who approached fair managers as early as May of 1928. In November, the De Saible [sic] Memorial Society, a predominantly black women's group led by Annie Oliver, began laying the groundwork for a concerted effort to carry the Du Sable exhibit to fruition. The two groups cooperated for the next five years; after many setbacks, the exhibit was approved in January of 1933, five months before the fair was to open. The fair management acceded to the legitimacy for the proposal and agreed to display a replica of the Du Sable homestead as part of the social science exhibits, an area reserved for nonmaterial aspects of progress. Funding for the replica was provided by the city through the efforts of black alderman Robert R. Jackson.

In promoting Du Sable's achievements, the De Saible Memorial Society and the Urban League never wavered from their position that Du Sable was to be recognized as founder of a great American city, not as a black man. The De Saible Memorial Society called him the "first settler, Negro, trader, pioneer, and business man" of Chicago. In the chambers of the city council, Alderman Jackson spoke of Du Sable as a "great pioneer," and of his cabin as "the cradle of a city which was destined to and has become the greatest city of the world." Consistent with the independence of the black middle class, the Urban League and De Saible Society rejected any suggestion that the memorial homestead represented special considerations for blacks. In a bit of irony, however, the Urban League did refer to Du Sable as the "first civilized man to settle in what is Chicago"—a possible offense to such American Indians as the Ojibwa (Chippewa), Potawatomi, Winnebago, and other indigenous groups of the Chicagoland area.

When opposition to the Du Sable project occurred, it usually appeared as part of the basically financial orientation of the fair management. From a business perspective, the fair was undertaken to generate profits for the investors and to promote the city's economic image and future. The sentimental causes posed by blacks promoting a pioneer or by Catholics promoting a memorial to Father Jacques Marquette were of secondary importance to profit-making. That policy, however, was not consistently followed. Fair leaders did not wish to offend any group and unnecessarily jeopardize profits; when possible, they acted to mitigate confrontation. Even though the fair's theme emphasized material progress, by 1933 the Du Sable memorial, as well as one for Marquette, had gained approval for display in the social science exhibits.

Two other attempts to memorialize black progress were unsuccessful. Black architect Walter Thomas Bailey had been working for three years on winning support for an exhibit that "would teach the world some of the interesting history of the Black people before the first boat load of slaves ever landed in this country." In 1931 an African prince named Modupe Paris persuasively argued for support of a similar project, except that he insisted that Africans, rather than Afro-Americans, should control the project. His group, the Africans and Descendants Centennial Committee, proposed a project with a budget of $132,166. The staging of such an extensive project covering the achievements and glories of so many diverse peoples over such a vast continent would have been difficult in the best of times, even if the city and its black citizens had not been in the grip of the Depression.

Upon scrutiny by fair investigators who looked regularly into the financial, personal, and organizational backgrounds of each prospective exhibitor, it was quickly determined that the Paris group had no chance of raising the funds necessary to mount the exhibit. From 1931 to 1932 the official fair position was to indulge the Paris group in its activities but to assume that the venture would stall indefinitely in its conceptual phase.

The next important effort aimed at producing an African exhibit came in 1932 from a white Chicago business, the Netherton Company. The motivation of Netherton's All-Africa Corporation is unfathomable from the Century of Progress records. The company promised "that no exhibit will be made which the World's Fair Administration shall deem might offend the American Negroes." But the Netherton Company had a questionable financial history, and there was some opposition from the black community. The All-Africa Corporation failed to come up with the financial guarantees required of exhibitors, and by late November of 1932 contact between the fair and the project terminated. The corporation's failure ended all serious activities directed at producing an African cultural and scientific exhibit. As a result, African contributions to world progress in mathematics, the smelting of iron ore, and other areas were not demonstrated on the Chicago fairgrounds.

Yet, support for such a project persisted. With the financial and organizational support of a small number of Africans and black Americans, Modupe Paris produced an independent project. The African and American Negro Exhibit opened along with the Century of Progress in May 1933 but under community auspices some two miles southwest of the fairgrounds at the National Pythian Temple at Thirty-Seventh and State Streets, in the heart of the South Side black community. The exhibit offered displays on ancient African architecture and artwork, contemporary African art and commercial products, and American Negro achievements in science, the military, the professions, and the arts.

Once the fair opened, a minor episode appears to have received press coverage and eventually historical significance disproportionate to its importance—the separate Negro Day at the fair. Black leaders who had worked on behalf of the Du Sable exhibit had always resisted a racially exclusive event. Jesse Binga, for example, had requested that "the race question be not brought up during the fair." The originator of the idea was Chandler Owen—orator, socialist, and promoter—who introduced the idea in 1932. A newcomer to the city, Owen was not a member of the middle-class leadership ranks. The only major endorsement for his plan was from black United States representative Oscar DePriest, and that turned out to be ephemeral. Other politicians ignored Owen's plan; Aldermen William L. Dawson and Robert R. Jackson failed to endorse the idea in the city council, negating a political custom.

The opposition that Owen encountered was consistent with the spirit of 1893, when a separate Colored American Day was held but with limited success. Ida B. Wells Barnett and other racial equalitarians boycotted that event, and Frederick Douglass reluctantly became involved because he was already at the exposition as an official at the Haitian Pavilion. Douglass's presence lent a semblance of legitimacy to the 1893 event, but the fair of 1933 had no one of Douglass's stature associated with it.

Negro Day, which was held August 12, 1933, was a colossal flop—both ideologically and financially. Owen had predicted that three hundred thousand persons would attend, but only fifty thousand did, establishing an all-time-low daily attendance record. It was such a debacle that the fair management had to intercede financially by assuming the debt in order to prevent the event from becoming an even bigger disaster. The *Chicago Defender*, which had reported but not supported the event, tersely summed up the popular feeling, "the less said about this day the better for all of us."

Throughout the rest of the fair, how were blacks treated? To be sure, in Depression-ridden Chicago there were apprehensions about racism, but at the fair it seemed that the apprehension of racism assumed a greater importance than its actual existence.

Containment of segregation, discrimination, and prejudice was directly attributable to the early and sustained involvement of black leaders with the fair managers. Civic and political interaction with the fair's hierarchy proceeded through stages and along conciliatory lines that prevented problems before they could fester. Even the militant Chicago NAACP attempted to work within the bounds of conciliation in order to prevent any explosive racial incidents. Because of the accessibility of fair president Rufus C. Dawes and his entire staff, contacts proved consistently cordial and productive. Dawes was personally committed to insuring racial justice, and on more than one occasion he did just that. Also important was the actively enforced Illinois Civil Rights Act, which provided legal redress for grievances.

The test of whether all citizens were to enjoy their rights occurred sooner than many expected. In 1932 one concessionaire rented the formerly public beach at Twelfth Street and set up a whites-only sales booth. The matter was investigated, exposed, and stopped. That action coincided with the formation of the CCWFC, which provided blacks a conciliatory vehicle to channel their grievances and to monitor racial progress at the fair.

Once the fair opened, the ugly threat of discrimination appeared to be real after all. The first victims were Urban League members Dr. Arthur G. Falls and his wife, Lillian. While on the fairgrounds late one evening, the Fallses were denied entrance to a restaurant. They seated themselves, were served, and brought the incident to Dawes's attention the next day. The concessionaire was warned to desist or to leave the fairgrounds. In the dozen or so other cases, the Chicago NAACP entered the battle at the confrontational stage. With a battery of well-trained volunteer attorneys who comprised its Legal Redress Committee, the NAACP repeatedly took offenders to court in an attempt to discourage other acts of discrimination.

Blacks also resorted to remedial political action through their representatives in the Illinois General Assembly. President A. Clement MacNeal of the Chicago NAACP induced Representative Charles J. Jenkins to act. Jenkins and Representatives Harris B. Gaines, William E. King, William J. Warfield, and Arthur T. Broche jointly introduced a resolution calling for more decisive action when civil rights violations occurred. On June 29,

1933, House Resolution 85 called on Cook County state's attorney Thomas J. Courtney to conduct grand jury investigations of those violations.

Discrimination cases dragged through the Chicago courts during the summer, and the NAACP led a delegation that included the membership of the CCWFC to the office of the Cook County state's attorney to demand swifter legal and judicial action. Although the delegation was met dispassionately, it might as well have been met antagonistically since its protestations fell on deaf ears. By the end of the fair's two-year run, remedy was finally at hand when the Chicago NAACP's suits were decided, all in favor of the plaintiffs. The branch won seventeen cases involving discrimination in or around the fairgrounds, amounting to judgments of $5,000 in the aggregate.

During the second year of the fair, black legislators redirected their focus. They planned to prevent discrimination and avoid the criticism from their constituents that they had suffered in 1932 when they failed to delay enabling legislation for the fair until passage of an anti-discrimination law that would have prevented the Twelfth Street beach incident. Now, they refused to support any fair legislation until they received a guarantee of an anti-discrimination law affecting concessionaries. The tactical move proved effective. House Bill 114, introduced by Representatives Gaines, Jenkins, and Warfield, passed the House by a 98–2 vote and the Senate by a 27–0 vote. With passage of the law, the number of complaints dropped considerably, and overt discrimination in private dining accommodations virtually ended.

Despite the legal guarantees, the atmosphere of prejudice was aided indirectly by the timidity of some blacks. Many members of the masses, as well as the southern black middle class who came to visit the fair, simply avoided eating at fair restaurants. Such action was opposed repeatedly by the Chicago Urban League, the Chicago NAACP, the *Defender*, and others, however. Blacks were chided to act like citizens and demand their rights in the same manner as they accepted their responsibilities as citizens. Blacks who partook of what the fair offered appeared to enjoy themselves.

Employment at the fair provided another opportunity to examine prejudice. After all, the fair was intended to show the nation and the world that Chicago was still economically viable despite the Depression. Blacks held positions from the top to the bottom of the employment rungs. Adam Beckley, for example, who was college trained, was visible in fair president Dawes's office as an administrative assistant. The major lecturer in the Lincoln room of the Illinois Host building was attorney Andrew Torrence.

Six of the uniformed policemen and three of the policewomen were black, and the men were conspicuous as members of the honor guard escorting Postmaster General James Aloysius Farley, President Roosevelt's representative at the fair's opening. The Walgreen drugstore chain employed a black clerk who served all citizens from a very visible position. Many entertainers, especially musicians and dancers, were prominent on the Streets of Paris, in the Midget Village, and on the Showboat. Most blacks were found at the bottom rungs, however. Most washroom attendants were black, and one of the fair's major concessionaires reported hiring four hundred to six hundred black laborers during 1933.

There were no black concessionaires, however, and without the owners of businesses ensuring equal access to work as other nationalities were prone to do, opportunities were limited. But the problem of black entrepreneurs was related to both discrimination and a lack of capital. Chicago black businessmen were suffering from the failure by 1932 of both the Binga State Bank and the Douglass National Bank, as well as the near-failure of three major black insurance companies. J. D. Carr, a self-appointed black spokesman, summarized the situation: "An investor has employment out there [on the fairgrounds] in proportion to his investments. Every concessionist has exclusionary charge over his employees." If blacks could not afford to be investors, they had to rely on the good will of those who could. Fair management might work to stop flagrant cases of discrimination, but it had never envisioned itself as a protector of employment rights or a provider of patronage.

The black effort to secure more employment was initiated in 1931 by Chicago Urban League executive director Albion L. Foster, who was joined by the staff of the Wabash YMCA and the director of public service for the *Chicago Defender*. From the ranks of the masses, the John Brown Organization of Cook County led by W. Thomas Soders joined the effort. Soders had already gained a reputation as a fighter for jobs based on his involvement in the streetcar riots of 1930, which involved massive street protests for jobs. Black employment improved only slightly at the fair, but in the middle of the Depression, improvements—even if only by degrees—were welcomed.

The Century of Progress proved to be a rather accurate indicator of how far Chicago blacks had progressed since 1833. Their racial image had improved considerably since slavery days, as the reception given the Du Sable homestead by blacks, whites, and the fair management demonstrated. Discrimination on the fairgrounds was controlled through the efforts of blacks and the fair leaders, who were supportive of justice from the onset. The problem of inequality in employment persisted as it had for decades, not only in Chicago but also in the nation. On balance, though, the fair turned out to be more of a benefit than a detriment to Chicago blacks. Therefore, it was a symbol of progress.

RELATED READING

August Meier and Elliott M. Rudwick, "Negro Protest at the Chicago's World's Fair, 1933–1934," *Journal of the Illinois State Historical Society* vol. 59, no. 2 (Summer 1966).

32

THE TRANSFORMATION OF HIGHER EDUCATION IN THE 1960s
Master Plans, Community Colleges, and Emerging Universities

David W. Scott

Journal of the Illinois State Historical Society
vol. 101, no. 2 (Summer 2008)

Located in only a few places in 1957, community college districts by 1971 were established or being planned throughout Illinois under the state's leadership and its expanded covering of operating and capital expenses. State teacher colleges emerged as state universities, and two new universities were created. Political conflict was intense in 1971 when Governor Ogilvie clashed over appropriations with the Board of Higher Education, created in 1961 to coordinate the development of Illinois colleges and universities.

In 1955 Illinois governor William Stratton and the General Assembly established the Higher Education Commission made up of legislators, public school leaders, and presidents of public and private colleges and universities. Its charge was to "make a thorough investigation, study, and survey of the problems facing Illinois higher education, public and private, which will be occasioned by the great increase in enrollment expected in the next decade. The provision of adequate facilities for the higher education of its youth is one of the most important responsibilities of the state; and ways must be found to discharge this responsibility in the most economical and effective manner."

Norris L. Brookens Library under construction on the campus of Sangamon State University (now the University of Illinois Springfield). *Photo courtesy University of Illinois Springfield Archives.*

Commission Plans for Higher Education

In 1957 the commission issued its report. The demographic basis for the commission's recommendations was increase in enrollments underway and projected for Illinois colleges and universities. All the commission members had to do was look at the rapid growth in elementary school enrollment, which reflected the annual increase in births in the state starting in 1946. The commission's report cited expansion of the number of jobs for which college training was needed, or at least thought appropriate, and it recognized and supported the growing participation of youth from lower middle-income backgrounds in postsecondary education. It identified strong needs for many more scientists and engineers and for teachers at all levels.

The commission gave much attention to junior (that is, two-year) college expansion. At that time in Chicago, four public junior college campuses were in operation, and four more were about to open. Outside Chicago, however, there were only ten public junior colleges, and they were geographically limited to the boundaries of school districts with a high school. Only such school districts were authorized by state law to provide public junior college programs. At the state level, the junior colleges were under the Office of the Superintendent of Public Instruction, which was concerned mainly with elementary and secondary education. Such colleges were established to provide vocational and technical programs geared to the training needs of local employers as well, as the first two years of a four-year liberal arts education. Public junior colleges were also to provide "a means of screening those not able to benefit from college work"—that is, to "cool off" the higher education ambitions of the academically inferior student. As "open door" colleges, they allowed the whole system of higher education to be "democratic"—that is nonselective—to allow universities to impose varying degrees of selectivity in admissions.

The two-year colleges were to be low cost to the student and the student's family. Students could continue to live at home; the programs were financed by local taxes, state aid, and low tuition. The commission called for a major expansion of two-year college availability across the state by means of the state's expanding its financing of operating and capital expenses. Such an approach would be less expensive to the state and more efficient overall than concentrating expansion expenses at the four-year state colleges and universities.

So would the commission's second recommendation, which called for the creating of state scholarships for students with financial need and academic ability. Such scholarships would make it more financially feasible for qualified students to choose a private college or university where tuition costs were higher than in a public institution of higher learning. Such scholarships were particularly needed to maintain the competitive position of the private sector, given the low-cost alternative being generated by the expansion of public colleges and universities. Although the state had no authority over the missions, plans, programs, and budgets of the private institutions, the commission took the position that it was in the overall interest of the state to encourage attendance there. For example, given the existing underutilization of academic and residential facilities in the private sector, it would be less costly to the state to pay for these scholarships than to build more public facilities.

Like expansion of community colleges, the idea of state scholarships had been around for a long time. By the late 1950s the General Assembly was ready to act. The Illinois State Scholarship Commission was established shortly after the 1957 report was issued, and in 1959 the legislature took a major step to encourage two-year college expansion by increasing state aid per semester hour from the level established in 1955 when the legislature first provided state support. Also in 1959 it authorized the formation of community college districts, a new unit of government to handle two-year college programs rather than school districts, governed by an elected board.

The commission was not ready to make a recommendation on the long-discussed matter of having a coordinating board for higher education in the state, However, it concluded that "recent surveys have pointed to the need for long-range planning and determination of priorities in the development of higher education on a state-wide basis, the coordination of budget request and fiscal policies, the elimination of unnecessary and uneconomical duplication of program and activities and so forth."

In 1957 there were three higher education governing boards. In 1949 Southern Illinois College at Carbondale had joined the University of Illinois at Urbana in having its own board of trustees and university status. It had broken away from Northern Illinois, Western Illinois, Eastern Illinois, and Illinois Normal state colleges, all of which remained under the State Teachers College Board well into the 1960s. However, by the late 1950s all four were renamed universities to reflect new programs outside of teacher education.

The commission made no recommendations on how to respond to the call for additional educational opportunities in the regional branches of Southern Illinois University (SIU) in the Illinois part of the St. Louis metropolitan area and of the University of Illinois (UI) in Chicago. The general—and controversial—question was whether there should be new universities in these two populous areas of the state and, if so, where they should be located. In 1959 the legislature acted. The legislative patrons—Senator Everett Peters for the UI and Speaker of the House Paul Powell for SIU—struck a deal that laid the foundation for second campuses for both universities." What had been extension programs in Alton and East St. Louis were to become a university campus in Edwardsville under the SIU board of trustees. The second university campus for the UI started as a freshman and sophomore program on Navy Pier in 1946 to accommodate returning World War II servicemen. The plans to have a comprehensive public university in Chicago were opposed by the Champaign-Urbana campus, business interests in the twin cities, and

Chicago-area private universities—notably DePaul, Loyola, and Roosevelt Universities. However, a Chicago campus of the UI had the strong support of Mayor Richard J. Daley and several state legislators from Chicago.

The 1957 Commission Report and its annual reports for the following three years stressed the need for cooperative arrangements between high schools and colleges, between institutions of higher education and their extension programs within the same area of the state, between the private and public sectors, between junior and senior colleges, and between private colleges and universities, all in the name of avoiding duplication and the efficient and effective use of state resources. For example, high schools and junior colleges needed to work cooperatively in developing vocational and technical curricula and junior colleges and universities transfer curriculum.

The commission's 1958 report cited existing laws forbidding the development of certain new and expensive programs at SIU and Northern Illinois University (NIU). Such prohibitions had been passed under the influence of UI. With specific attention to the proposal for an engineering school at SIU, the commission reviewed the engineering programs already available at four places: at the UI and three private universities—Bradley University, the Illinois Institute of Technology, and Northwestern University. It heard the case from David Dodds Henry, the president of the UI, that an engineering school at SIU would be duplicative and very expensive and hinder the strengthening of existing programs. Delyte Morris, president of SIU, argued that his university should have an engineering school because existing programs were failing to meet the increasing demand for engineering talent important for the economic development needs of the southern third of the state and, given the growing demand, that there would be no harm to the quality of existing programs. The commission agreed with the recommendation of the Illinois Engineering Council that "granting power to Southern to award degrees in engineering at the present time would be premature."

Coordinating Board Authorized

By 1960 the commission was ready to support a board of higher education and presented draft legislation for it. In 1961 the General Assembly overwhelmingly voted to authorize the creation of the Illinois Board of Higher Education (IBHE). Despite concern over a reduction in autonomy, there was no opposition from the UI or the other universities. Most of the board's members were to be appointed by the governor with Senate approval.

Legislators gave two major reasons for establishing the IBHE: "First, the legislature did not want to pick winners and losers in the rivalries among the universities. Second, specialized expertise was needed to conduct an orderly expansion of program, while minimizing expensive program duplication." Legislators knew they lacked the expertise to sort out competing appropriation requests and programmatic ambitions and whether and where to make cuts in budget requests from each of the governing boards. That was to be the job for the IBHE and its staff experts. The legislature came to think of its own role as being limited to the statewide organization of higher education, to annual overall appropriation numbers, and to major policy matters with significant fiscal implications such as tuition charges and whether a university should have a major new program such as a law school.

A review of the minutes of the IBHE in its first two years—1962 and 1963—shows that IBHE members and its executive director and other staff members occupied themselves with the three missions defined in the authorizing legislation—developing a budget for all of higher education, formulating a master plan, and reviewing and generally approving the requests for "new units of instruction" in the universities. The IBHE was developing procedures to evaluate whether a proposed new program would likely be of good quality and would meet a demonstrated need. As an example, it approved at its September 1962 meeting a master's degree in history for Illinois State Normal University. It also decided at that time that this action would be the last such action until it finally adopted a master plan that would provide overall criteria for decision-making.

Members and staff were well aware of the IBHE's ambiguous and dual role: on the one hand, to be an advocate for higher education and the needs and goals of each university and, on the other, to achieve an effective use of public funds for the coordinated development of higher education in the state based on some overall statewide plan of priorities and fiscal restraint. In its advocacy role, the IBHE would be responsive to the university presidents and the governing boards; in its statewide planning and prioritizing role, it was responsible to the governor and the General Assembly. An illustration of these conflicting expectations is a story told by James Furman, who was the executive director of the IBHE from 1975 to 1980. He told of a conversation he had with the president of the Washington State Senate when he held a similar job in that state before coming to Illinois. If he heard from the university presidents that the executive director was doing a good job, the president told Mr. Furman, he would know that it was not true.

In its January 1963 meeting, representatives of the three governing boards—those from the UI, SIU, and the four teachers colleges—requested that the IHBE restore the minor cuts it had made in each governing board's budget request. In this test case, board members held firm and, following staff recommendations, voted against restoration. The board was developing the procedure of discussing pending issues with the staff and then almost always following their recommendations.

The process of formulating a master plan was complex as it involved synthesizing the work of many committees, each with representatives from the state's universities and colleges and other subject matter experts. The committees presented data and made recommendations on two-year colleges, accommodating commuter students, technical and semitechnical educations, extension and adult education, enrollment projections, graduate and research programs, efficient use of existing facilities and the need for new ones, admission standards, faculty quality and salaries, undergraduate curriculum needs, and public service programs.

Community Colleges and Universities Expand

A major theme of the IBHE's first master plan in 1964 was the expansion of public two-year colleges, coming to be called community colleges rather than junior colleges. In 1965 the General Assembly followed up with the landmark Community College Act passed with general support and shaped by the Illinois Association of Junior Colleges as well as the master plan. Having earlier created community college districts, the General Assembly further developed organizational arrangements to sever the tie between the two-year colleges and the public school system, all with the intention of clarifying their identity and status as part of the system of higher education. It created the Illinois Community College Board (ICCB), replacing the Office of Superintendent of Public Instructions at the state-level junior college regulatory and planning agency. At the same time, it transferred authority for Chicago junior colleges from the city's board of education to a newly created Chicago Community College Board. The 1965 act created a system of financial incentives designed to encourage the formation of community college districts across the state. A school district not part of a community college district and without its own two-year college had to pay from its high school budget part of the expenses incurred by any two-year college in the state that enrolled a resident of the school district. To get such costs out of the high school budget, school districts, state planners expected, would be motivated to work with neighboring school districts to form a community college district. The act boosted state aid from the 1959 level, but provided higher levels of state aid to community college districts than to junior colleges remaining outside such districts. Only community college districts qualified for state construction aid.

Emerging universities and the shaping of university governance were major themes of the Master Plan, Phase II, adopted in 1966. Both the Edwardsville campus of SIU and the near west side Chicago campus to the UI began operations in the mid-1960s. Further development of a mission for each university was part of the Master Plan, Phase II. While the UI was defined as a fully developed, complex, multipurpose university, SIU was deemed a rapidly developing, complex, multipurpose university. In accordance with this mission, by 1971 state authorities had approved not only an engineering school, but also approved medical, law, and dental schools for SIU. With the establishment of the board and its role in determining needs and priorities, the laws forbidding the development of new expensive programs and schools were repealed. The 1966 Master Plan identified NIU and Illinois State University (ISU) as liberal arts universities, authorized to offer advanced graduate programs in these areas. NIU advanced more along these lines than ISU. However, there would be no competition from Eastern Illinois University and Western Illinois University for students and funding for doctoral programs. Under the Master Plan, these two institutions were to have a more limited scope and were to retain a focus on their traditional teacher college training mission, as well as on other undergraduate and master's degree programs.

The 1966 Master Plan addressed the rapid growth of working adults seeking more university education and of junior college graduates seeking to transfer to the junior year of universities. The General Assembly responded by authorizing two new universities in the late 1960s rather than the four originally proposed by the IBHE. These new schools had courses only for the junior and senior years and for the master's degree. One was Governors State University in south suburban Chicago, a populous and underserved area, with a special mission to serve minority students. The other was Sangamon State University in the capital city of Springfield with a specific mission in public affairs and administration.

The number of intermediate or governing boards increased from three to five with the creation in 1965 of the ICCB and in 1968 of the Board of

Regents. The Board of Regents (Regents) and the Board of Governors (Governors), a new name for the Teachers College Board, divided between them the four former downstate teachers colleges. ISU and NIU were paired under the Regents because they had developed beyond their sister institutions in terms of their orientation to research and graduate work. The newly created Sangamon State University (SSU) was added as a third Regents university despite its different mission, character, and much lower enrollment. Western, Eastern, Governors State, and the two campuses of the Chicago Teachers College made up the Governors cohort. The two Chicago teacher's colleges had been transferred in the mid-1960s by the General Assembly to Governors from the Chicago public school district. By the early 1970s these two institutions with missions similar to the other three Governors schools had been renamed Northeastern Illinois and Chicago State Universities.

The whole complicated governing arrangement in place by the late 1960s was called the System of Systems, designed to provide checks and balances among the separate and competing governing boards and universities. The creation of the Regents—and placing SSU under it rather than under the board of UI—"divided the power and influence to the extent that no single system, even the UI, could dominate state higher education policy making as had been done in previous years."

Although there was interest by SIU-Edwardsville and UIC for its own board, NIU more than any other university sought to have the status and increased clout with state decision-makers by having its own governing board. The General Assembly in 1959 rejected one of several bills over the years to allow NIU to get out from under the Teachers College Board and later the Regents. These intermediate boards presented a combined budget for all the campuses under their jurisdiction, normally with some reduction in the requests of each of the campuses. Its own board, NIU interests thought, would help it in its competition with SIU to be perceived as "number two" in the state and to acquire law and engineering schools—perhaps even a medical school. NIU justified these ambitions with reference to its location on the fringes of the Chicago metropolitan area with all the students and varieties of educational needs there.

The IBHE also played a role in the allocation of funds available from the federal government, mainly for construction and research. The many new programs of federal aid to education established by Congress in the 1960s also contributed in the transformation of higher education in that decade.

David W. Scott

Conditions in the Early 1970s

In 1971 the legislature responded to calls for direct aid to the private universities and colleges by finally agreeing to a formula for such aid, a formula
that took into account increased demand for transfer opportunities for community college graduates. Providing crucial support were Governor Richard
Ogilvie, the IBHE, the Federation of Independent Colleges and Universities,
and several state legislators. Backing up the considerations in the legislature
was a 1969 report that identified a deteriorating financial condition at many
private colleges, concluded that financial assistance was "imperative," and
strongly urged direct aid to the private sector. According to the report, Illinois' private sector consisted of nine universities—Northwestern University,
the University of Chicago, and seven others—plus thirty-eight liberal arts
colleges, thirteen junior colleges, four health institutes, two law schools,
and five institutes for the fine arts.

Accordingly, as it developed Master Plan revisions in 1971, the IBHE
reaffirmed its policy of support for the viability of private colleges and universities and for cooperative arrangements between the various segments
of higher education. It developed the concept of a "Collegiate Common
Market" to "utilize the existing and developing resources of the public
and private sectors to broaden and maximize educational opportunities
and reduce duplication," saying, "The Board will give high priority, in
its review of new and existing programs, to those that reflect efforts toward interinstitutional thrusts." It also called for using "the capacity of
the private sector in the assessment of need in the evaluation of demand
for programs."

The IBHE's workload in the early 1970s was heavily focused on reviewing and generally approving start-up activities of the state's two newest
universities and the new program and capital requests of the many recently
formed community college districts submitted by the ICCB, which reviewed
and adjusted the requests by the individual colleges. The percentage of total
higher education enrollment in two-year colleges rose from 14 percent in
1955 to 37 percent in 1971. Although by this time about half the territory of
the state was covered with community college districts, all the downstate
metropolitan areas were covered except Bloomington-Normal, Decatur,
and their surrounding areas.

In the six-county Chicago area, only the North Shore suburbs remained
outside a public community college district. In suburban Cook County,

seven community college districts had been formed by cooperative effort among twenty-seven neighboring high school districts. Outside Cook County in the northern and western Chicago metropolitan area, community college district boundaries tended to be based on county boundaries. The procedure for the formation of these community college districts involved a demonstration of local interest and planning, then state-level approval, and finally voter approval in a referendum. By 1971 plans were developing to allow the ICCB to force unaffiliated school districts to become part of a community college district.

Using a base of 100 in 1958, enrollment in the public sector rose to 382 by 1970 and 243 in the private sector, yet the total Illinois population rose only to 114, and the number of seventeen- and eighteen-year-olds rose to 151. These seventeen- and eighteen-year-olds were born in the early 1950s, near the peak of the number of births during the baby boom. These figures demonstrate the increasing percentage of people in this age group going to college. The percentage of general state tax revenue spent on higher education, excluding capital spending, increased to 20.9 percent in 1969 from 15 percent in 1958, higher education having benefited from expanding sales tax revenue generated and its favored status during the prosperous 1960s. With additional revenue from the newly authorized income tax, the share of state spending for higher education declined to 17.4 percent in 1971.

The Period of Great Expansion Ends

By 1971 there was talk of "cutback management" and "a new ball game." The minutes of 1971 meetings revealed IBHE members talking about overexpansion in higher education; for example, the discussions dealt with graduates trained to be teachers who could not find jobs in their field. What a difference from the 1957 report of the Higher Education Commission, which wondered how the state would ever get enough school and university teachers to meet the demand of surging enrollments! Some board members showed skepticism of the pressure and need for college graduates in many fields of work, a contrast with the 1957 report that identified an "urgent need" for a great expansion of educational opportunities. The IBHE adopted in its December 1971 meeting the following policy statement:

Advisors at all levels should increase their efforts toward career counseling so that individuals who would benefit more from community

college entrance or work experience, rather than by entering senior
institutions, be properly directed. . . . The Board of Higher Education,
through appropriate channels, should advise leaders in business and
industry of the desirability of employing personnel on the basis of the
applicant's past experience, realistic job specifications and appropriate
tests rather than on the possession of a college degree.

As there would be fewer students in senior institutions if this policy were
carried out successfully, the IBHE at the same meeting adopted a policy that
"[n]o new senior institution be planned at the present time."

The IBHE asked reluctant universities to identify 15 percent of their
budgets as low priority for reallocation to higher priority programs. Enrollment increases in higher education had recently leveled off. Although
Illinois legislators and governors had previously been very supportive of
higher education requests and budget reductions had not been large, starting
in 1969 higher education's budget requests were getting cut substantially.
Many thought it was time to put a leash on the rapid increases in spending
for higher education. One such person was Richard Ogilvie, who had been
elected governor in November 1968.

The year 1971 was a time of heightened tension between the various elements involved in or affected by state-level higher education decision-making, in part because of the development of Master Plan, Phase III that year.
Master planning with its centralizing tendencies and constraints on institutional ambitions inherently generated some criticism from the universities,
institutions that treasured their independence. In 1971 James Holderman,
the executive director for the IBHE, was charged with "power grabs," "empire building," and "high-handedness." Dr. Holderman, his staff, the IBHE
chairman, and other members were under heightened pressure to be what
each university thought they should be: its advocate at the state level for its
desired and needed programs and budgets.

The most visible conflict in 1971 was between the IBHE and its executive
director and the governor and his Bureau of the Budget. The governor had
the upper hand. The 1970 Constitution gave the Illinois governor additional
powers: the amendatory veto and the reduction veto. Governor Richard
Ogilvie further strengthened the executive by establishing a Bureau of the
Budget in his office in his first year as governor in 1969, which provided
him and subsequent governors with enhanced expertise and influence in
state budget-making.

The board called for a large increase for the Fiscal Year 1972 (starting in July 1971) over that allocated for Fiscal Year 1971. Governor Ogilvie and his Bureau of the Budget responded with a budget that called for a modest increase and called upon the board to reallocate its budget to the governor's bottom line number. The IBHE refused to do this, instead following its existing policy of having its recommendations introduced in the General Assembly and lobbying for passage. As far as the governor's people were concerned, the board had become captive of the universities' budget-busting demands and inadequately responsive to its proper role of making recommendations based on an overall statewide plan of priorities and sense of fiscal restraint. While the IBHE reduced the university requests from $975.2 million to $860.0 million, it was still a substantial increase over the $639.6 million appropriated for the Fiscal Year 1971—and still substantially above the governor's figures of $672 million. Although the General Assembly reduced the number to $707.4 million, the governor reduced the bottom line to his original number. There was a strong outcry made to override the veto. However, the IBHE successfully discouraged the systems and institutions from attempting to override the veto, but encouraged concentration on increasing tuition. Ogilvie's reduction veto was not overridden.

By the early 1970s higher education in Illinois had undergone a major transformation in just a decade and a half. The pace of change would be greatly reduced in subsequent years. During this decade and a half, enrollments had increased dramatically. Community colleges proliferated. New senior public institutions of higher education were created. Existing ones gained many new programs. A five-board governing arrangement for the public sector and a coordinating board for all of higher education had been put in place. Private higher education was receiving some state financial support. The governor as the dominant force in the state's budget for higher education had been clearly revealed to all concerned. The democratic goal expressed in 1957 had been reached: publicly supported education beyond high school was becoming available to all who sought it.

RELATED READING

Thomas L. Hardin, "The University of Illinois and the Community Junior College Movement, 1901–1965," *Illinois History Journal* vol. 78, no. 2 (Summer 1986).

33

PERSONAL REFLECTIONS ON THE SIXTH ILLINOIS CONSTITUTIONAL CONVENTION OF 1969–1970

John Alexander

Journal of the Illinois State Historical Society
vol. 99, no. 2 (Summer 2006)

The result of the Sixth Illinois Constitutional Convention was submitted to and approved by the voters in December 1970. John Alexander (Virden, Illinois) was a member of that convention, and in the years following became dissatisfied with some of its major provisions. Rather than strengthen cities through home rule, Alexander contends, it should have found means to facilitate consolidations and annexations.

Unexpected effects resulted from other provisions; for example, the governor was given amendatory veto power and the state "primary responsibility" for funding schools. A central concern at the convention, and one on which opinions differed greatly, was determining what is constitutional and what is legislative. No subsequent convention has been held.

The backdrop of the Sixth Illinois Constitutional Convention was the wild but wonderful decade of the 1960s, which featured the Kennedys, the civil rights movement, among others, and the dreaded war in Vietnam that never seemed to end. Illinois got the national spotlight in 1968 when Chicago hosted the Democratic National Convention. The state's most significant event of the decade, however, began a year later in

Springfield when the gavel fell on Illinois' first constitutional convention in fifty years.

Including the election of convention delegates in 1968, this event consumed nearly three years of my early adulthood, from ages twenty-six to twenty-eight, beginning as a field worker for the Illinois Committee for a Constitutional Convention and ending as a vocal opponent of the current charter. It provided the basis for lifelong learning. The most significant learning has resulted from literally years of thought about the meaning of the event to me as a person and to the millions of people in Illinois for whom it holds some considerable significance as well. The convention was a bittersweet experience in my life. Time has provided the perspective in which I can now better evaluate the event. Initially, it was too confusing and too painful to ponder at any length. I had invested too much energy and emotion. No wonder in hindsight it was so disappointing and disillusioning. Like many in my generation who reached maturity during the turbulent sixties, I set out to change the world. In a very small way, I did. In a much larger way, though, it changed me. I learned major lessons from my foray into social reform efforts at the constitutional convention.

(1) First, my convention experience confirms the notion that an idea whose time has come will, indeed, come. For decades before 1968 the Illinois Constitution of 1870 was depicted as old, obsolete, and detailed. It was the civics teacher's model of the "bad" constitution. The older but less detailed United States Constitution was the "good" one. Reformers spent years creating the impression that Illinois had become an important state despite the straitjacket restriction of its "horse and buggy" constitution. I know, because I was one of those teachers turned reformer who helped create that impression. A new constitution was necessary if Illinois was to maintain its rightful rank among the states. Events leading to the convention indicated widespread support for a new constitution. Except for opposition from the AFL-CIO and a few township officials, the referendum in the fall of 1968 revealed widespread support from citizens for a convention to create an improved, updated charter. Two years later voters approved the new constitution in less overwhelming numbers, but approve it they did on December 15, 1970. For many Illinoisans it was probably just an idea whose time had come. Many remembered, no doubt, the knocks against the old constitution and felt that a twentieth century effort would certainly be an improvement. I really didn't consider the possibility that a new document would not improve the old one until it was too late.

(2) Second, I learned that real reform is often illusory. Reality and reputation can be two different things. To my way of thinking, the 1970 convention laid the groundwork for a modern myth, namely that with the document produced by the convention Illinois now has a modern, improved constitution. We had erased our constitutional straitjacket. Major political problems would now be more easily addressed. The constitution got its renovation. It was probably okay now for another hundred years. Illinois could be proud of its new charter and even prouder of itself. We, after all, had succeeded in revising our political system when other states had failed. Illinois, scene of much unrest so characteristic of the 1960s, was "right on" once again. We had quietly and effectively changed our institutions in accordance with the law. We had responded to outcries for institutional reform and had accomplished ours not in the streets but in the convention hall. We spent months making ours one of the best state constitutions. The Illinois constitution was now in good shape. The challenge would be to keep it that way. In reality, though, we had simply deceived ourselves into believing that all was now well with the constitutional system. We had created the illusion which, in turn, would create the myth of our constitutional well-being in Illinois. The constitution was no longer viewed as a source of major political problems in Illinois after 1970.

(3) The third lesson I have learned is that many ideas are constitutionally ripe, unfortunately, at the very time they become obsolete. Such an idea at the 1970 Illinois constitutional convention involved home rule. The home rule concept extends greater authority to local governments to solve problems. However, "local" problems seldom respect local boundaries. The most effective efforts to deal with such wider problems often come from higher levels. Metropolitan or even state action is often required when problems extend beyond a local jurisdiction. Otherwise, local governments armed with additional home rule authority are better able to obstruct such solutions. In some cases, in other words, local governments are part of the problem and not part of the solution. This is especially true in Illinois, which leads the nation in units of local government. This shift in thinking away from home rule solutions began, ironically, about the time of the convention. Noted political scientist and former University of Chicago professor Theodore J. Lowi argued forcefully in *The End of Liberalism* that the Chicagos of the nation were in decline, in large part, because of growing fragmentation of the metropolitan regions. A progressive provision in a 1970 Illinois constitution might have facilitated consolidation and annexation instead of

fragmentation of government and dispersion of people into far too numerous local jurisdictions. Instead, we caved in to the demands of an urban political machine in decline and its surrounding suburbs that oversold the home rule remedy to local problems. At the very time that prophetic observers like Lowi were warning against home rule approaches to problem-solving, Illinois constitutionalized it.

(4) As a result of post-convention observations and reflections, I learned that solutions create new problems. Some of these were not unexpected. For instance, I supported the shift to electing state officials in non–presidential election years knowing full well the implications for lower voter turnout. We knew there would be a smaller electorate in the off year. The problem, though, is that this smaller electorate appears to favor one party almost exclusively and to weight the elections toward incumbents. Looking back at history makes this obvious. Between 1928 and 1972 Illinois voters elected eight governors, four Republicans and four Democrats. Since then, Republicans have clearly had the upper hand in gubernatorial elections under terms set forth in the 1970 constitution, which switched the election of the governor from the presidential year to the off year, beginning in 1978. Following the change, Republicans reeled off six wins in a row before Rod Blagojevich in 2002 became the first Democrat to win the governor's chair in thirty years. And it's certainly arguable that his victory might better be viewed as George Ryan's defeat, making the Democrat's win a deviation from the norm.

The convention made the shift to the off year to focus more attention on state races. Both parties bought the argument, but results indicate that one party made a huge mistake in accepting the change. Lower turnout in the off year has worked for Republicans and against Democrats. The new constitution has made possible, I would contend, almost one-party rule of the state's executive branch.

Another problem causing change consented to by leaders of both political parties and nearly all convention delegates, was the "new and better" mechanism for redistricting the legislature every ten years. Previous General Assemblies had often ignored or butchered this task. Most delegates were convinced that the two parties, evenly represented on a redistricting commission, would draw reasonably fair new districts rather than allow one to gain the upper hand by the lottery addition of an additional member. Neither party, it was hoped, would risk the nearly "winner take all" approach of an additional member. We were all wrong. Experience now shows that the prospect of adding a tiebreaker to the legislative redistricting process is not feared; it's favored by the parties. Each relishes the 50–50 opportunity of imposing its dream map on the other party for ten years at a time. Never mind that the constitution mandates compact and contiguous districts that should produce a typically competitive Illinois General Assembly. What we've gotten instead is an even more gerrymandered, contentious, and controlled leadership, more of a "top-down" assembly, if you will. Leaders create safe districts for members in both parties (read incumbents) and few competitive districts where voters actually make a difference. Incumbents are generally grateful to their mapmaker leaders. All told, constitutional change has given Republicans the upper hand in the executive branch and the tiebreaker winner a huge advantage in the legislative branch.

(5) Acts of omission can be as significant as acts of commission in reform efforts. The 1970 convention delegates, for example, failed to limit the number of terms a governor can serve. Never mind that about half the states, like the federal government, limit a chief executive's tenure. Illinois didn't have a history of longtime governors until the new constitution opened the door. No one at the convention foresaw a four-term governor of either party. Anyone for five? It was an act of omission not to limit governors, like presidents, to two terms in office.

(6) It was an act of rather innocent commission, however, which further strengthened the governor's hand in his relationship with the General Assembly. In a significant move, but only in hindsight, the new constitution armed the governor with an amendatory veto. Most delegates expected this veto to be employed in a housekeeping fashion to "clean up" minor mistakes of language in proposed legislation. Instead, almost from the outset governors have used this new toy to rewrite legislation. The expanded authority has altered the relationship between the two bodies and, maybe more importantly, become a major source of tension between the two. Speaker Michael Madigan, a former convention delegate, knows firsthand how this provision has changed the balance of power between the governor and the legislature and has led several unsuccessful efforts to limit the governor's amendatory veto power. The governor's liberal use of the amendatory veto has also contributed to the legislature's occasional abdication of its lawmaking power; legislators send over to the governor's office more imperfect forms of legislation than they would otherwise, knowing that the governor's censors will clean it up. Having done that, the legislature gets its final shot not on third reading but in the veto session. There, however, a three-fifths

vote is required to override. In effect, then, the new constitution provides the governor a constitutional way to write legislation that takes effect unless an extraordinary majority in each house disapproves. This imbalancing tool of tension was produced in 1970.

(7) Constitutional conventions held in legislative chambers look and act an awful lot like legislatures. No wonder they are tempted to act on occasion as super legislatures. Having been elected from state senate districts, the 1970 convention delegates represented legislative constituencies. They first met in the Illinois House of Representatives and later moved to the same legislative chamber in the historic Old Capitol. The convention was organized much like a legislative body, albeit of the one-house variety. The delegates adopted much of the legislature's language and customs. There were calendars, journals, committees, chairmen, officers, rules, staffs, a public gallery, a press box, member proposals, etc. Members included current, former, and future lawmakers. They possessed political skills, though many were not professional politicians. Nearly all were proud Republicans or Democrats. Membership ranks included men and women, young and old, wealthy and middle class, blacks and whites. The typical delegate, however, was a white, middle-aged, upper-middle-class male attorney, a lot like the typical Illinois legislator over the years. So was Con Con president Samuel W. Witwer's choice for chairman of every important standing committee. Expressing that concern to him, incidentally, earned me the aristocratic Witwer's wrath for the balance of the convention. Youngsters like me were supposed to be seen and seldom heard. A lot like the legislature.

(8) Fundamental law to one person is often deemed statutory by another. What belongs in a constitution, in other words? The common view is that constitutions are written to establish, grant, and limit governments. In reality, however, these are often very fine lines. The test of inclusion is simply votes. State constitutions include many items of legislative detail. The current Illinois document is no exception. Nearly every delegate brings an agenda including one or more such ideas. They rationalize as follows: the item is fundamental enough to merit inclusion, or there is a place for some nonfundamentals. Should a convention act, then, in some cases as a "super legislature" of sorts? Or should it write a bare-boned document, refusing to touch so-called legislative items? According to my definition, the 1970 convention dealt with many such items. A few were my own. I didn't care to leave some problems to a General Assembly which had not recognized or solved them in the past. This is especially true for reform measures which

directly affect that institution. My proposal to reduce the length of our campaign period, for example, was determined by our rules committee to be legislative in nature and was therefore not brought to a vote on the floor. Likewise, my attempt to name Springfield the seat of state government was rejected in a floor vote, in part because many viewed it as a question better left to the legislature. The new revenue article's language, lifted from a 1969 statute that favorably tied the corporate income tax rate to that on individuals, on the other hand, was elevated to constitutional status. An item is constitutional if the votes are there.

(9) A constitution is not much better, if any, than the people who must implement and interpret it. I cite the example of education funding. The new constitution, quite simply, assigned "primary responsibility" for funding local schools to state government. Delegates desired a greater future role for state revenues in public school finance. The problem was they didn't demand or mandate it clearly enough, at least according to the state supreme court. In a later interpretation the high court said that the constitutional declaration of state "primary responsibility" for school funding was "hortatory," meaning nothing more than a constitutional sermon. Never mind that the convention deliberated the issue for months. Never mind, either, that it was a selling point in the ratification campaign. Illinoisans thus continue to live with a school funding formula rooted in the property tax. Regardless of whether the language is labeled "hortatory" by the supreme interpreters of the constitution, it's clear that implementers of the constitution, including the governor and the legislature, have chosen not to heed language most laymen would easily comprehend. They talk about and around inequities in school funding. They disregard the basic law they are sworn to uphold. They have literally thumbed their noses at the education article of the new constitution every year since its enactment. The high court ultimately condoned their position. The situation may change with the makeup of the court, the legislature or the occupant of the governor's chair. Constitutional language created in 1970 wasn't enough.

(10) Leaders of the 1970 convention tried to author a relatively noncontroversial document that would meet with voter approval. Thanks to a wide margin in Cook County, they succeeded. Only a slight majority (55.5 percent) of a low voter turnout (37 percent) approved the new constitution. Nevertheless, the constitution will soon complete its fourth decade of history. Has it been a better document than the one it replaced? Has Illinois prospered as a result? The answer to the first question is arguable. The second question

is not as difficult to answer. Illinois has not prospered under the new document. It is, I would submit, a less important state today than the Illinois of thirty-seven years ago. Citizens remain burdened with a regressive tax system. They remain frustrated that schools are still underfunded and have not produced better students. These, among others, are ongoing problems. The culprit in part is the state constitution.

The 1970 Illinois constitution needs a tune-up. Several parts of the document have caused problems of much consequence in state government. Every defect, however, has a defender, and every change will be contested. No Illinoisan under fifty-seven years of age has had a chance to vote for a new constitution. No Illinoisan under sixty-two years of age has been afforded the opportunity to rewrite the state charter. Voters will soon get a rare chance to revisit important constitutional questions, and that opportunity should not be wasted. We deserve much better state government than we get here in Illinois.

USING JSTOR

CONTRIBUTORS

INDEX

USING JSTOR

Contributed by the University of Illinois Press

The *Journal of the Illinois State Historical Society* is available online at JSTOR.

JSTOR is a digital library of academic journals, books, and primary sources where researchers, students, and scholars have complete access to the *Journal of the Illinois State Historical Society*, which has been in continuous publication since 1908. (From 1984 to 1998 the *Journal* was renamed *Illinois Historical Journal*.) Members of the ISHS have free access to the online *Journal* on their home computers or handheld devices with their current paid membership/subscription. Many other journals on JSTOR are freely available to read online by creating a JSTOR account; individual subscription and article purchase options are also available.

Students and faculty at universities and colleges may also have access to content on JSTOR through their library. Some institutions also offer JSTOR access for alumni.

Need to read a *Journal* article but forgot your issue at home? As an added benefit of your membership to the Illinois State Historical Society, you not only receive a hard-copy version of the *Journal* but you also have access to it electronically through JSTOR.

If you are an ISHS member, you should have already received a welcoming email message from JSTOR with detailed instructions for accessing the latest *Journal* content in the online archive. If you didn't receive access instructions or no longer have your email message from JSTOR, please contact Paul Arroyo, parroyo@uillinois.edu, at the University of Illinois Press, Journals/IT Section. He will send you personalized instructions for establishing your online access to the electronic *Journal.* If you have already set up your JSTOR account, you can reach the electronic *Journal* archive at http://www.jstor.org/r/illinois/jishs.

The ISHS and the University of Illinois Journals Department are very happy to provide you with access to the electronic *Journal* through our partnership with JSTOR, one of the most trusted ways of accessing scholarly information online. We are committed to providing long-term preservation and access to the *Journal* for researchers and general readers worldwide.

CONTRIBUTORS

DAVID WALLACE ADAMS is professor emeritus of history and education at Cleveland State University. He authored *Education for Extinction: American Indians and the Boarding School Experience, 1875–1928* (1995) and *On the Borders of Love and Power* (2012).

JOHN ALEXANDER (1942–) was a delegate to the 1970 Illinois Constitutional Convention. He lives in Macoupin County, where he owns and operates Books on the Square, an independent antiquarian book dealership.

RICHARD F. BALES is an assistant vice president and assistant regional counsel for Chicago Title Insurance Company, Wheaton, Illinois, and the author of *The Great Chicago Fire and the Myth of Mrs. O'Leary's Cow* (2002) and *Land Surveys: A Guide for Lawyers and Other Professionals* (2012).

RICHARD LAWRENCE BEYER coauthored *A Handbook of Illinois History: A Topical Survey for Teachers and Students* (1943) with Paul M. Angle.

RAY A. BILLINGTON (1903–81) was an American historian whose work focused on the western frontier. He was a cofounder of the Western History Association (1961), the author of *The Protestant Crusade, 1800–1860: A Study of the Origins of American Nativism* (1938), and a William Smith Mason professor of history at Northwestern University.

ARTHUR W. BLOOM (1903–92) served as an academic administrator in visual and performing arts at Loyola University, Chicago; Loyola Marymount University, Los Angeles; and Kutztown University in Pennsylvania. He is the author of *Edwin W. Booth: Biography and Performance History* and *Joseph Jefferson: Dean of American Theatre*.

ROBERT GEHLMANN BONE (1906–91) was a president of Illinois State Normal University (1956–67) and a professor of history at the University of Illinois (1932–56). He coauthored *Frontiers in Teacher Education: Proceedings in the Inauguration of Robert Gehlmann Bone* with William G. Stratton (1957).

VIRGINIA R. BOYNTON is a professor at Western Illinois University, Macomb, and a former director of the Illinois State Historical Society. She specializes in American women's history.

STEPHEN J. BUCK is a professor of history at Joliet College.

JOHN D. BUENKER (1937–), professor emeritus of history at the University of Wisconsin–Parkside, is the author of several books on the Progressive Era, including *The Historical Dictionary of the Progressive Era, 1890–1920* (1988), *The Encyclopedia of the Gilded Age* (2005), and *Progressive Reform: A Guide to Information Sources* (1980).

GERALD CARSON (1954–) is a retired advertising copywriter.

JASPER W. CROSS (1916–70) was a professor of history at St. Louis University.

F. GARVIN DAVENPORT (1905–75) taught history at Monmouth College and was the author of *The Myth of Southern History: Historical Consciousness in Twentieth-Century Southern Literature* (1967).

LISA CUSHING DAVIS teaches Indian and United States history at Loyola University of Chicago.

SUSAN KARINA DICKEY (1955–) was the director of archives and diocesan history for the Roman Catholic diocese of Springfield in Illinois. She wrote *Come to the Water: The Diocese of Springfield in Illinois, 1853–2003—A Sesquicentennial History* (2002) and coauthored with Sister Therese Uhll *The Love of Christ Impels Us: A Short History of St. Dominic* (2006).

TIMOTHY DEAN DRAPER teaches history at Waubonsee Community College in Buffalo Grove, Illinois, and is the book review editor for the *Journal of the Illinois State Historical Society*.

WAYNE N. DUERKES received an MA in history from Northern Illinois University in DeKalb in 2015 and is pursuing a doctoral degree from Iowa State University.

ROBERT S. ECKLEY (1921–2012) was the president of Illinois Wesleyan University from 1969 to 1986, and he served as president of the Abraham Lincoln Association from 2002 to 2004. His *Lincoln's Forgotten Friend: Leonard Swett* was published by Southern Illinois University Press in 2012.

LARRY GARA (1923–) has been a historian, a teacher, and a part-time activist living in Wilmington, Ohio, where he retired from Wilmington College after forty years in the classroom. Gara wrote *The Presidency of Franklin Pierce* (1991) and *The Liberty Line: The Legend of the Underground Railroad* (1961).

CHARLES A. GLIOZZO (1932–) was the dean of international studies and programs from 1993 to 2001 at Michigan State University and was a professor of history there from 1989 to 2001. He authored "The Philosophes and Religion: Intellectual Origins of the De-Christianization Movement in the French Revolution," published in *Church History* (1971).

EVARTS BOUTELL GREENE (1870–1940) was an American historian who began his teaching career in 1894 at the University of Illinois, where he also served as dean of the college of arts and literature from 1906 to 1913. He was the first DeWitt Clinton professor of history at Columbia University, and his principal works include *The Provincial Governor in the English Colonies of North America* (1898) and a *Guide to the Principal Sources for Early American History (1600–1800) in the City of New York* (1929). Greene was an early leader of the Illinois State Historical Society.

ERNEST G. HILDNER was the author of several books on Morgan County and a member of the faculty at Illinois College.

STANLEY B. KIMBALL (1926–2003) taught history for forty-one years at Southern Illinois University. He was an expert on eastern European history but also wrote on Latter-Day Saint history, specifically the Mormon Trail and his ancestor Heber C. Kimball.

MICHAEL P. MCCARTHY taught at the State University of New York at Stony Brook.

ROBERT W. MCCLUGGAGE (1922–89) was a professor of U.S. history (1952–87) at Loyola University, Chicago.

ROBERT MCCOLLEY (1932–) is a professor emeritus of history at the University of Illinois. Past president and past editor of the *Journal of the Illinois State Historical Society* (1998–2002), he is the author of *Slavery and Jeffersonian Virginia* (1964).

CARL R. MILLER (1894–1980) was a journalist with a strong interest in early Illinois history who became a newspaper owner and editor.

MARK A. PLUMMER (1929–) was a professor of history at Illinois State University and is the author of *Lincoln's Rail-Splitter: Richard J. Oglesby* (2001), which won the 2002 Book of the Year Award from the Illinois State Historical Society. He is also the author of *Frontier Governor: Samuel J. Crawford* *of Kansas* (1971). He was the president of the Illinois State Historical Society from 1985 to 1986.

CHRISTOPHER ROBERT REED (1942–) is known for his expertise on the African American experience in twentieth-century Chicago. He was a professor of history at Roosevelt University (1989–2006) and is the author of *The Depression Comes to the South Side: Protest and Politics in the Black Metropolis, 1930–1933* (2011).

DAVID W. SCOTT (1936) is the chair of the Illinois State Historical Society's publications committee and a former president of the society (2003–5). Three of his articles have appeared in the *Journal*.

DANIEL W. STOWELL is a former director and editor of the Papers of Abraham Lincoln. He is the author or editor of several books, including *The Papers of Abraham Lincoln: Legal Documents and Cases* (four volumes; 2008) and *Rebuilding Zion: The Religious Reconstruction of the South, 1863–1877* (1998).

FREDERICK MERCER VAN SICKLE (1957–) has held a number of positions in fund-raising, alumni relations, and related activities in higher education.

JESSIE PALMER WEBER was the Illinois state librarian from 1898 until her death in 1926, and she served as the first secretary of the Illinois State Historical Society. She was also involved in creating the society's *Journal of the Illinois State Historical Society* and was its editor from 1908 until her death.

INDEX

Italicized page numbers indicate figures and their captions.

Lowi, Theodore J., 388–89
Lucas, George L., 191, 194
Lundin, Fred "Poor-Swede," 272
Lydon, Father, 350
Lynn, John A., 175

MacKenzie, Alexander, 38–42
MacKenzie-Isherwood theatrical
 company, 39–42
MacNeal, A. Clement, 369
Macomb, Illinois, 309, 311, 315
Macoupin County, Illinois, 62
Madigan, Michael, 389
Malony, Joseph B., 145–46
Mansion House, Chicago, 35
Markers Program, Illinois State His-
 torical Society, 3, 8, 10
market economy: development of,
 in DuPage County, 100–111; grain
 warehouse operators in transition
 to, 106; transportation system in
 development of, 101–2
Marquette, Fr. Jacques, 366–67
Marshall, Albert O., 179
Martin, George, Jr., 108
Mason County, camp meetings and
 murder, 141, 143, 146–48
Masonic Hall, Nauvoo, 116
Massachusetts, first normal school
 authorized, 93
Mather, Thomas S., 177
Mathews, William Smythe Babcock,
 225–26
McAndrew, William, 334
McColley, Robert, 15
McCormick estates, Great Depres-
 sion and, 361
McCullough, David, 324
McDermott, Douglas, 33–35, 38, 41
McDonough County, 315
McDowell, Mary, 241
McKinley, William, 286
McLaughlin, Catherine and Patrick,
 214–15, 218–19

McPherson, James, 175
McVicker's Theatre, 34
Meeker, Arthur, 354
Meier, August, 362–63
Memoirs of Theodore Thomas
 (Thomas), 230
Merriam, Charles E., 273, 281–82
Methodist circuit riders, 142
Methodist Episcopal Church, 142, 147
metropolises, as targets of Prohibi-
 tion, 279–80
metropolitan regions, fragmentation
 of, in 1970s, 388–89
Metzker, James Preston, murder trial
 in death of, 147–52
Mexican War, 160, 165
migration, early, to Illinois, 22–25
"Milker and Militant" clipping, 307
milk production (1870–1890), 110
millionaires, in Illinois, 274–75
Moody, Dwight L., 226
Moore, Clifton H., 195–96
moral geography, Prohibition and, 281
Morgan, Thomas, 294, 296
Mormons, Illinois period, 112–13,
 115–19. See also Nauvoo, Illinois
Morrill Land-Grant Act (1862), 95,
 133
Morris, Delyte, 377
Morrison, Hugh, 235
Morton, Oliver P., 195
Moulton, Samuel W., 98
Mound City, Illinois, and 1937 Ohio
 River flood, 336
Mowry, George E., 276, 278
Muller, Melusina, 226–27
Municipal Science Club, Chicago, 239
Munroe, George J., 261–62, 264, 266
murder, at Methodist camp meeting,
 141, 143, 146–48
Murray, Bronson, 97
Murray, R. N., 108
Musham, Harry Albert, 209–10, 212
Musham, William, 212

music, classical, 222–24, 226–27, 235–36

musical presentations, at Auditorium Block, Joliet, 267

musical societies and colleges, 225–26

musicians, in Chicago, 224–25

musician's union in 1890s, 232

"Music of the American Indian" (Eames), 321–22

Music-Study in Germany (Fay), 227

My State Reader (leaflet), 5

NAACP, Chicago branch, 365–67, 369–70

Naper, Joseph, 105, 108

Naperville, Illinois, 105, 107–9

National Anti-Slavery Standard (newspaper), 68

National Lincoln Monument Association, 159

National Recovery Administration (NRA), in Lake Forest, 359

Native Alaskans, in Eskimo village, *300*

Native Americans: Bureau of Indian Affairs and, 294, 296; Illinois State Historical Society's campaign to preserve Indian mound at Cahokia, 322; Indian Arts and Crafts Act (1935), 299; "Music of the American Indian" (Eames), 321–22; Pokagon on evolution of communities, 297–98; Society of American Indians, 299; tensions between Euro-Americans and, in 1812 War, 293; treatment of, by writers, 47–48; and World's Columbian Exposition, Chicago (1893), 290–92, 296–98, 300–301

Nauvoo, Battle of (1846), 120

Nauvoo, Illinois, *113*; business and commercial enterprises established at, 116; charter authorized by Illinois legislature (1840), 115–16;

decline and fall of, 119–20; hopes for establishment of city-state at, 112; land purchase and platting of, 115; periodicals published at, 116

Nauvoo Expositor (periodical), 119

Nauvoo Neighbor (periodical), 116

Nebraska Bill, 67

"Negro Protest at the Chicago World's Fair, 1933–1934" (Meier and Rudwick), 362–63

Netherton Company, 367

New Almaden quicksilver mine, 165, 169–70

New Deal, Lake Forest and, 359

newspapers, early: advertisements and subscriptions, 56; combined qualities of local recorder and literary journal, 55; as moulder of public opinion, 57; political character in early 1800s, 54–55

New York Philharmonic Society, 231–32

New York Telegraph (newspaper), 287

New York Times (newspaper), 287–88

Nineteenth Amendment to U.S. Constitution (women's suffrage), 288–89

Noble, Henry T., 161

normal schools, 93, 96–99, 133

Norris, James H., 147–48

Norris L. Brookens Library, Sangamon State University, *374*

Northeastern Illinois University (NIU), 381

Northern Cross railroad, 30

Northern Illinois University (NIU), 376, 377, 381

Northwestern Female College, 136

Northwestern University, 136

Northwestern University Settlement, 239

Northwest Ordinance (1787), 43, 90–91

Norton, John, 183

Index — page content continues.